D1695665

ARCHITECTURE IN INDIA
SINCE 1990

Rahul Mehrotra

ARCHITECTURE IN INDIA
SINCE 1990

PICTOR

DEDICATION

For my teachers at CEPT and the GSD who taught me to appreciate the simultaneous validity of the multiple ways of making architecture

PROJECT MANAGER Jemma J Antia
RESEARCH ASSOCIATE Kamalika Bose
BOOK DESIGN Anne Marie Koster
DESIGN SUPPORT Fravashi Aga
COVER DESIGN Verena Gerlach
TYPEFACE Akzidenz and Myriad Pro
PRODUCTION AND REPRODUCTIONS prints professional Berlin
PAPER EUROBULK 135 g/m²
PRINTING AND BINDING DZA Druckerei zu Altenburg GmbH

© Rahul Mehrotra, 2011

PUBLISHED BY

Pictor Publishing Pvt Ltd
17 Eruchshaw Building, 3rd Floor
249 Dr Dadabhai Naoroji Road
Mumbai 400 001
India
www.pictorpublishing.com

and

Hatje Cantz Verlag
Zeppelinstrasse 32
73760 Ostfildern
Germany
www.hatjecantz.com
ISBN 978-3-7757-3245-1

Printed in Germany

Distributed in Europe, United Kingdom, and the Americas by Hatje Cantz, www.hatjecantz.com
Hatje Cantz books are available internationally at selected bookstores. For more information about our distribution partners, please visit our homepage at www.hatjecantz.com.
ISBN 978-3-7757-3245-1

Distributed in the rest of the world by Pictor Publishing, www.pictorpublishing.com
ISBN 978-81-920432-0-3
Although the author and publisher have made every effort to ensure that the information in this book was correct at press time, they do not assume and hereby disclaim any liability to any party for any loss, damage, or disruption caused by errors or omissions, whether such errors or omissions result from negligence, accident, or any other cause.

Cover illustration: Detail of Indian Institute of Management, Ahmedabad, designed by HCP Design and Project Management, photo by Dinesh Mehta
Frontispiece: Nestle HQ, Gurgaon
Page 302: Detail of trellis at Lakshmi Machine Works corporate office Coimbatore (1997), designed from scrap metal by Yogesh Rawal and Rajeev Sethi in collaboration with RMA Architects

CONTENTS

Preface	6
Landscape of Pluralism	9
Global Practice: Expressions of (Impatient) Capital	57
Folios	75
Regional Manifestation: Local Assertions	117
Folios	139
Alternate Practice: Towards Sustainability	187
Folios	211
Counter Modernism: Resurfacing of the Ancient	249
Folios	269
Envoi	303
Chronology	304
Project Data	306
Acknowledgements	308
Photo Credits	309
Bibliography	310

PREFACE

This book is a personal account of architecture in India since 1990—the year I established my architecture studio in Mumbai. That year also marked the beginning of the decade in which India liberalised its economy and commenced the process of dismantling the shackles of self-imposed economic sanctions. This was to be the beginning of the country's engagement with the contemporary globalising world. As an architect starting to work in India at that time, I could only go by the precedents and models of architectural practice that I could visibly observe: models of practice that responded to defining the role of an architect in a socialist economy, with the state serving as the patron for all major building projects. This was a model that extended out of the modernist paradigm of the architect as change-maker—the visionary who saw spatial possibilities all the way from a residential commission to the potential of city design! Ironically, our first commissions were interior renovations and slowly (painfully slowly), over four or five years, we built our first architectural commissions. It was only after 1995 that we felt the surge of economic growth, frenzied building activity and India's confidence to embrace the globalised world.

Through a series of sheer coincidences, our commissions began gravitating to the southern states in India— where the economic boom, or at least the effects of the liberalisation policies, could be more squarely felt. Here we observed a strange combination in the emergence of new entrepreneurs who unhesitatingly engaged with the new economy but simultaneously reinforced their beliefs in the ancient. They were inspired by the West but even more so by their own religious beliefs and practices—an interesting 'schizophrenia', which we continually dealt with through our building projects. At our home base in Mumbai, our commissions veered towards conservation work—largely, I suspect, on account of the several books I co-authored with Sharada Dwivedi as well as the deference for private commissions that I had unknowingly created with potential clients as a result of my advocacy work in Mumbai through the Urban Design Research Institute. In fact, advocacy work was an interesting dimension to the practice that evolved naturally without any preconceived strategy. Over the years these disparate forms of work—ranging from smallscale design projects to larger architectural commissions in different parts of the country, as well as preservation and advocacy work in Mumbai—exposed us not only to varied scales of work but also to diverse constituencies. We worked with the non-governmental-organisation (NGO) sector, government and institutional clients and corporations, on private commissions as well as self-initiated projects in the city. We engaged with fifth- and sixth-generation craftspeople, large-scale construction companies, the Public Works Department and first-generation contractors. We became deeply interested in traditional construction practices in the regions in which we were building, and grew obsessed with mining local knowledge wherever we worked.

It was through these varied exposures and engagements that I became acutely aware of the different worlds, practices, processes and procedures that make up the pluralism that we see so vividly in the built landscape in India. While a major portion of this is not made or even influenced by architects, trying to understand the small percentage that we as professionals did make and influence intrigued me. It was only in the late 1990s that these patterns became clear to me, as economic conditions had now changed since the liberalisation process had finally taken off. I had thus projected in my mind that the practice paradigms would also shift; I imagined, and feared (as did my peers), the emergence of large corporations and the death of the individual practitioner. However, this did not happen. Instead, I witnessed a flourishing of varied models of practice that continued to fashion the built environment, and I also discovered that even our small studio in Mumbai was simultaneously engaging with different modes and procedures of practice. Therefore, it was with this experience that I finally formulated the structure of this book—a coalescing of field notes from my two decades of working in India.

Besides these felt and experienced moments in the practice of architecture in India, this book is also partly a response to my own frustration with the publications that have emerged in the last decade on contemporary Indian architecture. While my studio's (RMA Architects) works have been featured prominently in much of this literature, I could not help but feel that this was an obviously narrow representation of the pluralism that makes the Indian landscape so unique. My frustration was really triggered by the fact that I could not, and still cannot, accept that mould of sameness and the small box that architects in India are being compressed into by the media, both national and international. These readings all use modernism and its aesthetics and values as a benchmark to judge the variants! This is a limiting and, I believe, possibly useless framework for practitioners in India or those wanting to work there.

Thus, I set out to compile in one document a record of the major projects that represent the nature and unique process for the formal production of contemporary architecture in India. The intent was not only to map this emerging work but also to make sense of the aspirations it was representing. However, more importantly, it was to present a synchronic cross-section of the spectrum of positions that characterise architectural production in India in the face of both its liberalised economy and the large transformations that have resulted from the processes of globalisation.

This book is not intended to be encyclopaedic; it does not attempt to represent every significant Indian project produced in the last two decades. It is inevitable that there have been some inadvertent omissions, for which I offer apologies in advance to the architects not included— many of whom are my colleagues and (at least, up to this point) friends. This is not intended as a survey, but rather a provocation for us to see the multiple, and often simultaneously valid, streams of architectural thought and engagement in India. In fact, the book is a plea to all those who are responsible for the built environment to see the power and relevance of architectural pluralism as critical for our democracy as well as the continuing relevance of our cultural fabric. It is an appeal for us to not be blinded by the paradigms of Shanghai, Singapore and Dubai, which grow out of autocracies—it is not the way India should go! I have been particularly fascinated by the different paths that India and China have taken to achieve economic mobility and the betterment of the lives of their people. India, being a democracy, has clearly offered a different spectrum of resistances to the forces of globalisation, which has amazing implications for the physical expression and form of the built environment in general. Thus, to map the form of these resistances is, I believe, a useful way for the profession to understand and resituate its agenda.

The book lays out observations and ideas that have most often been culled 'on the ground', and are personal accounts or a selection of curated projects that have influenced my own understanding of the emergent Indian architectural landscape. In method and style, I have consciously steered clear of the pretence of formulating theory or validating with (maddening) cross-references what are intuitively felt observations—credits are provided in the text, where due (as references, listed in the first section; and in the form of a bibliography for the second section of the book). My observations have then been organised thematically in the form of essays that precede the selection of each portfolio of projects. The book is thus divided into five sections. The first section is an introductory essay, 'Landscape of Pluralism', which outlines my understanding of the architectural landscape in India from the era of colonial influence up to the present. This essay also establishes (in its summary) the rationale for the four models of practice that are presented in the following sections. These are organised with a lead essay and a portfolio of selected projects, which are emblematic of the mode of practice being discussed. The first of these, 'Global Practice', discusses practices that are focused on constructing global identities, often in response to and facilitating the expressions of what I term 'impatient' capital, and that in many ways characterise the globalisation process itself. The second is 'Regional Modernism', wherein the lineage of modernism is studied in its present variants. This model, conscious of its own presence both in the local and global arenas, is more about local assertions that are region-based than resistances to broader global forces. Following this is a section entitled 'Alternative Practice', in which new emergent models of engagement are examined. This model is posed as one that aspires towards sustainability and new ways of making, producing and situating architecture. The final section is titled 'Counter Modernism', and explores the incredible phenomenon of the resurfacing of the ancient in the built landscape of India.

There were many moments in the writing of these essays when I was tempted to expand more substantially on my views on the larger urban and rural landscapes that these practices are situated in and explain how they were making the emergent, broader built environment in India. This was a critical question in explaining how the pluralism I describe can potentially coalesce into a coherent construct at the urban or regional scale. I was similarly at a crossroads when discussing questions of conservation, as well as the conditions of adjacencies in which old and new come together physically. However, after much discussion with my publisher, I decided not to expand on these questions but rather to limit the scope of the book to new architecture for the sake of clarity and focus. So, while I have not explicitly expanded my perspective on these questions in this book, I think their presence is embedded in the choice of projects and the developing cultures I have described for each model of practice.

The architects referred to in the essays are people I have encountered over the two decades during which I have been a practitioner in India. With some, I have shared deep conversations and with others brief exchanges or just email contact. I have two regrets regarding the formulation of the final form of the book. The first relates to the resistance and often lack of openness from a number of professionals in sharing their work for public discussion—the book would have been far richer had more material been accessible. I can only think that, as professionals, it is our lack of confidence and a 'fuzziness' about our role in contemporary society that would dissuade us from sharing more openly. Today in India, there exist approximately 180 schools of architecture, which produce an estimated 4,000 graduates each year. The Council of Architecture has 30,000 architects registered, and there are a few thousand more unregistered ones that I imagine also practise. This is a strikingly low figure for a country of a billion people! So then, how can the influence of such a small segment of professionals have any impact on the built environment? It surely cannot be one of any consistency or visual coherence, as the built environment will continue to be shaped by forces that do not in any way intersect with the architectural profession and its aspirations. Thus, for us to find ways collectively of making sense of the plurality that will surround us is critical to our own future work and engagement. It is heartening to see the growth of multiple forums across India, where young architects band together to organise lectures and discussions on the state of architecture. This collective spirit is one that we need more of, and I hope the book can contribute to this movement. My second regret is that such a small number of women practitioners emerged in the process of the research. I know for a fact that, today, the bulk of architectural students are women, and perhaps as this is only a recent phenomenon it is too early to expect their emergence as practitioners in the same numbers as their male counterparts. In any case, the women architects that have been represented in the book more than make up for their modest numbers with the power of their ideas, commitments and passion.

The selection of projects in each portfolio is by no means exhaustive, but rather emblematic of the different modes of practice as well as representative of the wide cross-section of building types that we will see emerging with some fervour in the coming decades in India. The profession cannot avoid dealing with these types and adapting them for our condition and use. The book, however, has been organised by models of practice (processes of production, modes of instruction, etc.) rather than building type, e.g. airports, office complexes, private homes—mainly because organisation by type excludes hybrids or new programmes and ensuing building types, and assumes that they are not relevant. More importantly however, the intention was to focus on a categorisation by method of engagement and the formulation of models of practice. This, I believe, will be a more useful format for the young practitioner or the student of architecture—who will, after all, define the future of architecture in India—and I hope that it will make their choices more nuanced and conscious. While all categorisation is, of course, destined to fail eventually, it is but one of the many ways of producing and organising knowledge by naming the sensed phenomenon. Categories, maps and classifications are, by nature, instruments of controversy—always a personal view and never a description of the absolute truth, and the categories here must also be viewed in that spirit. Finally, the book is clearly intended for students, architects and patrons with the hope that it can help situate their own choices, engagements and patronage in a broader framework of architectural production in India. It will, I hope, serve as an instrument for critical reflection for the profession, as well as for those who patronise architecture in India.

Rahul Mehrotra
April 2011, Mumbai

Landscape of Pluralism

Introduction
Reassembling the Past
Indian Modernism
Architecture and Indian Identity
Emergent Landscapes
Notes

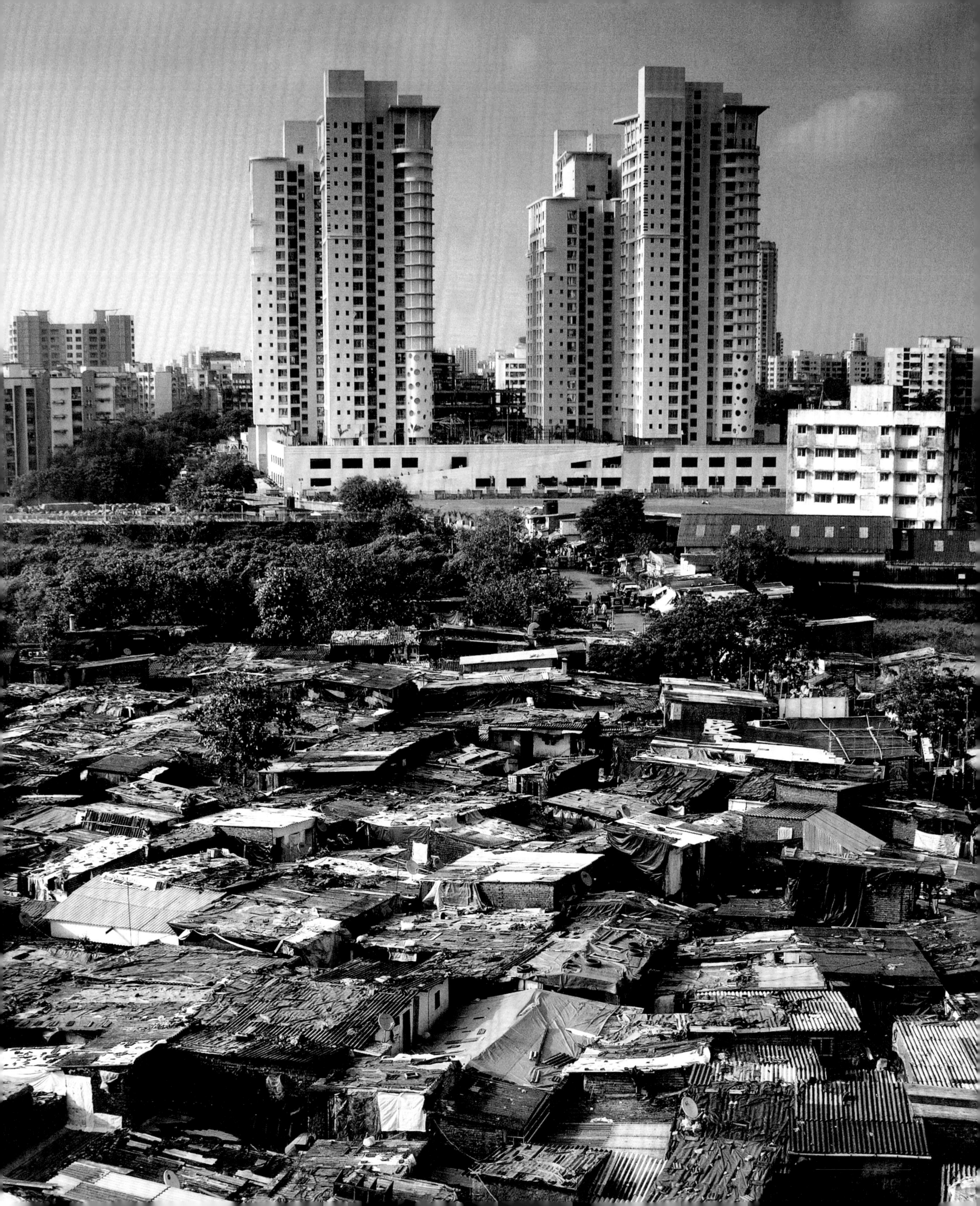

Architecture in India since 1990 | Landscape of Pluralism

The period starting in 1990 marks a particularly fascinating phase in the history of architecture in India, for it overlaps neatly with the liberalisation of the Indian economy and the massive transformations in the built landscape that have characterised this process. Liberalisation has resulted in the surfacing of many contradictions inherent in the rapid economic mobility that has engulfed the country. The consequence of this is a complex construct, in which disparate forms of architecture and built paraphernalia coexist in close proximity to each other, thereby creating some bizarre visual and physical adjacencies.

Yet this emergent landscape is a true representation of the simultaneity with which numerous histories, aspirations and cultures have played themselves out in India. In fact, it is this cultural diversity that has endured through the many dramatic changes that the country witnessed over the years, particularly in the twentieth century, when the new Indian nation transitioned from colonial rule to embrace modernism as the vehicle for constructing a national identity. In the process of encountering modernity, the nation was to simultaneously also resist the modernisation project on account of the uneven development that had characterised it in its formative years. The dual aspect of this phenomenon not only generated a multiplicity of 'alternative modernities' in architectural expression, but also blurred the boundary between the modern and the contemporary. These alternative modernities embrace the handmade and industrial as well as the oral and written traditions with equal ease, setting up varying hybrid architectural conditions not previously imagined. As the nation evolved and the range of architectural production expanded, the question of identities became far more complex than was initially imagined at the threshold of the country's birth. This complexity has been further exacerbated in the 1990s due to economic liberalisation and the contradictions inherent in rapid economic mobility. Indeed, globalisation brought with it glamour as well as marginalisation and displacement.[1] However, this phenomenon was not without resistance—political, social and cultural—which resulted in varying configurations being used to formally and informally construct the built environment. Thus, the emergent architectural and urban landscape in India is one in which global flows concurrently transform the local while being transformed by them in turn. It is a landscape of global flows particular to India and is characteristically enmeshed in adjacencies and polarities that are unique to the place.

Today the built landscape in India is characterised by physical and visual contradictions that coalesce in a landscape of incredible pluralism. Historically, particularly during British colonisation, the different worlds—whether economic, social or cultural—occupied different spaces both in urban areas and elsewhere in the pan-Indian geography. They operated under different rules, often resulting in vastly different physical manifestations of their values and aspirations in the built environment. However, today these worlds often share the same space, although they understand and use it differently. Furthermore, after independence the newfound social and economic mobility, starting in the early 1960s, brought about massive demographic shifts in the country, resulting in a blurring of cultural landscapes. The consequent pluralism in architectural expression was astounding. With globalisation and the emergence of a post-industrial service-based economy, at least in larger urban centres in India, urban space has been fragmented and polarised, bringing to light the inherent dualities and multiplicity of architectural expressions visible in any given physical locale.

Today, India is experiencing a shift in the position occupied by the state in the production of architecture. The state has more or less given up the responsibility of projecting an 'idea of India' through the built and physical environment. The major state-directed building and infrastructure projects, such as they are, are no longer destinations or buildings and places for consumption, but routes of approach: highways, flyovers, airports, telecommunications networks and electricity grids. The state no longer represents itself through monumental edifices but through its ability to steward statistics, such as growth rates and social indicators: it is a new statistical 'architecture' through which the state seeks to legitimise itself.[2] Unfortunately, with this new thrust comes a disinterest in placing a premium on the built environment as an indicator of progress; success is measured rather by how the numbers play themselves out. Thus while envisioning or projecting the end condition of

Indian urban landscape The coexistence of 'slums' and high-rise buildings in extremely close adjacency creates a visual duality that has come to characterise most Indian cities

these processes, were previously the purview of physical planning agencies in the country, it is now market forces that determine the form that the built environment will take.³

In India's post-liberalisation economy, cities and their burgeoning peripheries have become critical sites for the shifting of responsibilities and an evolving relationship between the private and the public, resulting in new negotiations between the elite and 'subaltern' cultures. Relationships between social classes in this new economy are quite different from those that existed in state-controlled economies, where the government provided critical safety nets in terms of housing and employment. Today, private capital chooses to build environments that are insulated from their context, without the burdens of facilitating citizenship or place-making necessary in a real city. In the words of Sunil Khilnani, "rather they take pride in the fact that they exist in international time zones, in an orbital relation to their immediate physical neighbours and surrounds. These are zones where the 'Non Resident Indian' and 'Resident Non-Indian' come together in a bleached cosmopolitanism."⁴

Furthermore, in the state-controlled economy the physical relationship between different classes was often orchestrated according to a master plan founded upon entitlement to housing and proximity to employment. In the new economy, the fragmentation of service and production locations has resulted in a new, bazaar-like urbanism that has woven its presence through the entire urban landscape. This is an urbanism created by those outside the elite domains of the formal modernity of the state—a 'pirate' modernity that slips under the laws of the city to simply survive, without any conscious attempt at constructing a counterculture.⁵ With the retreat of the state during the 1980s and 1990s (in different measures across India), the space of the 'everyday' became the place where economic and cultural struggles were articulated, and the physical shape the city took manifested itself in the informal landscape of the bazaar city! In fact, these common spaces in both rural and urban India have been largely excluded from the cultural discourses on globalisation, which focus on elite domains and the physical landscapes they create. Outside the elite domain of architectural production, architecture is often not the only 'spectacle' upon which society relies to express its aspirations, nor does it even comprise the single dominant image of most Indian cities. Quite in contrast, festivals such as Diwali, Dussera, Navratri, Muhharam, Durga Puja, Ganesh Chaturthi, and many more have emerged as the visual and representational spectacles of contemporary India. Their presence on the everyday landscape pervades and dominates the popular visual culture of India's cities, towns and villages.⁶ The increasing concentration of global flows has exacerbated the inequalities and spatial divisions between social classes. In this context, an architecture or urbanism of equality in an increasingly inequitable economic condition requires a deeper consideration, so as to locate the wide range of places that signify and commemorate the cultures excluded from the spaces of global flows. Such places do not necessarily lie in the formal production of architecture, but often challenge it with a counterculture that takes on multiple forms. They are set apart not only by the physical differences in how their architecture is produced, but also by the values and aspirations that they come to encode. These are the landscapes of the self-help settlements often referred to as slums or the periphery of cities that grow outside the formal state-controlled urban limit. Similarly, the over 300 small towns in India that are expected to become cities of one million people and more in the next two or three decades are actively producing forms of urbanism outside the mainstream discussion on architecture.

Thus, in this emergent condition, any real or accurate reading of the (broader) contemporary architectural landscape must necessarily recognise and accept the simultaneous validity of the diverse architectural forms in multiple locations in the country that act as expressions of the culture or society. This is a complex matrix that must be read with both a historic, or 'vertical', perspective and a 'horizontal' view across a contemporary time slice. The vertical time slice is critical for mapping the shifting scenario through the last century, leading up to the post-colonial Indian nation state, especially given the consistency of attitudes and institutional structures by which the Indian landscape continues to be moulded.⁷ Meanwhile, the horizontal, contemporary reading aims to make visible the plurality in the present production of architecture in India. The overlaps, slippages and potential cross-connections between these vertical and horizontal views would allow a reading of this matrix to permeate beyond the familiar images that most often emblematically represent contemporary Indian architecture. This common or popular interpretation is often limited by a recognisable imagery and a complex disjunction in synchronising and collapsing tradition and modernity in several permutations. Such a conscious attempt at grappling with this (often non-productive) reconciliation of tradition and modernity was triggered during the British intervention in India (throughout the late nineteenth and early twentieth centuries), which continues to pervade the formal debate about architecture in contemporary post-independence India.[8]

Ganesh immersions in Mumbai are perhaps a more powerful spectacle than the city's architecture, and temporal landscapes and events have come to exert a great presence in the representation of Indian cities

REASSEMBLING THE PAST

For the British in India, architecture served an important symbolic function—one that provided the European community with a visible assurance of its identity. It served as an affirmation of authority and "a rallying point for ourselves, and raising a distinctive mark of our presence, always to be held by the native of the country."[9] The colonial shift in values and attitudes towards architecture dealt a fatal blow to traditional modes and approaches to building in India (at least in the urban centres). The establishment of the Public Works Department (PWD) from the mid-seventeenth century onwards resulted in a centralised, standardised building system, with little response to the locale and cumulative traditional wisdom. James Ransome, the first Consulting Architect appointed to the Indian Government in 1902, summarised his experience of working in India at a Royal Institute of British Architects (RIBA) lecture more than 25 years later: "In India where ingenuity was required more than anything we were forcing purity of style, I was told to make Calcutta Classical, Bombay Gothic, Madras Saracenic, Rangoon was to be Renaissance and English cottages were to be dotted about all over the plains of India."[10]

Although the British in India perpetuated this rigid imperialistic view towards architecture until the 1920s and 1930s, it did not remain unchallenged. In the last decades of the nineteenth century, fuelled by current thought such as the Gothic Revival and Arts and Crafts Movement in England, there emerged British architects who looked more sympathetically upon the architectural traditions of the region in which they were building. In addition to the early attempts by revivalists,[11] the work initiated by Swinton Jacob had a definitive impact on Indian architecture in the early twentieth century.[12] Jacob perceived architecture in India as a 'composition' or 'assembly' of elements and details serving their various structural, ideological, and aesthetic functions. Thus, the logical step for him was to categorise or 'disassemble' these compositions.

A format was developed under the auspices of Jacob's patron, the Maharaja of Jaipur, and in 1890 Jacob published six large volumes entitled *The Jeypore Portfolio of Architectural Details*, in which he presented more than 600 large-scale drawings of elements chosen from various buildings in northern India dating from the twelfth through to the seventeenth centuries. What is of particular importance is the fact that the work was not organised by period or region, but by function: stone copings and plinths in one volume, arches in a second, brackets in a third, and so on. In fact, in the introduction, Jacob outlined that the portfolio was intended as a set of working drawings "and presented on loose sheets in order that different examples of architectural details may be compared and selections readily made." Jacob actually constructed a framework to enable this task of 'synthesis'. In the format of the portfolio, he had 'disassembled' traditional forms in order to disengage them from the buildings in which they appeared and so facilitate their reassembly into a composite architectural style suitable for modern buildings in India.

Jacob's approach was not free from political overtones. The complete erasure of regional origins implied a broader definition of Indian territory (for which the approach was valid), much like the idea of a 'Greater India' that the British used to define the limits of their South Asian colonies.[13] Architecture was put in the service of creating a composite identity for the region in order to validate colonial boundaries. The British had admired the Mughals for having successfully achieved such a synthesis through which they had evolved a new architecture for the region, combining their architectural sensibilities with the resources and skills that existed in the South Asian territory that they conquered. For the British, the Mughal buildings expressed a certain 'classical' simplicity that was easier for them, and most Europeans, to appreciate and comprehend than the complex and rich imagery of high Hindu art and architecture. Therefore, sites like Mandu, Bijapur and Fatehpur Sikri became great sources of inspiration for British architects working in the South Asian region. Mughal architecture was perceived as a blend of Hindu and Muslim elements; as a result, buildings inspired by this architecture came to be known as Indo-Saracenic (referring to the Saracenic tribes of the Mughal lineage), a term by which they are still described today. In addition, with the publication of Jacob's volumes this distinctive style of architecture came of age as his publication formalised this process of 'reassembling' as an instrument for producing the architecture of synthesis—the way Mughal architecture was perceived.[14]

In a sense, the Indo-Saracenic style attempted to promote itself as a counter-point to imperial architecture, but its influence began to wane in the second decade of the twentieth century. Indeed, its practice was restricted to particular official commissions, although it also found favour with local patrons like the princely states, whose territories comprised almost forty per cent of India. The Indo-Saracenic style was really a superficial attempt at synthesising local traditions and attitudes; although the buildings were made to look Indian in appearance, they never addressed any of the broader architectural concerns of spatial concepts and standards, technology and end usage. These buildings were still essentially European or colonial. Yet the initial popularity of the style ensured the importance of traditional craft, which was crucial to the assembly of the various components that Jacob had disassembled in his portfolio. These elements were usually decorative in nature; although they did not inspire building technologies they did support crafts ranging from woodworking to stone masonry and carving. As a result, albeit inadvertently, and although the trade of the master craftsman was being replaced by the architect, craft and traditional building technologies continued to flourish and be supported by a range of patrons, though not with the same reverence and social status that they had enjoyed in earlier historical periods.

In this scenario, European classical buildings began to simultaneously reappear, with banks and commercial establishments being the chief patrons of this style. Classicism, in fact, remained entrenched as the architecture of political imperialism and of commerce, and the underlying deterrent to the establishment of the Indo-Saracenic style was perhaps this strong official control of architecture, which made it difficult to divorce building from political ideologies. This conflict became abundantly clear in the planning of the city of New Delhi in the 1920s. Despite being politically pressured into using the Indo-Saracenic style (the government appointed Jacob consultant to the project), Sir Edwin Lutyens transcended the overly simple approach of the Indo-Saracenic architects by attempting a fusion between what he referred to as essentially Western classical and carefully selected traditional forms.

Architecturally, Lutyens achieved much more success than his predecessors. Through abstractions, he invented details that he then integrated with his classical language. Recognising *chhatris*, *chhajjas* and *jalis*[15] as the stylistic characteristics of the place, he naturally tied them to his classical features through functional uses, thereby achieving a balance between the requirements of a harsh climate and the symbolism demanded by politics. Lutyens perceived New Delhi as an Indian Rome, giving appropriate expression to the existing colonial ideology of commanding the ruled through the use of their own language and symbols. Thus, by cleverly superimposing Indian motifs, ranging from details to larger elements like the stupa from Sanchi for the main dome of the Viceregal Lodge, Lutyens took the Indo-Saracenic style to its logical conclusion by denouncing the symbolic content of the motifs and sufficiently abstracting them for use in his design vocabulary. Although this methodology inspired a number of works in a similar genre in New Delhi and other parts of the colony, by the 1930s the paradigms and issues were already beginning to shift substantially. The Nationalist Movement and the advent of modernism had by then established their presence in India, and had begun to use architecture as a vehicle to further their own ideologies.[16]

Architecture in India since 1990 | Landscape of Pluralism

Mubarak Mahal, a nineteenth-century building by Chimanlal, built under the patronage of Maharaja Madho Singh in Jaipur, was designed as a reception space for guests. It displays a rich fusion of Rajput, Islamic and European architectural styles. An early example of the Indo-Saracenic style, this delicate yet rigorous composition is a magnificent complement to the broader architectural landscape of Jaipur

Jeypore Portfolio plates showing details of columns from Birbal's Quarters, Fatehpur Sikri; Nizamudin's Tomb, Delhi; and Suraj Pole Bowri, Udaipur

Jeypore Portfolio plate showing column base from Rai Samand, Udaipur

Jacob perceived architecture in India as a 'composition' or 'assembly' of elements and details serving their various structural, ideological, and aesthetic functions. Thus, the logical step for him was to categorise or 'disassemble' these compositions

FROM RAI SAMAND, UDAIPUR.

Scale 1 ½ 0 1 2 3 4 5 6 7 inches

Architecture in India since 1990 | Landscape of Pluralism

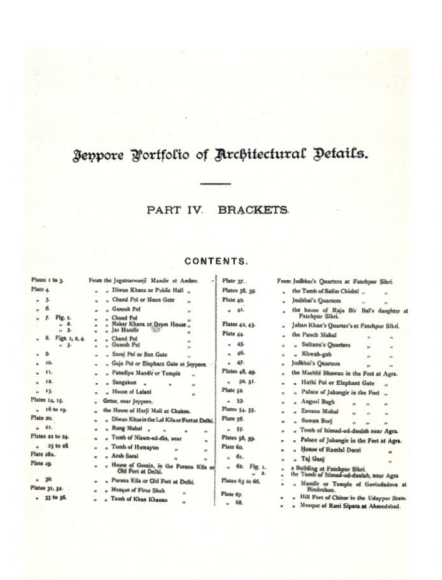

Jeypore Portfolio plates

Chatris and Domed Roofs: Akbar's Tomb in Sikandra

Contents Page from Part IV: 'Brackets'

Brackets from Mussaman Burj, Agra Fort

Brackets from Hathi Pole, Agra Fort

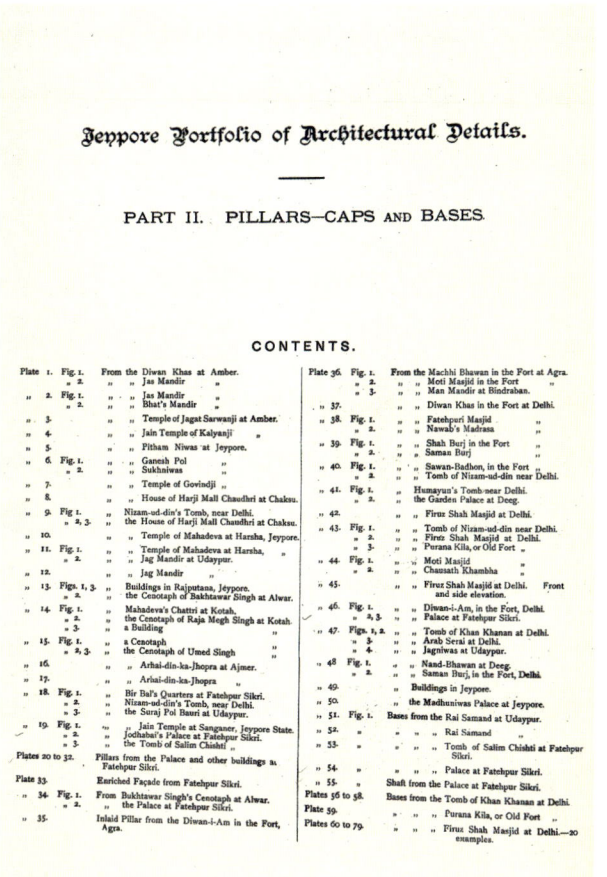

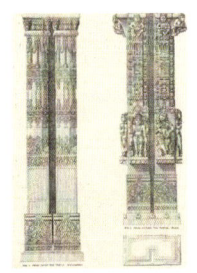

Contents Page from Part II: 'Pillars, Caps and Bases'

Pillars from Bakhtawar Singh's Cenotaph, Alwar

Pillar from the Diwan Khas, Red Fort, Delhi

Pillars from Diwan Am, Red Fort, Delhi

Pillars from Jagat Surwanji Temple, Amer

Pillars from Hursh and Udaipur

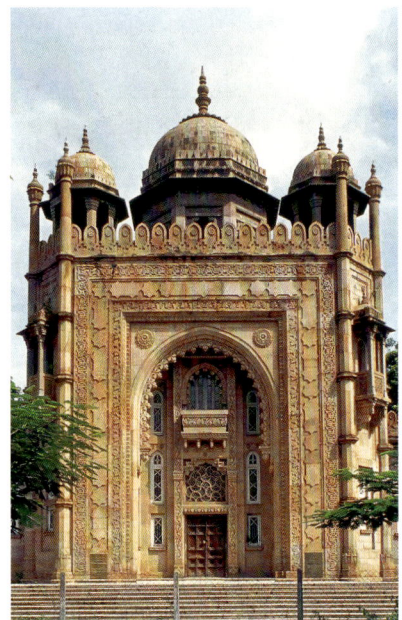

Jeypore Portfolio plates Turret over Tomb of Itmad-ud-Daulah, Agra

Built in 1910, **Daly College**, Indore was designed by Samuel Swinton Jacob. It is an example of the Indo-Saracenic style for residential (or boarding) schools, which imparted a Western education to the princes of central India

The **National Gallery**, Chennai was designed by Erskine Irwin, as the Victoria Memorial Hall in 1909. This ornate sandstone structure draws inspiration from the Buland Darwaza in Fatehpur Sikri—an example of the hybrid fusion of the Indo-Saracenic style

Architecture in India since 1990 | Landscape of Pluralism

The **Prince of Wales Museum** was commissioned in 1909 from George Wittet, to commemorate the Prince of Wales' visit to Mumbai. An Indo-Saracenic edifice in basalt and Kurla stone, it refers to Golconda Fort for its central dome while incorporating several architectural elements from Maratha and Jain traditions

Built in 1873 for departments and offices of the University of Madras, the **Senate House** in Chennai by Robert F. Chisholm is an example of Indo-Saracenic architecture that blends elements from Byzantine traditions

Designed by John Begg and built between 1902 and 1913 in black basalt, Mumbai's **General Post Office** makes a clear reference to the Gol Gumbaz in Bijapur in its central hall with the imposing dome

Architecture in India since 1990 | Landscape of Pluralism

Rashtrapati Bhavan, New Delhi was built as the Viceroy's Palace between 1912 and 1929. This seat of power, designed by Sir Edwin Lutyens, incorporated Indian motifs into a classically Western building plan with great subtlety, and was distinctly different from the work of Lutyens' counterparts across the country in that period

An iconic third-century BCE hemispherical structure in brick, the **Sanchi Stupa** in Madhya Pradesh is symbolic of a rich period in Buddhist art and architecture in India. Its dome is believed to have inspired the dome of the Rashtrapati Bhavan, which correlates with it rather accurately in its form and design

Detail of the dome of the **Rashtrapati Bhavan** which is visually lifted off its supports and made to feel lighter on account of the verandah wrapped around its circumference at the base

Stone carvers at building sites and workshops. The role of traditional and decorative crafts remained paramount in injecting a sense of rootedness into colonial building stock in the early twentieth century. This live and continous tradition enriched and made possible the seamless integration of ornament in the buildings of the Indo-Saracenic style, and in the architecture of colonial India more generally

Architecture in India since 1990 | Landectape of Pluralism

INDIAN MODERNISM

In September 1920, the Indian Congress met in Kolkata and launched the non-cooperation movement, ultimately demanding Home Rule—an event that would eventually reconfigure all of South Asia. The Nationalist Movement had begun emerging as early as 1905 with the establishment of the Swadeshi Movement, which emphasised non-cooperation with the government and the call to evolve a national style of life. A central emphasis of the campaign was the use of self-reliance as a tool against colonialism and to exert an 'Indian' identity. With this movement, the first ideas of combating imperialism, both politically and architecturally, took root.

In 1915, Mohandas Karamchand Gandhi's arrival in India signalled a new era for the South Asian region. Gandhi applied the process of passive resistance and civil disobedience, which he had developed in South Africa. His influence on nationalist themes in art and architecture was indirect, being predominantly spiritual rather than stylistic, and his thoughts affected the debate about architecture more than the actual design of buildings.[17] However, the most influential forum for the translation of the ideals of the Swadeshi Movement into architecture and art was the Bengal School of Art along with the contribution of Rabindranath Tagore, who founded the educational centre of Shantiniketan with the specific objective of furthering the Swadeshi cause, or the impulse for self reliance. In its architectural expression, Shantiniketan synthesised various influences from the South Asian region and made explicit the desire to evolve a pan-Asian sensibility. It wove these influences together using a sort of folk paradigm for the design of buildings, devoid of any sense of the monumental. Traditional forms and materials were combined to create buildings that ultimately seemed unresolved and incongruous. This lack of resolution in the building designs minimised the impact that the architecture of Shantiniketan had on the larger architectural scene in the region.

Meanwhile, the architecture of Gandhi's ashrams was one of simplicity, with many intellectual antecedents and parallels, including modern architectural precepts, but without the formal vocabulary of modernism. These ashrams displayed a frugality of design and the spirit of Gandhi's political and social ideas, in which architecture became a vehicle for manifesting these ideals as directly as possible. Gandhi's buildings were minimal. Unlike Tagore's experiments, which used built form as a symbol of national identity, Gandhi's ashrams were built more in the spirit of the sustainable environment movements of today. In fact, neither the revivalist nor the folk traditions formed any part of Gandhi's architecture. In that sense, his ideas were closer to what was simultaneously emerging in South Asia as the modern movement.

Thus, what eventually emerged in the nationalist agenda was a duality that was becoming difficult to reconcile: one strand being the folk tradition, which in spirit associated itself with the revivalists; and the other being the stream propagated by Gandhi, of simplicity and minimal means. In many ways, this Gandhian approach implicitly suggested modernism (perceived as a Western import) and thus perhaps was inappropriate to serve as an icon of a newfound identity, especially when the freedom struggle was still going on. As such, the revivalists finally gained currency as their movement was in more tangible ways seen as the counterpoint to the emerging modernism (as manifested through the 'international style') and Art Deco. Both these styles had, by that time, become associated with either the decadence of the affluent and the princely states or with the newly emerging manifestation of imperialism in the form of the new cinemas springing up across the country, and the construction of new office buildings for business corporations in the colony.

The revivalists believed that these 'alien' movements (i.e. Art Deco and modernism) did not reflect the soul of the region. They contended that modern architecture for South Asia, and India in particular, should be based on traditional styles. They looked to the region's ancient past for inspiration, and ironically endorsed the works of Indo-Saracenic architects like John Begg.[18] In fact, from 1900 to 1940 a constant struggle existed between revivalist ideas and those of the modernists as expressed in Art Deco and the international style. The revivalists among the British architects turned to classicism as an expression of imperialism, whereas the Indian revivalist architects looked to Buddhist- and Gupta-era prototypes—namely, a distant past that was free of any perceived colonial influences. However, the revivalist ideas did not hold strongly with the politicians who were to be the future leaders of South Asia—men like Jawaharlal Nehru, who were all set to embrace modernism as the vehicle to represent the agenda of the unfolding future. In their projections, architecture went beyond icons and façade design to also fulfil a social agenda firmly situated in the future.

Modernism emerged in various circumstances in different parts of South Asia between 1920 and 1940, and resulting in different manifestations of this style. However, its common thrust was anti-romantic, which meant the innovation of an idiom that was essential to articulate the new perception of life in the context of industrialisation and urbanisation. In India, the first manifestation of modernism was Art Deco; although it was strongly associated with modernism, it differed from the latter in that it was less functional and initially more aristocratic in both its form and patronage. In many ways, the opulence of 'princely India' that Art Deco perpetuated was an interesting contrast to the sensibility introduced by Gandhi— the austere and the elegant together attempting to evoke the spiritual. Although modernism rejected decoration, Art Deco incorporated decorative themes and motifs, facilitating a continuity in expression that was critical for South Asia. Similarly, although Art Deco grew out of industrial means of production, in India its buildings continued to be built by manual labour. Yet the import of Art Deco from urban centres was quickly achieved within the hinterland regions through cinema and other seductive technological innovations, which were rapidly assimilated in smaller towns. As such, Art Deco served as the harbinger for modernism and its establishment in the 1920s and 1930s, which essentially allowed for an easy transition by the 1940s into a modernist idiom.

The first 'onslaughts' of modernism in the South Asian region were felt in the 1930s, when international architects outside the British mainstream began designing buildings for the elite in India without official patronage. As this was not a coordinated effort, its influence on the architectural scene was minimal and localised.[19] Consequently, perhaps the first truly modern building in India was the Golcunde Ashram in Puducherry, designed and built between 1936 and 1948 by Antonin Raymond. Much like the sensibility of the architecture in Gandhi's ashrams, this building was also built as an ashram—for the Mother in Auroville[20]—and was free of political self-consciousness in terms of expressing an identity for a new nation. This was an autonomous project, totally 'under the radar' of architects in the rest of the country and built in direct response to climatic, social and technological constraints. It imposed on itself the need to create a sensible architectural solution in a modern idiom, but completely rooted to the place and the community that it served.

For elite patrons, modernism answered the nationalist cause as it was devoid of references to the past and was brimming with optimism about the future. These early modern experiments in India were free of the baggage related to addressing the issue of identity, enabling architects to take their experiments with modern architecture to their logical limits: pristine forms, new paradigms in space conceptualisation and organisation, and the use of new technologies. However, with India being part of a galaxy of new nation states in the process of their formation, these modern works were soon to confront ambiguity and anguish. This struggle sought to address questions of collective identity in the light of the inherent cultural pluralism that existed in the region—a challenge that architects across South Asia would have to face in the coming decade.

Gandhian architecture was an architecture of simplicity, with many intellectual antecedents and parallels including modern architectural precepts, but without the formal vocabulary of modernism.
Displaying a minimalism of design and the spirit of his political and social ideas, the architecture of Gandhi's ashrams became the vehicle for manifesting these ideals as directly as possible

Gandhi's ideas of simplicity and asceticism resonated in the conception and representation of his **Sabarmati Ashram**, Ahmedabad as well as in other locations such as Wardha. The *charkha* (spinning wheel) symbolised his ideals, and the simplicity of space and its occupation reinforced the minimal and frugal lifestyles that he was propagating

During his stay at the **Sevagram Ashram**, Wardha between 1936 and 1948, Gandhi's use of appropriate building technology for the ashram *kutirs* (huts) furthered his idea of frugality

Architecture in India since 1990 | Landscape of Pluralism

Bharatiya Vidya Bhavan, by Doctor and Vajifdar, Mumbai, 1938

Aurora Theatre, Mumbai, by GL Kulkarni of Marathe & Kulkarni Architects, early 1930s

Metro Adlabs, Mumbai, by Thomas Lamb and DW Ditchburn, 1938

In India, the first manifestation of modernism was Art Deco; although it was strongly associated with modernism, it differed in that it was less functional and initially more aristocratic in both its form and patronage. In many ways, the opulence of 'princely India' that Art Deco perpetuated was an interesting contrast to the sensibility introduced by Gandhi—the austere and the elegant together attempting to evoke the spiritual

Architecture in India since 1990 | Landscape of Pluralism

Golconde Ashram
Interior view of a typical residential room at the ashram in Pondicherry. The armchair and bed were designed by Japanese-American architect George Nakashima

The drying verandah at the ashram

View of the garden courtyard from the entry lobby of the ashram. The plinth, finished in black cuddapah stone, receives the staircase that leads to the residential quarters on the upper floors

The overall massing and articulation of the buildings reflect sensibilities that the architect, Antonine Raymond, perhaps imbibed from his training in, and exposure to, Japan

The teakwood sliding panels that separate the residential rooms from the vernandah create a porous inner skin that facilitates passive cooling through the building, while ensuring privacy when required. The large, operable louvres were custom-made and allow great flexibility in controlling air and light in the building

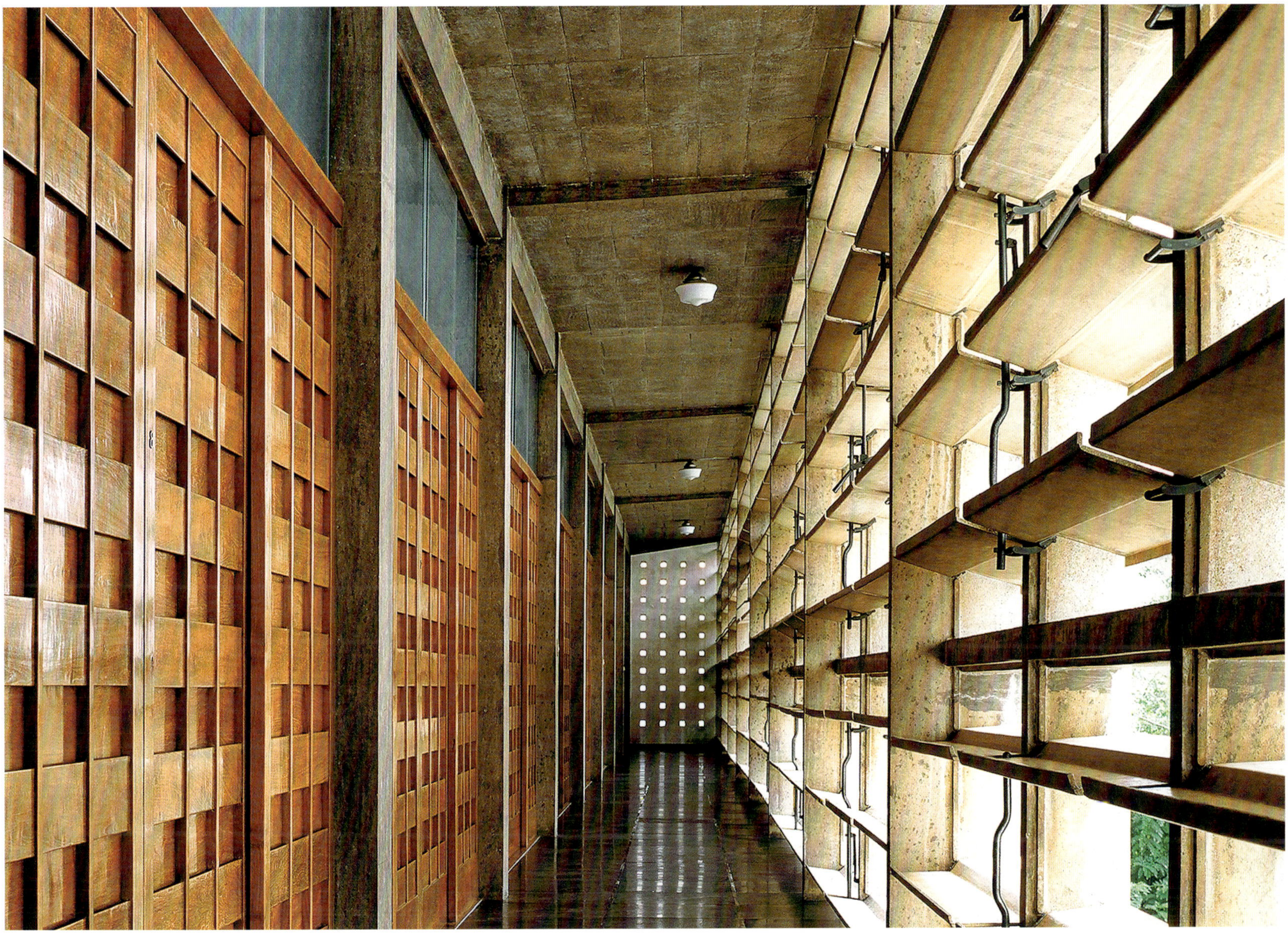

ARCHITECTURE AND INDIAN IDENTITY

The late 1940s and 1950s in India (and, indeed, all of South Asia) were characterised by the drive among architects and patrons to create a collective identity for the emerging nation states that grew out of independence from colonial rule. In the South Asia of the time, Mahatma Gandhi, Rabindranath Tagore and Nehru in India, Muhammad Ali Jinnah in Pakistan, and Solomon Bandaranaike in Sri Lanka emerged as the dominant leaders who embodied different visions of nation building. Although the idealism and austerity of Gandhi, the poetic vision of Tagore and the zealous rhetoric of Jinnah inspired generations, ultimately Nehru's socialist programme emerged as the prevailing model in the region. Nehru compelled the leaders of South Asia to look to the future—"not go abroad in search of the past, [but] go to foreign countries in search of the present. The search is necessary, for isolation from it means backwardness and decay."[21]

Ironically, the immediate architectural response to independence was a major revivalist phase throughout India. Official government architecture was most susceptible to this phenomenon, with each nation digging into its past repertoire for images to represent the bursting confidence of its new government and to symbolise this newfound power through public buildings.[22] Others, like the established firms and practitioners (many of which were Anglo-Indian companies) drew the middle ground, straddling the views of both the revivalists and modernists. Their modernism was rooted in the Art Deco style, which allowed overlays of symbols and decoration; this was the extent to which they localised their designs.[23] As a counterpoint to these approaches, young intellectuals and architects returning from Europe or North America proposed modernism as being more relevant to the spirit of the period.[24] Modernism was perceived as the natural approach for expressing the new nationalism: it was unhampered by historical or cultural restraints, and reflected the optimism of a free people in their aspiration for economic development as well as a desire to link to the rest of the world.

The first heroic modernist phase of modern Indian architecture comprises roughly the period that may be described as the Nehruvian state (1947-75). At the threshold of India's independence in the 1940s, men like Nehru clearly embraced modernism as the appropriate vehicle for representing India's future agenda. For the elite patrons (of architecture), modernism was also attractive as it was specifically focused on the future, with no reference to past styles. In fact, Nehru's orientation made India the most vibrant site for the 'modern project,' where the East-West relationship was constantly redefined and the modernising experience was key in forming the nation's identity. Furthermore, Nehru was convinced that India, a new nation, was the most potent site for ushering in what Le Corbusier had referred to as a second, more humane machine age.[25] This resulted in an invitation to Le Corbusier to design Chandigarh, his proposals for which became the symbol for the modern, independent India of Nehru's imagination.

Thus, while the rest of South Asia struggled for the next few decades to resolve its issues of national identity, India solved its problems by default, with Le Corbusier coming to design Chandigarh. In retrospect, Le Corbusier's greatest impact was that he thereby instantly solved the debate between revivalists and modernists (the modernists won). His progressive social ideals and architectural concepts fitted in neatly with Nehru's ambitions for India. For almost two decades, Le Corbusier's work served as a model for an independent democratic India, while other countries in South Asia struggled with reconciling the international style and revivalist ideas to represent their political ideologies.

However, outside official patronage what characterised the period from the 1950s through to the 1970s, perhaps around the world, was the idea that architects could shape the form not only of the physical environment but also of social life. Modernists' ideas, and the optimism of reconstructing society through the re-orchestration of the built environment, pervaded the debate in India. The sphere of the architect in India thus expanded considerably in this period through the building of both physical and social infrastructure. Museums, hospitals, schools, colleges, housing projects and new towns presented many fresh possibilities for architects. Yet the challenge was how to celebrate, through this architectural production, a new identity for the region. In fact, this era witnessed a phenomenon in which disparate attitudes and aspirations for the future, which had earlier been subordinated to the focused agenda of independence and political freedom, began to be expressed, with the central question being what vision should guide planning for the future? Although Le Corbusier and, later, Louis Kahn were the most influential figures in the formation of these directions, the development of a localised elite patronage in different countries served as crucibles for the birth of a new architectural direction. Throughout the 1960s and 1970s, an architectural 'spine' of awareness and patronage developed in India, running from Chandigarh through New Delhi to Ahmedabad, Vadodara and Mumbai. In addition, building programmes of some significance in Puducherry, as well as Colombo and later Dhaka in Bangladesh, became new centres in the post-colonial scenario.

What characterised all these efforts across India was the phenomenon of the simultaneous acceptance of and resistance to Western ideologies. In fact, Indian architects found many impediments along the path to developing a modern visual idiom. Isolated from the philosophical origins of modernism, architects in India were perhaps unable to comprehend the depths of its intricate mechanism and purpose. Thus, Indian architects in the 1950s and 1960s struggled to make modernism work—not only in regard to their existing traditions, but also in how they would situate their modernity within a cultural context. As a result, this period and the subsequent decades saw numerous attempts by Indian architects to reconcile Western forms and local issues, using ideas and lessons from the past.[26] In addition, this struggle was set in the context of South Asia, where divergent problems had to be addressed—ultimately resulting in varied solutions and architectural forms, and thereby further reinforcing the pluralism that had historically characterised the architectural landscape of the region. Moreover, with the broadening of the architect's role, urbanisation and its related concerns began to draw the attention of architects and planners. Projects for new towns, including low-cost housing with affordable infrastructure, found their way into the architectural debate in India.[27] Simultaneously, a greater sensibility evolved, leading to attempts to revive traditional crafts and of looking deeper into tradition for clues to address issues of both cultural continuity and economic appropriateness.[28]

With all these dimensions, the modern project in India found its greatest expression in the city of Ahmedabad, after its first celebration in Chandigarh. However, Chandigarh was a *tabula rasa* situation, in which modernism did not really confront the many layers of tradition or the cultural milieu that, for example, Ahmedabad presented. Chandigarh was also a unique attempt at a synthesis of the monumental with the decorative without being forced to confront any existing built context, or even society as such. Meanwhile, in Ahmedabad, Le Corbusier built in an existing context, sparking off a series of potent processes for modern architects in India as well as all of South Asia. He did not mimic, but rather absorbed, recreated and pointed toward the potential remaking of the context.[29]

Ahmedabad offered the kind of patronage that modern architecture in India had perhaps not experienced before. The families who owned the city's cotton mills, particularly the Sarabhais, were more representative of the New India than the constituency for which Nehru was building in Chandigarh. These families saw the necessity of combining modernity and tradition in order to compete in a world market. Indeed, the Sarabhais were instrumental in bringing Frank Lloyd Wright, Le Corbusier, and Louis Kahn to India. They were also responsible for inviting Ray and Charles Eames to assist in creating a framework for establishing the National Institute of Design (NID) in Ahmedabad. This resulted in the famous *India Report* (1958), which served as a manifesto for the NID and its pedagogic thrust. Essentially, they facilitated a context in which modernism could interact in the truest sense with the culture in which it was now set. These mill-owning families also played a significant part in the liberalisation from British rule, together with Gandhi, whose ashram was located in Ahmedabad. Through the Ahmedabad experiment,[30] modernism finally put its roots down in all of India, with an entire new generation of architects inspired and committed to all that it stood for.

India's independence, although apparently closing the debate on architecture and identity, did not produce the society for which the country had hoped and yearned; instead, all efforts were directed toward dealing with the splintered society that the nation had inherited. A society fractured by caste, class, economic disparities, rural-urban divides, and a multitude of beliefs and religious affiliations was welded together as a nation state.[31] Through this process, issues of uneven social and economic mobility threw up disparate aspirations, with their satisfaction becoming increasingly challenging. In fact, in the decades after independence the struggle for identity really played itself out; these modern works soon ran up against ambivalence, resistance and the struggle to address the issues of multiple identities. It became overwhelmingly evident during these years that aesthetic modernity seemed to have arrived before social modernity, through the small community of architects who had become host to these new ideas.[32] Similarly, architecture in India continued to be largely handmade and dependent on craft. Reconciling these modes of production with the modernist tenets of pre-determinacy and predictability was difficult for practitioners trained in Western sensibilities of architectural production. This resulted in crafts staying at the fringes of formal production of architecture even as they engaged in the creation of common everyday structures that were outside the influence of trained architects. Thus, Indian architects struggled for the acceptance of modernism in the popular imagination, and grappled with the challenge of placing their aesthetic modernity within the complex cultural context of India.

The Nehruvian state came to an end not with Nehru's death in 1964, but in 1975, when Indira Gandhi as prime minister of the country abrogated democratic freedoms and imposed the Emergency (more correctly, the State of Emergency), arising from internal disturbances (1975-77), in order to contain popular unrest against her policies and political style. The year 1975 marked the beginning of the next phase of Indian architecture, which was both post-heroic and post-modernist in nearly equal measure.[33] In the aftermath of the Emergency, the then Indian nation state lost a certain momentum. In architecture, this general situation was reflected in a degree of exhaustion. By the late 1970s, nationalism was less of an issue for architects than merely attempting to resolve the contradiction of trying to intensify development while also preserving the best of the inherited culture and societal values. Interestingly, although not being inspired per se by nationalism, these efforts were driven by an obsessive drive toward fabricating a pan-Indian identity. The 1980s saw many moves by architects to create this Indian identity, or an 'Architecture for India' as it was phrased at that time.

The Festivals of Architecture (1983-86), organised by the Government of India at the initiation of Pupul Jayakar (who was often referred to as the 'Czarina of Culture') were an amazing spectacle of international travelling exhibitions covering the arts and architecture of India. These events celebrated India's coming of age as a nation and its confidence to confront the world on its own cultural terms, and they worked to reinforce this pan-Indian identity. The Festivals were held in Britain, France and Japan, and celebrated the ability of the arts to connect to the wellspring of tradition. Through their sophisticated representation of ideas, ancient tradition demonstrated its continuity in nourishing contemporary architectural and artistic production. Founded on strong modernist principles, the architecture of the 1970s and 1980s was crucial in terms of both internalising modernism and setting it off on a trajectory to confront the past—namely, to challenge and be challenged by tradition. The festivals became instrumental in articulating this otherwise ambiguous relationship with the past, and they broadened the scope of discussion to perceive the traditional heritage of Indian architecture as not merely in terms of monumental edifices but as being intrinsically linked to the expression of our innermost aspirations. In particular 'Vistara', the exhibition curated by architect Charles Correa, posed a highly pluralistic view of architecture in India. It spectacularly made the range of architectural production in India, from the vernacular to the monumental, appear seamlessly interconnected by the idea that architecture was myth-based, expressing the presence of a reality more profound than the manifest world in which it exists. The exhibition inadvertently challenged the architect to move in and embrace more divergent directions, in such a way that the past and present could be configured to construct the future. The exhibition's message emphasised the fluidity of identity resulting from the many layers of history characterising this kaleidoscopic pluralism of the Indian architectural landscape. More importantly, it also implicitly shifted the gaze from an industrial, urban and modern India to the village, rural and ancient one as the seat of intellectual nourishment for architects and the production of architectural identity.[34]

Architectural education perpetuated this phenomenon of the rural as a wellspring of nourishment for new directions in architectural thinking. Although older schools of architecture established under the British continued to thrive in terms of popularity, they merely extended the tradition they were set up to propagate—that is, of producing draughtsmen. Schools such as the one established at the Centre for Environmental Planning and Technology (CEPT) by architect BV Doshi first made the search for an Indian identity in architecture an intellectual project.[35] Architects like Claude Batley had attempted this reconciliation between tradition and modernity through their teachings,[36] yet it took the next generation of architects in free India to confidently define this new direction. The creation of the school in Ahmedabad coincided with the establishment of the National Institute of Design and the presence of several young intellectuals and designers in the city; thus, its founding moments were nourished with ideas and visions from disparate sources.[37] Over the years, the school in Ahmedabad set a precedent for new forms of architectural education in India and became a pace-setter in its detachment from government controlled education. This created a new model of education for thinking architects and prepared them to embrace the challenges facing the country as it transcended the multiple anxieties it had grappled with at its birth and moved forward as a nation into the 1980s.[38]

This resurrection of the dialogue with the past took on a fiercer form in the later years of the 1980s in many aspects of life in India. Indeed, the idea of asserting regional identities in the face of globalisation was becoming more important than that of national identities per se. Since architecture is not easily identified according to political boundaries, the overlap between culture and nationalism is not always clear. From this ambiguity and the resultant 'churning' and search for identity, regionalism, playing upon both modernity and a traditional vocabulary, emerged in a renewed form as the focus of the profession in India. This position attempted to relocate the architect within broader social processes, thereby linking the profession to a renewed sense of the past, to local building traditions and to the importance of a continuing dialogue with the user.[39]

Such developments accelerated throughout the 1990s with the liberalisation of the Indian economy, which witnessed the rapidly disappearing role of the state in the influencing or creation of the built environment and a swiftly fading emphasis on a pan-Indian identity.[40] The most significant shift in the 1990s was that regional identities, facilitated by the fragmentation of the political power structure in the country, asserted a coalition of regional parties rather than the centralised two-party system.[41] However, implicit in this broadening approach was a fundamental shift in attitudes toward the construction of identities, whereby the singular pan-national identity was replaced by fluid identities in which the metaphors of hybridity and pluralism became more significant than any kind of authoritative orthodoxy or superior, singular identity. This understanding highlights the notion of identities as dynamic and ever-shifting rather than static. To quote Homi Bhabha, "Each time the encounter with identity occurs at the point at which something exceeds the frame of the image, it eludes the eye, evacuates the self as a site of identity and autonomy and—most important—leaves a resistant trace, a stain of the subject, a sign of resistance. We are no longer confronted with an ontological problem of being but with a discursive strategy of the moment of interrogation, a moment in which the demand for identification becomes, primarily, a response to other questions of signification and desire, culture and politics."[42]

Although the idealism and austerity of Gandhi, the poetic vision of Tagore, and the zealous rhetoric of Jinnah inspired many generations, it was ultimately Nehru's socialist programme that emerged as the dominant model in South Asia

Gandhi and Tagore at Udayan, Shantiniketan. The synergy between these two minds galvanised distinct visions on nation building, but it was ultimately the Nehruvian agenda and the ensuing aesthetic that dominated the post-independence era

Tagore's mud house, Shyamali, at Shantiniketan, by Surendranath Kar and Nandalal Bose, advocated Gandhi's ideas of simplicity in living while reflecting an 'aristocratic-folk paradigm'

Vidhana Soudha, Bengaluru by BR Manickam, chief engineer of the Public Works Department. This seat of assembly, built between 1952 and 1957 by the PWD for the state of Karnataka, symbolises the direction in which the revivalists would have liked to take architecture in the post-independence era

The **Ashoka Hotel** in New Delhi by EB Doctor in 1955 mounted traditional elements onto its main façade, and is one of the few examples of 'official' Indian architecture designed with revivalist tendencies

Architecture in India since 1990 | Landscape of Pluralism

Le Corbusier's greatest impact was that he instantly solved the debate between revivalists and modernists (the modernists won). His progressive social ideals and architectural ideas fit in neatly with Nehru's ambitions for India. For almost two decades, Le Corbusier's work served as a model for an independent democratic India

Nehru's vision of a new India, that was 'unfettered by traditions of the past' found expression through Le Corbusier's **Capitol Complex** at Chandigarh

As an emblem of the first legislative building in postcolonial India, the **Assembly Building** in Chandigarh emerged untouched by historicity, showcasing a new, robust use of form and material as well as a bold experimentation with form. Le Corbusier's influence shifted instantaneously the direction of post-independence architecture in India

High Court, Chandigarh by Le Corbusier

Architecture in India since 1990 | Landscape of Pluralism

Architecture in India since 1990 | Landscape of Pluralism

Chandigarh was a tabula rasa situation, where modernism did not really confront the many layers of tradition or the cultural milieu that Ahmedabad presented.

It was also a unique attempt at a synthesis of the monumental with the decorative, not forced to confront any existing built context or even society as such. Meanwhile, in Ahmedabad, Le Corbusier built in an existing context, sparking off a series of potent processes for modern architects in India as well as all of South Asia. He did not mimic, but rather absorbed, recreated, and pointed toward the potential remaking of the context

Architecture in India since 1990 | Landscape of Pluralism

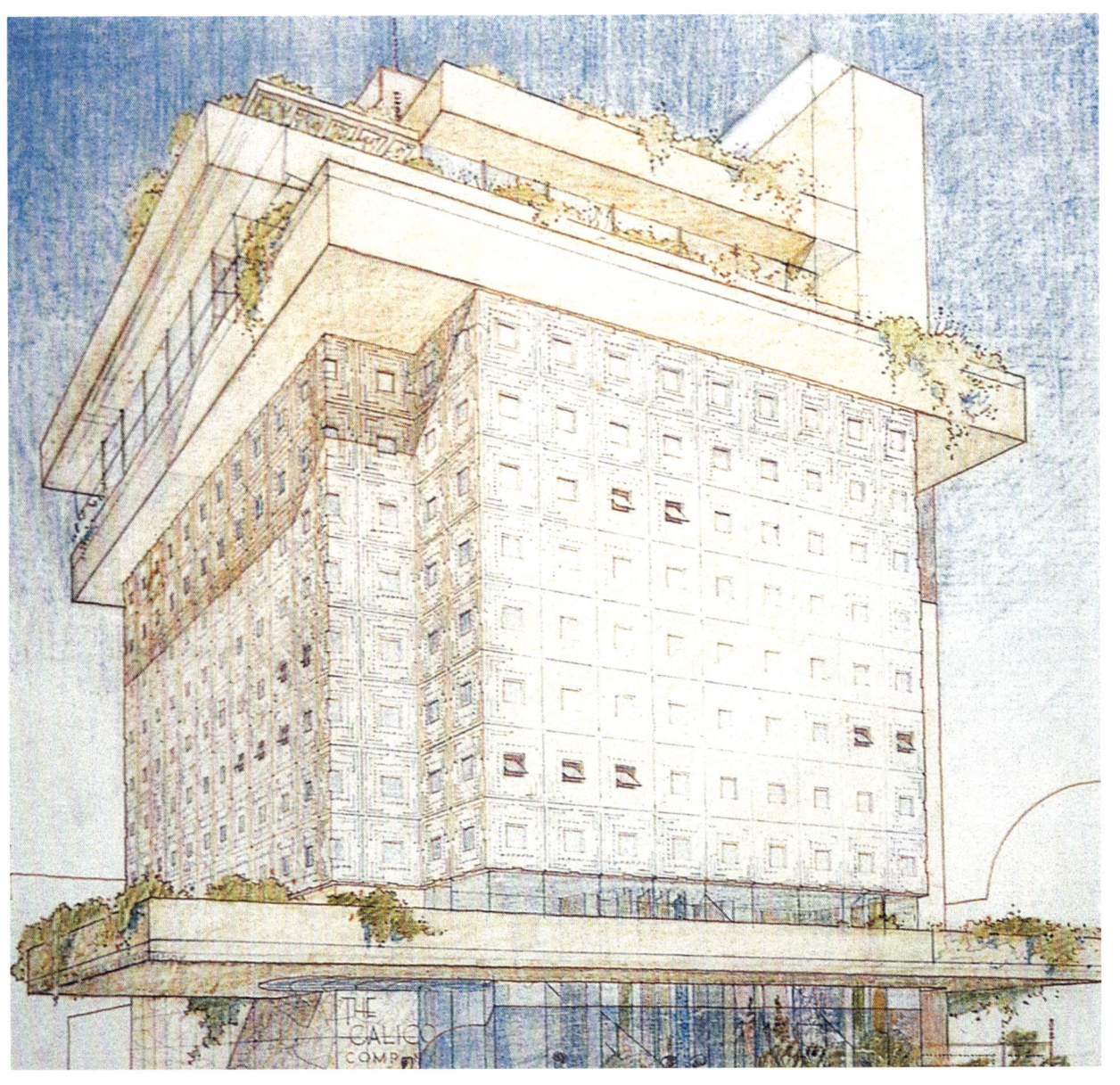

Shodan House by Le Corbusier, Ahmedabad, built in 1956

Unbuilt project by Frank Lloyd Wright for the **Calico Headquarters** in Ahmedabad. This city experienced amazing patronage in the 1960s and 70s. Had this Wright design been built, Ahmedabad would have had the distinction of containing buildings by perhaps the three greatest architects of the twentieth century—Wright, Kahn and Le Courbusier!

Louis Kahn Plaza at the **Indian Institute of Management**, Ahmedabad

Western façade of the **Mill Owners' Association** building, Ahmedabad, showing ramp and *brise soleil*. This headquarters for the textile guild wholly demonstrated Corbusier's tenets of the free plan on *piloti*

In the decades after independence the struggle for identity continued to be the central issue for architects in India. Modern works soon ran up against ambivalence, resistance and the struggle to address the issues of multiple identities. It became overwhelmingly evident during these years that aesthetic modernity seemed to have arrived before social modernity through the small community of architects who had become host to these new ideas

Mill Owners' Association building by Le Corbusier, 1954

Collage by David Wild, juxtaposing the modernist building agenda in India with the political, social and cultural milieu—represented skilfully and with a critical edge

Vigyan path
Himalya Marg
Madhya Marg
Udyog path
Udyan path
Sarovar path
Sukhna path
Chandi path
7 - 8
17 - 57 38 -
30 जनवरी सन 95 सोमवार को
2 5
02 - 96 75 -
जनवरी सन 95 मंगलवार
0
05 -

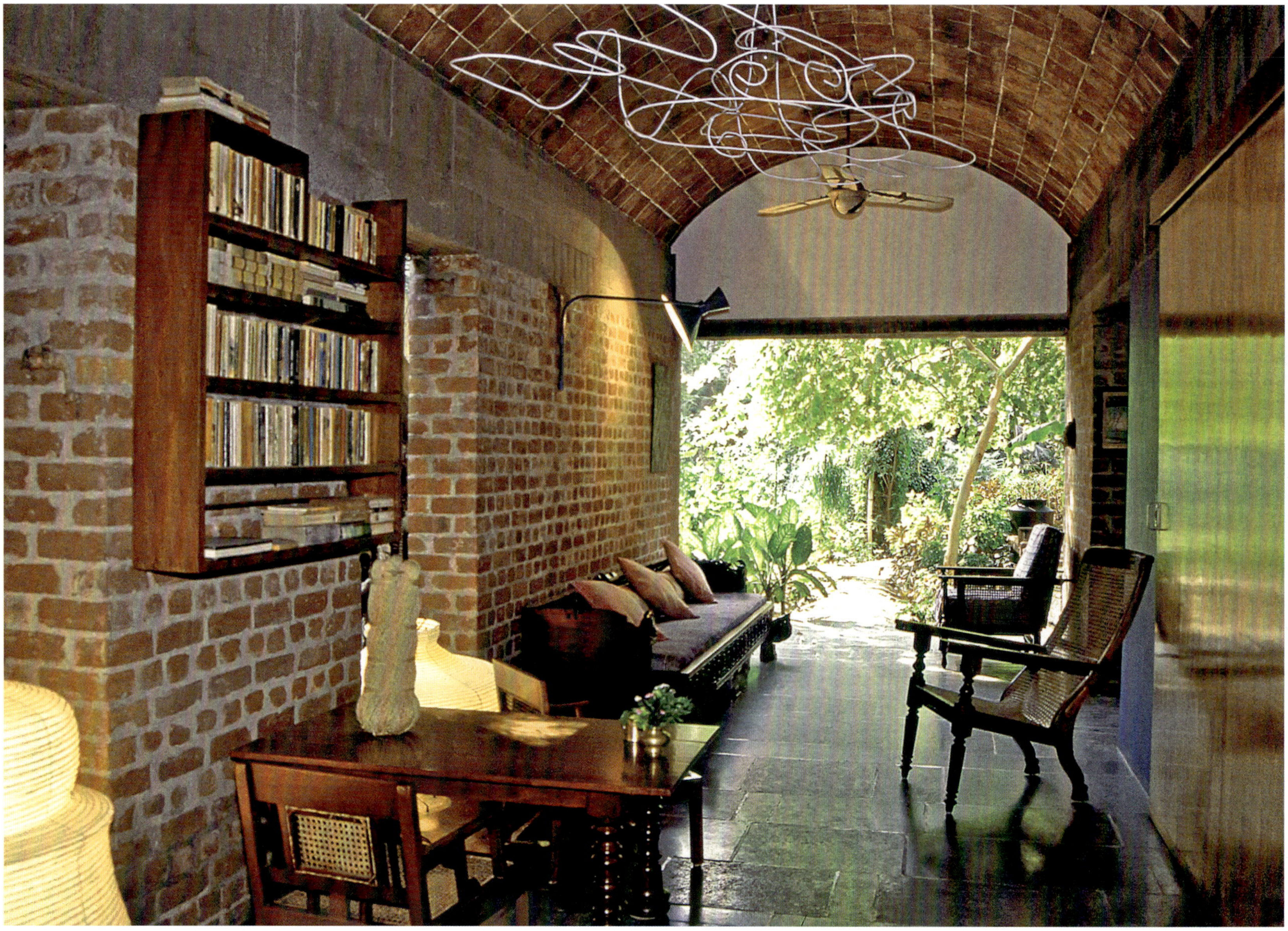

Architecture in India since 1990 | Landscape of Pluralism

Sarabhai House
For this family residence in Ahmedabad, Le Corbusier employed parallel bays in exposed brick with a vaulted ceiling, a clear deviation from the beton brut expression of his buildings in Chandigarh

Collage by David Wild, layering the interior of the house with imagery from the popular visual representation of India together with European images—provocatively suggesting the sensibilities that the Sarabhais represented as major patrons of architecture in Ahmedabad

View of the garden façade

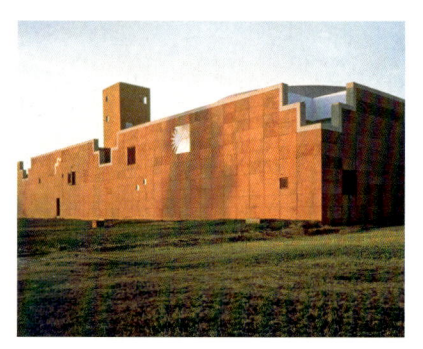

Architecture in India since 1990 | Landscape of Pluralism

The Indian government's invitation to **Ray and Charles Eames** to assess and recommend on the establishment of programmes for training designers in India gave great impetus to design education and research in the country

Jawahar Kala Kendra by Charles Correa Associates, 1992, Jaipur. A brilliantly provocative integration of deep abstract traditions and a modern sensibility

Pupul Jayakar, with J Krishnamurti and Indira Gandhi

View of one of the inner courtyards at the **Jawahar Kala Kendra** by Charles Correa Associates, 1992

Hall of Nations, **Pragati Maidan**, New Delhi by Raj Rewal Associates, 1972

Charles Correa (*right*) with Moshe Safdie (*middle*) and Christopher Alexander (*left*) at the Aspen Conference in 1967

Views of the **Vistara exhibition** at the Nehru Centre, Mumbai. This international exhibition, held between 1983 and 1986, presented a narrative of India's architectural traditions in a format that emphasised the philosophical and pluralistic nature of architecture in the country. It also highlighted how urban and folk paradigms had, through the ages, been seamlessly integrated into the architecture of India

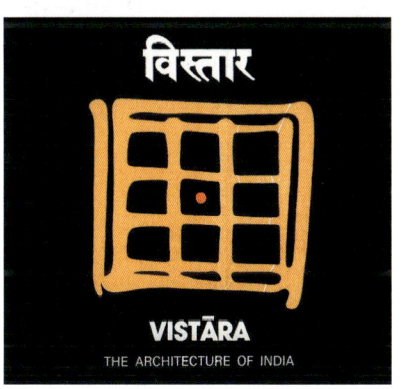

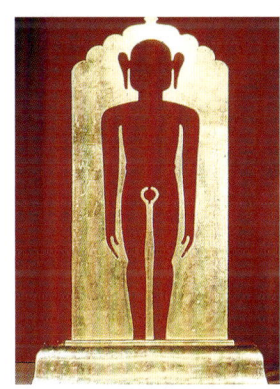

CEPT, Ahmedabad
The academic buildings and surrounding landscape of the School of Architecture, are designed to encourage intellectual exchange in order to create a 'thinking architect'

Internal view of the architecture design studio. The north orientation allows uniform light to flood the work place

Entrance to the studios—an intersection point for multiple circulation systems

BV Doshi introducing Buckminster Fuller (seated next to Doshi) when the latter visited CEPT in 1977. Also seated is architect Hasmukh Patel, who took over as Director of the School of Architecture from Doshi in 1976

B V Doshi's design for his own architectural studio **Sangath**, in Ahmedabad, was a clear departure from an earlier strict modernist approach towards a more humane vocabulary. In this partially subterranean building, natural means of insulation and cooling, and its physical rootedness to the site, makes this a special project in his seminal oeuvre as an educator and practitioner

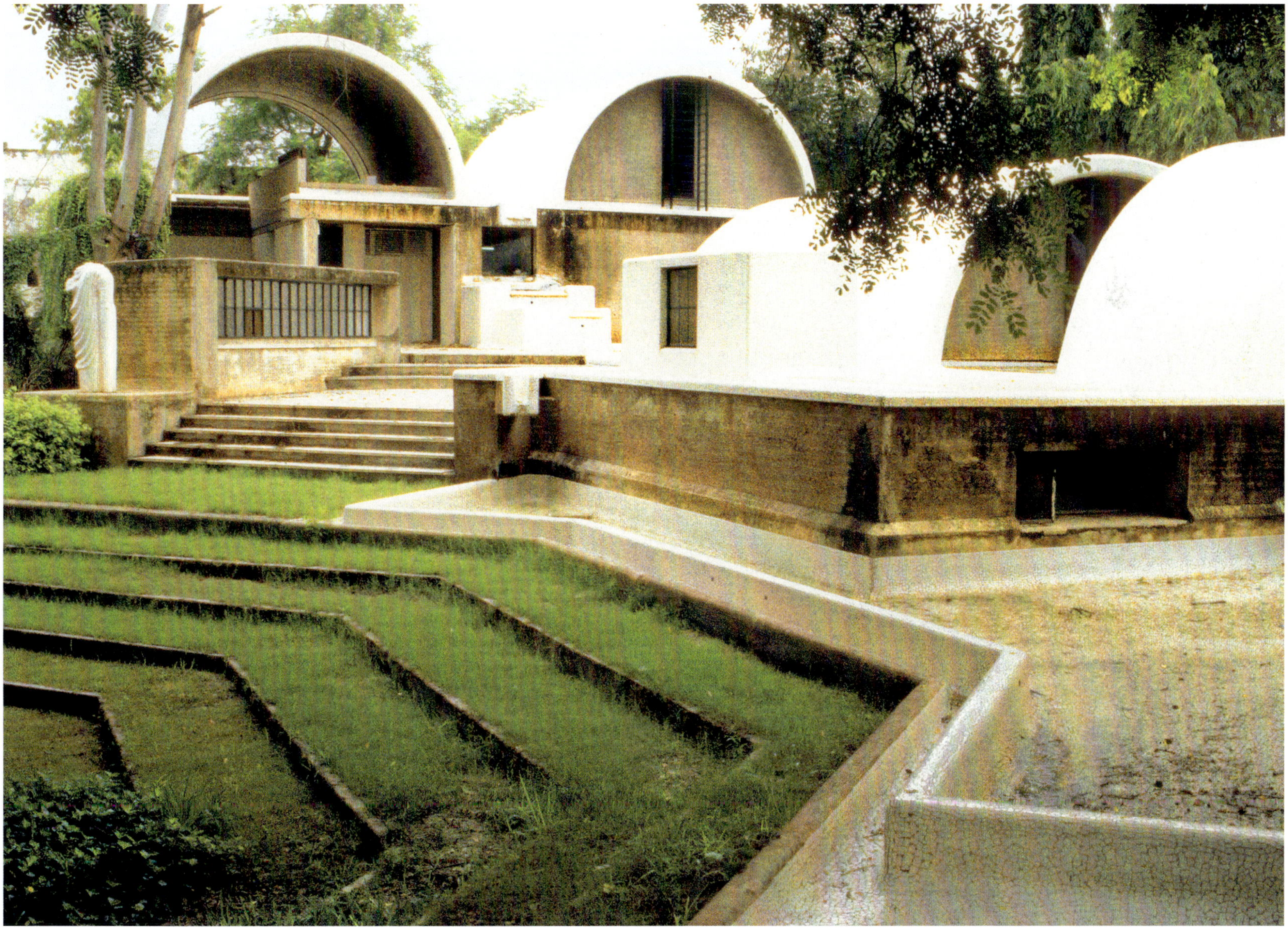

EMERGENT LANDSCAPES

It is here that the notion of cultural significance is of importance, where culture and place seminally influence the production of architecture—especially in the face of globalisation. In fact, over the last two decades, starting in the 1990s, the discussion of architecture in India has witnessed popular notions such as context, genius loci, sense of place, vernacularism, regionalism and heritage conservation—all informing in some way this all-encompassing notion of cultural significance. When viewed from this perspective, architecture is perceived to be culturally significant in so far as it embodies a definable difference—typically, the product of a distinct society, history and geographic condition. In short, it is representative of a particular culture. Unfortunately, more often than not these trajectories between identity and culture rarely intersect. Identity is discussed in terms of the discovery, rather than the potent possibilities inherent in constructing or inventing it. Cultural significance in a pluralistic society like India will be ever evolving and transforming to continually encompass changing aspirations and needs, as well as to respond to new confrontations. Only through this process of recognising the kinetic nature of cultural significance will architecture respond to contemporary realities and experiences and be truly put to the service of emerging aspirations. Discerning and understanding identity in this way will broaden our perceptions, enabling us to encompass and engage with reality beyond its formal readings through the mainstream of architectural production. This reading will be more open than before to other processes of architectural production, and to the multiple identities that are emerging or made manifest through varied practices. Thus, for any exploration concerned with the contemporary landscape in India, it is imperative to represent the multiplicity of architectural production in that context. It is precisely in the multifaceted nature of production processes that we might find clues about the form and nature of the emergent architectural landscape in India—the new practices that are responding to the contemporary.[43]

These emerging practices are in fact the indicators of the architectural landscapes that we can anticipate in the future, as they represent issues that society in India aspires to as well as patronises. Moreover, such models of architectural practice can easily be seen as a response to these needs. Whatever form these practices take, they strive for authenticity and identity while attempting to resolve the monumental complexity and cultural dynamics of India. Although the nature of these responses is diverse, four distinct patterns of practice have become evident as being emblematic of the divergent approaches emerging to give expression to contemporary societal aspirations in India. These are: the practice of constructing global identities which manifest and give expression to the arrival, most often, of global capital; the practice of regionalism which responds to local resources and concerns; the alternative practice, which recognises the presence of the subalterns, or the unrepresented voices and communities in society; and a pattern based on a sort of counter-modernism, which thrives on the revival of the ancient and closes the loop (on this range of practices) through its single-minded resistance to the global aspirations of the nation.[44]

Global Practice

In today's India, rocketing levels of consumption—spurred by a rapidly increasing and economically mobile middle class—are driving the construction of a new landscape of global derivates, which constitute images of globalisation. Given this condition, when capital arrives in such an environment it is expected to take on a particular character and is supported by freeways, shopping malls, new corporate centres and global suburbs. The pattern of architectural practice concerned with the construction of these global identities is largely a corporate one, and its influence is today probably one of the most visible in the public realm. Assuming a sophisticated building industry, this pattern of practice communicates its design intentions through a well-detailed set of instructions and documents that are translated into buildings. The practice is usually organised in the form of a large firm with in-house specialisation and services. Although this pattern thrives on client confidence to deliver competent and predictable products, it perpetuates the rigid landscape of global architecture devoid of any responses to the local setting and social milieu. In the recent past, with the acceleration of India's economic liberalisation, several

Asian, American and European corporate architectural firms have begun to build in India, further perpetuating this pattern of construction as well as the images that go with it. Curtain-wall-glazed, metal-clad façades; central air conditioning; and an emphasis on providing adequate parking, security systems and numerous other such features, all combined with the overarching sense of total containment, make these 'implants' eminently recognisable in the Indian landscape.

This pattern of global practice has been patronised by multinational corporations and developers and, from the mid-1990s, by the government as well—usually for their financial institutions. Similarly, given the boom in software exports the information technology industry has been a large emerging patron of this global architecture. Software campuses in the outlying areas of Hyderabad, New Delhi, Bengaluru and Mumbai are becoming sites for the manufacture of this imagery, which is rapidly being emulated by smaller operators across the country. This architectural response is desperately trying to seek a dialogue with its client base in the United States or Europe rather than establish any connection with its locality. Glass-clad buildings of over-articulated forms, all held together by (water-consuming) manicured lawns, are the form of these campuses.[45]

The quantity of such architecture is increasing as globalisation gains a foothold in India, thus amplifying its influence on the profession as well as people's perceptions of it. Projected to make India appear more efficient and competent, this representation also makes Indian architecture look similar to manifestations of globalisation elsewhere in the world. However, the limitations of architecture in these circumstances are only too evident: a predictability and detachment of the built form from its ambient environment, a divorce from place and community, and an indifference to the imperatives of tectonic innovation and material resources. The resulting gated communities and privately initiated housing projects are emblematic of the emerging global suburbs characterising the landscapes of India's post-liberalised economy. The manufacturing of global identities is also patronised by the diaspora Indian community, who have become a significant economic force as a result of the government's new liberal policies that permit the easy flow of funds and legalise the purchase of property by foreign investors—with those of Indian origin receiving a special status and incentives.[46]

Historically, or at least since the country gained independence, work in the Indian private sector has always been small scale, focusing on artesian practice or a boutique approach. This was a natural outcome of the larger scale of work, whether it was institutional or housing, being delivered directly by the government through its own design agency.[47] In the socialist economy, any large private sector establishment was equated with capitalism, and consequently, was viewed as 'commercial' and morally on the fringe of societal acceptability. As a result, India was ill prepared for large-scale global practice as the country has had no tradition of this form of working. Thus, until the 1990s, no substantial tradition or capability existed in the profession that could respond to large-scale infrastructure or building projects. With the sudden opening up of the economy, firms from Singapore, Europe and the United Sates took the lead in bidding for the new commissions that accompanied the liberalisation of the economy and the processes of its globalisation. Often the first capital that arrived was foreign capital, from investors who brought their own architects to design the form it took on the ground. These, often large, corporations were capable of deftly and swiftly responding to the 'impatience' of capital as well as traversing the obstacles on the ground through their confidence, detachment and disengagement from local politics. This situation introduced a new cultural paradigm for the profession in India, with the bulk of indigenous firms aspiring to remake themselves throughout the 1990s in the form of corporate large-scale architectural offices.

Regional Manifestation

A counterpoint to the corporate model of practice is posed by the regionalist approach, which has evolved beyond its modernist roots to respond to the locale. Today, this form of practice does not reject modernism but rather the new form of internationalism perpetuated by the corporate pattern of practices in the face of globalisation, and seeks to resist these flows on their terms. In fact, regionalists see the importance of modernism as a mechanism to view tradition anew. They recognise that modernism demands a respect for the inherent qualities of building materials, expressiveness of structure, the functional justification for form and the subtle integration of the icons and textures of the larger landscape in which they are set. Regionalists clearly focus on the concerns of the region, which is their context, their endeavour being to create a distinct identity without resorting to clichés or literal references.

The chief patrons of the regionalist approach are the various cultural and social institutions as well as private bodies (e.g. schools, resort hotels and private homes). In addition to institutional buildings, mass-scale housing was very much in the realm of engagement of the regionalist architects until the government began to patronise and produce social housing. Since the liberalisation of the economy, this area has been squarely pre-empted by the corporate pattern of practice—a contentious issue in the architecture profession in India, and perhaps globally. However, regionalist architects continue to build socially and climatically responsible projects within this model of practice. Despite patronage for previously government-controlled projects transferring from the public to the private sector, regionalist practice seeks to retain the social and environmental commitment of these programmes. As a result, these practices constitute 'centres of local resistance', which produce alternative modernities within the overarching narrative of globalisation. In other words, while their patronage has shifted their ideals remain.

Alternate Practice

The notion of the architect as the custodian of the vernacular traditions of a region extended the regionalists' approach. This model emerged in India in the 1970s as a counterpoint to modernism and the perceived elimination of tradition that the modernist project implied. This model first manifested itself in the form of the architect as craftsperson, working directly with the builders, more or less eliminating drawings as a medium by which to communicate design intentions.

The buildings being constructed by these practitioners displayed an energetic adoption of local materials and vernacular building practices. This approach constituted a genuinely participatory process, with the craftspeople and builders making the bulk of the decisions. The flexibility in design intentions and the open-endedness demonstrated in these cases, where the final product is determined by the construction process, facilitated the easy incorporation of symbols and icons and also linked this architecture to the larger religious and cultural traditions of a region. Non-Government Organisations (NGOs), cultural institutions and intellectuals are often the chief patrons of this architecture.

In the 1990s, with the onslaught of globalisation and the marginalisation and displacement that ensued from its arrival in the altered economy, this model of practice re-energised itself. Today, it encompasses architect-activists and practitioners who have consciously chosen to be more reflective and consider the consequences of their actions as well as the ways in which they can effectively counter global flows that marginalise both tradition and people. These practitioners enter into a potentially more fulfilling relationship with a site, its history, the community of users whose needs they address and the members of the workforce who are their collaborators. Yet these practitioners are viewed with great suspicion by mainstream architects—perhaps because they challenge the more customary models of professional practice. In fact, they focus on experiments and subversions that are carried out at the margins of conventional practice. By electing to work at the periphery of the prevailing model, these alternative practitioners have declared their moral retaliation against the forces of globalisation. Their approach with respect to both patronage and technology, is pioneering; their projects may occasionally be commissioned by the state or corporate sector in a benevolent mood (trusts, foundations, etc.), but they originate more usually with NGOs, charitable trusts, and similar patrons. In fact, these practitioners reject certain sources of patronage, such as developers and real-estate speculators, and treat technologies of mass production (such as reinforced cement concrete, glass andsteel) with suspicion.

The most frequently recurring theme in the architecture of this practice is the exploration of alternative technologies and construction methods that are often experimental in nature and highly innovative. Moreover, attempts to engage technology and building processes with community participation aims to rescue architecture from formal production processes and weave it decisively into the fabric of the lived experiences of its users. It further acts as an important counterpoint to the protocol-driven corporate pattern, emphasising intimacy of scale, direct involvement in the building and an activist's preoccupation with political and civic issues that impinge on architecture. These practitioners represent an argument for architectural diversity and an acknowledgement of the differences that are critical to the evolution of relevant architecture. Furthermore, the recognition of human creativity acquires special meaning in the age of atomising privatism. This access to a wider base of skills is especially important in the face of globalisation, which has reduced the character of the built form to a thin veneer of glamour.

Although operating at an often limited scale, this model of practice is entrenched in its socio-economic setting. It incorporates regional social networks into the construction process, and offers cost-effective solutions. The latter often involve the conversion of social assets into financial ones, in terms of the use of local labour and sourcing of materials. Unencumbered by aesthetic concerns, the resultant buildings are often designed and located with a 'looseness' that permits a welcome degree of flexibility in terms of materials and the building process. This mode of practice has seen popular support among institutions, NGOs and intellectuals, producing as a result a significant amount of building—yet it lacks the cohesion in physical articulation emphasised by the regionalists, and is often reduced to caricatures of local icons and images. Thus, although it may appear to extend tradition and attempt to express economy of means its literal visual nature often subverts rather than enhances vernacular traditions, and it can lack the aesthetic robustness that renders the genuine vernacular timeless. However, and more importantly, this model of practice demonstrates new directions and interpretations for sustainable design in the Indian context.

Counter Modernism

Simultaneously, an emerging phenomenon perpetuates a pattern of practice that facilitates the 'resurfacing' of ancient Indian building traditions—with the master craftsmen as decipherers of ancient texts and scriptures. This resurfacing of the past is a growing phenomenon, with numerous temples and an entire range of institutional buildings being built by these practitioners. In addition to religion-driven fundamentalism, the quest for greater economic mobility has triggered a growing interest in ancient treatises, as industrialists and the business community in India are seeking refuge in the security of ancient props wherein pre-industrial, and even primitive, images are confidently labelled as integral to regional identity. These trends not only constitute clear strains of resistance to the modern identity, but are also symbolic of the collision course that religious chauvinism has embarked upon with the integrative mechanisms of globalisation, creating a situation in which communities are concerned about the threat to their very identities as well as their autonomy and freedom to dissent. This phenomenon challenges the very foundations of the Indian nation state, and its long-established ability to absorb external influences and integrate them into the forging of its own identity. In short, it is challenging the inherent pluralism that has hitherto been integral to the identity of the nation.

This model manifests itself in two clear ways. The first is the construction of religious buildings, often employing ancient imagery as a natural expression of the fundamentalism that has grown to coincide with the process of globalisation. These temples are built by master craftsmen (often a hereditary position).[48] The thousands of smaller temples and mosques appearing across urban and rural India are examples of the fervour with which this counter-modernity has been asserting itself on the country's architectural landscape. Furthermore, an entire landscape of faith-based architecture is also simultaneously exerting its presence, wherein new forms of expression are attempted but infused with inspiration from familiar ancient imagery. The second way in which this counter-modernity is manifesting itself is the amazing resurrection of a belief in Vastu—or the sacred rules of building. Much like feng shui, Vastu probably had its roots in geomancy and was later codified in religion. Today, specialised practitioners hold the power of interpretation and have turned Vastu into a full-blown practice.

The rise of the interest in Vastu coincides rather accurately with the liberalisation of the Indian economy in the late 1980s and early 1990s—just when global flows were sweeping across the Indian landscape. Today, most middle- and higher-income families (especially in the southern states of India) would claim to follow Vastu principles in the design of their habitat. Although it has no particular or specific physical expression, the teachings of Vastu are often limiting in what they permit. These rules determine the disposition of rooms in a plan as well their topological relationships in terms of the articulation of the lowest and highest locations on a site. The rules further micromanage the design in terms of door locations, directions of staircases and the placement of water bodies. Interestingly, these tenets are codified with a certain abstraction that is not limiting to the aesthetics of the building itself. The practice of Vastu and its popularity are clearly bringing a new conservatism to the realm of architecture and the innovations of form, without necessarily challenging the emerging vocabulary and imagery of global identities. Yet its practitioners and patrons are setting specific rules for the operation of Vastu, thereby localising the spirit of global flows and constraining their operation, thus implicitly resisting the universalising effects of globalisation.

Conclusion

India seems to be experiencing an emergence of polarities or extreme positions taken by corporate aspirations: the assertion of global identities on one hand and the resurfacing of the past on the other, with the attitudes of regionalism and subaltern expression poised in between. These are not merely models of practice, but are also indications of the 'cauldron' that constitutes the emerging built environment—namely, the inherent multiplicity of identities simultaneously emerging on the Indian landscape in the face of globalisation. From this churning, a celebration of fluid identities seems to have emerged rather than an assertion of the 'pure' and 'indigenous'. Interestingly, these identities often coexist simultaneously, creating a unique landscape of pluralism.

Architecture in India has clearly developed its own resistance to globalisation, creating in the process a kaleidoscopic rendering of identity rather than a singular, clear and tangible representation of an Indian identity. Perhaps this process of forging identities must necessarily be accompanied by ruptures and confusions while, in the process, highlighting the notion of identities as dynamic rather than static, growing out of multiple as well as ever-changing societal aspirations. In the words of Amartya Sen, "identity is not a matter of discovery—of history anymore than of the present—and has to be chosen with reasoning … and we have to resist an often implicitly invoked assumption that we 'discover' rather than choose our identity."[49]

Today, with its liberalised economy, unprecedented social mobility and mutinous democracy, India is at a critical crossroads and faces the challenge of choosing, inventing and constructing its identity—a process that focuses on questions and choices. One challenge stems from how to facilitate the coexistence of multiple identities—how they relate, contradict, oppose and yet coexist, and are negotiated. Can extreme social diversity and coexistence be addressed and manifested in the designed built environment? Can architects design with divided minds? This situation has resulted in critical questions about the role of architecture in such conditions and the immense possibilities thus available to the profession.

It is perhaps through the articulation and expression of these differences, rather than subsuming them in a single identity, that we can truly read the aspirations of a nation and its regions—thus moving closer to ways of interpreting these emergent architectural landscapes where differences are no longer a source of animosity, but are instead valued as the essential ingredient for global and human harmony. Reading this diverse landscape and representing it as accurately as possible is critical for understanding India's diverse architectural practices on their own terms and accepting their simultaneous validity. Through such reading, we may capture the potential pluralism being expressed in the form of new architecture in India.

Craftsperson at work in temple workshop near Chennai

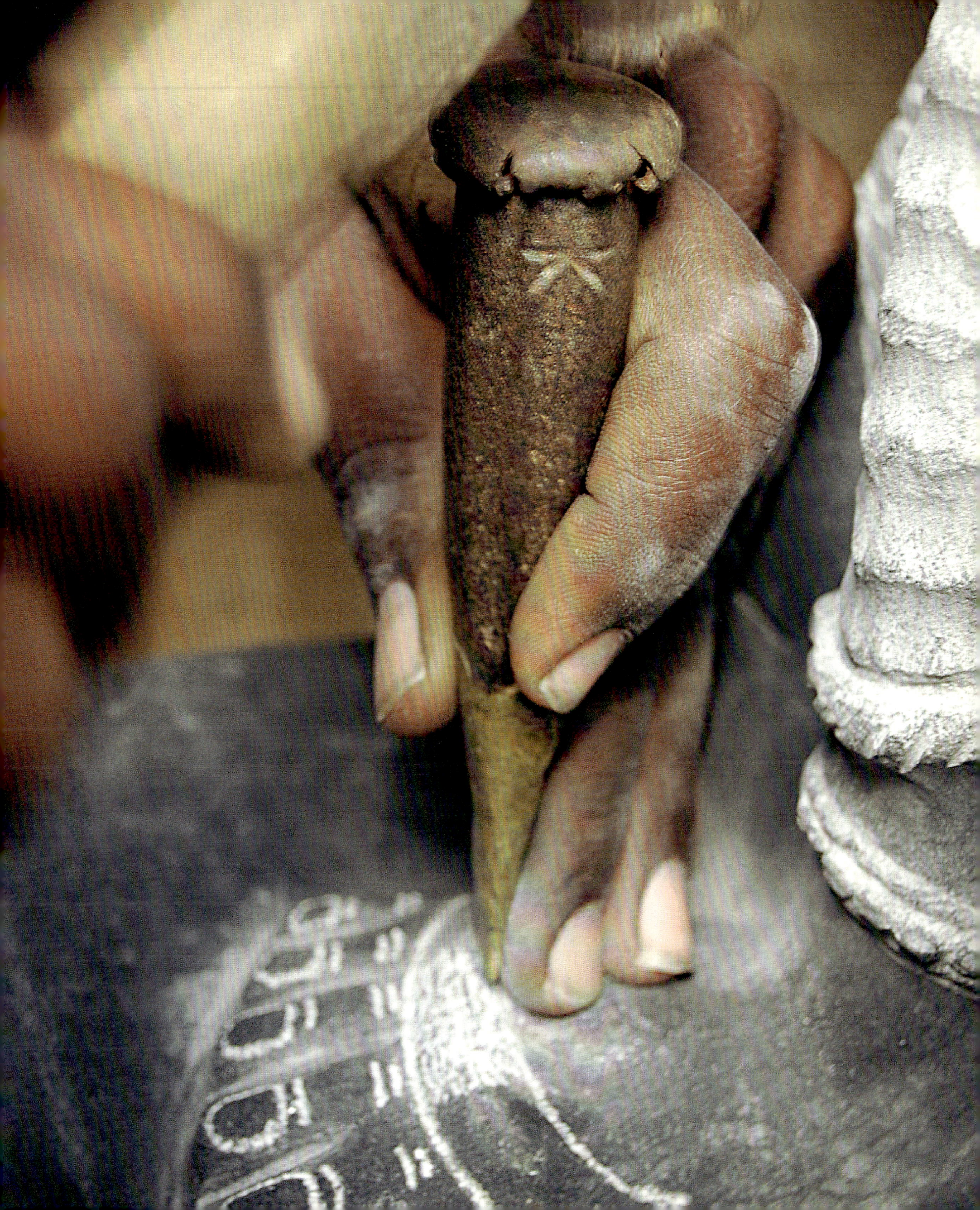

NOTES

[1] Sassen, Saskia. "Whose City Is It? Globalization and the Formulation of New Claims", *Public Culture* 8.2, 1996, pp 205-23.

[2] Khilnani, Sunil. "The India Project" in *Made In India, AD*, John Wiley and Sons, London, 2007.

[3] Agencies like CIDCO—City and Industrial Development Corporation—in Mumbai, HUDCO—Housing and Urban Development Corporation—in Delhi and the development authorities in each megacity and state were set up throughout the 1960s and 70s to provide a vision for those cities. They orchestrated growth and infrastructure, and their mandate was to make the two criteria (land-use planning and infrastructure) work in tandem. Unfortunately, these agencies were not effective and this resulted in infrastructure and land use becoming totally disjointed in most Indian cities, resulting in chaos and abrupt adjacencies in the built form.

[4] Khilnani, "The India Project".

[5] Sundaram, Ravi. "Recycling Modernity: Pirate Electronic Cultures in India" in *Sarai Reader: The Cities of Everyday Life, The Public Domain*, Sarai, New Delhi, 2001.

[6] Mehrotra, Rahul. "Negotiating the Static and Kinetic Cities" in *Urban Imaginaries*, ed. Andreas Huyssen, Duke University Press, Durham, NC, 2007.

[7] These include the bureaucracies by which building is regulated as well as the education system. The latter has largely been skill-based and completely devoid of critical thinking, a rigorous study of history or a broader culture of situating architecture in the larger cultural landscape of India. Instead, a greater part of the education system has perpetuated the training of the 'draughtsman' (a British legacy), which has now resulted in the all-pervasive cut-and-paste, or Photoshop, culture in imagining, designing and often producing buildings! For a more detailed argument on this deficiency, see Menon, AGK. "The Invention of the Modern Indian Architect", *Architecture and Design*, Vol xxv, no 3, March 2008.

[8] This debate and categorisation of the traditional and the modern, and their reconciliation, has dominated the imagination of architects in India as well as Asia as a whole. This is the Western obsession of viewing the 'other', where tradition must necessarily play a role in the discussion. American architects, for example, do not need or want to address tradition; nor do their European counterparts. The Western position often sits free of the baggage of tradition, but implores the East to be conscious of it!

[9] Smith, Roger T. "On Building for European Occupation in Traditional Climates especially India", Royal Institute of British Architects Transactions, 1st series, Vol 8, London, 1867/68.

[10] James Ransome in discussion with George Wittet following a paper presented by John Begg at the RIBA on 22 April 1929. RIBA Journal, issue 1, June 1929. Ransome was appointed the first consulting architect to the Government of India in 1902.

[11] EB Havell, Principal of the Calcutta School of Art in 1913, published the History of Indian Architecture, wherein he discerned a host of modern Indian buildings fit for praise, such as the palaces of Jaipur, Deeg and Lucknow; the domestic architecture of Rajasthan; and the temples on the banks of the Ganges. FS Growse was an outspoken Indian Civil Service officer. Though not trained in architecture or crafts design (he had an academic Master of Arts from Oxford), in the district where he held charge (Mathura from 1870-77 and as collector in Bulandshahr from 1878-84) he erected public buildings conceived in the spirit of Ruskin and constructed wholly by local artisans. His structures, like the Church in Mathura, the New Town Hall and the construction of Market Square in Bulandshahr, with their use of indigenous methods of construction, probably represent the most sustained efforts to incorporate the ideals of the Arts and Crafts Movement into architecture in the South Asia region.

[12] Sir Swinton Jacob (1841-1917) was a graduate of the East India Company's college at Addiscombe, and member of the Bombay Artillery. He served for five years as a field engineer in Aden (1861-66) before taking up his position as Executive Engineer for the public works in Jaipur. After his retirement in 1896, he stayed on in Jaipur at the Maharaja's request, first as Superintending Engineer (1902) and then (1905) as an adviser to the Maharaja. While in the service of the Maharaja, Jacob began to employ students from the Jaipur Art School to copy the ornamentation on the palaces, temples and other ancient structures in the neighbourhood. A large number of these details, which comprised measured drawings and impressions or casts transferred to paper, were subsequently reproduced, together with many others, in the volumes of the *Jeypore Portfolio of Architectural Details*. Jacob himself designed Victoria Memorial Hall, Peshawar; St Stephen's College, Delhi; the State Bank of Madras; Lalgarh Palace, Bikaner; and extensive works in Jaipur (Albert Hall Museum), Lucknow (Canning College) and Lahore.

[13] The term 'South Asia' was a Western invention, a neutral post-colonial term popularised by journalists and academics to replace the phrase 'Indian Sub-Continent'. The terminology was endorsed in the establishment of the South Asian Association for Regional Co-operation (SAARC). That was in 1985, and scholars and the media everywhere readily pressed 'South Asia' into use.

[14] By the end of the nineteenth century, and in the first decades of the twentieth, the 'Indo-Saracenic' was well established, and was perhaps the most officially favoured style of building in South Asia. Buildings in the Indo-Saracenic style were produced in all major cities of South Asia, extending from Lahore and Karachi to Chennai and Colombo, Yangon, and even in the cities of Malaysia—with architects like RF Chisholm (1840-1915), John Begg (1866-1937) and George Wittet (1840-1926) being its great propagators.

[15] *Chatris*—a small domed kiosk or open umbrella-shaped pavilion, usually placed on top of a roof for decorative or symbolic purposes. *Chajja*—a thin projection of stone, resembling a cornice, running along the side of a building or an eave over a door or window. *Jali*—a pierced stone lattice screen to a window/opening, often intricately carved, to provide protection from direct sunlight and permit ventilation.

[16] The first signs of this shift to modernism among the officially patronised British architects of the time were seen in the works of Walter George and Arthur Gordon Shoosmith. These young architects, who started off as assistants to Lutyens, began working on smaller private commissions in which they explored a synthesis of traditional motifs set in more abstract compositions of massing and overall plan articulation. This was a particularly important signal of a shift in approach within the otherwise 'architecturally sanitised' zone of New Delhi!

[17] This is an insight I attribute to Jon Lang and Madhavi and Miki Desai: Lang, Jon, Madhavi Desai and Miki Desai. *Architecture & Independence, The Search for Identity – India 1880-1980*, OUP, Delhi, 1997.

[18] John Begg worked as the Consulting Architect to the Government of Bombay from 1908 until 1921. In these 13 years, his influence on the city was substantial, and besides designing important buildings like the General Post Office in Bombay in the Indo-Saracenic style his most important contribution was the acceptance of the style for public buildings generally. He was succeeded by George Wittet, who was extremely prolific and built several commissions such as the Prince of Wales Museum and Gateway of India, thus extending the reach of the Indo-Saracenic style after Begg.

[19] Architects such as Eckhart Muthesius and Otto Koenigsberger were some such practitioners. In Mumbai, Messerschmidt and Stefan Noblin (a Polish artist) were among several European refugees who made India their home.

[20] Puducherry, a former French colony (between 1742 and 1954) in Tamil Nadu, was a fortified town distinctively divided into two by a canal and the Quai de Gingy. The Tamil town (Ville Noire) and the French town (Ville Blanc) follow a grid pattern of street planning. While the primary thoroughfares follow a north-south orientation, all feeder streets take on the perpendicular axis. Twelve km north of Puducherry lies Auroville, an experimental township founded by the Mother and designed by architect Roger Anger.

[21] Nehru, Jawaharlal. *The Discovery of India*. The Signet Press, Kolkata, 1946.

[22] Some examples of these post-independence revivalist buildings are the Ashoka Hotel in Delhi, designed by EB Doctor (1900-1984) in 1955; The Supreme Court in Delhi by the PWD in 1954, based on the design approach of Lutyens; and the Vidhana Soudha in Bengaluru, designed by the PWD in 1952.

[23] Several examples of this approach can be found in Mumbai. The city's Life Assurance Building is an otherwise modern edifice capped with a sculpture of Laxmi—the goddess of wealth—and other symbols adorn the entrance. Besides these, the building is totally without decoration.

[24] These architects included Habib Rahman, the first Indian architect to be trained at MIT; Achyut Kanvinde, who was trained at Harvard; Gautam and Gira Sarabhai; Durga Bajpai; Piloo Mody and Vina Colgan; Mansingh Rana; and, later, Charles Correa and Balkrishna Doshi.

[25] Professor Mary Wood brought this idea to my notice in her unpublished paper on Luc Durand's "Photographs of India". For this theorisation of the second machine age by Le Corbusier in the 1930s, see: Mardges, Bacon. *Le Corbusier in America: travels in the land of the timid*. MIT Press, Cambridge MA, 2001, pp 255-56.

[26] Charles Correa and BV Doshi were the first to articulate a new position about this relation in the context of modernity. Their contribution was to abstract the essential lessons of tradition—climate, light modulation, sequences of spaces, etc. This was a fundamental shift in viewing tradition not as a 'grab bag' of visual and aesthetic elements, but as embodying the fundamental structure of space and its relationships to place.

[27] The planning of New Bombay, the establishment of HUDCO and state level housing boards, as well as the building of several company towns centred around industrial production, opened up new questions about the architect's role and engagement with the built environment.

[28] As the projects by Le Corbusier in Ahmedabad were being completed, the Museum of Modern Art in New York premiered the first film of a new cinematic talent from West Bengal—Satyajit Ray. The film was *Pather Panchali*, a saga of village life. Besides Ray, the film also introduced the master musician Ravi Shankar to Western audiences. From then on, it was not just Le Corbusier who was entrenched by the culture of post-colonial South

Asia (and especially India)—musicians and artists all turned their eyes on the sub-continent just as the last building in Chandigarh, the Palace of Assembly, was being completed. Source: Wild, David. *Fragments of Utopia – Collage Reflections of Heroic Modernism*. Hyphen Press, London, 1998.

[29] Ahmedabad also became the crucible for the first generation of post-independence Indian architects. Built works by Le Corbusier and Louis Kahn paved the way for young Indian practitioners, who had recently completed higher education or apprenticeships abroad, to return and establish their practice in Ahmedabad. Of these, BV Doshi, Anant D Raje, Hasmukh C Patel, Kamal Mangaldas, Kulbhushan Jain and Leo Pereira are notable.

[30] The main patrons were the Sarabhai family, with Vikram Sarabhai (scientist) and Gira and Gautam Sarabhai (architects). The Sarabhais invited Surendranath Kar to design their family house 'Retreat', in Shahibaug in Ahmedabad, which was started in 1932 and completed in 1937. Le Corbusier was invited to design Manorama Sarabhai's house and Frank Lloyd Wright to design the Calico Headquarters—which was (unfortunately) not built. They were also instrumental, together with the Lalbhai family, in inviting Louis Kahn to design the Indian Institute of Management. They also invited Charles and Ray Eames who were asked to study the state and potential of Indian design, which led to the founding of the National Institute of Design in Ahmedabad. Their India Report was developed after a careful study of the many centres of design, handicrafts and general manufacture. Recommendations were made after thorough dialogue with several officials and personnel in the fields of small and major industry, design and architecture.

[31] Tagore, Sundaram. "The Legacy of Anti-Tradition", *The Art News Magazine of India*, Vol II, Issue I. This post-independence scenario is described by Sundaram Tagore: "Independence unleashed waves of violence that seemed to be the wrath of supernatural powers. Indeed, in a metaphorical sense, the violence embodied the Indian philosophical tenets of creative and destructive forces – the cycle of chaos leading to order to only return to turmoil. Although modernity claims to decry chaos, its determination to oppose tradition breeds confusion." This is a phenomenon that continuously resurfaces in the coming decades, and plays itself out in far more potent manifestations as the nation evolves.

[32] Bozdogan, Sibel. *Modernism and Nation Building*. University of Washington Press, Seattle, 2001.

[33] A contention of Hoskote Ranjit, in notes exchanged with the author in 1999 when discussing the possibilities of writing a book on emerging alternative practices in India. This followed a conference on the subject organised by the Urban Design Research Institute in Mumbai.

[34] Anoma, Peris. "The Search for Tropical Identities: a critical history" in *New Directions in Tropical Asian Architecture*, ed. Patrick Bingham Hall, Periplus, Singapore, 2005. Besides 'Vistara', the other exhibition on 'Architecture in India' was curated by Raj Rewal for display in France. Designers such Rajeev Sethi and Martand Singh, while not focusing on architecture per se, made references to the discipline through the allied design exhibitions that they curated. The 'Golden Eye' exhibition, for example, curated by Sethi, actually incorporated a collaboration between cutting-edge Western designers and Indian craftspeople—often evoking architectural imagery.

[35] The School of Architecture at CEPT, the Centre for Environmental Planning and Technology (a university since 2004), was founded in 1962 by BV Doshi, who had returned after working in Le Corbusier's Paris atelier; French architect Bernard Kohn, who was a student of Louis Kahn; and Dr RN Vakil. The school's philosophy and pedagogical approaches were deeply rooted in the modern movement. Wide exposure to international architects, design educators and scholars as visiting teachers, propagated in its initial years, laid the foundations for its future direction. In its founding years, the school was supported solely by the Ahmedabad Education Society, and so was free of the shackles of the government-run university system. This allowed it to be more experimental in that it was a clean break from the pedagogic thrust of most professional institutes, which had a great technical leaning with little space for the humanities. The other facility that, a decade later under the stewardship of architect Jhbavala, took on a similar direction was the School of Architecture and Planning in New Delhi. However, as this was a government-founded institution it had many constraints and limitations, and had to operate under the norms of technical education as defined by the state.

[36] For details on Claude Batley's contributions, both as an educator and a practitioner, refer to Mehrotra, Rahul. "Response to a Tradition", unpublished thesis, CEPT, 1985.

[37] CEPT benefited from the input of many visiting scholars and Fellows who spent time on the campus. Prominent among them was Christopher Benninger who was instrumental in designing the school's planning programme.

[38] The Council of Architecture recognises over 180 colleges offering an undergraduate programme in architecture in India. Approximately 30,0000 architects are registered with the council. For more details, refer to: http://www.coa.gov.in

[39] Critical regionalism (a category coined by the academics Alexander Tzonis and Liane Lefaivre, and then expanded and popularised by Kenneth Frampton, the renowned architectural critic) can be seen as a Western construct through which to view the 'other'.

[40] In this new era, commencing in 1992, Narasimha Rao was Prime Minister and Manmohan Singh the Finance Minister who introduced the new economic policy. This marked the end of the era of self-sufficiency—a sort of self-embargo that India had placed on itself—and opened the door for foreign investments and a connecting to the outside world for trade. However, unlike China, India did not take its investment in infrastructure seriously enough before opening the doors on its economic policies. Thus, the process of investment as well as development was much slower in India, and it took the whole of the 1990s before any palpable difference on the India landscape was even noticed.

[41] This era of liberalised economic policies was also marked by a shift to coalition politics from the former, almost two-party system. This transferred the power balance for the first time to the southern states, which were also now emerging as economic powerhouses. Thus, the period of economic liberalisation also resulted in a more 'mutinous' form of democracy for India and an assertion by the states regarding their own identities. One of the many fallouts from this was the renaming of cities using references to their names in regional languages—e.g. Bombay to Mumbai, Bangalore to Bengaluru, Madras to Chennai.

[42] Bhabha, Homi. *The Location of Culture*, Routledge, London, 1994.

[43] For a more nuanced and detailed argument about the politics of representation and the question of identity, refer to: Mehrotra, Rahul, Prasad Shetty and Rupali Gupte. "Architecture and Contemporary Indian Identity" in *Constructing Identity in Contemporary Architecture*, Technical University Berlin, 2009.

[44] This overall concept, of the different models of architectural practice, was first proposed in Mehrotra, Rahul, ed. *World Architecture A Critical Mosaic 1900-2000 – Volume VIII, South Asia*, a book documenting canonical works of architecture of the twentieth century in South Asia, General editor: Kenneth Frampton, published by the Architectural Society of China, Beijing and the Union of International Architects, Beijing, 2000.

[45] Mehrotra, Rahul. "Bangalore Dysfunctional Boom Town", *Harvard Design Magazine*, Spring/Summer 2007.

[46] The NRI (Non-Resident Indian) and PIO (Person of Indian Origin) population across the world is estimated at over 30 million. As per a UNDP (United Nations Development Programme) 2010 report, after China, India has the second largest diaspora (comprising first-generation emigrants living abroad) in the world, estimated at 25 million—besides being one of the largest 'sending' nations in Asia, with an emigration rate of 0.8 per cent, out of which 72 per cent work in other Asian countries. Also, as per UNESCO's Institute for Statistics the number of Indian students abroad tripled from 51,000 in 1999 to over 153,000 in 2007, making India second after China among the world's largest sending countries for tertiary students. Source: http://en.wikipedia.org/wiki/Non-resident_Indian_and_Person_of_Indian_Origin. The NRI has, in the last decade, begun investing in India more substantially. This group is also characterised by a conservatism that is known to support and fuel right-wing politics and fundamentalism.

[47] The Public Works Department (PWD) was a legacy of the British era, yet it was powerful and held (and often continues to hold) a monopoly on large-scale housing and infrastructure projects. Similarly, each state had its own housing board which was responsible for 'turnkey' delivery of the various components of infrastructure or housing in which that state was investing. In the late 1990s, these bodies began slowly to be replaced by state agencies responsible for delivering infrastructure and housing, as the responsibility of the state is gradually being devolved and left completely to the private sector.

[48] Although temples form the bulk of this new construction, a number of these structures are not specifically religious but are faith based. Several new mosques have also been built recently, but do not compare in terms of numbers to the Hindu temples that have been constructed. However, the presence of religious and faith-based architecture, and of cultural practices, has shown a manifold increase in the last two decades, exerting a certain visual presence that cannot be ignored.

[49] Sen, Amartya. "Culture Matters and How" in special issue on Culture and Development, *Humanscape*, April 2002.

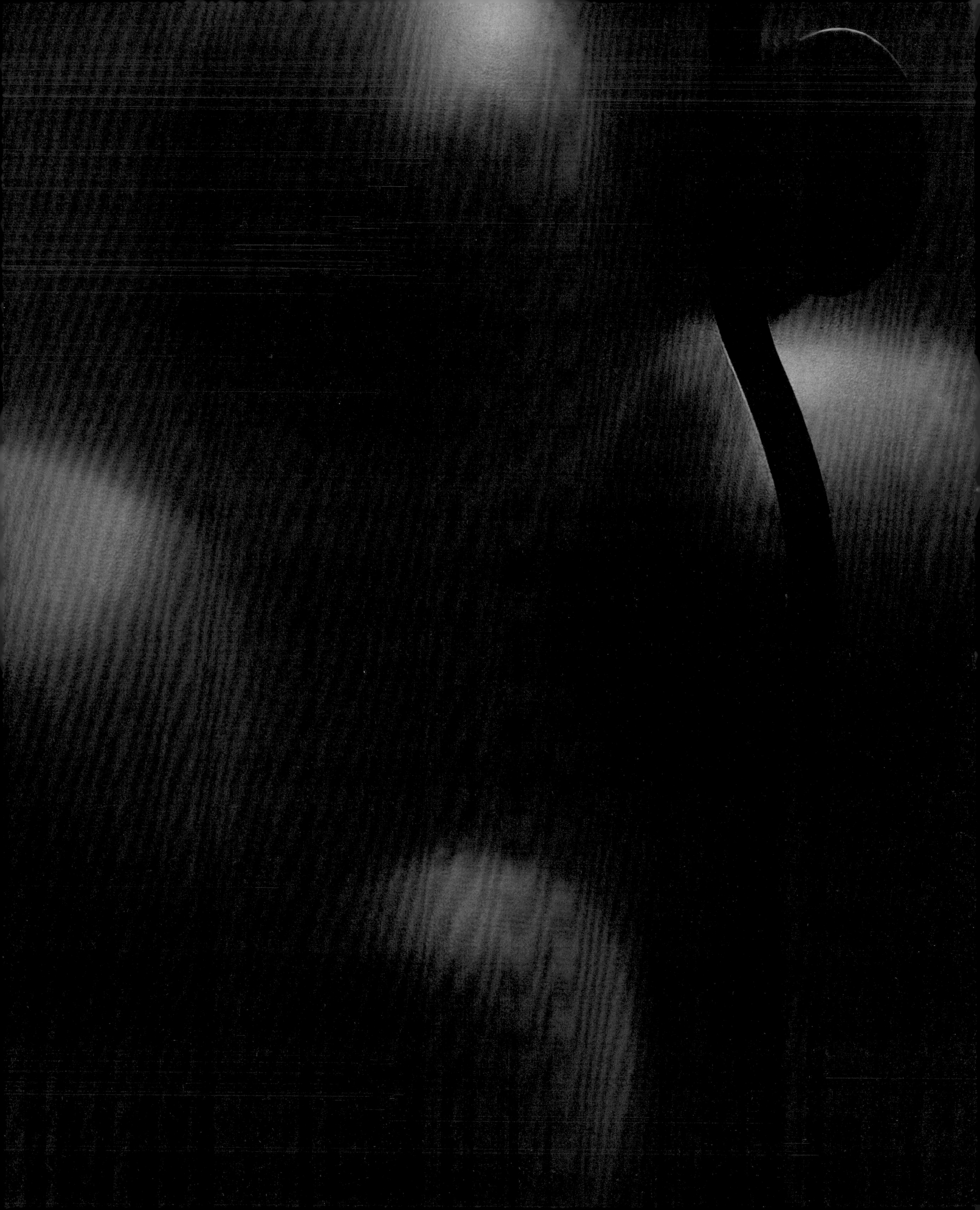

Global Practice
Expressions of (Impatient) Capital

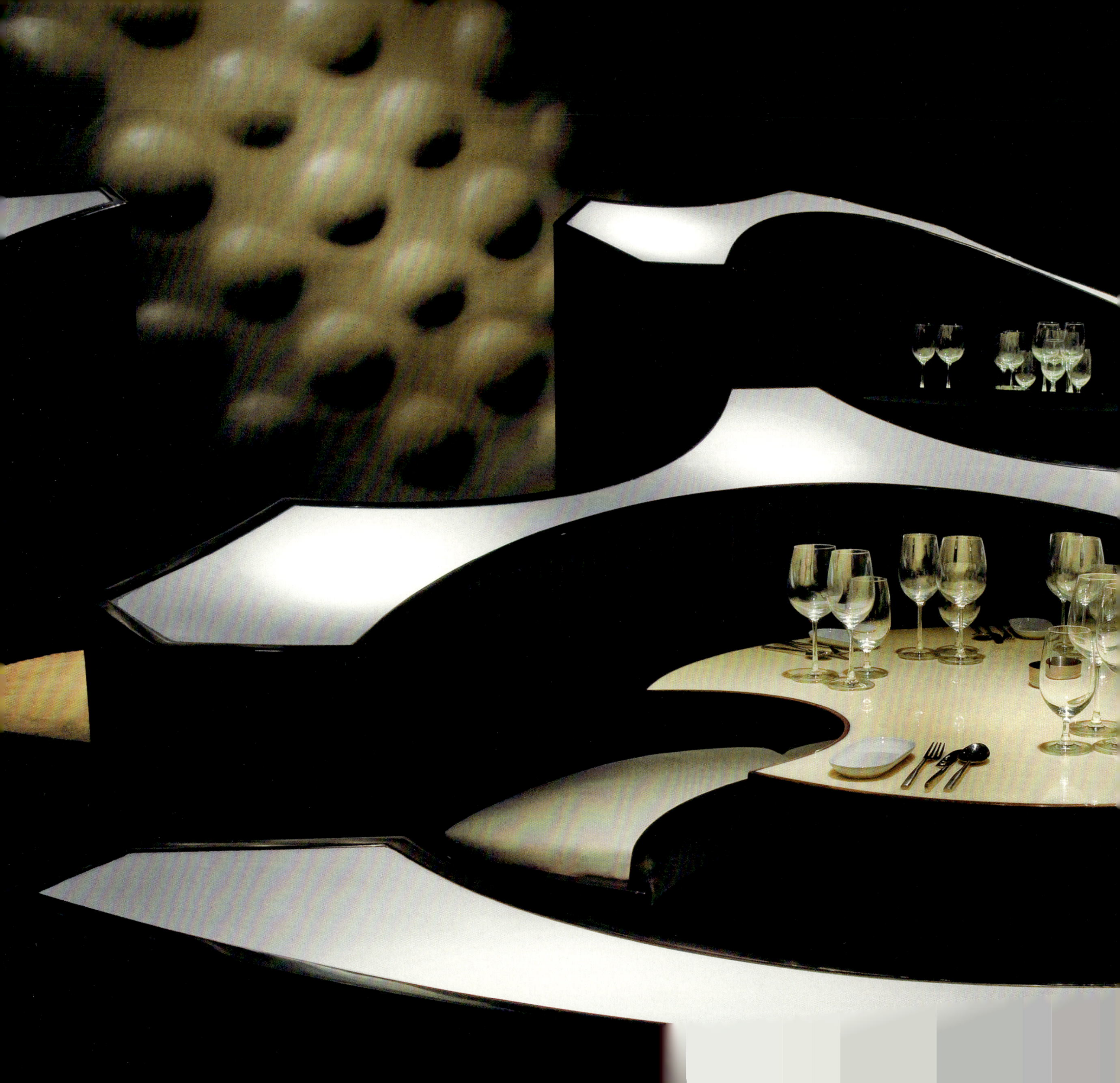

With the liberalisation of the Indian economy in the mid-1990s and the opening up of the design and construction sector to global flows of capital, massive transformations in the built environment became starkly visible on India's landscape. Architecture in India experienced new forces as an emerging generation of international design firms asserted their presence and influence on the country's architectural scene. These firms were harbingers of new trends and shifts that grew out of the confidence with which global capital began to locate itself in India.

Interestingly, the process of economic liberalisation was preceded in previous decades by an emphasis on social integration. This was manifested in the shift to regional politics, stemming from a series of negotiations throughout the country on issues of class, caste and social mobility. Once the political system settled these concerns, it shifted its emphasis to economic integration. Indeed, the resolution of social issues was critical in setting the foundations for the liberalisation of India's economy, allowing it to open and embrace the forces of globalisation. Infrastructure, both physical and social, was imagined as an important instrument for integrating the Indian market as a whole. Consequently, India saw significant investment in infrastructure and a frenzied acceleration of physical development, but it was only in the early 2000s that architecture emerged as a visible manifestation of this process.

In India today, hyper-consumption, fuelled by a rapidly growing economically mobile middle class, is resulting in the construction of a new landscape of global derivates or the images of globalisation. The quantum of such architecture is increasing as globalisation 'hits the ground' with a tremendous impact on the profession as well as on society's perception of it. The architecture that results from this phenomenon often displays a complete detachment from its ambient environment as well as the place and community in which it is set. Furthermore, its tectonic quality and materiality is most often unmindful of local resources and traditions of building. Such architectural production is usually a quick response to large-scale infrastructure projects (such as housing, hospitals, schools, colleges and commercial development) that allow private participation in otherwise largely government-controlled sectors. Most importantly, this form of global architecture thrives on its perceived competence to provide predictable and stable services for (often impatient) capital searching for a host terrain in which to invest. Consequently, design services are often outsourced to Western firms perceived to be competent and well experienced in configuring global buildings—namely, those well versed in the use of new materials and technologies that meet international standards and facilitate the predictable value of the building's performance. This notion of design by a remote agency enhances, rather than diminishes, the perceived value of this form of global architecture. Most importantly, it epitomises a reversal of outsourcing, in which Indian patrons have to outsource the design work to the West in order to receive instructions on how to make the buildings that eventually house the activities outsourced to India from the West!

In the post-independence era from the 1940s to the 1980s, most architectural practices in India focused on modest building commissions as the private sector was engaged in construction activity of a limited scale, barring the few townships that private entrepreneurs such as the Tatas, Birlas, Singhanias, and others initiated for their industrial establishments or manufacturing units. Most large-scale building was the purview of government or public sector entities, which often had an in-house department for design. The few large firms engaged in architectural design were largely sustained by work from private developers and from within the architectural fraternity; these firms were deemed commercial and not seen as ideologically committed to the socialist state's nation-building agenda. As a result, private enterprise never engaged in large-scale architecture; indeed, the market for it did not exist until only after 1990, when a liberalised economy stimulated the government to divest itself of the responsibility of managing and delivering large-scale housing and infrastructure projects. Clearly, the 'big firm' culture had not arrived in India, and the profession was, at the time, ill prepared for the international corporate practice that is ardently patronised today. In fact, the government's failure to efficiently deliver architectural projects and infrastructure on this scale ultimately facilitated the

Blue Frog by Serie Architects (Chris Lee & Kapil Gupta). Detail of dining alcoves that allow individual group seating defined by low partitions

India Land and Properties Limited by Zaha Hadid Architects (*left top*) and **Software Technology Park** by FXFOWLE (*left centre*). The profusion of IT parks over the last decade opened the arena for prominent international architects and firms to enter the Indian market propounding a 'global' visual language in these new buildings

National Institute of Fashion Technology by Hafeez Contractor (*left bottom*) employs open, pavilion-like buildings in combination with more traditionally configured structures to create a new image for institutional buildings

Infosys Progeon (*right top and centre*) and **Infosys SDB Park 6** (*right bottom*), both by Hafeez Contractor. The vital partnership between Infosys Technologies and the architect for several campuses in South India resulted in a proliferation of such facilities across the country, with Bengaluru and Gurgaon emerging as key centres. Contractor has been at the forefront of exploring the potential of this 'impatience' of global capital in an array of projects that juxtapose autonomous architectural forms in the local landscape

unquestioned embrace that the emerging middle class in India provided for private sector engagement in the delivery of these services. Although this has also been true of the provision of several other non-physical or social infrastructures such as health and education, the entry of the private sector in the delivery of physical infrastructure manifests itself more directly on the landscape. However, the Indian practitioners' inability to respond to large-scale infrastructure projects with the same competency and speed as a global firm resulted in outsourcing to international firms from Singapore, the United States and some parts of Europe, which have come to command the largest share of such projects in India.

These projects range from developer-initiated housing schemes for the upper and middle classes to high-end luxury apartments and hotels, hospitals and shopping malls, and master planning for large-scale townships and Special Economic Zones (SEZs). However, more recently, the most representative and visible projects have been Information Technology (IT) parks set up outside growing IT cities. Cyberabad in Hyderabad, Electronic City in Bengaluru (formerly Bangalore) and Tech Park in Chennai are good examples of such development, in which special incentives in the form of stable infrastructure are provided to attract IT companies to these cities. Naturally, as IT parks cater to multinational global companies, their architecture is global in its treatment. Zaha Hadid Architects' India Land and Property Limited (ILPL) Project in Chennai

An unrealised vision for a **Software Development Centre** in Chennai (*top*), and the built **DLF Gateway Tower** in Gurgaon (*bottom*), both by Hafeez Contractor, are early examples of global architecture 'landing' on the new terrains that were emerging to receive global capital

(2006-present), FXFOWLE's Software Technology Park (2008-present) in Noida, Pei Cobb Freed & Partners' Wave Rock in Hyderabad (2006-10) and the recent (2005) work by Indian architect Hafeez Contractor for the National Institute of Fashion Technology (NIFT) building in Navi Mumbai and on the Infosys campus in Mysore (as well as several other buildings for Infosys across India) are poignant examples of global flows landing on the ground as alien objects without a 'reality check' of the locale. Designed, crafted and engineered with completely Western sensibilities, they represent the impotency of global architecture (if this can be called a style) to inspire or respond to its location—yet perhaps it awes the local population momentarily? Furthermore, these projects are driven by the impatience of capital, which must be realised and physically manifested as soon as it arrives in a locality in order to make visible its worth. Large, open floor plates (for maximum user flexibility) are used, that can be assembled very quickly using dry construction. The employment of steel, glass and several prefabricated cladding products, not manufactured in India in the 1990s but now freely available, are seen as new expressions that are attractive for investors. In fact, often the vendors of these new products actually provide designs and details as a service to encourage the use of their products and hasten the process of building conception and construction.

However, the inefficient response of these buildings to basic parameters such as climate, light and airflows, as well as their dogmatic use of energy-unfriendly materials such as metal and glass cladding, make them uneconomical and unsustainable propositions. On the other hand, their power lies in their ability to potently represent the power of capital and its universalising symbolism. Thus, they serve as iconic beacons for investment in new terrains, reassuring external investment and capital that it is safe to 'land' there. Interestingly, though, it is the local developers with large stakes in SEZs or IT parks that usually underwrite these iconic buildings as they serve to inflate the value of much larger tracts of land around them and consequently the value of the buildings themselves. In short, it is the patronage driven by international capital that supports these (global) follies.

The buildings in IT parks and the numerous Singapore-style shopping malls under construction in Bengaluru, Hyderabad, Gurgaon and Mumbai testify to the blatant and aggressive onslaught on India's terrain as Arjun Appadurai says, "by these weapons of (global) mass construction". While demonstrating an incredible skill for assembling international-standard building artefacts in the Indian context, which is otherwise largely dominated by labour-intensive construction processes, the buildings fall short of any innovative design moves for an emergent economy or for the ground realities of the country. In fact, the malls and gated employment enclaves work counter to the otherwise incremental and fine grained organisational texture of places of work and commerce in the Indian

The remodelling of Terminal 1B at the Mumbai Airport by Architect Hafeez Contractor and DV Joshi & Co opened up this sector for public-private partnerships, where international design expertise was deemed desirable for equipping new terminals and upgrading existing facilities to meet global standards. The new **Chhatrapati Shivaji International Airport, Terminal 2** in Mumbai (*this page*), being designed by SOM, presents a further example of this emergent infrastructure

context, and consequently reconfigure this landscape completely based on an imagined economic condition in the country. Such practices challenge construction norms and tradition, and are built with prescriptive instructions and often in partnership with vendors who develop the palette of materials via a series of negotiations involving costs, schedules and predictability of delivery. Indeed, therein lies their disjuncture with the context in which they are situated: they attempt to transfer to a context alien processes and forms, rather than engaging with transforming existing processes and ways of building with visionary aspirations of the common good.

Another programme that demonstrates the same characteristics in the way it manoeuvres itself onto the landscape is the luxury hotel. Often driven by brands or chain hotel corporations, in conjunction mainly with local investors, these buildings exert their uninhibited presence in the form of large-scale structures. They too need no reality check from the locale and are insulated, gated enclaves that are often designed to isolate the tourist or business traveller from the realities of the neighbourhood. Several such buildings are being constructed across India at as rapid a rate as the growth of the economy and the increase of traffic of business travellers and tourists. Located generally in the boomtowns of India such as Mumbai, New Delhi, Gurgaon, Hyderabad, Bengaluru and Chennai, these buildings put great premium on efficient functioning and lavish interiors without any investment in the exterior form or their configuration in the city urbanistically. The one exception perhaps is the fully Indian Park Hotel group, which has consciously employed design as a way to represent the locale and has drawn on a talented pool of both foreign and local designers to work collaboratively. Building in Kolkata, Navi Mumbai, Chennai and most recently in Hyderabad, the Park Group of Hotels has set an interesting precedent that will challenge the multinational hotel chains as time goes on.

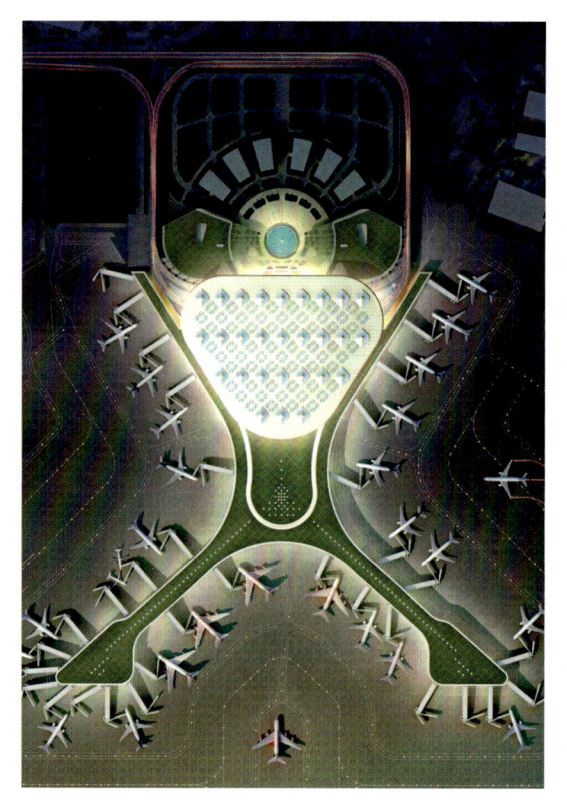

Interestingly, other infrastructure-related projects such as new airports, educational institutes and housing estates, are subject to greater reality checks from the locale and so tend to become somewhat more culturally specific. Social norms, densities of occupation and many other related aspects must be negotiated in these projects, unlike the autonomous nature of IT parks and office buildings. Airports, for example, have to accommodate spatial innovation to respond to teeming crowds that accompany

Architecture in India since 1990 | Global Practice

Other metro cities followed suit by the addition of new terminals, as in the **Indira Gandhi International Airport, Delhi** (*left top*), by HOK and **Chennai International Airport** (*left bottom*) by Gensler and Frederic Schwartz Architects, adapting the global formulae to local needs and Indian social paradigms

Vadodara Airport (*right, top and bottom*) by Gensler and Frederic Schwartz Architects, an unrealised vision. Airports at smaller urban centres, like Vadodara and Raipur, have witnessed rapid industrialisation in the recent past and become points of transit into newer developing zones. They are also keeping pace with new architectural trends

passengers in arrival and departure lounges for traditional ceremonies that are still the social norm in the country. They confront a high level of resistance due to the fact that they are often extensions to, or renewals of, existing airports. The nature of some of these projects is one of accommodating a functioning transition between the old and new. Adaptations evolve naturally, and global formulae are modified and localised quickly. Examples include the retrofitted Mumbai domestic airport designed by Architect Hafeez Contractor and DV Joshi & Co. (2006-08); the Indira Gandhi International Airport, Terminal 3 in New Delhi (2006-10) designed by HOK; Chhatrapati Shivaji International Airport, Terminal 2 in Mumbai by Skidmore, Owings & Merrill (SOM) (expected completion 2014); as well as the Chennai (2009-present), Raipur (2007-present) and Vadodara (2008-present) airports designed by Gensler in collaboration with New York-based Frederic Schwartz Architects. These projects, in addition to integrating responses to social conditions, struggle (most often unsuccessfully) to be more sensitive to their orientation, siting and the manner in which they address issues of sustainable design parameters. Such questions are critical for their success as efficient investments by public agencies, which are more accountable today in India than they were in the earlier post-independence decades.

In addition to the new infrastructure projects, the government in India's liberalised economy tends to use this global imagery for its financial institutions, such as ICICI and LIC (Life Insurance Corporation of India) across the country as well as for state capitals in the past. A case in point is the Tamil Nadu Legislative Assembly building (2008-10) designed by the Berlin-based gmp architects. The domed capping of this building bears an uncanny resemblance to the Reichstag dome; moreover, its imagery is removed from any reference to the cultural milieu in which it is set. Instead, it boasts of energy efficiency and the integration of sustainable design principles as

Architecture in India since 1990 | Global Practice

Imperial Towers (*left top*) by Hafeez Contractor is an example from Mumbai that demonstrates the adoption of the steel-and-glass skyscraper model as a compelling signifier of 'kinship' with world markets

These proposed projects in the heart of Mumbai, all commissioned by international firms, indicate the architecture's intention to stake a claim to a global position. **World One, Lodha Place** (*left centre*) by Jay L Berman, Pei Cobb Freed & Partners and **Mixed-Use Tower** (*right*) by FXFOWLE clearly reinforce this claim

Antilla (*centre top*), a residence by Perkins + Will, is symbolic of the rising capitalism gripping cities like Mumbai through such disruptive interventions within an existing fabric. Out of scale, out of proportion, this single-family house epitomises the crassness of capital expressing itself on the landscape, unmindful of context

Aerial view (*centre bottom*). A downtown image similar to that of several world cities is emerging in the residential and commercial districts of Mumbai

its driving logic. Governments find the narrative of sustainability and the obvious qualification for the internationally recognised LEED rating (Leadership in Energy and Environmental Design) attractive. Global practitioners use this aspiration to their advantage, whereby the rigorous challenges of a place are sidestepped in order to embrace the more universally attractive and easily marketable sound bites of sustainability. This is often packaged in a limited rhetoric of energy efficiency addressed through mechanical fixes rather than any systemic or typological invention. Such rating is an example of the narrowness of this approach, in which the broader ecology of a building and the place in which it is set is ignored in the quest of focusing on more quantifiable parameters. In particular, the LEED rating tends to perhaps unwittingly create a hegemony of Western codes. These ratings do not necessarily lead to more ecological solutions, as they provide a chemical or mechanical fix to any design problem (to meet the rating requirements). It is possible to see an entire 'green' industry developing around this idea. Thus, while global practices in India have expanded the debate around green buildings, it has been detached from the locale, narrow in its arguments about sustainable design and self-serving in propagating global imagery.

Similarly, the housing sector is one in which the paradigms of global flows have caused often-irreversible destruction of landscapes in many of India's urban centres due to the government's clear failure to deliver housing, or the conditions necessary for good housing, for millions of homeless people. As a result, in the liberalised economy, private enterprise has stepped in to bridge this gap. The squeezed land markets and the spike in land values make this a viable and attractive proposition for private developers who work with local politicians to form a new 'land mafia' in most Indian cities.

Global flows, in the form of large high-rise building complexes in the city's fissures, have physically manifested the inherent dualities that exist within Indian urban centres and have poised these extremes in bizarre adjacencies. The midtown landscape constituting areas such as Tardeo and Parel in Mumbai is symbolic of this transformation and the iconic presence of capital. Similarly, on the outskirts of growing centres such as Gurgaon outside New Delhi, the landscape of global 'storm troopers' is omnipresent in a laissez-faire formation. The proposed World One, Lodha Place in Mumbai by Pei, Cobb and Freed, Mixed-Use Tower by FXFOWLE and the brutal intervention by Perkins + Will for Antilla, the Ambani family house (2006-10) in Mumbai are emblematic of the disruptions these extraneous interventions cause in cities that have been characterised by accretive and fine-grained additions as they evolve. This medley of office towers, malls and gated housing communities is symbolic of the emergent landscapes that globalising processes are creating across the world. Such segregated communities are almost completely dependent on individual mobility, high-level security and complete exclusion of economic and social diversity. In fact, these communities in essence secede from the city and no longer rely on the formal or informal urban system for services. Rather, they have become an emergent 'third space' in India's urbanism.

The recently established Lavasa Township between Mumbai and Pune, designed by the American firm HOK, is an example of the global suburbs that are based on the New Urbanism model that propagates a low-rise, high-density and walkable city paradigm while being limited by its nostalgic references to traditional European urban imagery. Fuelled by speculative investments in what is an unprecedented new township made possible by massive land-use changes—and, thus, obviously politically patronised—the Lavasa Township struggles to achieve its purpose despite the fact that, in this case, its physical infrastructure has led the development. A complete counterpoint to the 'business as usual' Indian urbanism that thrives and is buoyant without substantial infrastructure, Lavasa seeks out this social and economic buoyancy after it has developed in physical terms. Similarly, the Mahindra World City near Chennai (2008-present), also by HOK and the Special Economic Zone (2007-present) designed by Robert AM Stern Architects in Gurgaon suggest the popularity of the New Urbanist paradigm as well. Unfortunately, all these projects have either densities too low to imagine in the Indian urban context or feature

Lavasa Township (*left, top to bottom*) and the proposed **Mahindra World City** (*centre*), both by HOK. Based on New Urbanism principles, these recent townships set in verdant surroundings draw references from the imagery of European townscapes and operate as gated communities, insulated from the Indian urban reality

The proposed **Iridium Tower** (*right top*) by FXFOWLE is emblematic of the new emerging landscapes in India's financial centres

Greater Noida Housing (*right bottom*) by FXFOWLE is one of the upcoming new multi-hectare developer-led housing schemes in suburban centres, which create gated enclaves with an array of facilities inviting the upwardly mobile to invest in 'new-age' living

high-rise apartment blocks in farmlands! Conceived clearly in Western imagery, it is hard to imagine how Indians would occupy these spaces. Thus, while the international studios of firms like FXFOWLE, under the leadership of Indian architect Sudhir Jambhekar, have attempted to respond to the locale through colour, texture, material choices and a more rigorous understanding of lifestyles, most other firms have merely translated their standard designs into a context entirely different from where these ideas originated. The isolation of these proposed settlements within the Indian context at best makes them global suburbs, gated and buffered from the reality of the diverse and economically disparate urbanism of India.

Most importantly, the new paradigm for residential projects in the context of these global practices serves as a model in which housing and settlements are imagined as finite artefacts incapable of absorbing change. In other words, it is the predetermined form of buildings that has become the image of a safe and predictable city where architecture and its iconic presence are given precedence over the lives that would potentially occupy these settlements. As such, these imagined locations seem to be at odds with the incremental strategies that otherwise appear to characterise traditional organic housing patterns in India. Although this is an area in which India faces immense challenges, such global practices are apparently unable to address this crucial problem in any sustainable manner. They are often built on difficult ground, involving displacement and contested conversion of land uses. Their big, bold, powerfully represented plans and images, together with the incisive objectivity of professionals detached from

Indian School of Business (*left, top and bottom*) by John Portman & Associates, a Hyderabad management school, an American university campus concept, is a comparatively humane intervention. Its planning and facilities nonetheless are high on energy consumption

The boost in the privatised higher-education sector saw the emergence of an architecture reflecting diverse pedagogical philosophies. The **Vedanta University** (*right, top and bottom*) by Ayers Saint Gross and Dhiru Thadani is an ambitious project that draws from tenets of ancient Indian philosophy and sacred geometries to inform its large-scale campus planning

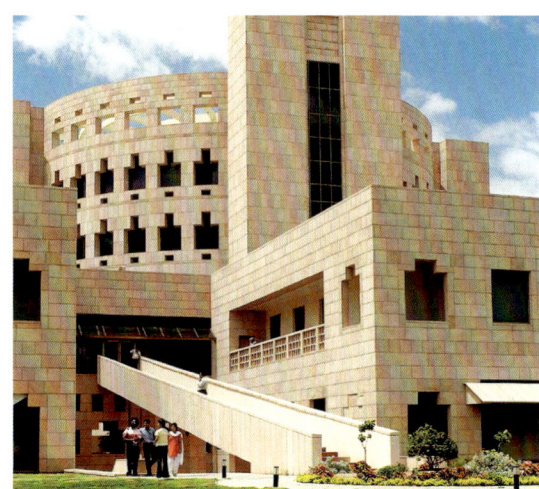

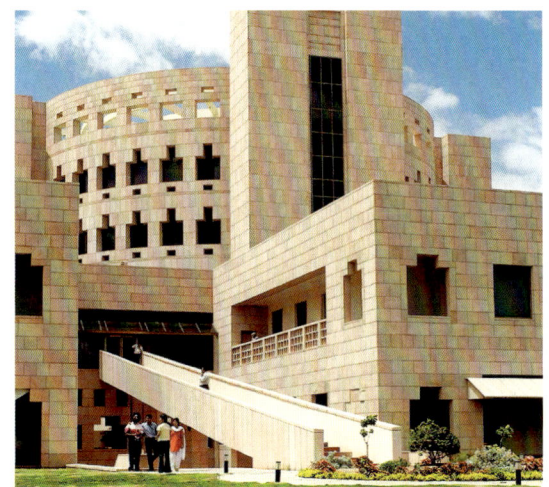

the locale, become instrumental in cutting through the thick layer of local resistance—often successfully. These practices have become instruments for developers to legitimise land conversion, and also to secure quick master plans and design schemes to jump-start the process of selling these dreams in the form of artistically rendered images of the projects. Such places and projects have rarely come to fruition.

A softer space for these global flows and the engagement of international practices is the education and culture sector. The funding that fuels the creation of this space is often a form of 'patient capital' that has no contingencies on design and is flexible and inherently responsive to people, locales and places. These programmes are often funded through foundations or not-for-profit companies that are far more patient with the realisation of capital, and that are willing to pay a premium for its manifestation in an appropriate manner. Museums, art galleries and educational institutes are prominent in this cluster of programmes, which are also being shaped by global practices today. An early example of this engagement was the Indian School of Business in Hyderabad (2001) designed by John Portman & Associates. The form and organisational content of this self-sufficient American-style campus are governed more directly by the user interface and its diverse requirements, thereby creating a more humane environment. However, its formal moves tend to be Western imports, thus burdening the infrastructure with unsustainable pressures on energy consumption and allied services. Similarly, the proposed campus for Vedanta University in Orissa, designed by the US-based firm Ayers Saint Gross and Dhiru Thadani, is fraught with a rigid disposition and a powerful formal gesture that has emerged out of planning traditions that clearly emanate from the West. In spite of such limitations in their formal moves these campuses set new benchmarks and standards in design for the education sector in India, which is projected to be one of the fastest growing in the world. In the case of the Vedanta campus, an ambitious proposition for a large private university, the architects have attempted to evoke ancient Indian principles within the rather formalistic tenets of the New Urbanist approach. The importance of this project lies in its being an early example of large scale campus planning, a field which will preoccupy architects in India in the coming decades as social infrastructure assumes greater priority by both the government and the private sector in equal measure. A smaller example of this building of educational infrastructure, and symbolic of a similar disjuncture while infused with great creativity, is the Sri Siddhartha Institute of Technology (SSIT) Library in Tumkur by Geodesic Techniques (P) Ltd. Here, the designers have adapted Western technologies for Indian conditions

The Kolkata Museum of Modern Art (KMOMA) (*left top*) by Herzog and deMuron and the **Kolkata International Convention Centre** (*left centre*) by RMJM (both proposed). With a renewed interest in contemporary icons of art and culture, new institutions representative of the times are underway through a series of public—private commissions in the metro cities Civic buildings such as the proposed **Bombay Arts Society** (*right top*) by Sanjay Puri Architects and **Writer Warehouse** (*bottom, left and right*) by Khanna Schulz allow the public to engage directly with the new global idiom propagated through their architecture, while responding to the local context through material and climatic concerns

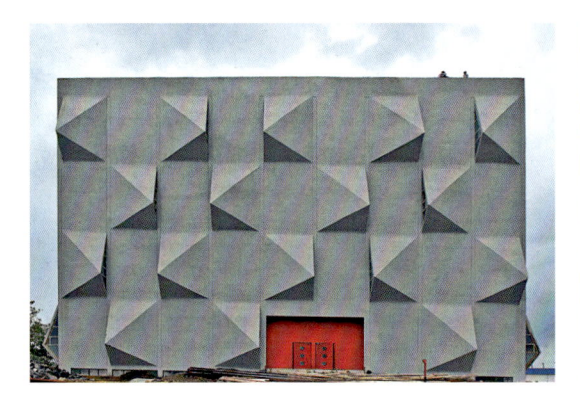

and construction methods while not really addressing the question of sustainable paradigms by inventing a new one that grows out of the Indian context.

Other civic buildings, such as the proposed Museum of Modern Art by Herzog and de Meuron and the International Convention Centre by RMJM (both in Kolkata), the proposed Bombay Arts Society by Sanjay Puri Architects and Writer Warehouse by Khanna Schultz, both in Mumbai (2003), encode distinct global strains while still holding to the promise of localising their responses, even if only through materials, textures, modulation of light and climatic considerations. These are pioneering projects comprising new investments in cultural and educational institutions that India has to take seriously in the coming decades.

Both the Indian Institute of Management (IIMA) in Ahmedabad (2007-present) by HCP Design and Project Management Pvt. Ltd. and the Khalsa Heritage Centre (1998-present) by Safdie Architects from Boston in collaboration with Ashok Dhawan set important precedents in responding to difficult cultural landscapes. The IIMA extends Louis Kahn's campus by expanding the original building's geometric logic while basing its expression in its construction—and, in this case, in exposed concrete rather than brick. The incorporation of art, exhibitions and local references link it to the tradition of the institution. As a result, although the building does not invent new paradigms for building institutions in India it is at least respectful of an existing institutional tradition which it extends in

Banyan Park (*this page*) by Tod Williams Billie Tsien Architects, headquarters for Tata Consultancy Services, weaves Indian planning and craft traditions into its architectural narrative, thereby localising its response for a global IT company. Identifying labour-intensive construction as a reality in India, the project utilises this effectively through prototyping. The simultaneous incorporation of art and craft at a large scale is significant in this project

a subtly new and sophisticated way. Meanwhile, the Khalsa Heritage Centre is an architectural response to hundreds of years of Sikh culture and represents for the first time since the Golden Temple (the holiest Sikh shrine) that an architectural icon on this scale, representing Sikh history had been commissioned in India. The architect here draws from a wider Indian landscape, but encapsulates it within the form's references to the headgear, or turban, that characterises the Sikhs as well as to the ancient ramparts of fortress towns. The buildings are intelligently sited and use a masonry base and metal clad roof profile—once again, obvious references to a broader Islamic and Sikh tradition of building in India. Another potent example of this negotiation of the locale is Mumbai's Banyan Park project (in progress) by Tod Williams Billie Tsien Architects. Designed as the headquarters for Tata Consulting Services, the project extends the Indian tradition of buildings located around courtyards while weaving a narrative of circulation to amalgamate complexly diverse programmes in a wooded site. The engagement with local crafts, textures, materials and ornament somehow localises these buildings while addressing a global IT programme and allied services. Recognising the labour-intensive processes of construction in India, this project's buildings are using a prototyping process integral to the construction sequence. Naturally, this feedback loop, replete with trial and error, is only possible when the project is afforded the luxury of time and financial resources.

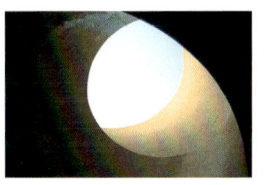

In the global projects and practices described thus far, adaptation to the locale varies in direct relation to the level of impatience of the capital driving these projects. The IT parks, malls and developer-driven housing schemes are manifestations of the most impatient capital, while institutional projects respond more authentically to the locale's contingencies. Unfortunately, in this first phase of the liberalisation of India's economy most capital seems to be impatient. The tradition and culture of giving have not yet become the norm. Foundations and other not-for-profit institutions are restricted to responding to the needs of the poor, not the rich or middle class; consequently, galleries, museums and universities are only just beginning to enter the imagination of the country's political, industrial and financial elite. Hopefully, this space will eventually transform the global flows of ideas and root them to the locale.

However, a younger generation is emerging in India of recently returned Western-trained architects who are using these global flows to their advantage. This young breed uses new techniques and narratives of sustainable design and digital technologies, fabrication interfaces, etc. with great ease. Most importantly, they seem to demonstrate an ability to root their projects more squarely and honestly in the contexts in which they operate without overt references, stylistically speaking, to their Indianness or regional affiliations.

Romi Khosla Design Studio in New Delhi, Serie Architects (Chris Lee & Kapil Gupta) in Mumbai and Morphogenesis in Delhi have been engaged in a range of projects giving us a glimpse into how these recent global flows can actually be translated into elegant solutions: buildings that feel completed, rooted, and are generated out of the material as well the construction capacities of the locale. Romi Khosla Design Studio's Castro Cafeteria at the Jamia Millia Islamia University (JMI) (2005-07) has skilfully taken the now standard technology of the cantilevered canopy that is extensively used by gas stations (or petrol pumps) and crafted its application into an elegant semi-open canteen facility for students. Similarly, in their gallery at JMI screens are employed in a contemporary and fresh configuration to filter light while subtly suggesting a universal language that straddles both the locale (the Islamic university in which it is located) and its aspiration to relate to a global style.

Serie Architects, on the other hand, engage more easily with cutting-edge software and new technologies that allow the exploration of an incredible amount of spatial and formal possibilities. Their obsession with pushing the limits of digital and construction technologies is refreshing. Their optimism at the arrival of robotic construction and a more enmeshed interface between design and potential fabrication possibilities makes their work relevant to the discussion of architecture in the Indian context. Their early projects in Mumbai for the Jewel Tech building (2002) and Thanks Boutique (2004) first hinted at these sensibilities. More recently, their project of recycling a mill shed in Mumbai into a jazz club, Blue Frog (2006-07), demonstrates the robust use of new digital technologies in generating an intelligent and elegant spatial modulation whereby a perfect hybrid between an auditorium and dining facility displays a new type of architectural configuration. In another recent project in Mumbai, for the Tote restaurant (2006-09), they have similarly engaged with complex forms while remaining sensitive to both the natural landscape and the historic architectural context in which the building is situated. Thus, a new hybrid emerges in which an extremely creative articulation of the structure inspired by the rain trees around the building is integrated with a tiled roof to resonate with the existing historic Turf Club structures on the site.

Meanwhile, the New Delhi-based firm Morphogenesis, besides being a larger operation in terms of personnel is also the most ambitious of the younger generation in terms of the scale of projects in which they have engaged. Their Apollo Michelin Corporate office (2002) in Gurgaon engages with global imagery while attempting to make local specific gestures related to sustainable design. Although these are sometimes superficial gestures, the project struggles with this reconciliation. The Pearl Academy of Fashion (2008) is more successful in this respect. Here, a large academy is organised in a courtyard deftly modulated to integrate circulation as well as act as a great source for light and the natural flow of air. A finely articulated screen along the outer perimeter of the buildings suggests a filter

Jamia Millia Islamic University Gallery (*left, top and bottom*) by Romi Khosla Design Studio. This gallery space utilises the traditional concept of light-filtering screens in a contemporary way through material exploration. Projects like these bring a fresh perspective by successfully straddling the global and the local without being overtly conscious of either

Jewel Tech (*centre, top and bottom*), an early project by Serie Architects for a jewellery manufacturer, demonstrated the possibilities of using digital and computational techniques to generate new spatial models

Blue Frog (*right, top and bottom*) by Serie Architects combines software-generated design with local fabrication skills to generate new forms that reinterpret the usual spatial configurations for commercial activity

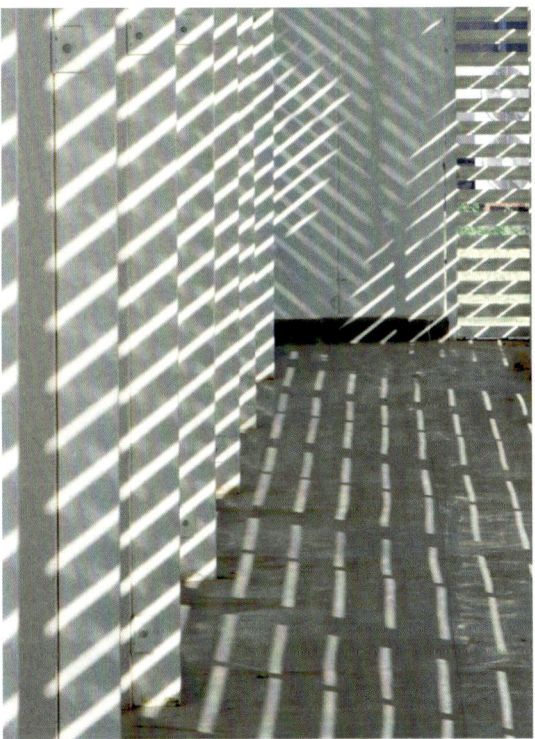

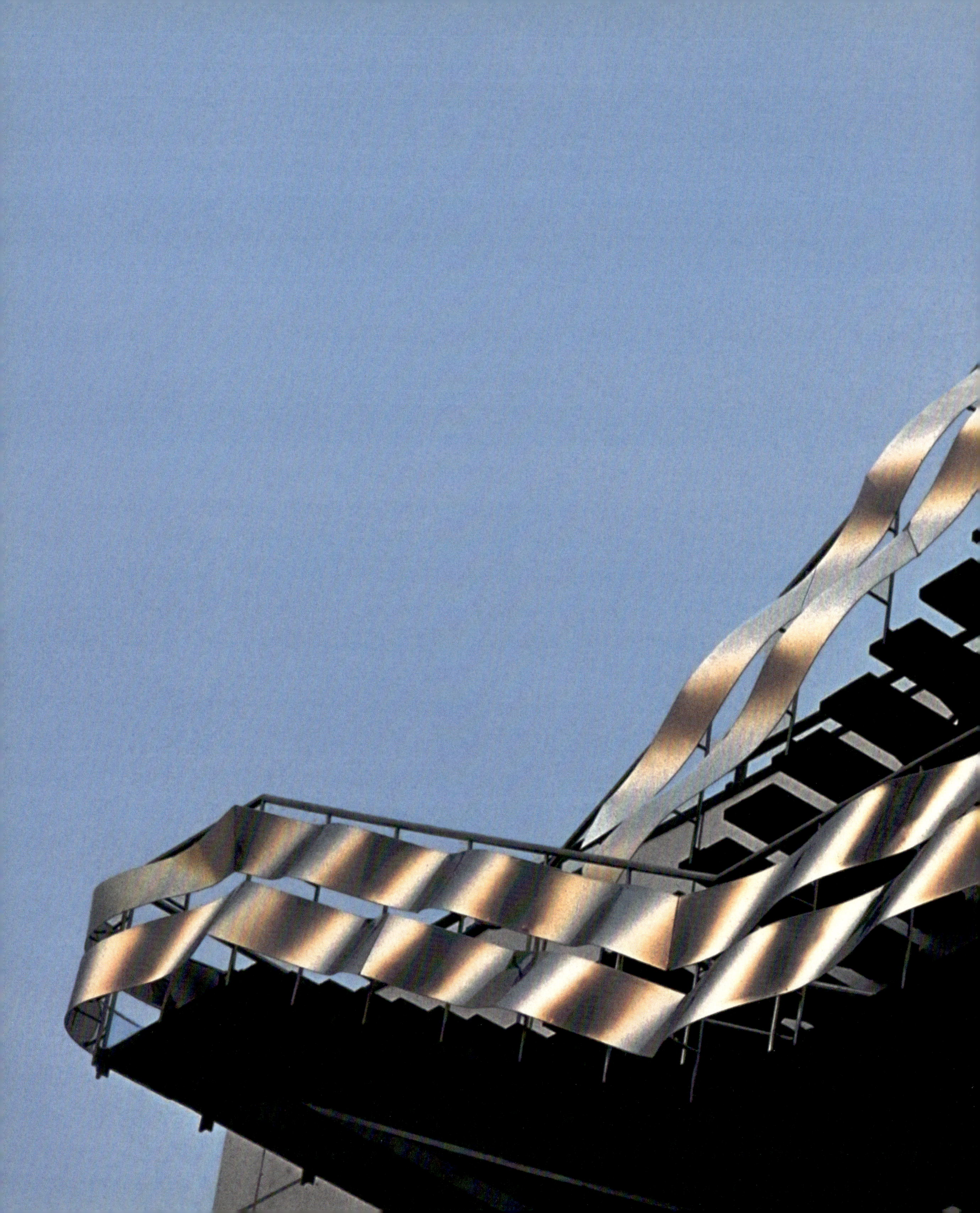

Architecture in India since 1990 | Global Practice

of light and air while having obvious references to the traditional *jali*, or screen, element characterising architecture in Rajasthan, the state in which the building is set. Morphogenesis has successfully picked up on the narrative of sustainable design and attempted to make this more plausible and transparent in the Indian context. This narrative is consistently demonstrated in the several larger commissions they have been engaged in, such as the India Glycols Limited (IGL) offices (2009) in New Delhi and the Uppal Business Centre (2006-9) in Gurgaon. Both these projects also demonstrate schematic but sophisticated propositions in addressing the challenges of sustainable design in the new building programmes of the country.

At any rate, what these practices symbolise is the evolution of approach with the emergence of a new generation of Indian architects—a generation that has the ability to synthesise these external flows and craft a new practice that will respond to India's global aspiration while still being mindful of the locale in an intelligent manner. This approach could potentially establish fresh paradigms regarding how new emergent aspirations and (often impatient) capital can manifest themselves more gently (or successfully) within the Indian landscape.

Apollo Michelin corporate office by Morphogenesis showing detail of stair and railing

Folios

INFOSYS SOFTWARE DEVELOPMENT BLOCK 4	76
PARK HOTEL	81
SSIT LIBRARY	85
CHHATRAPATI SHIVAJI INTERNATIONAL AIRPORT	89
TAMIL NADU LEGISLATIVE ASSEMBLY COMPLEX	93
INDIAN INSTITUTE OF MANAGEMENT	97
PEARL ACADEMY OF FASHION	100
KHALSA HERITAGE CENTRE	105
CASTRO CAFETERIA	108
TOTE	113

folio 1
INFOSYS SOFTWARE DEVELOPMENT BLOCK 4, Mysore

Architect Hafeez Contractor

This folded glass building occupies a heavily contoured site forming the software development block of the Infosys campus in Mysore. A five-storey structure housing 2,500 IT professionals, its form and language were inspiredby the jagged profile of the surrounding landscape and the tenets of origami, the Japanese art of paper folding. The open-plan layouts on all floor plates have a rectilinear profile featuring skewed atrium pockets at the edges. These atriums are intended to create an array of spatial experiences by following the changing form of the outer skin, which becomes pronounced at certain levels when it modulates inwards—pressing against the structure of the building. The texture of the skin of the building, which is made in glass, is ever transforming on account of the reflections produced by differing light conditions, which appear to give it varying dimensions.

Although the building was produced using materials now popular and easily accessible in India, the architect made a leap of faith, and pushed the boundaries of the local construction industry in a valiant effort to generate forms that were uncommon in the Indian context for that time.

Elevation drawing of exterior façade The folded glass exterior, which takes reference from origami—the Japanese art of paper folding—creates a translucent, net-like envelope

Front façade under a night sky Unlike during the day, the building now begins to showcase the office spaces and activities within. A welded steel framework supports the curtain glazing that creates the jagged forms and edges

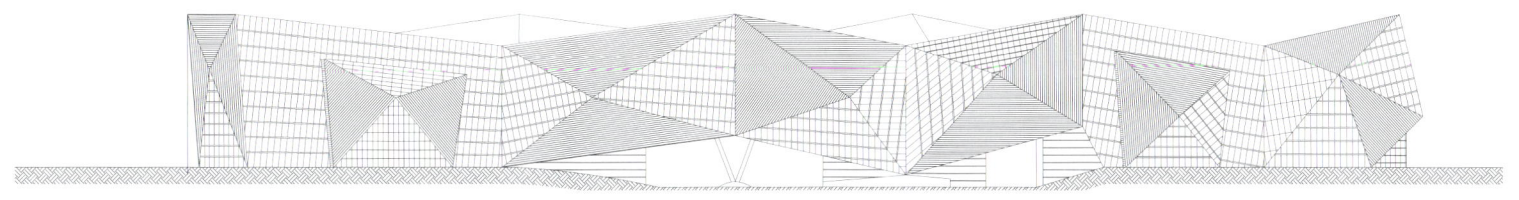

Architecture in India since 1990 | Global Practice

Architecture in India since 1990 | Global Practice

Exterior façade The imposing glass-clad façade reflects changing light conditions through the day, transforming and dematerialising the building's bulk in differing lighting conditions

Interior support structure A structural system in steel holds the curtain glazing while creating skewed pockets of atrium spaces that bring natural light into the public areas

Undulating façade by day A combination of reflective and ceramic-fritted glass is supported by hinged steel members cantilevered from the floors to create the fractured façade geometry

Decks overlooking the atrium The jagged edges of the interior spaces penetrate the overall spatial volume and command a view of the surrounding landscape through an internal glazed skin

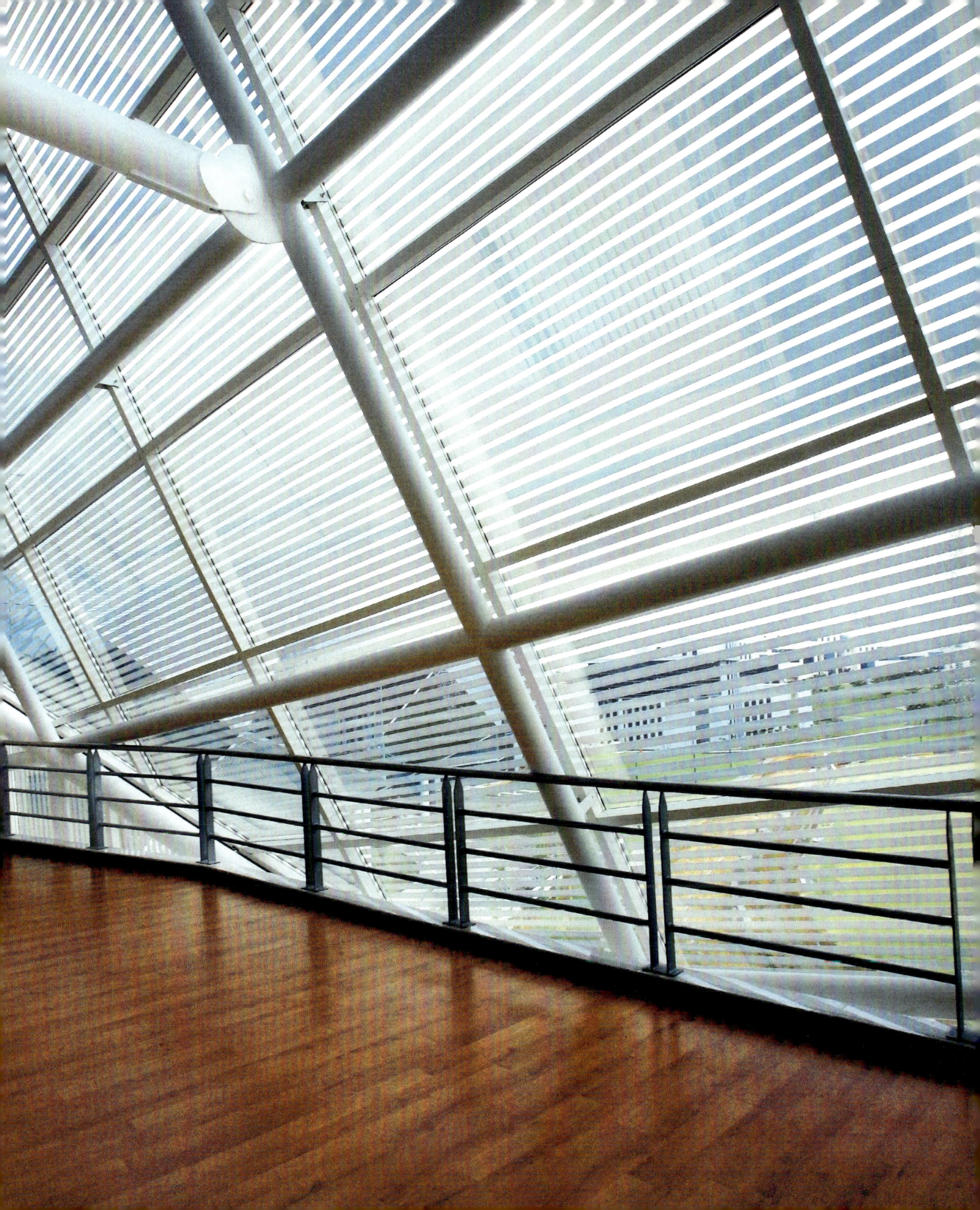

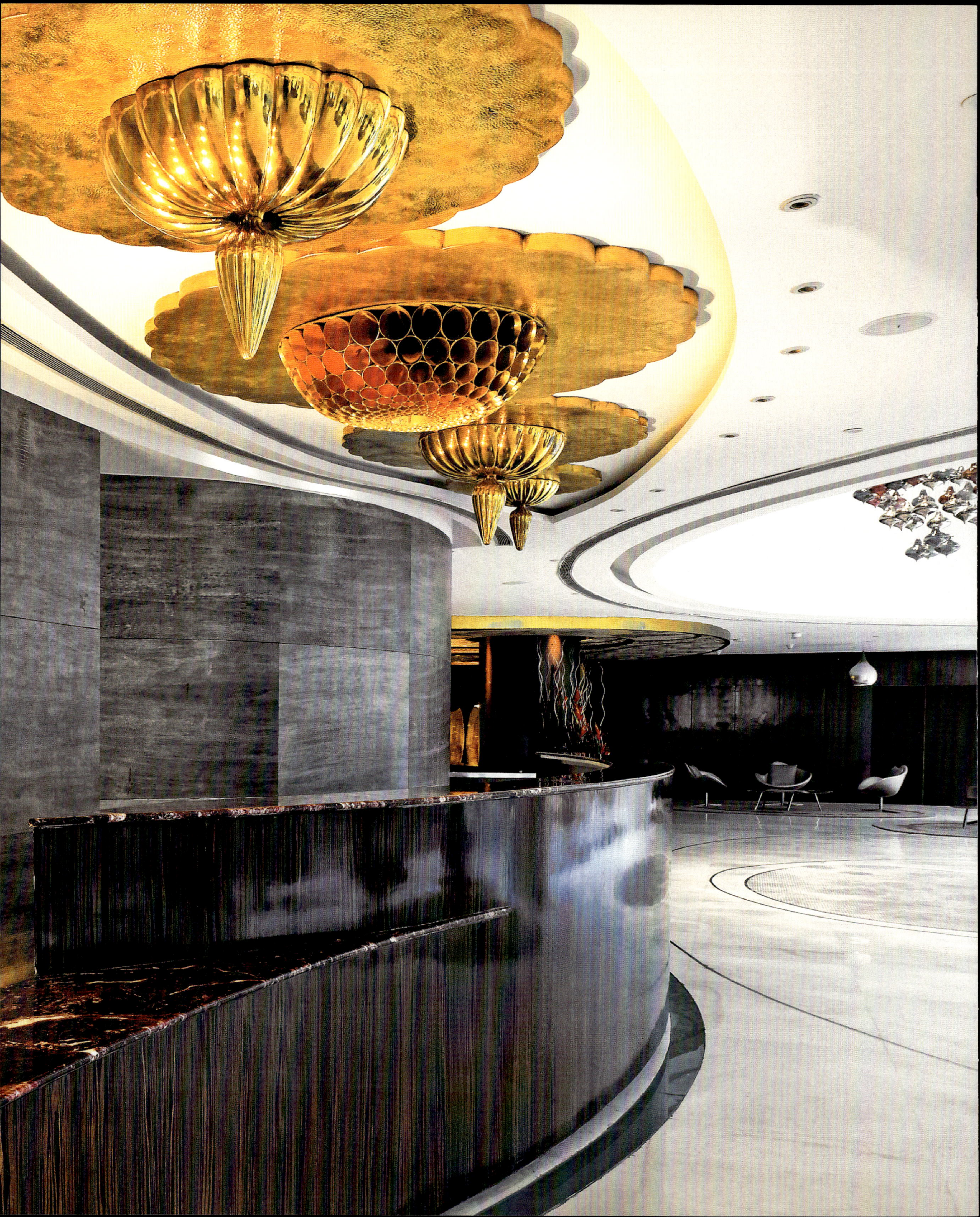

folio 2
PARK HOTEL, Hyderabad

Skidmore, Owings & Merrill

This new flagship hotel, located by the Husain Sagar Lake, alludes to Hyderabad's traditions in the crafting of precious stones and distinctive textiles. The hotel's dull-aluminium external screen cladding and interior surface finishes, including mosaics, reflect local craft traditions, patterning and style.

In a departure from the general trend, a slew of internationally reputed firms from different disciplines were brought on board. The American firm SOM has conceived the main building, including the exterior, while other spaces are designed and decorated by Conran & Partners, Chhada Siembieda from Australia, fashion designers Tarun Tahiliani, Rohit Bal and Manish Arora, artists Bharati Kher and Subodh Gupta, and textile designer Jean Francois Lesage—all designing a suite or restaurant each. The Hyderabad hotel is one of the many buildings that the Park Group has installed across the country using diverse and talented designers. In this way it has drawn attention to the importance of evolving place-specific designs, rather than importing the international-hotel typology that characterises the juggernaut of globalization in India.

Arrival lobby and concierge These copper-capped ceiling medallions over the reception area showcase local craft traditions within this contemporary facility

Poolside view overlooking the city The timber deck in the pool area is strategically located to take advantage of commanding views of the city's skyline and the Husain Sagar Lake, while being in close proximity to the hotel's restaurants and reception areas

Architecture in India since 1990 | Global Practice

Interior view of foyers on various levels Back-lit perforated sheet metal recreates a starry-sky effect, while a similar pattern is woven into the floor carpets to allude to the effect of shadows on the floor

Interior view of a guest room Specific colour and design themes characterise the guest rooms, a number of which are designed by noted artists and international designers

Lounge area A contrasting array of materials and colour palettes lends distinction to the various zones within the hotel that also have custom-made floor covers and international furniture lines

Streetside view of hotel exterior The hotel sits imposingly by the lakefront, with its undulating façade surfaces clad in glass and perforated aluminium screens. LED back-lighting, programmed to change periodically, makes the building look like a glistening jewel at night

Corridor adjoining lounge space Monotony of a typical long hotel corridor is broken by the playful articulation of the partition wall complemented by the warm, mood lighting

Architecture in India since 1990 | Global Practice

Internal staircase with views outside This stair in stone and metal is placed along one edge of the dome, and has an independent structure that allows changing vistas of the surrounding landscape

Junction detail and glass façade An interplay of light and shade on the façade allows its visual character to change through the day while also reflecting fragmented images of the adjoining buildings and landscape on the campus

Approach way to the library building The facility, housed within a glass geodesic dome, sits on a high plinth that is accessed through a series of steps in a landscaped mound

Architecture in India since 1990 | Global Practice

folio 3
SSIT LIBRARY, Tumkur

Geodesic Techniques

This library is located on the campus of the Sri Siddhartha Institute of Technology (SSIT) in Tumkur, 80 km from Bengaluru. Designed as a glass-clad geodesic dome, it houses a building within, which forms the bones of the overall structure, while the outer shell is treated like an independent skin. Entirely prefabricated as linear members to be assembled on site, the form of all structural parts was carefully considered at design stage for ease and precision of assembly. Lightweight steel components that could be easily handled by semi-skilled workers, without the need for cranes and heavy scaffolding, were part of the practical design considerations.

The inner building is constructed using standard reinforced-concrete frames and a series of slabs that create the floor plates and house different functions. The importance of the project lies in the juxtaposition that is created between these two systems of construction. The project also demonstrates how a building which requires precision in the way its components are assembled can be fabricated in glass and steel in the Indian context, where precision in construction is often difficult to achieve.

Architecture in India since 1990 | Global Practice

Mezzanine floors within the dome structure The different levels in the building are staggered in plan to overlook each other, and are interconnected through multiple stairways. The landscape within the atrium visually extends to the outside, while maintaining appropriate levels of privacy in the library reference areas

Reading area on the upper level A frame structure supports all intermediate floors that are detached from the geodesic shell. Book racks also create spatial enclosures for the inner areas, while the reading tables look onto the outside

Stairway connecting the lower levels The polished granite stair is profiled to the dome's perimeter in plan, and the sharp shadows of the structural members create changing patterns on its surface

Detail of pyramidal units forming the geodesic dome The faceted profile of the structure creates changing kaleidoscopic images externally, which transform as the light shifts during the course of the day

External view of the airport
A simple yet elegant wraparound structure created an extension to the existing Mumbai Airport with minimal disruption throughout its construction

folio 4
CHHATRAPATI SHIVAJI INTERNATIONAL AIRPORT, Mumbai

Architect Hafeez Contractor and DV Joshi & Co

As part of the government's initiative of modernising and restructuring airport infrastructure, the Mumbai Airport terminals were selected for upgrading. The Domestic Airport Terminal-1B has a large column-free check-in area with thirty-eight counters and an elaborate security hold wrapped in an aluminium composite-panel envelope with a glass roof and large skylights. A mezzanine cafeteria overlooking the departure lounge, landscaped areas and the extended car park were some of the new facilities that were provided.

The primary task for the architect was to not only give new form to what already existed but also to create a new image. The challenge was to retrofit an existing airport while keeping the facility functioning and adapting an old structural system for the new terminus. In working with these existing systems the architect brought about a remarkable transformation to the airport, making it far more efficient than had been imagined. With this project the importance of design in airport infrastructure and rehabilitation opened up across the country—in that sense it set an important precedent, and provided the confidence for architects to undertake well-designed airports and infrastructure building nationally!

Arrival foyer leading towards the exit This space is flooded with light, as the entire side of the building is clad in glass

Side view of terminal by night Foyers at the lower level lead up to waiting lounges and retail space on the upper level, all housed within this large volume

Architecture in India since 1990 | Global Practice

Approach to the departure lounge A continuous membrane structure in steel and FRP creates a canopy over the driveway leading to the departure area. Lighting and signage are integrated within this system

Interior view of foyer and check-in areas A large column-free interior space accommodates check-in counters along with areas for refreshments and relaxation. Ceiling-hung banners herald a new approach to advertising, which was previously absent in public-transit facilities

Architecture in India since 1990 | Global Practice

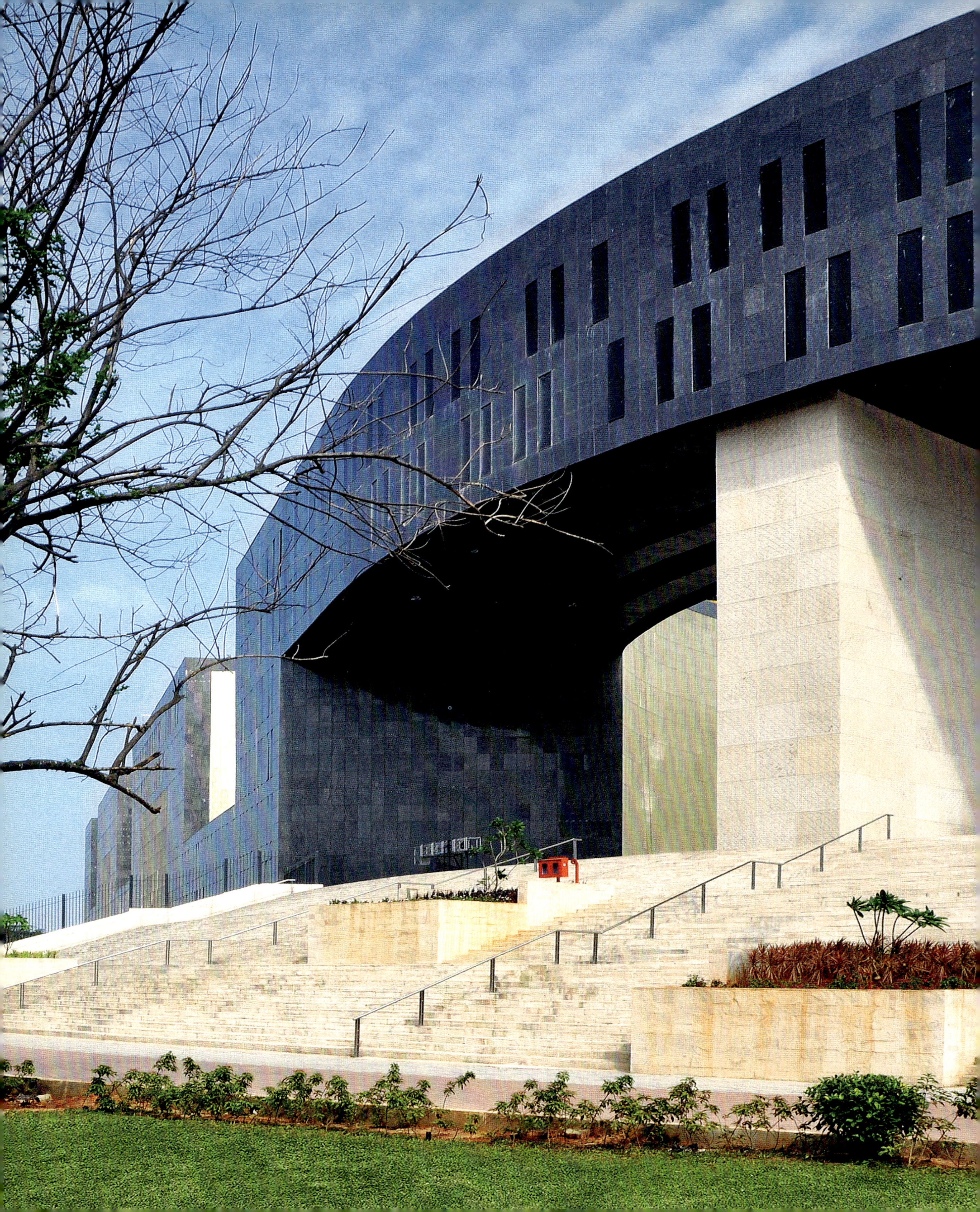

folio 5
TAMIL NADU LEGISLATIVE ASSEMBLY COMPLEX, Chennai

gmp · von Gerkan, Marg and Partners · Architects

One of the first examples of a state assembly building in the post-liberalisation era in India is the Tamil Nadu State Assembly, situated along the Koovam River in Chennai. While the building structure, derived from the chakra vortex column, is reserved for the actual parliament building, the outer circle on plan is a public urban plaza. This is coupled with a number of architectural structures and landscaped open areas—including administration buildings, an auditorium and guest houses—situated to the east of the legislative assembly. The urban-plaza circle marks the perimeter for all other subordinate bracketing structures, thus notionally forming the 'hinge' between the people and the elected government.

Apart from the philosophical, a critical aspect to the design development was the creation of a courtyard element for usage in various forms—a central plaza, an access and distribution area, and an open water tank—was critical to the design development. Four circular forms, connected by peripheral bridges, were created within the building mass to respond to the large array of functions. The first holds an open space, while the other three house the assembly hall, library and conference rooms respectively. The 'negative' spaces in between provide natural lighting for all rooms and floors.

The circular public plaza at the entrance An inner courtyard, circular in plan, is visible from the street, thus establishing a level of transparency from the outside

Rendered view of the assembly building by night A ceremonial flight of semicircular steps ascends to the urban plaza, which leads to the administrative blocks at the rear

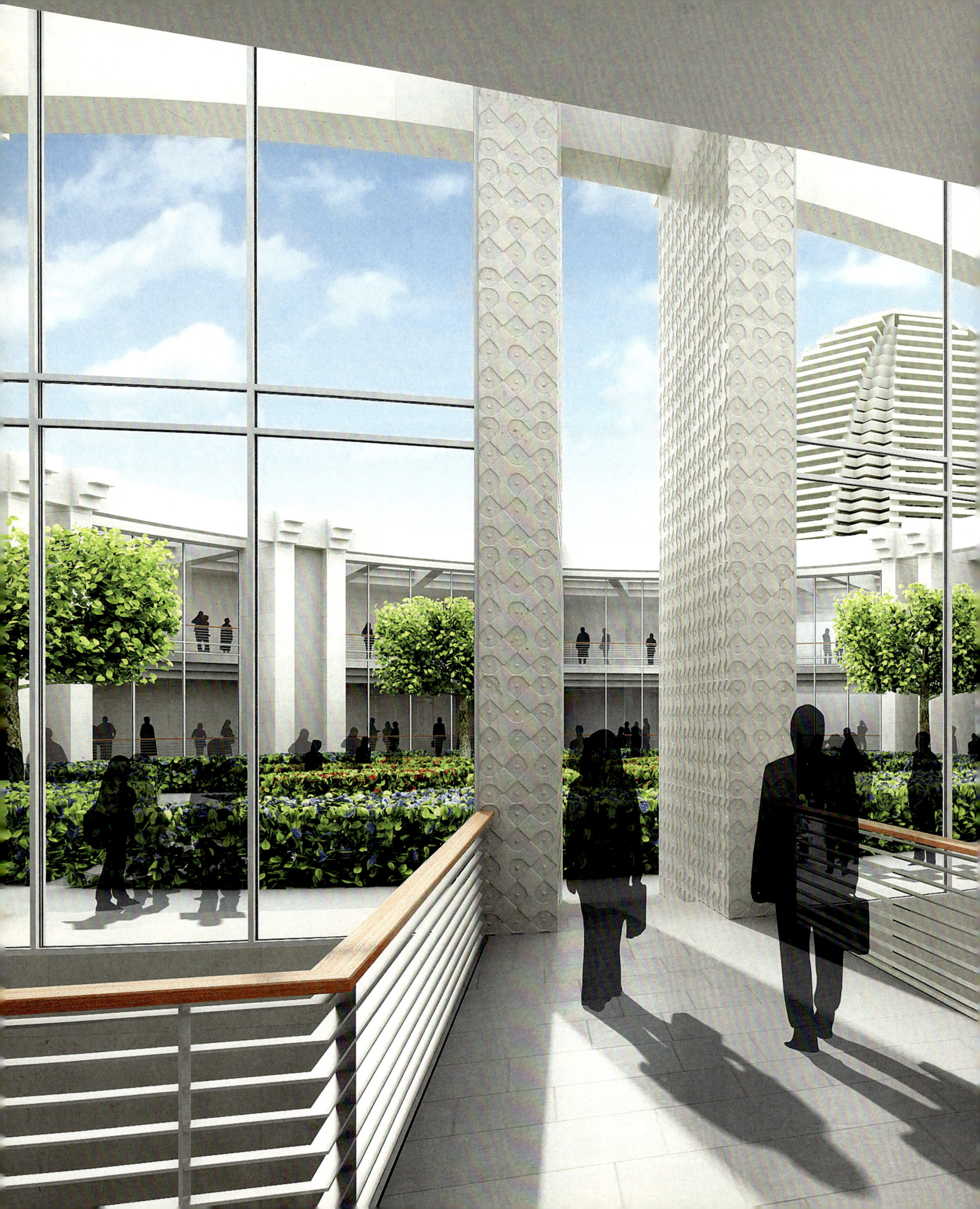

Architecture in India since 1990 | Global Practice

View of bridges and connectors Bridges form an integral part of the movement path, linking the various functional zones to the landscaped gardens and walkways

Model of assembly building This model demonstrates the translation of the *chakra* vortex into the building design, whereby functional blocks are sequentially placed one after the other in a diminishing proportion

Site plan of assembly complex The assembly building, on its corner site, is complemented by a series of buildings comprising the secretariat, state departments, guest houses and chambers for ministers

Rendered view from street side The domical structure houses the State Legislative Assembly and is positioned at the point at which the road bifurcates, thus exerting a visual presence on the street

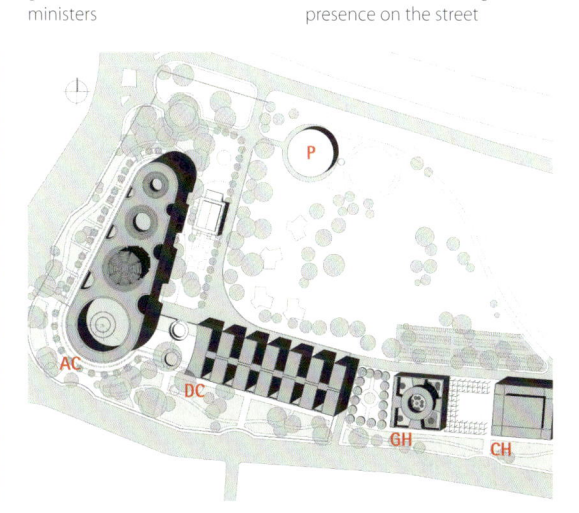

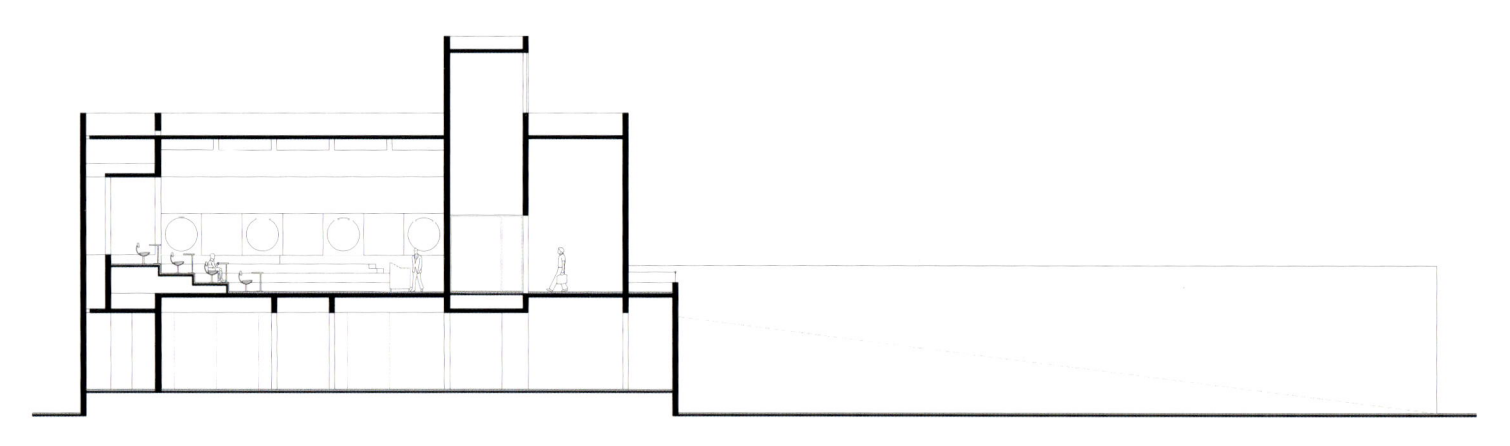

Architecture in India since 1990 | Global Practice

Architecture in India since 1990 | Global Practice

folio 6
INDIAN INSTITUTE OF MANAGEMENT, Ahmedabad

HCP Design and Project Management

The new campus for the Indian Institute of Management, Ahmedabad (IIMA) is located adjacent to the original building designed by Louis Kahn. Though both campuses function independently without any apparent link, they are connected by a pedestrian underpass creating easy access between them. This 16-hectare site houses new areas for teaching and residential purposes for the International Management Development Centre, the Centre for Innovation, Incubation and Entrepreneurship and also the Institute's post-graduate programme, along with guest rooms and dining and sports facilities.

The use of smoothly shuttered exposed concrete as the primary building material, with fenestration in a combination of mild steel and wood, gives the new facilities a distinct vocabulary while in formal terms the new buildings allude to the architecture of the original campus. A deliberate attempt seems to have been made by the architect to refer to, and provide continuities with the existing structures through the use of diagonal geometries in the dormitory layout, semicircular stairs and turrets, and materials and compositions using abstract forms and large surfaces. This is sometimes limiting in terms of the potential that could have been exploited in expressing a similar programme decades later. In spite of this limitation, however, and the looming presence of Louis Kahn, the architect has managed to correct a number of pragmatic problems with the old campus while creating a distinct identity for the new one.

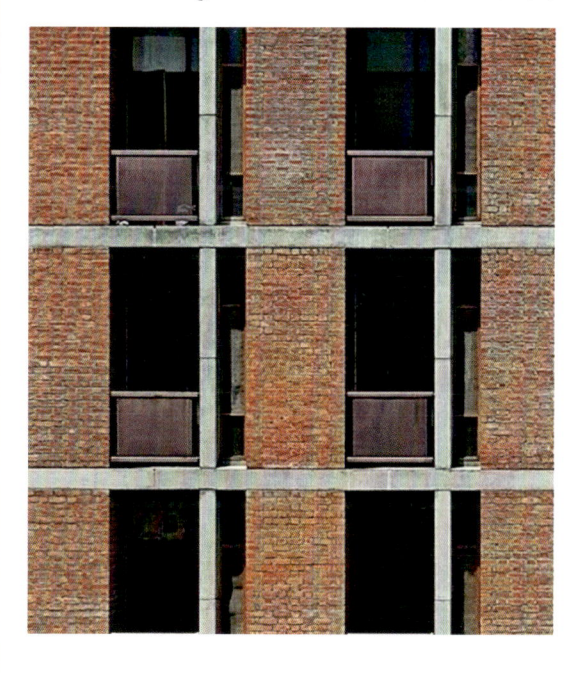

Cross-section through classroom The drawing shows how the classrooms are elevated in section, giving them a handsome spatial volume while segregating them from the functions on the lower level

Entry to classroom The ramp leads up to the academic block, whose stark modernist architecture is tempered with warm interior lighting, wood-finished furniture and panelling

Detail of dormitory façade The use of brick and metal offsets the stark exposed-concrete surfaces to create an interplay of light and shade along the balconies

Culmination of corridors Dead-end spaces are treated skillfully by allowing filtered light to flood these areas, creating an enigmatic moment in an otherwise monotonous circulation route

Entrance foyer of IMDC block
Large metal screens, by Walter D'Souza, serve as filters for the harsh light in Ahmedabad. The textural relief that these metal screens provide visually offsets the raw concrete and the otherwise diagrammatic nature of the buildings

Axonometric view of dormitories and seminar rooms Arranged on a diagonal grid, these multistoreyed living units make reference to the planning principles of the neighbouring older campus designed by Louis Kahn. The new water tower and underpass lie on axis with the dormitories on the existing campus, creating a promenade that divides the new residential quarters from the lecture halls and seminar rooms

View of the dormitory courtyard from the ground level An arcaded walkway around the courtyard provides covered circulation that in turn connects to the vertical access points

View from IMDC foyer Large openings provide framed views of the adjoining landscaped plaza and the built forms around it, thus serving as an orientation device as one moves through the campus

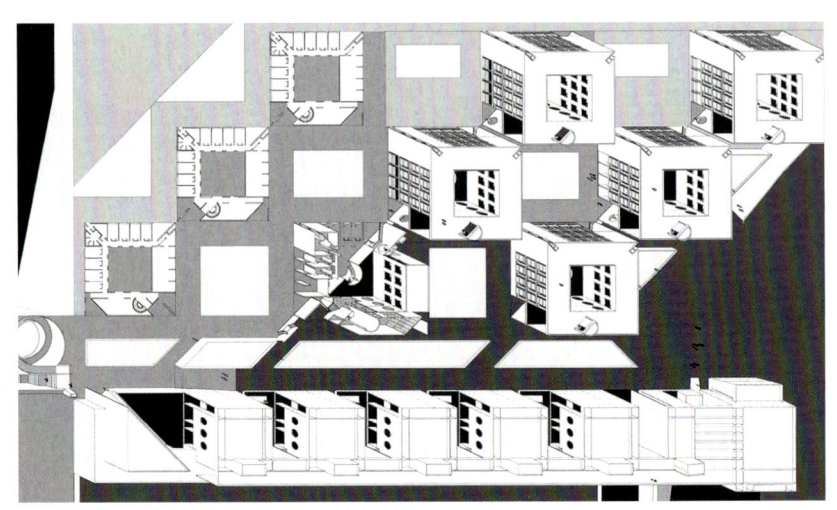

Architecture in India since 1990 | Global Practice

Academic block entrance plaza The visual articulation of the entry plaza breaks the monolithic horizontality of the academic block. The composition of the ramp, walkway, metal screens and lotus pond makes for a sense of welcome on arrival

folio 7
PEARL ACADEMY OF FASHION, Jaipur

Morphogenesis

Located on the outskirts of Jaipur, this institute offers programmes in fashion at both undergraduate and postgraduate levels. Its academic environment comprises studios and workshop areas, lecture and exhibition spaces, performance and refreshment zones, and a resource centre.

The design development was based on two main premises—achieving a satisfactory microclimate within the built space and reinterpreting traditional elements to derive an energy-efficient model. Computational shadow analyses based on façade orientations informed the creation of double-skin *jalis* (stone trelliswork) as a thermal buffer between the building and its surroundings.

Self-shading courts and open stepped areas facilitate light and ventilation through the academic and teaching blocks. The raised ground around the building allows the underbelly of the structure to form a natural thermal sink, using recycled water from the sewage treatment plant, through evaporative cooling. This thermally banked area houses the recreation and exhibition zone—the nucleus of the institute. A night-time drop in the surrounding temperature allows the floor to dissipate heat, thereby ensuring thermal comfort throughout the institute's working hours. This is an intelligent and elegant structure that fuses the pragmatic lessons of history with new technologies to create fresh architectural elements that facilitate operational efficiency.

Stepped sit-out areas Drawing inspiration from traditional *baolis* (step-wells), the ground is modulated to create levels and platforms that allow student exchange and interaction while serving as a break-out zone

View of courtyard Self-shaded sliver courts create a microclimate within the built form, ensuring thermal comfort for all functional areas. This is further aided by the thermal sink formed by the water body, which is surrounded by stepped walkways and connectors

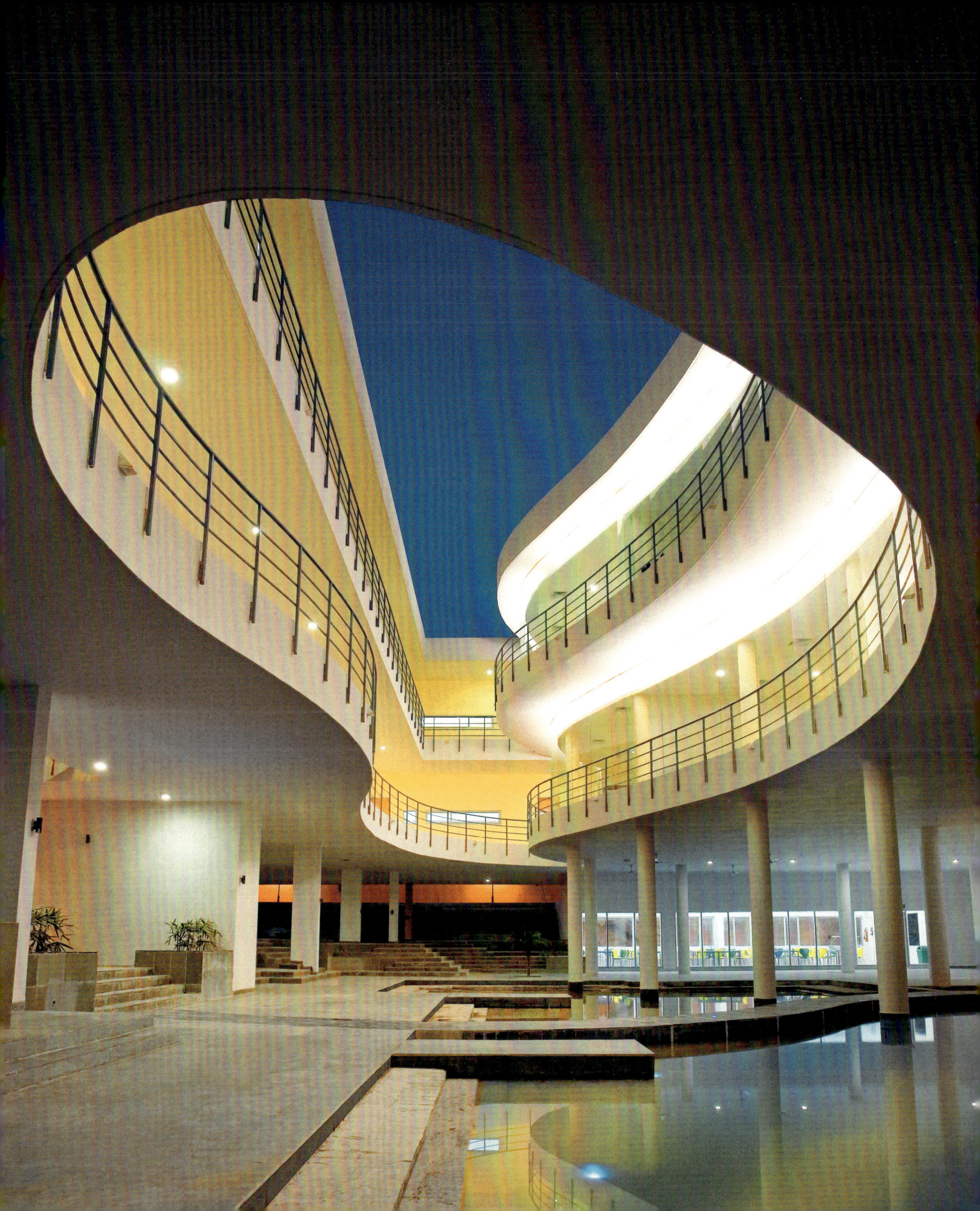

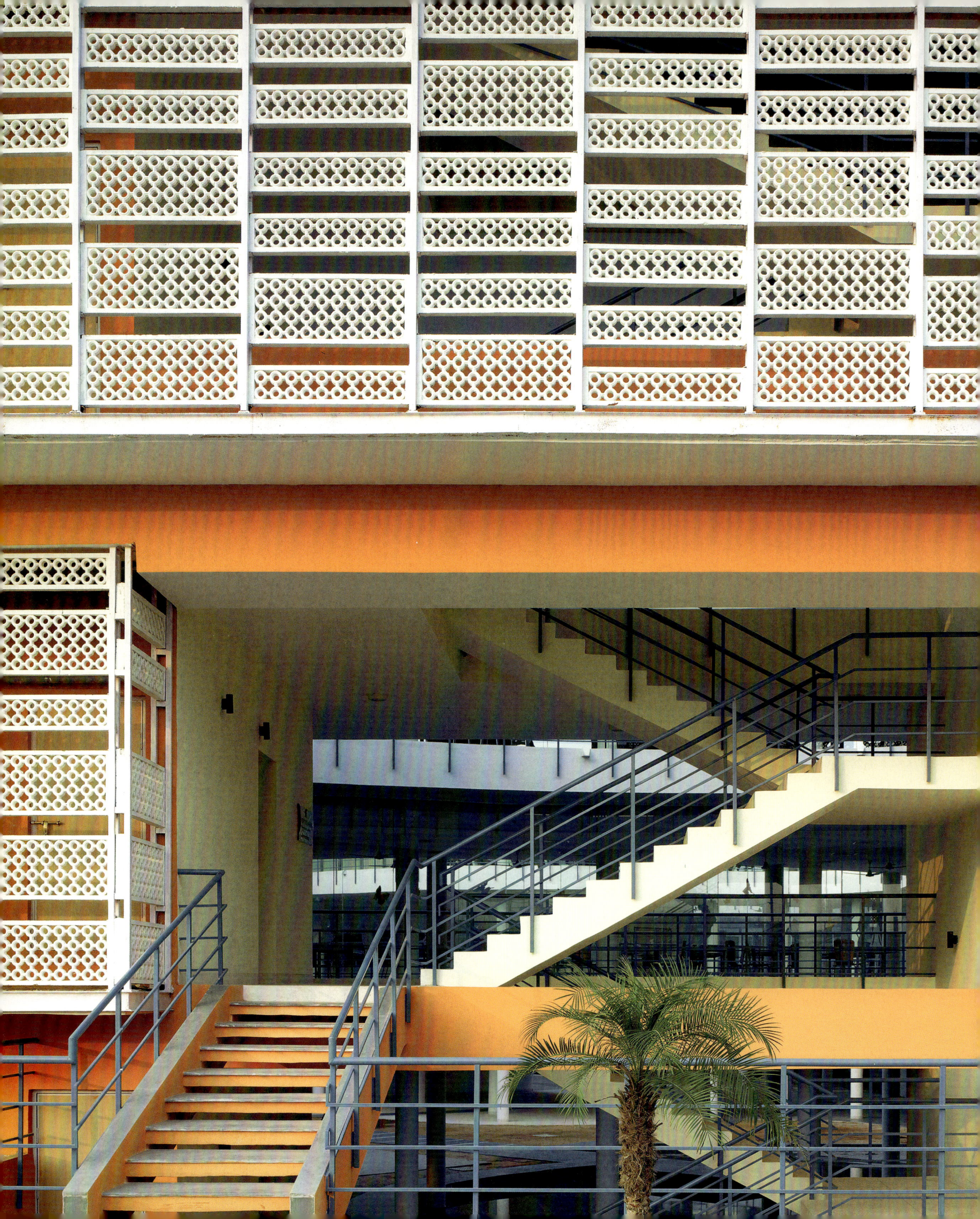

Architecture in India since 1990 | Global Practice

Entrance area and main stair The *jali* (stone trelliswork) façade frames the main entrance, while this free-standing staircase allows natural light into the movement areas

Simulation of lower-ground level 3-D modelling tools indicate the location of functional areas and their connections through various levels and pathways, which are interspersed with natural landscaping

Double-skin building envelope Contemporary use of the stone jali creates a thermal buffer while casting shadows onto the inner building skin. This means of passive cooling allows the spaces to remain almost 20 degrees below the outside atmospheric temperature

Night view of exterior façade Derived through shadow analysis using specialized software, this double-skin building envelope integrates evaporative cooling through drip channels that are integrated in the façade

canteen spill out

library spill out

performance area

103

Architecture in India since 1990 | Global Practice

Modulation of built form along undulating terrain Imposing sandstone façades, which are devoid of fenestration, dominate the landscape while being reminiscent of bastions in medieval fortresses

Architect's sketches Preliminary studies of the site and overall massing of the built forms, clearly indicating a reference to the fort at Jaisalmer

folio 8
KHALSA HERITAGE CENTRE, Anandpur Sahib, Punjab

Safdie Architects and Ashok Dhawan

Located on either side of a 30-hectare ravine overlooking the holy town of Anandpur Sahib, near Chandigarh, the Khalsa Heritage Centre is a new museum of the Sikh people. It demonstrates the architect's interpretation of a contextual response, integrating religious and cultural symbolism related to the history of the Sikhs. It is designed to celebrate 500 years of Sikh history and the 300th anniversary of the Khalsa, scriptures written by Guru Gobind Singh, the tenth and last guru and the founder of modern Sikhism.

The complex is divided into two parts, situated on either side of the ravine and linked by a bridge. The western section, connected to the town, is organised around an entrance plaza containing a 400-seat auditorium, a two-storeyed library and temporary exhibition galleries. The eastern part holds a permanent interpretive exhibition space and two clusters of undulating galleries. Conceptually, the clustering of the galleries in groups of five is reflective of the Five Virtues, a tenet central to the Sikh faith. Reminiscent of the region's fortress architecture, the built form is intended to exert a dramatic skyline against the surrounding terrain, which is characterised by sand cliffs. The building is a poetic expression of its programme as well as a sensitive response to the site, which creates an architecture that changes dramatically depending on the light conditions.

Architecture in India since 1990 | Global Practice

Eastern complex set around a water feature Exerting a dramatic skyline against the rugged terrain, the complex sits on a ground plane which is softened by dense landscaping while reflecting the structure in its water bodies

View from the Takht Shri Keshgarh Sahib Set in a picturesque ravine in the holy town of Anandpur Sahib, the memorial provides commanding views of the surrounding landscape and architectural edifices

Plaza leading to permanent exhibition gallery This cluster draws inspiration from the Five Virtues central to the Sikh faith. The gallery displays simulated recreations of historic events, animated period-settings and walk-through dioramas that represent Sikh history

Architecture in India since 1990 | Global Practice

107

folio 9
CASTRO CAFETERIA, New Delhi

Romi Khosla Design Studio

The Castro Cafeteria at the Jamia Millia Islamia University exerts a new and powerful presence on the landscape of the campus. The cafeteria essentially comprises a kitchen block and a long eating area, and attempts to challenge and alter the conventional notions of a campus canteen as an enclosed space. In this way, it also seeks to address the extreme climatic conditions of the region by providing a partially open-air environment, allowing ambient year-round temperatures without compromising on ventilation. With spatial elements delineated as distinct and independent from each other, the kota stone floor becomes the primary unifier that seamlessly blurs the boundaries between the interior and the exterior. The transition from enclosed to open occurs from a semi-covered space, defined by parallel marble walls and a floating galvanised iron roof supported on steel columns, to an open space demarcated only by the floor and fixed seating. The structure appropriates standardised building technologies (used commonly for petrol pumps or gas stations), making this a significant project in the context of a contemporary India. The use of creative innovations opens up novel ways in which the construction industry can contribute to evolving suitable building typologies for the new Indian landscape.

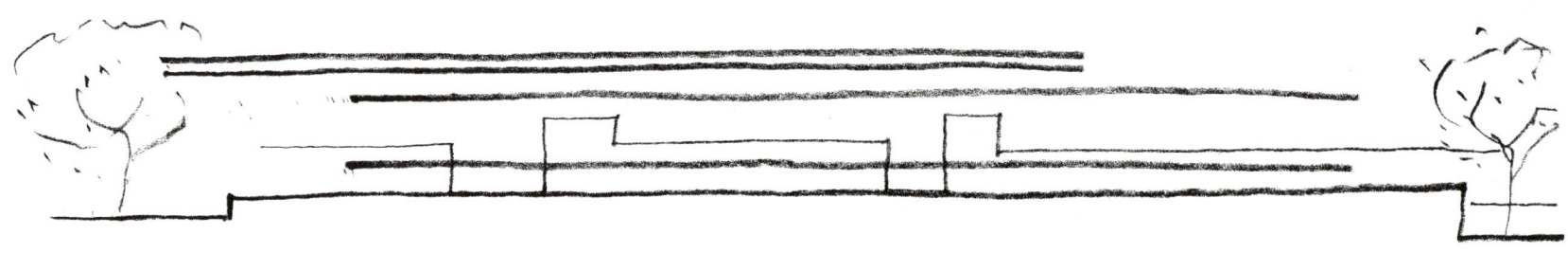

Translation of the design concept The side walls are detached from the floor and roof, allowing each horizontal and vertical element to be read as an individual entity enclosing the space

Conceptual sketch The cafeteria was designed as a floating pavilion that emphasises the horizontal plane, allowing the surrounding landscape to visually penetrate its enclosure

Detail of the façade Plastered surfaces and a stone-clad wall are placed adjacent to each other, subtly playing off different textures

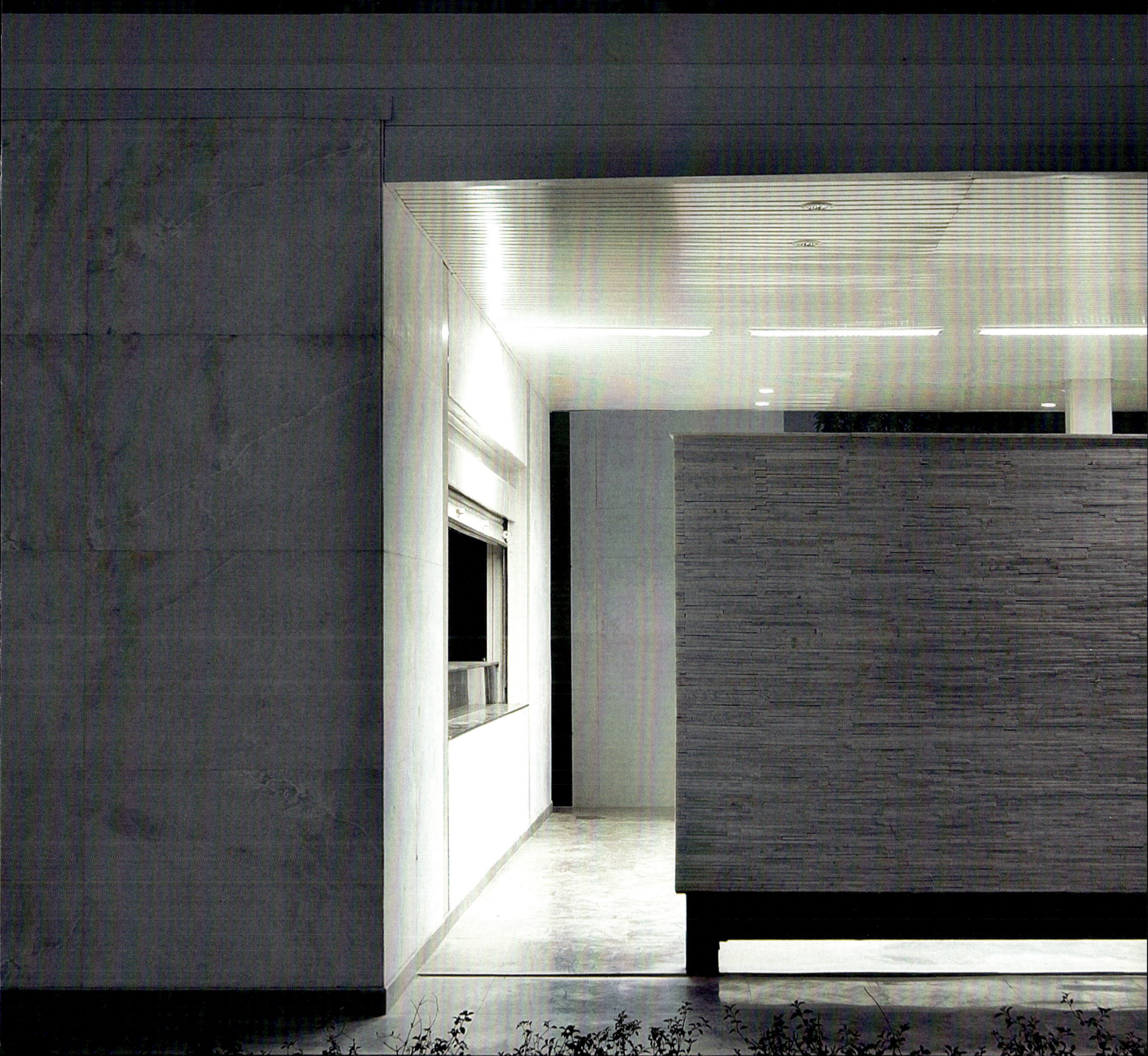

Architecture in India since 1990 | Global Practice

Seating area looking towards service block Guided by the structural supports, the linear furniture arrangement along the periphery allows for a clear movement path and ensures the alignment of seating in what is usually a chaotic student space

Side wall and edge condition The dining area explores varying degrees of enclosure that allow multiplicity of use while segregating the service areas from the main space

Architecture in India since 1990 | Global Practice

111

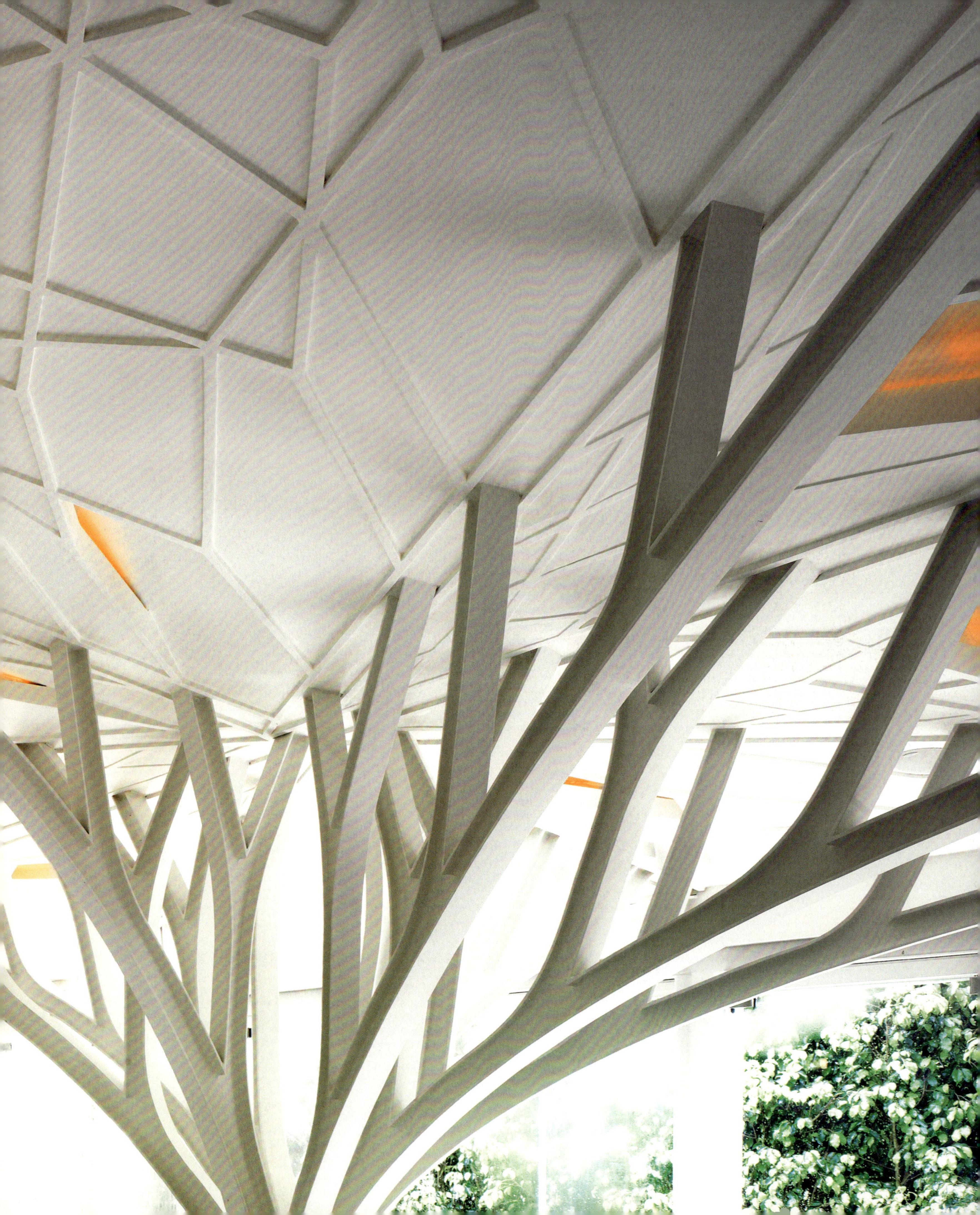

folio 10
TOTE, Mumbai

Serie Architects (Chris Lee and Kapil Gupta)

Set in a disused historic colonial structure in the Royal Western Turf Club at the Mahalaxmi Racecourse, Mumbai, Tote is one of many such buildings now converted into restaurants. Strict heritage regulations ensured complete conservation of a portion of the original building along with the entire roof profile. The abundance of mature rain trees surrounding this site became a feature that inspired both the design and structural logic of the building. The uses accommodated within comprise a lounge bar, restaurant, café and banquet areas.

The most seminal aspect of the project is the construction process and the interface with digital technologies in generating, and then fabricating, its form. With extensive use of CAD applications and 3-d modelling tools for form generation, branching pattern analysis and structural studies, the challenge was to marry cutting-edge technology with local manufacturing skills. Employing boiler fabricators and allowing for precise laser cutting, two sectional truss profiles in steel were devised, while metal fabricators ensured the accurate welding and assembly of flanges onto the trusses. The corten steel-clad roof is punctured with openings that correspond to the 'branch' intersections, with the envelope allowing light to filter in and penetrate the space, modulating its volumetric perception. False ceilings and faceted wall panelling are also generated using a similar method for computing, plotting and fabrication.

Detail of ceiling The ceiling, which integrates three different lighting systems, is built up in plasterboard and plywood coves, and is then patterned to match the structural truss. Punctures within the ceiling at appropriate places bring in natural light

Entrance into main level The space is spanned by a series of tree-like columns in steel, which further branch out to form the trusses that support the roof

Architecture in India since 1990 | Global Practice

Main-level lounge seating
The branching grid determines the lounge layout with its upholstered leather furniture, where the column structure creates a pavilion-like space

Interior view of lounge area
The faceted wall backdrop uses a walnut veneer finish that complements the warm hues and lighting in the lounge. Bronze channels create a branching pattern, echoing the external structural system

View of the restored colonial structure Adhering to heritage regulations, the building was converted into a restaurant while maintaining its original roof profile. A landscaped path leads to the restaurant, which is surrounded by the rain trees that inspired its structural logic

Drawings of structural systems CAD applications and 3-D modelling allowed various permutations and combinations in order to explore and analyse branching pattern and structural capacities

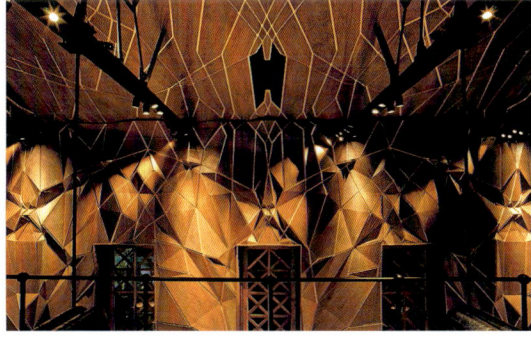

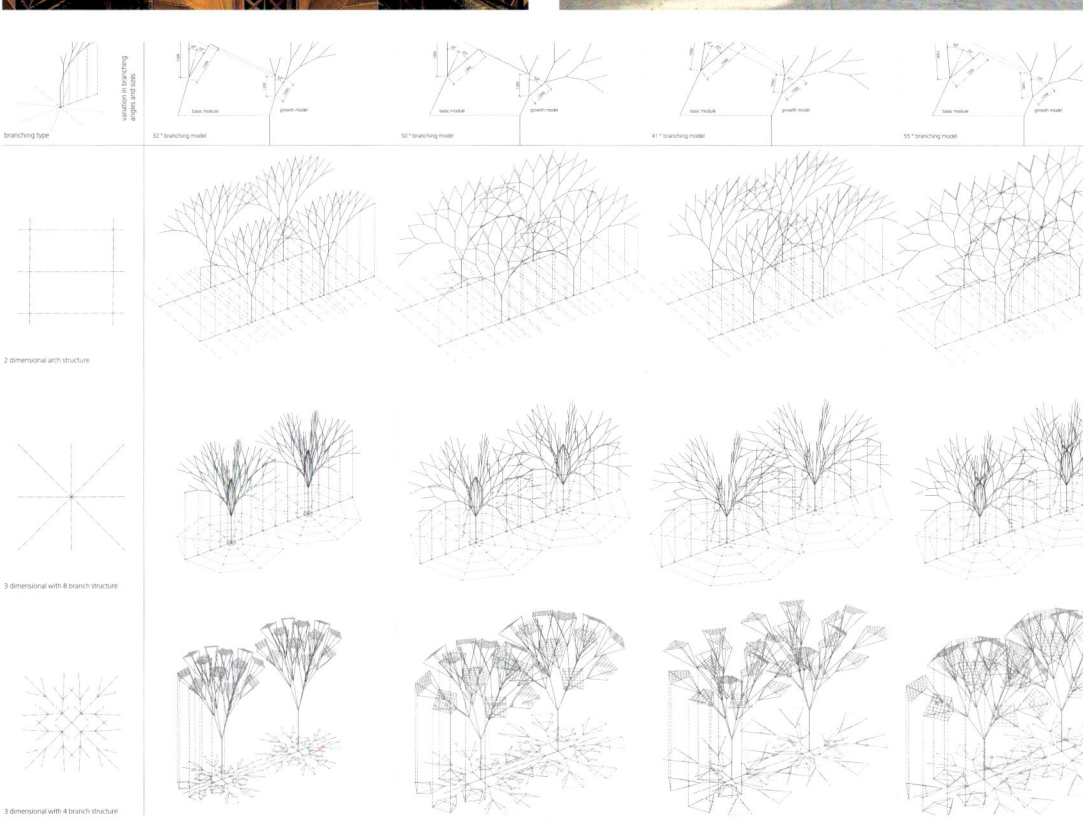

Architecture in India since 1990 | Global Practice

115

Regional Manifestation
Local Assertions

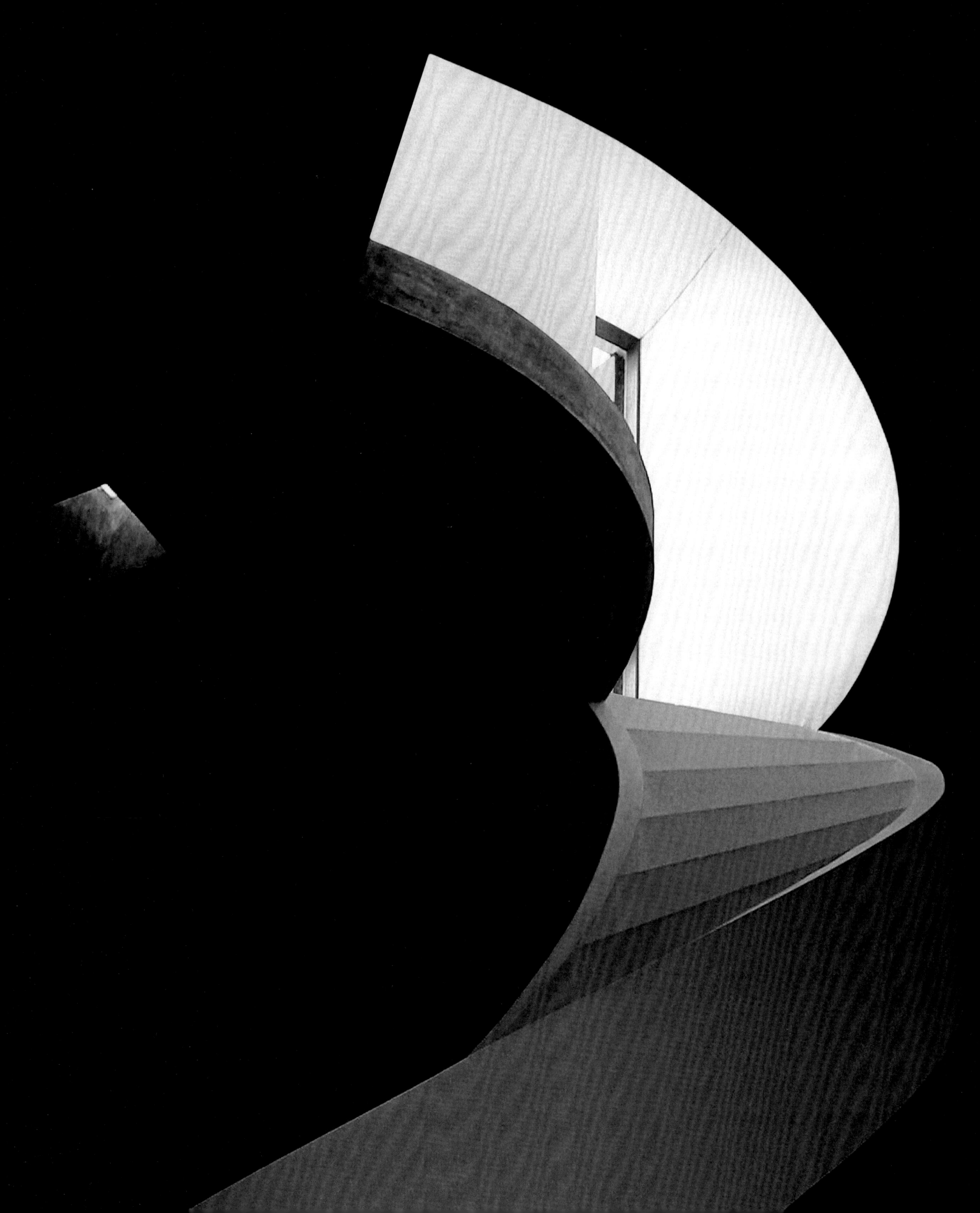

In a mutinous democracy like India, global flows do not effortlessly erase and remake landscapes; rather, they continually negotiate their space with the locale and are often (at least spatially) forced to occupy fissures within cities or along the periphery of urban centres. Furthermore, although the designs of the most obvious territory belonging to global capital flows have been pre-empted by the Western architect, an entire landscape of architecture inspired by spontaneous local resistance is emerging, driven by Indian practitioners. These practitioners, although limited by the scale of their operations, grapple with questions related to the relevance of the architecture of globalisation to India's social, cultural and economic milieu. The transformations that have occurred in the political and economic landscape in India have necessitated the construction of new meanings for this model of practice, or regionalist approach. Thus, the new and varied forms of contemporary architecture in India cannot be easily discerned when viewed using previously existing narratives of a neat and linear progression of modernism and its adaptation to the locale. Although pluralistic responses to this condition have emerged in the last few years, the projects that capture the imagination of both the profession and society are those that simultaneously result from global flows and yet resist the globalisation process.

What results from this local resistance to the otherwise all-unifying global flow of capital, building and cultural seduction, is a unique form of a sensitised international architecture—an architectural approach that is indigenous, regional in spirit, and rooted in the place. These practitioners bring in regional sensibilities when dealing with building, resisting global flows on their own terms. They are usually local Indian architects equipped with Western training yet insightful about the locale. They are the inheritors of the rich tradition of modernism in India, and recognise the rules and rigour that characterise it, but are also sensitive to the need to integrate the sensibilities of a place and the implicit rules of building embedded in the locale. They endeavour to create a distinctive identity without literal references or caricatures. Most importantly, they aim to make globalisation relevant for India in terms of the physical form it takes. This type of practice, with a regionalist approach (or critical regionalism, as it is often referred to in academic debates on architecture today), does not reject modernism, but rather the new form of internationalism perpetuated by the corporate pattern of practices. In fact, regionalists see the importance of modernism as a mechanism for viewing tradition afresh. Although this model of practice is organised much like the practice of global architecture, its mandate, agenda and aspirations are regional.

After gaining independence in 1947, India focused on a concerted political effort during the following four decades to weld the nation together socially and economically as well as to create a singular national identity. Ironically, starting in the 1990s this centralised thrust for nation building saw a reversal, as the country experienced the rapidly disappearing role of the state in all aspects of life (except perhaps economic policy) and a quickly fading emphasis on a pan-Indian identity. Central government institutions responsible for the delivery of housing and other forms of physical and social infrastructure were virtually dismantled in the 1990s. Similarly, the Public Works Department (PWD), a legacy inherited from the decades of colonial rule and the virtual custodian of all state building, had a diminished influence in the creation of the built environment from the 1990s onwards—especially the control over state-sponsored cultural and social institutions. These shifts were largely a result of both the devolvement of responsibility by the centre in delivering physical infrastructure at the state level and a shifting political landscape, with the emergence of regional parties and disaggregated power centres. In fact, in the 1990s, the most significant outcome of the liberalisation of the Indian economy, was the assertion of regional identities augmented by the fragmentation of the country's centralised political power structure into a coalition of multiple regional parties. This political decentralisation impacted on both the state as well as privately driven production of architecture—a kind of stylistic decentralisation (or regionalism) that has facilitated the expression of multiple strikingly different forms.

Although patronage for earlier socialist government-controlled projects has shifted from the public to the private sector, regionalist practice has attempted to resituate these programmes within the realm

Stair detail from **House for Inge Rieck** by Domnique Dube and David Nightingale

Architecture in India since 1990 | Regional Manifestation

Gandhi Smarak Sangrahalaya Ashram (*top left*) by Charles Correa Associates. In post-independent India, this project embodied a significant reflection of regionalist ideas and expressions within modernist architecture, while embodying Gandhi's principles of frugal means in constructing its image

Cidade de Goa Hotel (*bottom left*) and **Kanchanjunga Apartments** (*right*), both by Charles Correa Associates, were seminal in establishing a regionalist approach within the tenets and rigour of modernism

of social and environmental responsibilities. These practices have subsequently become forms of local resistance that manufactured alternative modernities within the broader narrative of globalisation. In the mainstream of the profession, this model of practice has the greatest currency among both colleges of architecture and professional institutions, with a new generation extending the powerful combination of modernist principles and a locale-inspired aesthetic and articulating it in their work. Today cultural institutions, schools, resort hotels and private (often second) homes are the chief patrons of this architecture.

The works of Balkrishna Doshi, Charles Correa and Raj Rewal are seminal examples of this mode of practice, and their early projects of the 1980s served as its foundation. They had international 'currency' in architectural discourse and were cited as potent examples of critical regionalism (a category coined by the academics Alexander Tzonis and Liane Lefaivre and then expanded and popularised by Kenneth Frampton, the renowned architectural critic). Early projects in the era of India's pre-liberalised economy—such as Charles Correa Associates' Gandhi Smarak Sangrahalaya Ashram in Ahmedabad (1958-63), Kanchanjunga apartments in Mumbai (1970-83) and Cidade de Goa Hotel in Miramar (1979-81)—brought the deepest values of regional sensibilities and aesthetics to modern Indian architecture. Similarly, the work of Doshi's Vastu Shilpa Consultants—particularly his firm's own office, Sangath in Ahmedabad (1979-81) and buildings for the School of Architecture at the Centre for Environmental Planning and Technology (CEPT) campus in the same city (1962 onwards)—demonstrated the immense possibilities for a localised architecture based on climatic and technological constraints that also resonated a deep cultural sensibility. Raj Rewal Associates' startlingly refreshing demonstration of localising technology in his building for the Permanent Exhibition Complex at

Sangath (*left, top and bottom*) and **CEPT** (*right top*) by BV Doshi's Vastu Shilpa Consultants, for their own office and the architecture school in Ahmedabad, demonstrated a keen inclination towards material and climate-responsive design while humanising the modernist idiom

The **Permanent Exhibition Complex** of New Delhi's Pragati Maidan (*right bottom*) by Raj Rewal Associates demonstrates the architect's ability to overcome existing technological constraints in order to create a series of space-frame pavilions in concrete, taking the regionalist expression to a different level of technological exploration

Pragati Maidan in New Delhi (1970-72) extended the regionalist approach to yet another level. Here, Rewal adapted the handmade technologies of cast in-situ concrete to fabricate the largest space frame in the country—an innovation that had local relevance in the most comprehensible ways.

Paralleling these efforts was the quiet evolution of a more humane and organic architectural response to regional concerns by Gira and Gautam Sarabhai in Ahmedabad. The Sarabhai siblings were way ahead of their time in that they sought to create architectural

The **Belgian Embassy** (*left, top and bottom*) by Satish Gujral, an artist with no formal training in architecture, was conceptualised through a series of sketches, reflecting a new approach in the use of brick and stone as well as plasticity of form. This project challenged the conventional expression of modernism, and brought a fresh 'spin' to the debate in the late 1980s

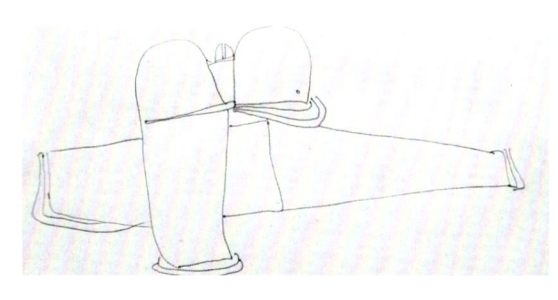

Tejal House (*right*) by Vastu Shilpa Consultants displays a looseness and plasticity that characterised a new phase in BV Doshi's work, marked by a more playful aesthetic

expression through tectonic exploration using local materials. They recycled and collaged components from historical buildings, used adobe techniques prevalent and alive as building traditions in rural India, employed bamboo screens and a host of other materials not 'on the radar' of the modernist. In short, they were liberated from the formality of modernism that often weighed down mainstream architects. Their affluent background supported the experimental nature of their work and allowed them to establish a place for the 'contemporary ethnic', which became a popular aesthetic for the rich in socialist India.

In the same vein, Joseph Allen Stein, an American expatriate, worked in New Delhi at a slower pace, and built a circle of followers and patrons that supported similar experimental explorations in adoption of the universalising influences of modernism locally. The several buildings he built there demonstrated a looser and less ideological representation of the Indian nation's concerns for constructing a modern identity. Committed to building in harmony with the land, both to minimise costs and to knit the building into the landscape, Stein blurred the lines between the inside and outside with visual ambiguity by using rough-hewn stone on the interior. He also employed a host of other materials, which transcended their local association, for different components in a building. In particular, his India International Centre in New Delhi (1959-62) represents this more organic and deep connection to the landscape and textures of the locale in an effort to inspire a separate stream of thinking within the regionalist approach. Simultaneously, a single project by artist Satish Gujral infused a sense of optimism with regard to the possibilities of manipulating the locale for inspiration. The plasticity and sculptural quality of his Belgian Embassy building in New Delhi (1980-83), albeit the one exemplary project that sliced effortlessly past the self-conscious regionalist gestures. This project also challenged the superficiality of postmodern approaches of applying historical references to modern and contemporary works as a veneer without grappling with the processes that localise architecture in much more sustained ways. This too, like Stein's work, inspired a generation of architects and triggered multiple streams of expression beyond the aesthetic of the pure modern.

Doshi's Tejal House (1998) and Hussain Gufa (1992-95) have, more recently, extended the regionalist architects' preoccupation with creating an appropriate intersection between tectonics and local material skills, as well as the visual fluidity and plastic nature of India's popular visual landscape. In the same vein, Correa's Vidhan Bhavan (1980-96), the Legislative Assembly building in Bhopal for the State of Madhya Pradesh, while representing a Palace for Democracy, is a plastic expression that weaves into its syntax the rich array of formal as well as visual tribal folk culture in its articulation, thereby representing a cross-section of society and its aspirations in the building. Importantly, it is perhaps the most powerful example in post-independence India of the use of a dominant form or clear theme as the starting point for the

The **Vidhan Bhavan** (*left*) by Charles Correa Associates is significant not only for its complex organisation and for constituting an inclusive symbol of democracy for the people of Madhya Pradesh, but also for its intelligent siting in the city of Bhopal

The **National Institute of Immunology** (*right top*) by Raj Rewal Associates, perhaps the most seminal work in the architect's career, embodies the spatial character and imagery of a traditional Indian town with a rigour that suggests a new type of institutional organisation

The **Mahindra United World College of India** (*right, centre and bottom*) by Christopher Charles Benninger Architects responds to the surrounding landscape of Lonavala through material and form, whereby the architect humanely translates the pedagogical agenda of this international institute

configuration of a spatial narrative. Here, the circle and its subdivision into nine squares alludes to the navagraha (or the ancient mandala diagram) while setting up a recognisable instrument that can accommodate multiple rich (spatial and visual) narratives, which Correa embeds in the building. Similarly, in the Inter-University Centre for Astronomy & Astrophysics (IUCAA) complex (1988-92) in Pune, Correa gives expression to the emergent cutting-edge research in astronomy using the most deeply traditional forms and spatial configurations as his inspiration to generate a unique and visually stunning design vocabulary. At a more formal scale is Rewal's Indian Parliament Library (2003), situated next to the Lutyens and Herbert Baker parliament complex in New Delhi. This building is an attempt to relate to the existing historic structures of the parliament complex without compromising its aspirations toward structural and material innovation. Rewal's National Institute of Immunology (1983-90) in New Delhi is perhaps his finest work, wherein the inspiration from the incremental and accretive quality of traditional towns finds a contemporary resonance in both spatial sensibilities and imagery. Similarly, Christopher Charles Benninger Architects' Mahindra United World College of India (1998) near Lonavala symbolises the quest to create localised expression, through form and material, for an international educational institute that represents the growing shift in the privatisation of education in the country.

More recently, the work of Kerry Hill Architects in Kolkata has provided a refreshing example of a five-star hotel by ITC in Sonar Bangla (2003), employing a rigorous reference to materials, textures and the character of a place by innovating at the level of both

Architecture in India since 1990 | Regional Manifestation

The **Aman Hotel** (*this page*) by Kerry Hill Architects, whose style is in stark contrast to that of a global hotel chain, is consistent with the architect's rigorous efforts to customise and utilise regional materials and techniques to create a formal yet organic expression

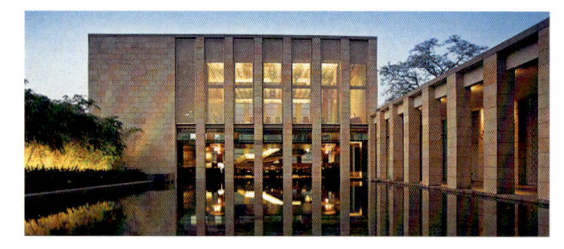

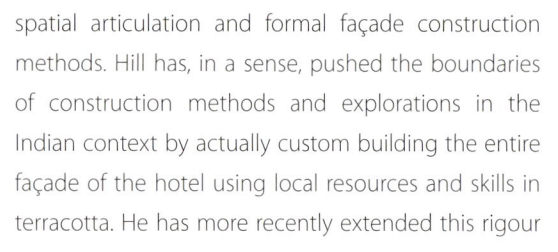

spatial articulation and formal façade construction methods. Hill has, in a sense, pushed the boundaries of construction methods and explorations in the Indian context by actually custom building the entire façade of the hotel using local resources and skills in terracotta. He has more recently extended this rigour in the use of material in the Aman Hotel, New Delhi (2009). Sen Kapadia in Mumbai, on the other hand, has consistently experimented with form and varying programmes and has attempted to straddle local sensibilities, arising from programmatic constraints and abstract, seemingly Western, forms. The deftness of his spatial articulation, with its minimalist aesthetic, suspends his buildings in an ambiguous space between the global and the local. His factory building for the Garden Silk Mills in Jolva (2009) is a powerful example of his ability to traverse this ambiguity between the universal nature of the programme

Shihor Farmhouse (*left, top and centre*) by Leo Pereira aspires to set itself firmly yet sensitively within the landscape of Bhavnagar through its spatial disposition and use of material and form

French Embassy Staff Quarters (*left bottom*) and **Housing for British High Commission** (*right top and bottom*) by Raj Rewal Associates. Such large housing projects, often used by international organisations and their staff, had also witnessed considerable experimentation from the regionalist perspective in India's pre-liberalised economy

and the specific context. With a completely different approach, KT Ravindran's memorial to Rajiv Gandhi in Sriperumbudur (2003) is an example of a building being rooted squarely in its place through the skilful use of local granite and a richly sculpted narrative of decoration using local craftspeople from the region. These architects and others such as Anant Raje, Leo Pereira, Minakshi and Kulbhushan Jain and Rabindra Vasavada in Ahmedabad; Romi Khosla, Gautam Bhatia and AGK Menon in New Delhi; and Ramesh Tharakan in Kochi (formerly Cochin) have extended these sensibilities in more localised yet innovative, rigorous, and socially and culturally relevant ways. They have addressed these questions through their engagements with education as well as their writings on the realities of the regions, establishing a broader critical framework for architects working in India.

Aside from institutional buildings and other private commissions (such as single-family houses), mass-scale housing was very much in the realm of engagement of the regionalist architects until such time that the government patronised and produced social housing in the early 1990s. Since liberalisation, this area has been squarely pre-empted by the corporate pattern of practice—a contentious issue in the architecture profession in India, and perhaps globally. However, regionalist architects continue to build socially and climatically responsible housing projects within this model of practice. Rewal's housing projects for the French Embassy and the British High Commission (1990 onwards), both in New Delhi, strive to create localised responses—albeit for expatriates working in India. Correa's Titan Township (1992) near Bengaluru, attempts to extend the local vernacular in the configuration of what is essentially a company town. Here, the attempt is to create an environment

Architecture in India since 1990 | Regional Manifestation

The **City Centre Mall** (*this page*) by Charles Correa Associates doubles as a housing project in Kolkata's Salt Lake City. It breaks away from the stereotype prevalent in similar mixed-use development across Indian cities by responding in its configuration to traditional Indian bazaars as well as to climatic considerations

Aranya Community Housing (*top*) by Vastu Shilpa Foundation and **Belapur Housing** (*bottom*) by Charles Correa Associates, both housing complexes built for the urban poor, recognise the incremental way in which a house may 'grow' with direct participation from its occupants

for employees of a premier watch manufacturer that respects local resources while creating a humane habitat that is soft and 'malleable' to the user. The same is true of the recently designed apartment blocks in Kolkata's Salt Lake City by Correa (2004), which attempt to respond to climatic conditions as well as contemporary aspirations in a high-rise configuration while situating themselves in a larger mixed-use development comprising malls, community halls and multiplexes. For the urban poor, Doshi's Aranya Community housing project in Indore and Correa's Belapur Housing (both established in the late 1980s but continuing to grow) explore and deftly extend the idea of sites and services in which the urban architectural pattern is generated by recognising the incremental nature of growth. This is especially true for the urban poor who invest piecemeal over time in the house. This notion of housing, as an instrument for habitation capable of absorbing change, has unfortunately disappeared from almost the entire housing delivery system, now dominated by private developers in India. This has left little room for innovation by architects as the model of the high-rise tower is sweeping across the country as the paradigm for housing—whether for the higher-income demographic, the middle class or even the poor. Furthermore, the privatisation of housing has also signalled a significant shift in the role of the architect and the relationship of the profession to the state. The housing sector was one of the largest areas in which the state patronised architecture and archi-

Mewar Complex (*left, top and bottom*) by Vijay Arya of Minakshi Jain Architects and **Bhishangarh Fort Hotel** (*right*) by Stephane Paumier of SPA Design show contemporary architects striving for an appropriate aesthetic through the honest and direct use of materials. While the former takes this rigour to an extreme, the latter walks the thin line between serious proposition and a folly

tects through the 1970s and 1980s, via both state-level and central agencies such as the Housing and Urban Development Corporation (HUDCO). Today, for the next generation of architects the state is virtually nonexistent as a patron for building.

In the recent past, since India's economic liberalisation in the 1990s, a new generation of architects has emerged which chooses to negotiate this complex landscape of reconciliation between the local and global in new ways and to engage with new forms of patronage. These include private institutions run by trusts and foundations, and private-sector projects ranging from single-family homes to corporate and industrial commissions. Interestingly, the spread of these new practices is geographically more diverse than before, and includes centres in the economically mobile southern states outside the architectural 'spine' of New Delhi, Ahmedabad and Mumbai, where the seminal practices of the previous generation were situated.

Some of the significant emerging practices are those of Sanjay Mohe, Prem Chandavarkar, Mathew & Ghosh, Kiran Venkatesh and Rajesh Renganathan in Bengaluru, a city that has seen an incredible building boom as it established itself as India's premier information technology hub. In Ahmedabad, architects like Gurjit Singh Matharoo, Meghal Jain, Vijay Arya, Aniket Bhagwat and Rajeev Kathpalia are extending the legacy of the previous generation of modernists but furthering their use of material and spatial sensibilities to create startlingly fresh forms. Meanwhile, in Kochi, Jacob George and Klaus-Peter Gast have evolved distinctive spatial responses to the locale without alluding directly to traditional forms. Samira Rathod and Bijoy Jain in Mumbai struggle to make a place for architecture in a landscape comprising largely interior-design commissions. Their work employs a rigorous material exploration, but one limited by episodic narratives rather than clear spatial propositions. On the other hand, Stephane Paumier in New Delhi, although an expatriate architect, demonstrates the most innovative approaches within the regionalist

Architecture in India since 1990 | Regional Manifestation

Arjun Machan – A Weekend Retreat (*left, top and bottom*) by Rajeev Kathpalia, Vastu Shilpa Consultants. This weekend house is experimental at a formal level with materials and tectonics, while sensitively responding to its verdant site

Leslie Pallath House (*right, top and bottom*) by Klaus-Peter Gast is so confidently modernist in its expression, in a Keralan landscape dominated by traditional and vernacular imagery, that it acts as a counterpoint to the facile caricature-like interpretation of local context and building practices often demonstrated by architects in that region

The **Indian Institute of Management Hostel Block** (*left top*) and **Hindustan Unilever Limited Research Centre Phase 3** (*left centre*), both by Mindspace Architects, are additions to existing facilities with global programmes—and here the architect, by using local materials and technologies, creates an expression that resonates with its surroundings

Design Combine Office (*left bottom*), by the architects themselves, demonstrates a synthetic approach that embodies industrial aesthetics woven seamlessly with a deep regionalist understanding of climate, landscape and local building skills

stream of work inspired by tectonic as well as historical precedents. These practitioners all belong to the first generation of architects in India's global economic era to consciously extend this critical regionalism as an architectural approach and, perhaps, style. They seek to reconcile their alliances to the locale while speaking the universal language of a globalising world. Their training (often Western) equips them to understand the dynamics of production using new technologies and materials, while their rootedness in the context layers their work with a deep understanding of the culture of place and the processes of building in India. They bring a Western rigour to their buildings while demonstrating an adept negotiation of labour-intensive modes of production.

Among these architects, most of whom started their practices in the early 1990s, some push the boundaries of imagery as well as technological innovation further, whereas others more finely and consciously articulate lessons from tradition and place. Mindspace Architects' Hindustan Unilever Limited Research Centre (2006) and Sanjay Mohe's NSRGIV at the Indian Institute of Management (2003), as well as the Karunashraya Terminal Care Centre (1999), all in Bengaluru, demonstrate a deftness with which global programmes can find alternative expressions using local materials, traditional space configurations and construction processes. Rajesh Renganathan, on the other hand, demonstrates the confidence to engage with new materials and minimalistic compositions with frugal dispositions. His addition to the International Institute of Information Technology (IIIT) Campus (2009) and 2DC817 house-studio (2001), both in Bengaluru, are varied and yet sensitively configured in order to make an architecture that is pragmatic yet poetic. Similarly, Jacob George's houses in Kochi create fresh, new expressions for the hot and humid climate using steel, glass and an array of new materials. Jacob manages to build with sophisticated industrial precision and well-calibrated proportions thus far unequalled in India. His own house (2004) and office for Design Combine (2005) are the strongest testimony to his approach and the rigour with which his buildings are made. Matharoo's various works in Ahmedabad and other parts of the state of Gujarat extend the modernist tradition in India of exposed reinforced concrete as well as its application to new programmes. Matharoo Associates' explorations of this material and its plastic expression for buildings as varied as the Ashwini Kumar Crema-

Architecture in India since 1990 | Regional Manifestation

Prathama Blood Bank (*left and opposite page right*) by Matharoo Associates evokes the sculptural through architectural expression, a key component of Gurjit Matharoo's work. Furthermore, his engagement with a series of social projects, such as this one and a nearby crematorium, has made his contribution special for the local community

House with Balls (*centre and right top*) by Matharoo Associates. The architect's design for this contemporary residence embodies the spirit of modernist projects in the post-independence era through a unique approach to material, form and technological experimentation

Tahiliani Design Headquarters (*centre bottom and right, centre and bottom*) by Stephane Paumier of SPA Design. This fashion studio and production unit continues in the spirit of New Delhi's modernist traditions of evocative exposed brick, while the inner spaces echo the stark assembly-line nature of the building's programme

torium (1999) in Surat and the Prathama Blood Centre (2000) and House with Balls (2009), in Ahmedabad have been refreshingly startling. Furthermore, he has brought architecture to social institutions that have never before been made evident or visible through architectural expression. In addition to his engagement with social programmes, he has designed among the most innovative single-family houses of his generation, unconsciously extending the traditions of Corbusier and Kahn, in that he straddles both sculptural and tectonic manoeuvres with equal ease.

From another perspective, Paumier's practice SPA Design's Tahiliani Design headquarters in Gurgaon

South Asian Human Rights Documentation Centre (*this page*) by Anagram Architects shows this team of young designers attempting to develop a fresh idiom in New Delhi's architectural context through experimental expression in exposed brickwork

(2005-07) is an important work in the New Delhi landscape. It simultaneously refers to the sculptural qualities of Satish Gujral's work as well as the more extended tradition of Shoosmith's Garrison Church and the exposed brick landscape that dominated New Delhi through the decades after independence starting in the 1950s. This resonates even more strongly in the works of Anagram Architects in their South Asian Human Rights Documentation Centre (SAHRDC) building in New Delhi (2005-08). Here, brick is modulated in innovative ways using new technologies to create not only an intelligent and low-cost screen but a completely new expression in the context of the historic landscape of the city.

Another stream that seems to be prominent among what might be classified as India's regional modernity is the aesthetic that could be referred to as the Auroville style, which grew out of the autonomy that the ashram township of Auroville near Puducherry enjoyed. Auroville provided its architects with fertile ground for experimentation, as rethinking lifestyle and human relationships with nature was one of its core agendas. Settled by architects and designers from around the world (but largely European), Auroville became a rich ground for experimentation in the exploration of local materials and their application in an architecture for contemporary life in India. Being an ashram, the area's autonomy and insulation in terms of cultural, as well as social and economic, imperatives put no pressure on its architects to respond to anything but the purity of material and tectonics. Although this did produce a minimalism and an earthy aesthetic (characterised by the use of exposed or pigmented cement floors and whitewashed or adobe and exposed stone walls), it in no way responded to the contingencies of the real India in terms of either densities or pressures to deliver architecture as a commodity for occupation in the context of high property values. Often limited by styling, these works seemingly do not recognise society or the broader economic landscape as an influence on form making—hence, they are often rendered soulless. Thus, despite the extremely well-crafted and evocative form of these buildings, they suffer from a detachment from the place beyond material and autonomy not dissimilar to the tropical resorts across Asia.

Within this landscape some architects have brought a rigour of questioning and engagement with issues that can be replicated across India. Fabian Ostner's Klara House in Auroville (2003), in its exploration of industrial materials opens up questions connected to mass-housing approaches. Dominique Dube and David Nightingale's House for Inge Rieck (2005) and Ganesh Bala's Learning Centre (2006) are examples of tectonic explorations that characterise the new regionalism emerging from Auroville. These projects offer many lessons for contemporary Indian architecture, especially through the discipline and fundamental integrity that they demonstrate.

House for Inge Rieck (*left and centre bottom*) by Dominique Dube and David Nightingale, situated amidst Auroville's climate of experimental thought, demonstrates a rigour of material expression and a grounding in regional ideas that are highly relevant to current practice

Vault House (*centre and right top*) by Samira Rathod Design Associates is representative of the weekend retreats of the affluent around Mumbai. These projects exercise restraint through materials and their articulation, mediating between global imagery and local contingencies

Bridge House (*right, centre and bottom*), also by Samira Rathod Design Associates, is another second-home retreat near Mumbai, which demonstrates the architect's ability to experiment and combine varied materials and architectural expressions

In addition to the numerous similar works in Auroville, this style and approach of an unhurried, 'insulated' architecture has found its expression in resorts and various weekend houses on the peripheries of Mumbai, Goa, Kochi and other regions where the tropical climate affords a replication of such conditions. Some examples of the extension of this style are the projects of Aniket Bhagwat in Ahmedabad as well as Samira Rathod and Bijoy Jain in Mumbai, whose highly stylised articulation of traditional forms and rigorous use of materials express a struggle to find an aesthetic minimalism relevant for India. These projects for resorts and single-family (often second) homes, largely for extremely affluent clients, are often not disciplined in spatial economy or severely constrained by costs. They nevertheless attempt to create an aesthetic that might speak of this reconciliation between the superficial glamour of global images and the rigour

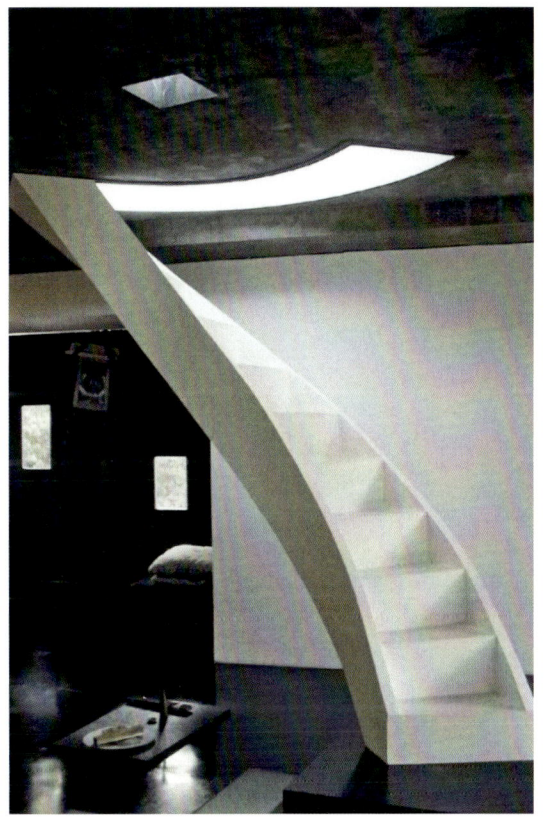

International Flower Auction Complex (*top*) by Chandavarkar & Thacker Architects is a fresh articulation for a new institution in Bengaluru, which suggests a search for new expressions for the social infrastructure of an emerging India

Indian Institute of Journalism and New Media (*left, centre and bottom*) by InFORM Architects. New and emerging programmes, such as this one for an Institute of Journalism, have also seen the innovative crafting of space and material, thereby resisting the global imagery that is often used for these building types

International Institute of Information Technology (*right, centre and bottom*), B-Campus Extension by Flying Elephant Studio. The architect's design for the new IIIT building carefully negotiates lessons from modernism with a contemporary use of material and technology in achieving innovative new solutions and expressions for the institutes of a new India

of localised material palettes and labour-intensive modes of construction. Bijoy Jain's Tara House (2006) in Kashid (near Mumbai) and Belavali House in Badlapur (2008) as well as Samira Rathod Design Associates' Vault House (2006) and Bridge House (2009), both in Alibaug, are stunning examples of this approach. Obviously inspired by Geoffrey Bawa from Sri Lanka and by the villas of Singapore, these architects seek to give expression to the buildings of the affluent in localised and architecturally sensitive ways while insulating themselves from the broader questions of economy and the speed of change confronting most architects in India.

More pragmatic in their approach are the architects in the fast-growing metropolitan regions of Hyderabad, Bengaluru and Chennai. These new centres of entrepreneurship and industry in India are emerging as the home of the most innovative work in the country, especially when viewed in the context of the speed of change and the challenges facing these architects on the ground. Chandavarkar & Thacker Architects' International Flower Auction Complex (2006) in Bengaluru, Kiran Venkatesh's practice InFORM Architects' Indian Institute of Journalism and New Media in Bagalpur in Tamil Nadu (2000) and Rajesh Renganathan's International Institute of Information Technology in Bengaluru (2008) all strive to find new expression for programmes emerging in the new India. Situated in the face of the onslaught of mindless global icons, these architects have valiantly negotiated

RRM 2 B8 House (*left and right centre*) by Mathew & Ghosh Architects characterises the designers' occupation with precision and minimalism. Their projects achieve levels of finishing not easily attainable in India

Mathew & Ghosh Architects Office and Design Studio (*right top*), by the practice themselves, deftly sculpts a roofscape to create a spectacular studio space flooded with light and a sense of openness

Freedom Park (*right bottom*) also by Matthew & Ghosh Architects is the result of a winning competition entry on the site of a former prison, now redesigned as a public park. A rich narrative has been woven using fragments of surviving buildings from the prison complex

the pressures of these global flows while attempting to craft an indigenous message through their architecture. Similarly, in the Good Earth Apartments (2002) in Bengaluru, Shibanee and Kamal bring to the discussion questions of sustainability and appropriate technologies in a landscape of rapid change. Mathew & Ghosh Architects demonstrate how abstraction can also be a technique for powerfully connecting to the locale, while resisting and challenging the tsunami of regular commercial material choices that flood the market place in Bengaluru, Chennai and Hyderabad. Their deep exploration of spatial possibilities and great attention to handcrafting precise modernist forms have led their architecture to take a prominent position in the landscape of India's emerging southern states. Their design studio (2004) and the SUA House office building (2002), both in Bengaluru, demonstrate a deft handling of both spatial possibilities and articulation through the sensitive use of light. Similarly, their RRM 2 B8 House in Bengaluru explores tectonic sensibilities in new ways. The spectrum of their involvement, which extends to making public spaces in the city, identifies their engagement in deeper ways than most architects of their generation. The Freedom Park project in Bengaluru (2003) and Bethel Baptist Church (2002) are rare examples of architects with such tectonic preoccupations also reaching out to fashion the public realm.

A growing trend embodying similar sets of values of place making is the interest among this new generation of practitioners regarding questions of the conservation of historic buildings. Some practitioners treat these as resources in India's challenged economy while others are engaged with deeper questions of memory and the conservation of continuity in India's built environment. Fuelled by the tourist industry, the most potent works in conservation have emanated from destinations in Rajasthan, Gujarat and Kerala. An early example of this approach was the Neemrana Hotel in Rajasthan by Aman Nath and Francis Wacziarg (1991), which led to several other historic properties being converted into heritage hotels. This was followed

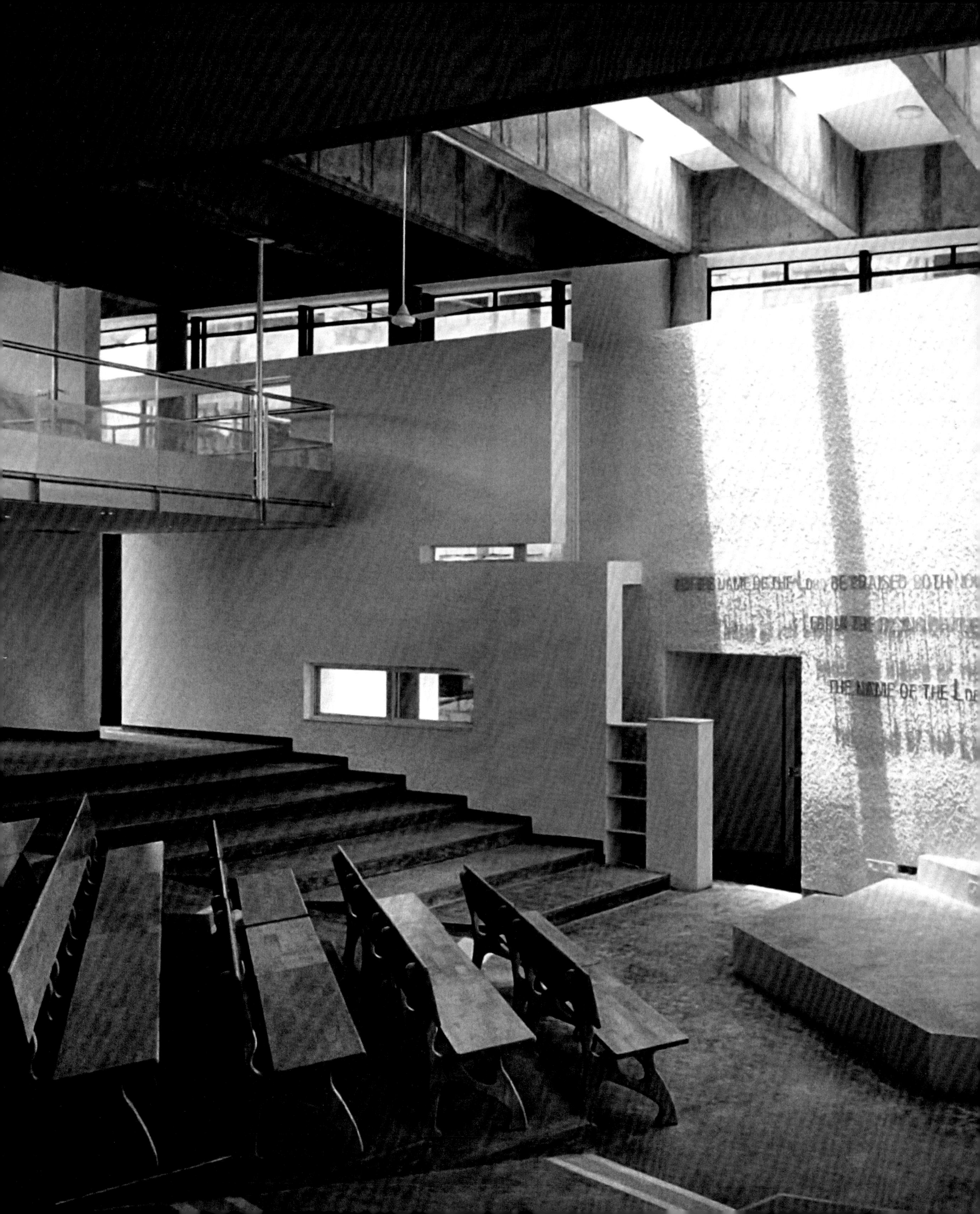

by the Devigarh Hotel in Udaipur by Gautam Bhatia, Navin Gupta, Rajiv Saini and Aniket Bhagwat, which took the idea of recycling a historic property to a higher level of sophistication and interplay between pure conservation and contemporary design. This approach has subsequently taken a more rigorous form, with several architectural and urban conservation efforts under way now in Mumbai, Ahmedabad, Hyderabad, Chennai and Puducherry. Such efforts have become a critical instrument in connecting practitioners to urban questions and larger environmental concerns and issues. This stream of practice within the regionalist tendency in contemporary India will take centre stage as society will use both environmental concerns and questions of conservation as instruments to moderate the pace of change in the future.

If anything separates the new band of regionalist practitioners from their predecessors, it is their disengagement with the public. This new generation, while producing the most potent possibilities in the field of architectonic solution, is characterised by a seeming myopia toward the broader issues (both urban and rural) that formed the natural repertoire of the previous generation—perhaps as a result of its modernist training. Their preoccupation with material (sometimes taken to the level of a fetish), texture and detail has created a short-sightedness and lack of ambition to take on the challenges of moulding and influencing the broader context in which their work is situated. These practitioners are also the most self-conscious among the different emergent models of practice in India. They generally cultivate an extensive network across the globe and exert a disproportionate presence in the international media, taking centre stage when architecture in India is projected to the world outside. In any case, at least at the level of architecture, these projects and practitioners all challenge global trends in that they present sensible climatic responses that use local materials and techniques, recognising the imperatives of the local economy as it makes the transition to its new avatar. In short, these deeply rigorous and committed struggles also resist the juggernaut of global expression and promise a potent new architecture for the varied regions of India.

Bethel Baptist Church (*these pages*) by Mathew & Ghosh Architects is spatially rich, and draws in light to visually expand the volume of the congregation area in a dramatic fashion

Folios

ITC SONAR BANGLA	141
IUCAA	144
HUSAIN DOSHI GUFA	151
KARUNASHRAYA TERMINAL CARE CENTRE	154
ASHWINI KUMAR CREMATORIUM	159
DEVI GARH FORT PALACE	162
PARLIAMENT LIBRARY	167
TARA HOUSE	171
RESIDENCE FOR JACOB GEORGE	175
SUA HOUSE	178
RISHI VALLEY SCHOOL	183

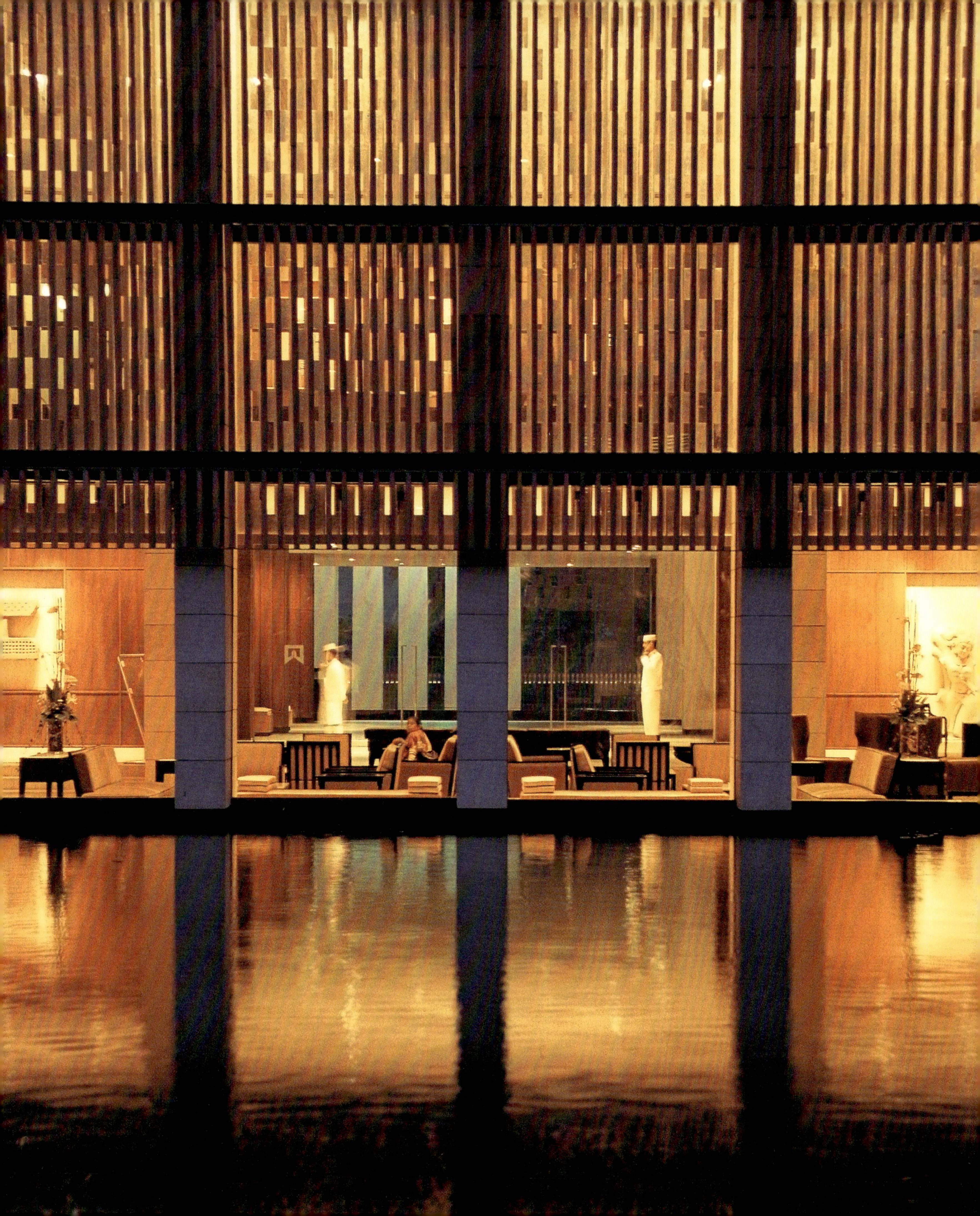

folio 1
ITC SONAR BANGLA, Kolkata

Kerry Hill Architects

This hotel is one of many new projects that intend to help re-establish Kolkata as a leading modern metropolis, breaking away from its earlier image of a decadent colonial city.

Central to the design of the hotel was the transformation of an existing water body, around which all public areas and guest rooms are placed. This organic way of planning takes references from vernacular settlements found in the region. Courtyards and colonnades are used to both separate and connect the various hotel blocks, thereby fragmenting the overall building mass. In keeping with its broader aspirations and ambitions to deal simultaneously with tradition and modernity, many building elements were developed specifically to create an appropriate visual expression as well as help the building function climatically in a sustainable manner. The most important of these elements were the façades, which are panelled with GRC (glassfibre-reinforced concrete) louvres, pigmented with locally made brick dust to provide an earthy quality.

The importance of this project lies in the precedent it set for the fabrication of custom-made building elements (using local resources) at the scale of a luxury hotel. The experimental quality of the screen and other spatial articulations will enhance its significance as a seminal project in the coming years.

View of the lounge A light wooden screen allows light to flood the lounge during the day, while allowing it to glow like a jewel box at night

Floating pavilions A series of detached wooden pavilions dots the periphery of the waterfront, enclosing private tea spaces within. Intricate screens of timber latticework surround these spaces, which house sunken seating areas that draw the viewer's eye level close to the water

Architecture in India since 1990 | Regional Manifestation

View from the internal court
Independent built masses accommodating various functions are placed organically around the water body and connected through colonnaded pathways. The rear tower houses guest rooms and business areas, and is detached from the public areas of the hotel

Waiting and lounge area Looking onto the central water body, the lounge brings in diffused light through its high perforated stone façade, which exudes a translucent quality when backlit at night

Stairway leading to guest rooms Rough stone-finished walls and flooring create a muted space that is washed by natural light from the central courtyard through the glazed wooden frames

Walkway leading to the entrance foyer These steel and FRP canopies edging the water body scale the entranceway and create a sense of arrival before reaching the main hotel lobby

folio 2
IUCAA, Pune

Charles Correa Associates

The Inter-University Centre for Astronomy and Astrophysics (IUCAA), was set up as an autonomous centre of excellence to help propel research and development in astronomy and astrophysics in the university sector.

A multipronged programme facilitates research and academic activities, balanced with observatory facilities and a science-popularisation programme for the general public and students of the school.

The site is divided into three sections—one area containing the Auditorium and Science Park; a second zone, with institutional buildings; and a third zone, the Akashganga Complex, containing staff housing and a recreation centre. Material explorations and variations in surface texture—with the use of a wide variety of materials such as local basalt stone, cuddapah, and granite—not only connect the building to the locale but are also used to evoke metaphysical connections, such that the shiniest surfaces seem to merge with the sky. At the heart of the institutional building lies a *kund*, used as a metaphor for the expanding universe. Diagonal connections from this centre suggest links to the other facilities on the campus: the computer centre, hostels and housing for visiting-faculty. The project, in its use of symbols and references, is a brave attempt at finding ways to represent a contemporary understanding of the cosmos, the mandate of the institute itself.

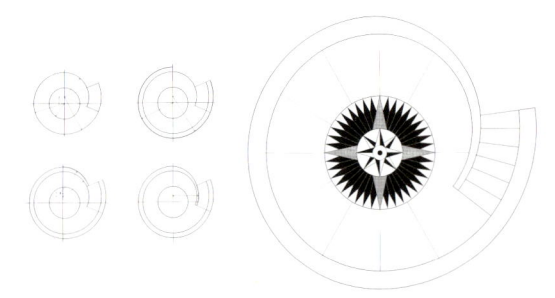

Installation outside the faculty offices Based on Foucalt's pendulum, which demonstrates the Earth's rotation, this structure uses calibrated markings at its base while spiralling upwards as a series of steps

Detail drawing of pendulum receptacle This drawing illustrates the calibrations and markings that structure the pendulum installation

Dome on one of the buildings that line the main courtyard Through articulated punctures, the cupola captures on its inner surface the position of the major planets in the sky on the day on which the building was commissioned

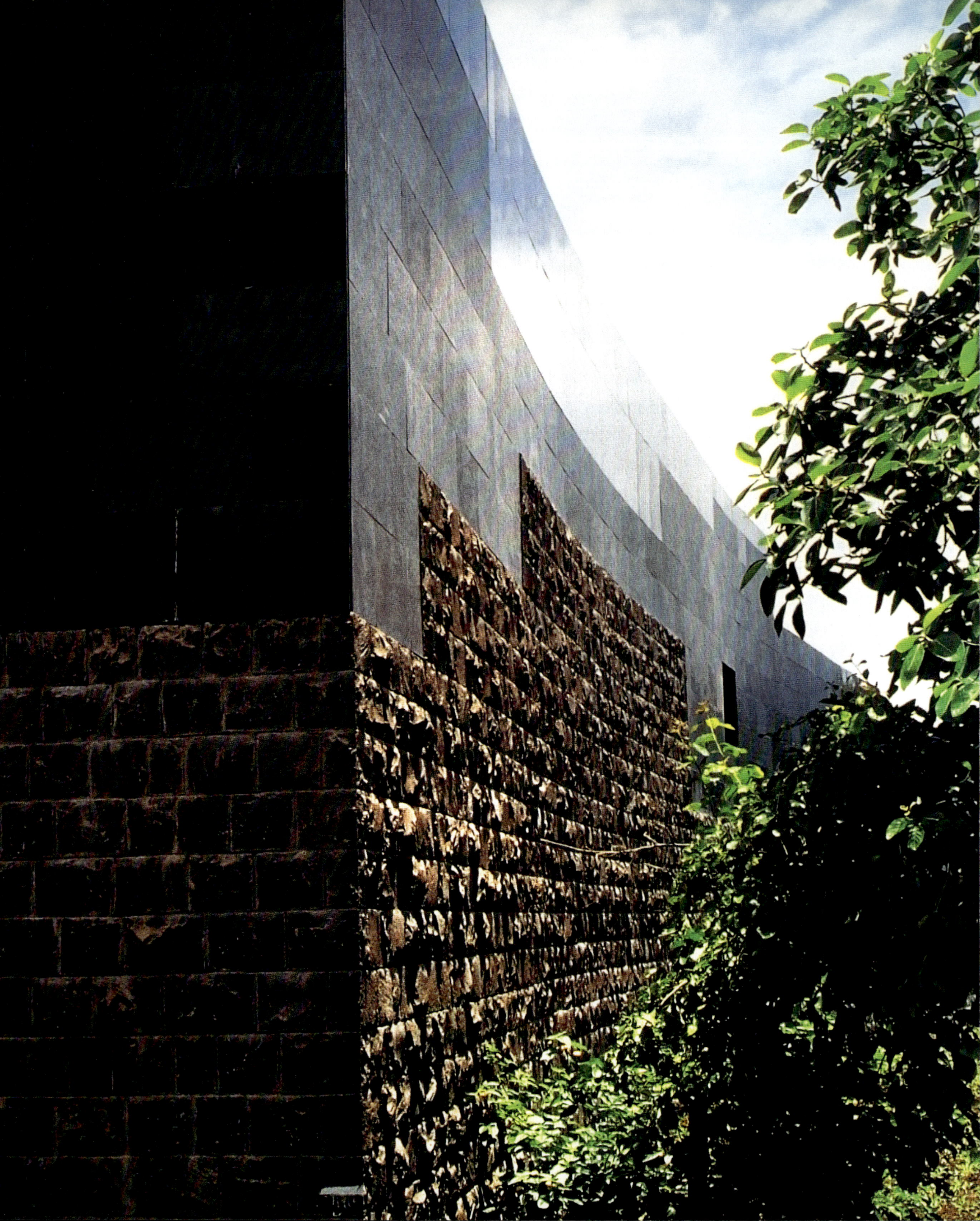

Architecture in India since 1990 | Regional Manifestation

Detail of entrance wall
A stratified wall using layers of local basalt, black cuddapah stone and polished granite creates a visual gradation from the earth to the heavens, while alluding to the darkness of the night sky

Approachway with indirect entry The twin free-standing exposed concrete columns are tinted blue at the top as a metaphor of their dissolution into the sky, while the textured back basalt wall creates a backdrop that leads visitors into the building

This statue of a thoughtful Albert Einstein stands alongside the central sunken space, or *kund*, which is populated with sculptures and inscriptions in a 'landscape' comprising models of the cosmos

Verandah outside the computer centre This verandah looks onto a landscaped garden with the Roche lobes at the centre representing stars and their gravitational theory

Architecture in India since 1990 | Regional Manifestation

Architecture in India since 1990 | Regional Manifestation

Courtyard The image of a black hole as seen through a radio telescope is represented in the planting arrangement marking the centre of the courtyard garden

View from the lecture hall The metaphor of the 'expanding universe' and the black-hole phenomenon are explored in this landscaped *kund*. The corner-stone arrangements signify a centrifugal energy that creates thresholds to the various sections of the institute that border the courtyard garden

***Kund* detail** The steps along the *kund* are shaped in rough grey granite. Varied fissures and grain in the stone add a rich texture to the space

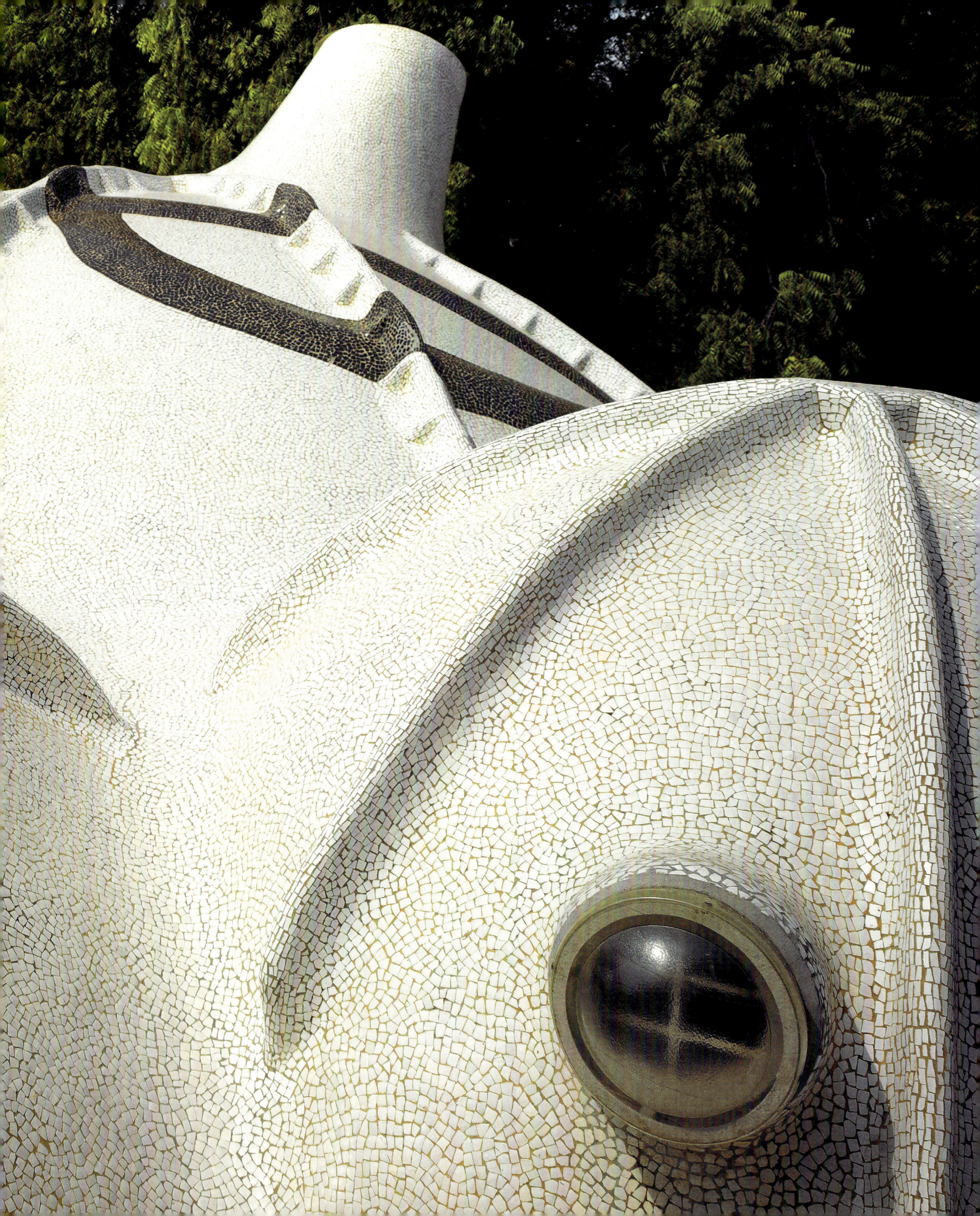

folio 3
HUSAIN DOSHI GUFA, Ahmedabad

Vastu Shilpa Consultants

Designed by BV Doshi, the Gufa is situated adjacent to the Centre for Environmental Planning and Technology University. Commissioned as an art gallery by the artist MF Husain to collect, curate and exhibit his work, it is also used for conducting art workshops and training programmes.

The contrasting paradigm of India and its realities find form through the spatial, climatic and constructional vocabulary of the Husain Doshi Gufa. A sense of the conditions of the subterranean, painting reminiscent of Palaeolithic art and visual reminders of caves have influenced the imagery of its form. The intersection of circular and elliptical forms has given rise to the basic plan organisation, developed into complex three-dimensional articulations of bulbous inclined domes, curvilinear planes, undulating floors and uneven columns. Dark, subterranean, amorphous spaces are then mystically illuminated by protruding circular skylights, while the interior lighting warmly accentuates the texture on the inclined walls.

Climatic responses and energy consciousness were important concerns at the Gufa, that were pivotal in the creation of buried spaces to avoid artificial cooling. Experimental applications of ferro-cement for shell forms, and to support large spans with optimum material consumption, have been compelling factors for the scheme. An unusual project in the India context, this structure blurs the lines between architecture as spatial containment and sculpture or art installation.

Detail of domes The domes were constructed using a ferrocement structure with a finishing layer in white china mosaic. Circular skylights are used to dramatically brighten the inner spaces

Roofscape Amorphous dome forms rise from the ground, while seeming to unite with grass mounds and plantations that envelope the building

Architecture in India since 1990 | Regional Manifestation

Convergence of art and architecture within Inclined columns and bulbous inner volumes are accentuated by circular skylights, and the brushstrokes, reminiscent of Paleolithic art, boldly characterise the subterranean experience

Husain's artwork on the interior surfaces As a gallery for the artist the inclined interior surfaces serve as a canvas for his artwork, some of which was site-specific and integrated through the process of design

Sculptural entrance door and arrival area Undulating floors and curvilinear planes merge to almost form a continuous surface that encloses the interior space, dramatised by the rough cement finish and bold dashes of colour

Bulbous spaces accentuated by sculptural metal cut-outs The cavernous spaces are mysteriously lit to create a play of light and shadow, while life-size cut-outs dramatise the artistic synergy of the project

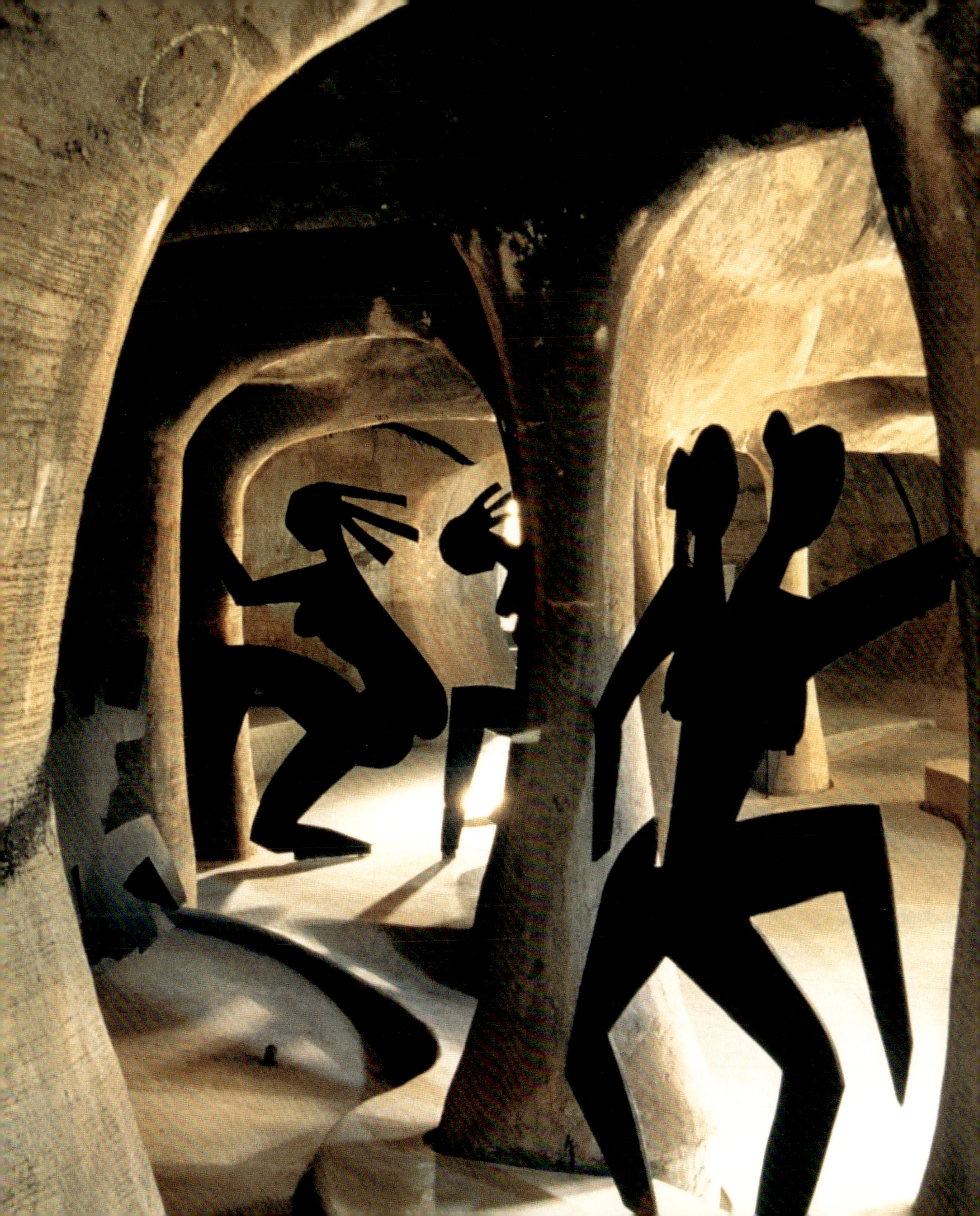

Architecture in India since 1990 | Regional Manifestation

folio 4
KARUNASHRAYA TERMINAL CARE CENTRE, Bengaluru

Sanjay Mohe

Karunashraya is located to the east of Bengaluru, beyond the old airport and on the road leading to the Whitefield Industrial Development Area. A socially committed project, conceptualised as a hospice to serve and care for the terminally ill, the architectural brief was to sensitively complement this context and concern.

The main sections consist of administrative and conference areas, a day-care centre and wards for the resident patients. The primary living units are located at the rear of the site, orienting themselves around a large water body, intended to be a central, metaphoric feature. Other secondary activities are placed nearer the main entrance plaza and transitioned through courtyards. The structural limits of locally available granite create a typical module—each having a centralised nurses' station and wash area, with individual spaces for each patient, and storage and access to the verandah with a sit-out area. These verandahs open onto the water body and have courtyards on the other side—offering a flow of continuous spaces.

In this project, the architect demonstrates both the rigorous use of an order and design discipline emanating from the choice of material, and also a sensitivity and skill in modulating a sequence of spaces that make for seamless transitions within the building.

View looking towards surrounding units The complex is articulated to frame views of the sky and water, which in turn reflect the surrounding landscape and the buildings themselves

Aerial view of site The built form is intended to 'grow', with individual units that accrete to create an open-ended pattern suggesting continual expansion. The courtyards, water body and landscape connect the individual units together

154

Architecture in India since 1990 | Regional Manifestation

Sit-outs along the water edge Twin staggered ponds allow a continuous vista of open spaces, while connectivity through the verandahs encourages interaction between residents

Architecture in India since 1990 | Regional Manifestation

Approach wall preceding entrance plaza This semi-dressed granite wall shields the administrative and activity zones from the main entrance

Detail of transition areas
The rough, textured stone is softened by the diffused light bouncing off the courtyard

Stair leading to terrace
The approach to the terrace from this open stair evokes a meditative moment as the sky becomes visible, the bright light momentarily overwhelming the viewer

Architecture in India since 1990 | Regional Manifestation

The funerary zone
The series of adjacent furnaces are arranged in full view of the public area, where the use of natural light and material expression become defining elements

River façade The furnaces all line the riverside edge of the building, allowing easy views and direct access to the river

folio 5
ASHWINI KUMAR CREMATORIUM, Surat

Matharoo Associates

Located on the banks of the River Tapti in Surat, and surrounded by industrial areas and migrant settlements, this project was floated as a design competition, in an attempt to upgrade Surat's sanitation and infrastructure levels after the plague outbreak in 1994. Building on the traditional framework of a crematorium, incorporating a pavilion and allied spaces for reflection, this facility responds to rituals associated with cremation as well as to the activities and emotional needs of the mourners. Using the river to compelling advantage, the building sets up interesting relationships with the water by strategically framing views of the Tapti in an attempt to give this place of death and mourning a quiet dignity and solemnity.

The crematorium unfolds, along an inner corridor, as a large hall marked by five gas-fired furnaces. Alongside this are two separate places for traditional cremation over a woodpile. These spaces are isolated from the surrounding building and road by structures that incorporate all the auxiliary functions. The use of exposed concrete as the single material throughout lends a stark brutality to the spaces, intensified by shafts of natural light.

Perhaps this is the first time in independent India that an architect has taken on the challenge of finding architectural expression for a programme such as a crematorium, complexes which were otherwise built regularly by Public Works Department engineers. The fact that he has done this so poetically makes the project truly emblematic of the potential that lies ahead for architects to mould the emergent social infrastructure of contemporary India.

Architecture in India since 1990 | Regional Manifestation

Detail of ceiling cut-out
The exposed concrete-framed structure is poetically punctured as a gesture to accommodate an existing tree on the site

Approach path from the main street A long, contemplative promenade buffers the transition into the main court that leads to the furnaces. Skylights wash the corridor with a warm hue

Contemplative spaces
Diffused light bathes the space along the rear wall, which accommodates seating for mourners as they wait to collect the mortal remains of their loved ones

160

Architecture in India since 1990 | Regional Manifestation

An individual chamber Five furnaces are enclosed by a circular wall to create a private space. The stark grey of the concrete resonates with the sombre mood of the mourners

Detail of furnace The detached furnace, painted in red, contrasts with the surrounding tones while commanding the focal point within each funerary chamber

Furnace enclosure and ritual space at the rear Curved concrete walls define each furnace area, which opens onto a terrace for rituals and also leads down directly to the river

161

folio 6
DEVI GARH FORT PALACE, Udaipur

Bhatia, Gupta, Saini and Bhagwat

The hotel, historically Delwara Palace situated northeast of Udaipur, was an eighteenth-century fort built by the ruler Raghudev Singh. In disrepair for many decades, this property was acquired in the early 1990s by Lekha Poddar of Devi Resorts with a view to restoring and converting it into a luxurious and modern boutique hotel.

Conceptualised and executed as three distinct phases, that of the 'restoration' of artistic and historic elements of the building, the 'renovation' of the existing structure with sensitive structural interventions in accordance with the proposed hotel layout, and its 'rehabilitation' as a contemporary hotel. Re-appropriating and updating locally available craft skills for contemporary applications, the project has set a significant precedent for the restoration and adaptive reuse of several hundred such buildings in India, Rajasthan in particular. Although the forerunner to this scheme was the Neemrana Hotel, the employment of architects, an interior designer and a landscape architect has made it an important example of diverse contemporary sensibilities occupying the shell of a medieval building. The interior design in particular plays a crucial role in the success of this building.

View from rooftop pool onto the landscape This black marble terrace pool, with a vaulted *chatri* (pavilion) adjoining a luxury suite, offers commanding views of the rugged surroundings

Step-well near the fort palace The fort towers over this adjoining *kund*, which is used by the residents of neighbouring Delwara village for their daily activities

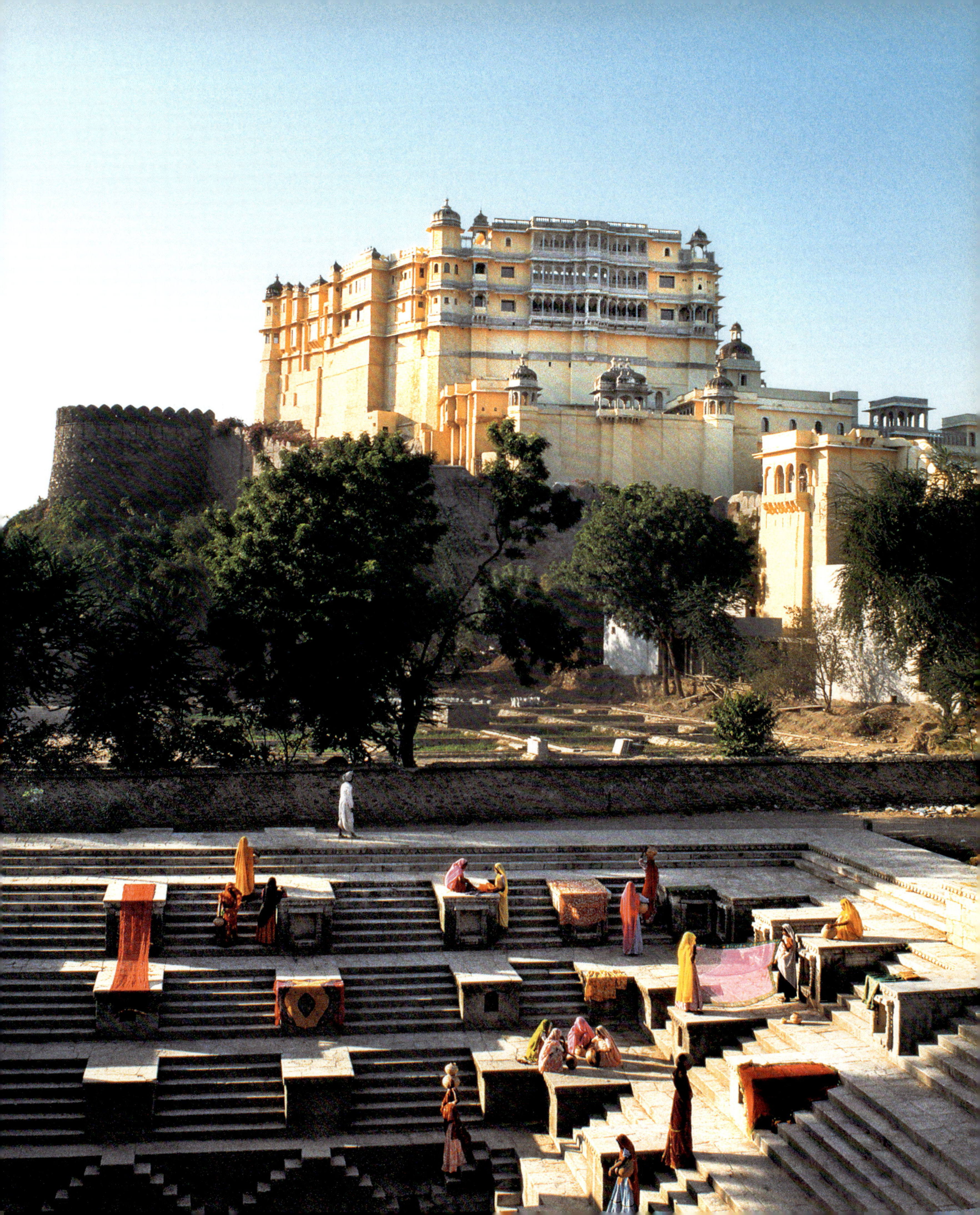

Architecture in India since 1990 | Regional Manifestation

Interior view of durbar hall
This space now forms a lounge area, with cushioned seating in earthy tones that contrast with the all-white building elements

The conference lounge
Tones of silver are used against a glazed wall panel that defines this zone. Upholstered sofas and large stone bowls characterise the space, while a wooden entranceway frames the path to the adjoining pavilion

Detail of the lotus courtyard
Conceived as a water maze in black marble, this motif is a contemporary interpretation of the traditional lotus

The fort palace against the natural landscape
Surrounded by the Aravalli range, the main palace is transitioned through a series of gateways and landscaped courtyards

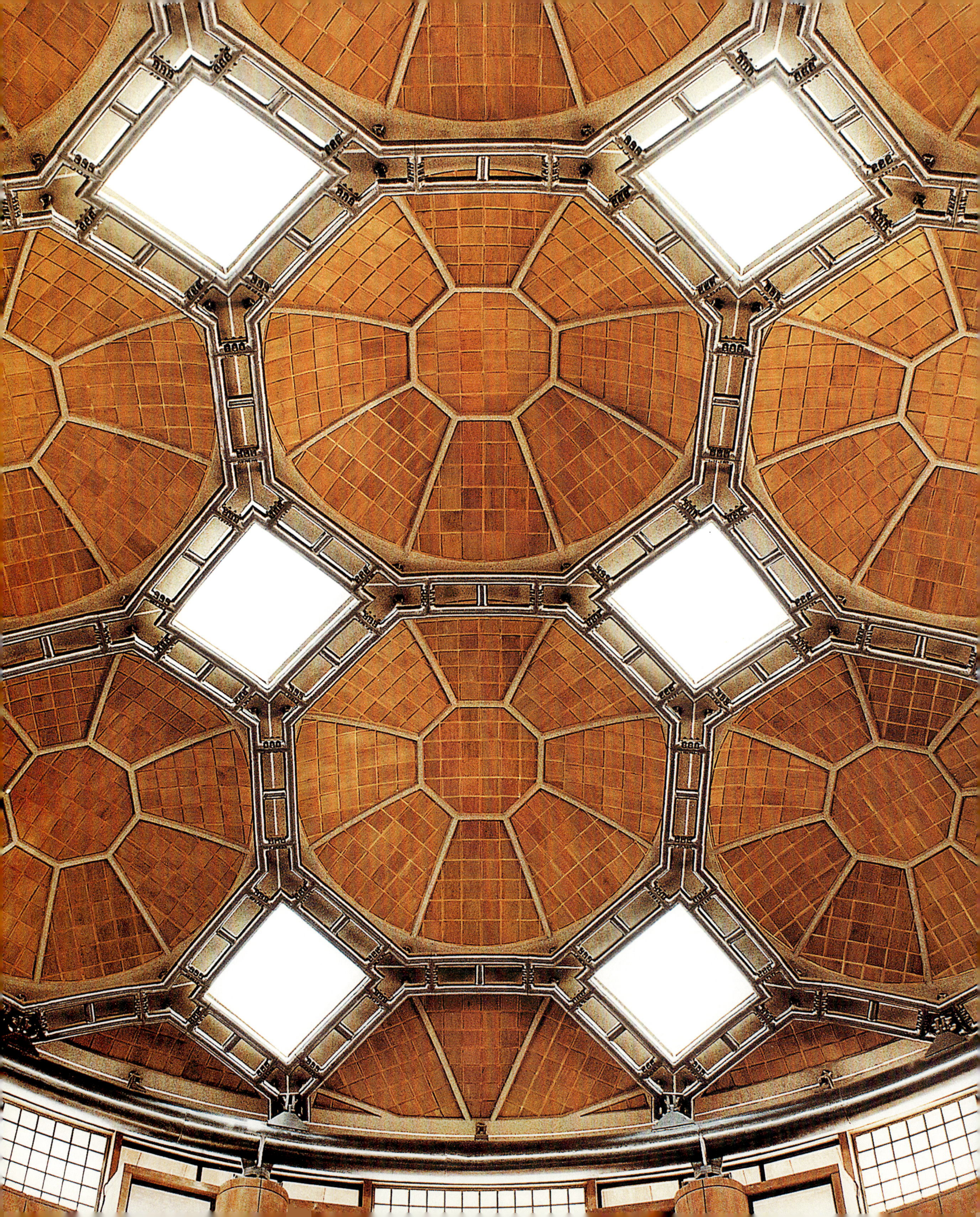

folio 7
PARLIAMENT LIBRARY, New Delhi

Raj Rewal Associates

Situated north-west of Parliament House, in the heart of Edwin Lutyens' New Delhi, this library project was required to house vital research and meeting facilities for the Indian Government. The building has three main components: the library and related facilities; a section for parliamentary functions, incorporating a training centre, museum and archives; and meeting halls with conference and auditorium spaces. Parts of the building were to function independently for simultaneous programmes and social events.

The primary design concern was to relate harmoniously to Herbert Baker's Parliament House, which stood right across the road. By submerging two floors below ground, the scale of the library building is minimised from all sides. Bubble domes atop the fifth level help the library to create its own landscape when viewed from afar, thereby subtly connecting visually to the parliament building. Light—symbolically representing wisdom, enlightenment and democracy—is a key design element. Courtyards, top-lit atriums, clerestories and the partial transparency of domical ceilings ensure an abundance of soft natural light into all spaces. Structural lattices, bubble domes in precast FRC (fibre-reinforced concrete) shells, and the central glazed dome with its filigree web of steel members contribute to this amalgamative process. Most importantly, the building is a culmination of a lifelong quest by the architect to make innovative architectural expressions for technological system.

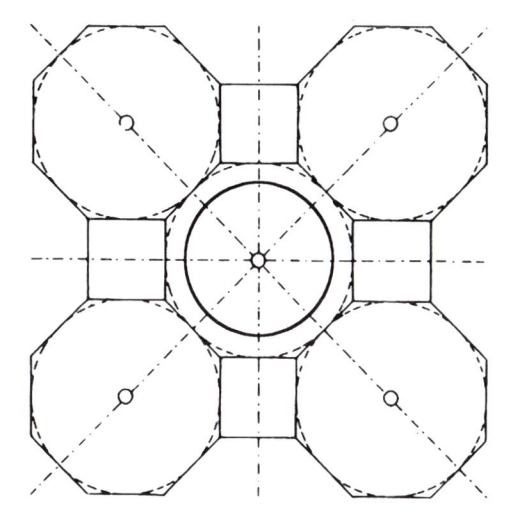

Structural lattice over the VIP entrance These steel and FRP bubble domes follow an octagonal latticework in doubly curved steel pipes and tiles, with skylights that bring diffused light into the atrium

Roof view towards Parliament House
Landscaped terraces with bubble domes and skylights allow a visual continuity with Baker's and Lutyens' edifices, while respecting their stature through the building scale

Drawing of the roof unit
Detail of lattice structure roofing over the VIP entrance; this octagonal geometry is used as the basic unit to generate the form for the building

Architecture in India since 1990 | Regional Manifestation

Glass dome over central atrium 'Petals' of the dome were welded onto a steel framework that incorporated reflective glass layered with the structural glazing to reduce heat gain

Architecture in India since 1990 | Regional Manifestation

North-east courtyard with pool Carved sandstone *jalis* and machine-turned circular-column cladding punctuate the corridors and walkways, set around a *kund*-like water body

Site diagram Concept development of the triangular site in relation to the geometry of Parliament House

Inspirational sources for the planning of the complex Datia Palace near Gwalior, Adinatha Jain temple in Ranakpur and Taj Mahal in Agra

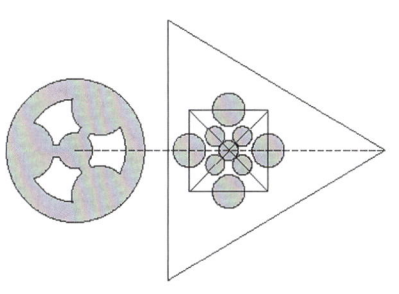

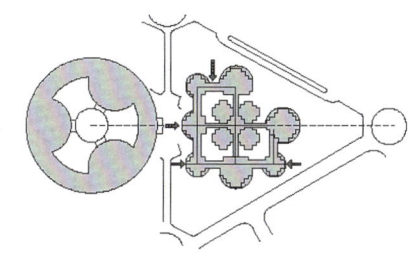

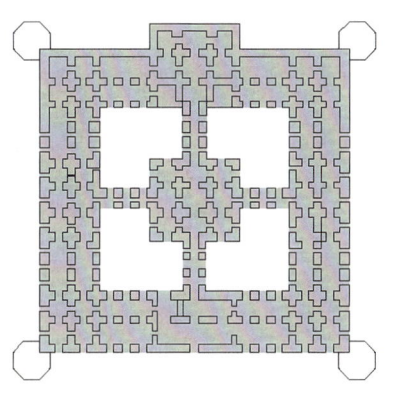

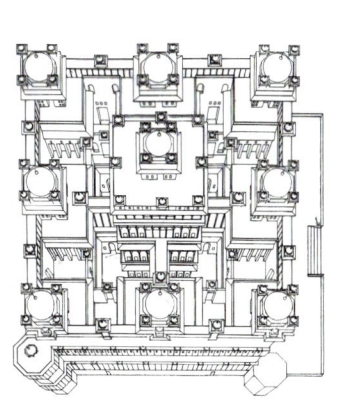

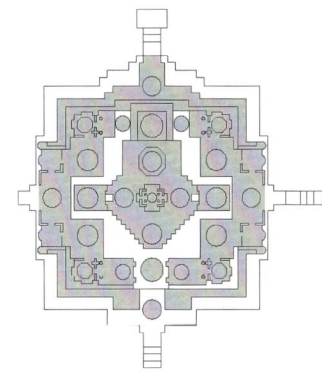

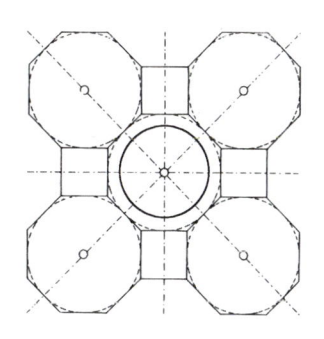

169

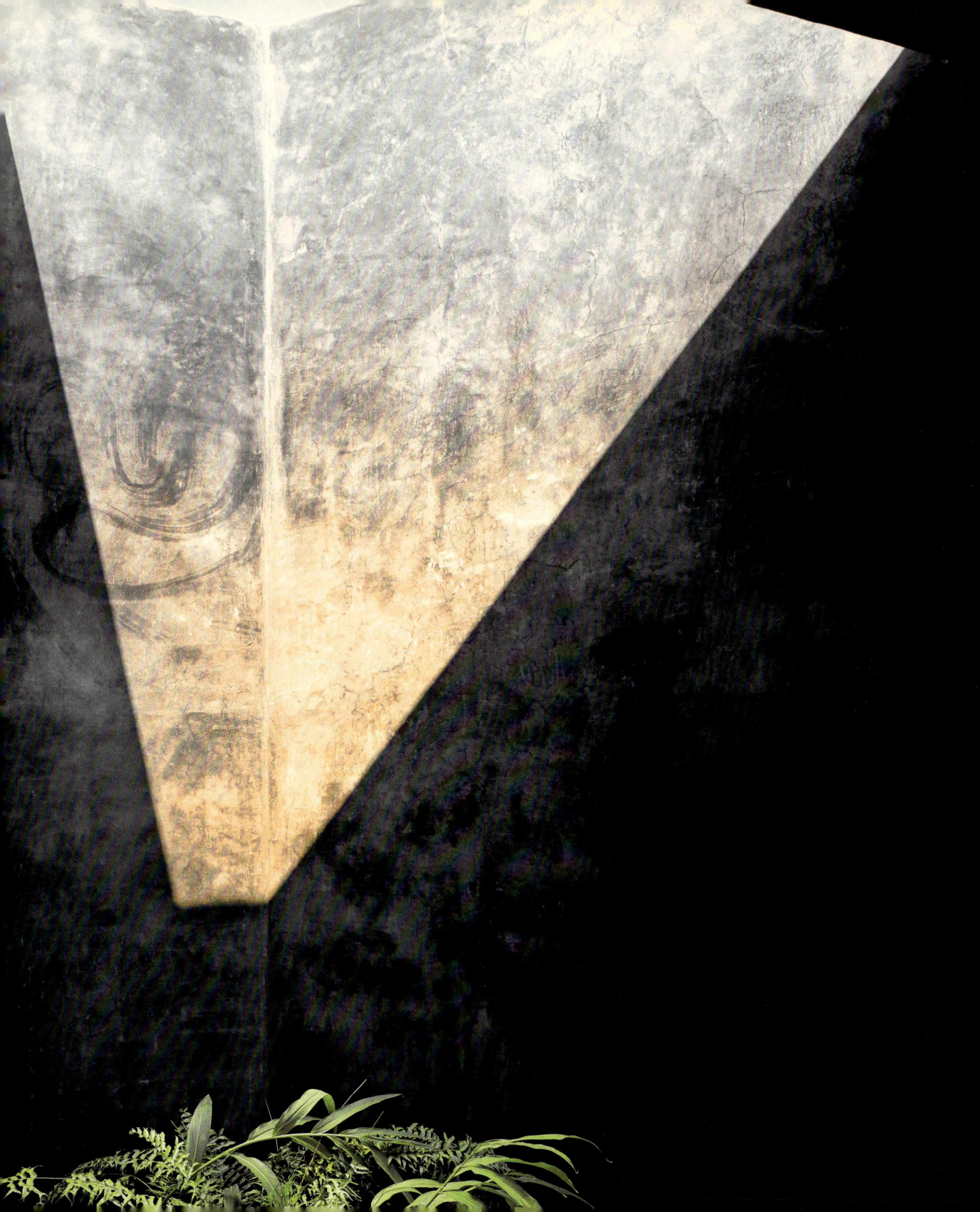

folio 8
TARA HOUSE, Kashid

Studio Mumbai Architects

This weekend retreat in Kashid on the Maharashtra coast is shared by a multi-generational family. Individual building units housing the functional areas are configured around a landscaped garden with dense vegetation. These units are interlinked as well as separated by paved walkways around the garden under which runs a subterranean aquifer providing water for the property through the year.

Exploring concentric layers of privacy, the centre of the residence is an open courtyard garden that can be traversed and occupied intermittently throughout the day. A hierarchical layout encourages the sequence of a gradual discovery of spaces and the treatment of materials used. Wood-framed structures form the 'skin' that contains the landscaped garden, while porous timber screens enclose the pavilion-like shared spaces. These spaces are covered under a large undulating clay-tiled roof. While luxurious in its spatial disposition and use of materials, the project displays a rigour in terms of the use of material and its minimalistic aesthetic. The building also demonstrates a symbiotic relationship with the landscape, the verdant quality of which embraces the house.

Detail of a courtyard wall
Finished in a dark-pigment cement plaster, this surface softens the bright light

Living spaces with operable wooden doors The light stone flooring offsets the heavy wooden ceiling structure, whose precise craftsmanship is highlighted through the delicate woodwork

Detail of wooden screen doors Large slatted screens enclose the verandahs while allowing diffused light to wash the spaces within

Detail of column base The wooden column merges into the peripheral black-cement floor, while the main circulation zone is marked with a change in material

Transition areas Continuous verandahs are articulated through the irregular flooring pattern and sloping wooden ceiling

Architecture in India since 1990 | Regional Manifestation

View of garden from a verandah space As a central space, the garden both unites and separates each functional unit, effectuating privacy for the occupants. The 'country-tiled' roof and deep verandahs link the house to traditional typologies

Architecture in India since 1990 | Regional Manifestation

Staircase detail This locally fabricated custom-made stair in steel and timber, which is suspended on cables, achieves a visual lightness in the space

Landscaped stairwell adjoining living area This slender timber-and-steel stair seems to float against the glazed façade, which floods the adjoining areas with natural light. The glazed side wall allows the house to extend further onto the external landscape

The traditional *kalvillaku* A customary stone lamp, which adorns traditional entrances, finds a position in the house, set amidst a lotus pool near the kitchen area

folio 9
RESIDENCE FOR JACOB GEORGE, Kochi

Design Combine

Built by the architect as his family residence in Kochi, this house follows a grid-based development and spatial arrangement organised around interior landscaped courts. Passive cooling techniques for comfort, and rainwater harvesting were concerns that have been addressed through design.

Through the use of materials, this projects moves away from the traditional building practices in Kerala to adopt a modernist, and perhaps systemic, approach to building. A modular bolt-on board-based construction system using pre-laminated and pre-painted cement board panels was devised, within which all glazing and electrical conduits were built. Stainless-steel window frames and continuous louvred ventilators just below the flat slab level allow for ventilation and visual connectivity. Customised interior elements, furniture and lighting fixtures add to the crafted quality of the spaces within. Highly innovative and bold in its disposition and use of construction systems, this is one of the rare examples in contemporary India of an architect engaging with new materials but confining himself to locally sourced skills.

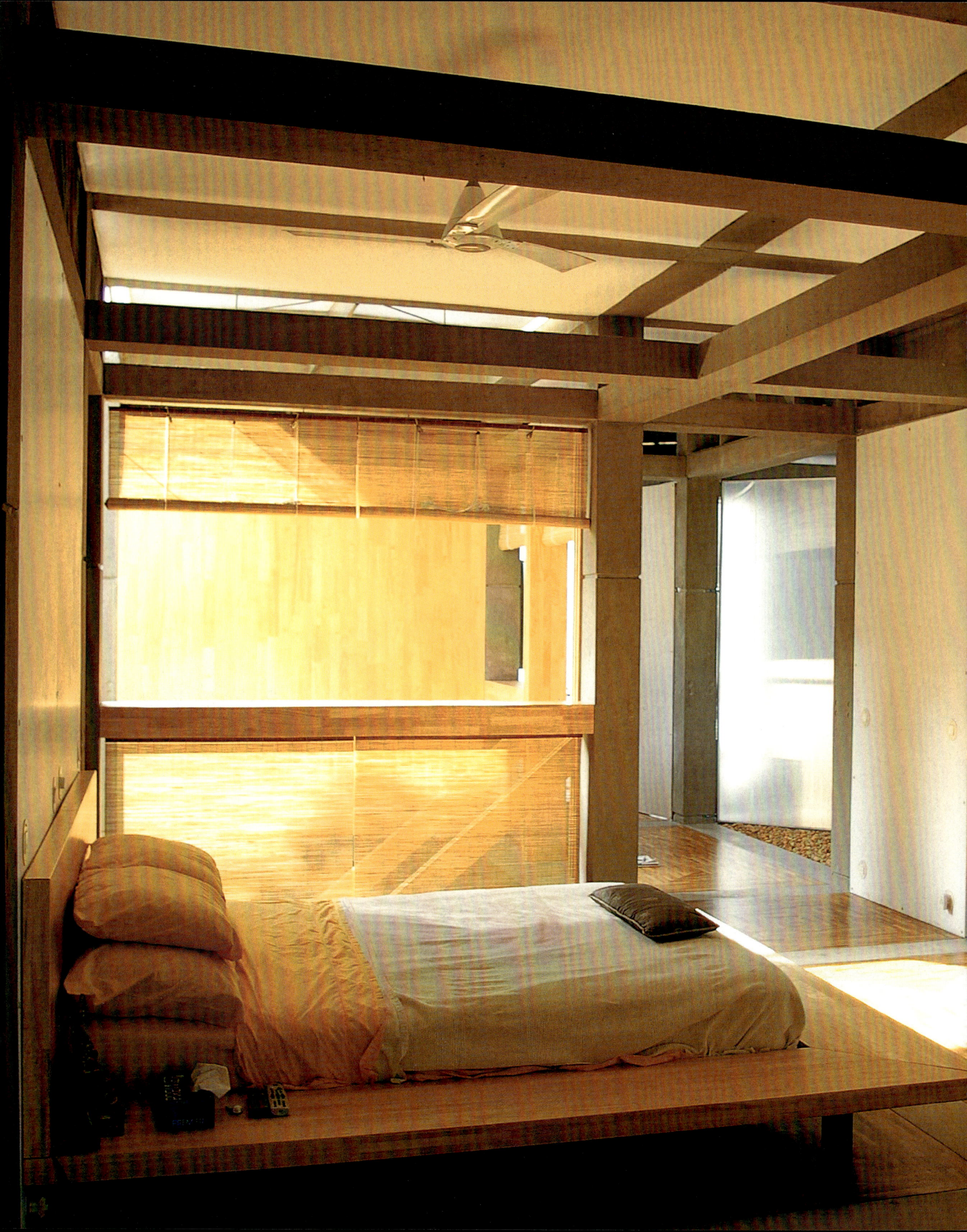

Architecture in India since 1990 | Regional Manifestation

Bedroom, extending onto verandah and sit-out The interior space, providing a neutral backdrop for the furniture, is constructed from local materials but contemporary in its expression

Corner view from rear garden The house opens up towards the rear with verandahs, pavilions and open balconies extending into the landscaped areas, all contained under a light parasol-like roof

folio 10
SUA HOUSE, Bengaluru

Mathew & Ghosh Architects

Sua House in Bengaluru is the corporate office of a business house with diverse interests. Designed for a client who is also an avid art collector, the spaces are responsive to his collection, blurring the lines between workspace and art space. The site, seen as a 'self-contained urban box', is sliced by three interstitial gaps which allow for movement, light, ventilation and extended views within the building. These also serve as functional divisions for the hierarchical office structure.

The front portion of the building contains private cells for managers, the middle houses meeting zones at each level, while the rear functions as a staff area. Each bay is structurally self-contained, allowing continuous strips of structural glazing to separate each section. A linear bridge forms connections within this tripartite building while skylights, which wrap around the building, architecturally create different zones, flooding the space with abundant natural light. The split vertical movement creates pause-points through landings and passages, and allows both occupants and visitors to engage with the artwork displayed all around while retaining the privacy of the upper floors, that are reserved for the management. The architecture is restrained and minimalist, thereby creating a neutral backdrop for the art.

Detail of light shafts The idea of the 'three interstitial gaps', which generated the overall organising principle of the plan, creates slices of light within the building

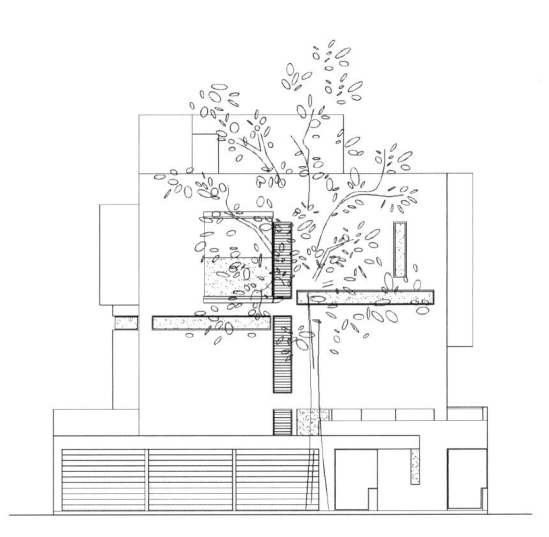

Street-side façade A low, landscaped entranceway offsets the main office building from the street and lengthens the transition into the arrival space

Drawing of front façade The façade is punctured by horizontal and vertical slit windows that control light within the spaces, while a balcony mass projects on this side at the upper level

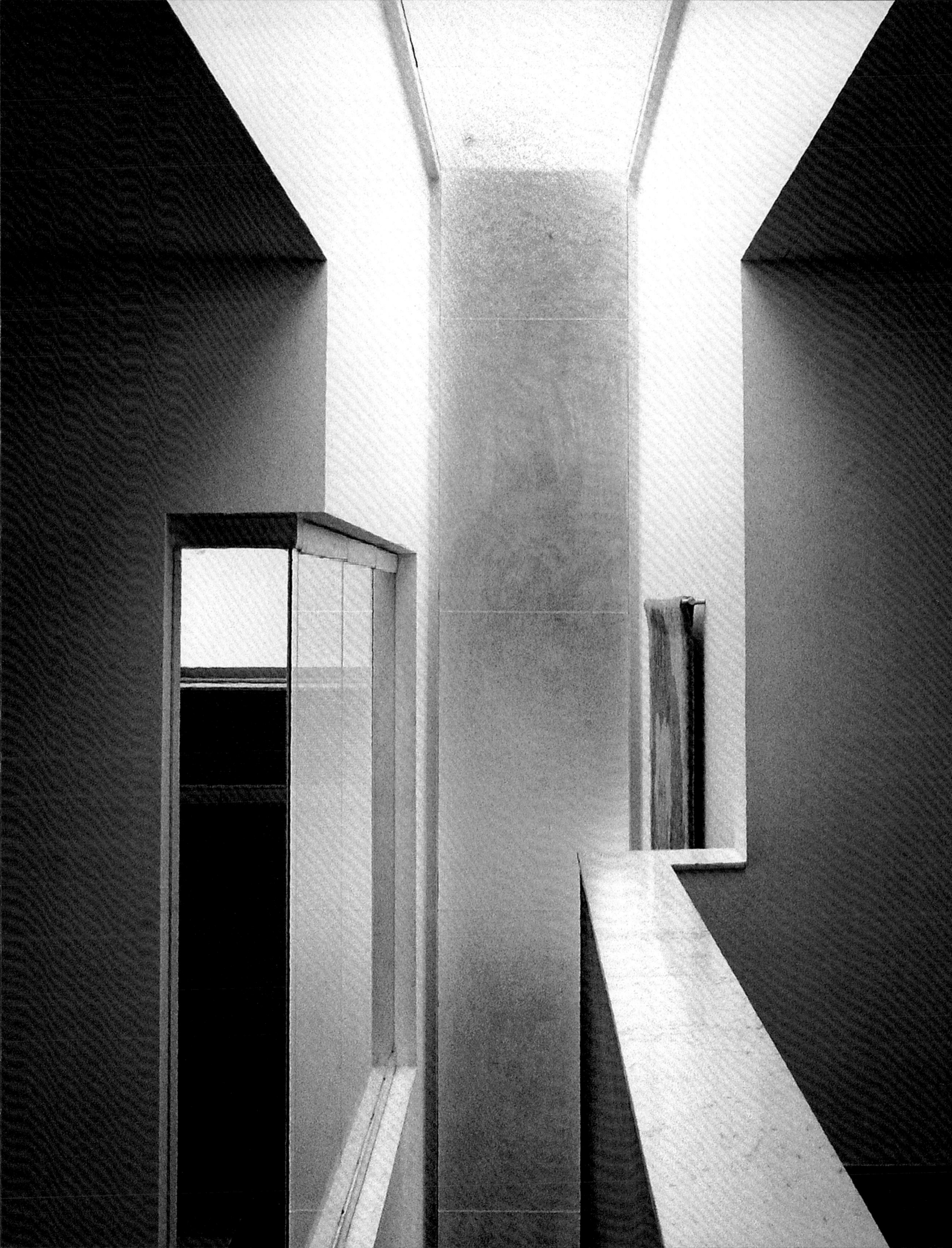

Architecture in India since 1990 | Regional Manifestation

Stairwell with adjoining meeting areas Skylights along this shaft bring abundant natural light into surrounding spaces, where it is reflected off the white walls

Split levels as display areas Deep landings and extended platforms allow sculptures and art pieces to informally integrate with the space

Meeting and lounge spaces The split vertical movement enhances vistas and spatial connections to the formal areas, and art is placed at strategic locations along the circulation route through the building

Central bay with meeting room Self-supported structural glazing is carried on up to roof level, also allowing visual continuity through the transparent enclosures

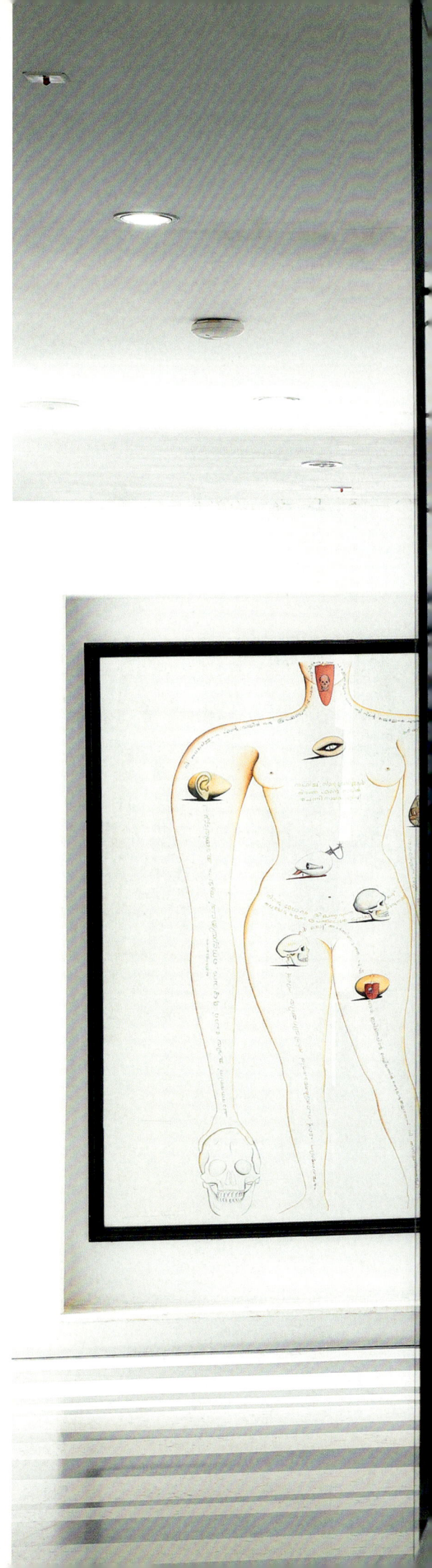

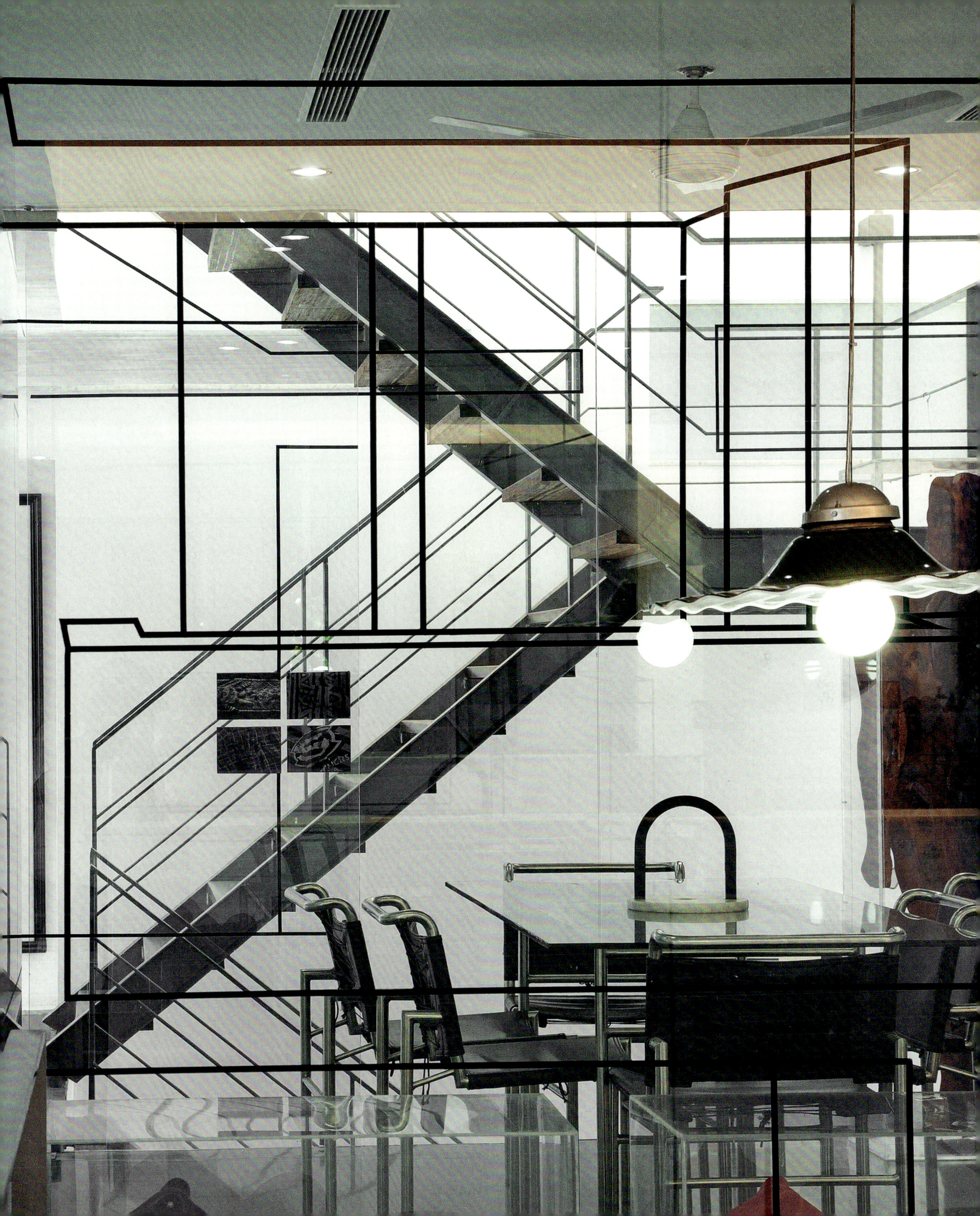

Architecture in India since 1990 | Regional Manifestation

Courtyard surrounded by dormitories A combination of single- and double-storey units fragments the scale amidst lush green surroundings

Exterior façade of senior girls' dormitories All rooms are shaded from direct sunlight by deep overhangs that run as a continuous architectural feature. The articulation of stone surfaces with metal grillework also addresses security concerns

folio 11
RISHI VALLEY SCHOOL, Madanapalle

Flying Elephant Studio

This 160-hectare rural campus in Madanapalle in Andhra Pradesh, founded and mentored by the twentieth-century philosopher and mystic J Krishnamurti, is an educational institute modelled on the system of the traditional Indian forest retreat, or *vanashrama*. This school of thought instils an introspective spirituality and an intimate communion with nature, both of which were critical to the design brief for the project. The commission for this phase of the campus comprised dormitories for senior girls and residences for supervising teachers around an existing courtyard and school wing. Water scarcity, unavailability of skilled building agencies and budgetary constraints were significant challenges at hand.

Cross-ventilation and visual transparency were key factors in the design, as the dormitories were open on two sides to encompass the greenery around the court. A rainwater-harvesting system finds visual expression in the architecture and landscape detailing. Frugal use of materials and a rigorous economy in the use of space make this an intelligent expression for a school and a 'neutral ground' for the students, who come from varied backgrounds. The choice of materials and the scale of the building all reinforce the idealised landscape of an ashram of free-standing simple pavilions.

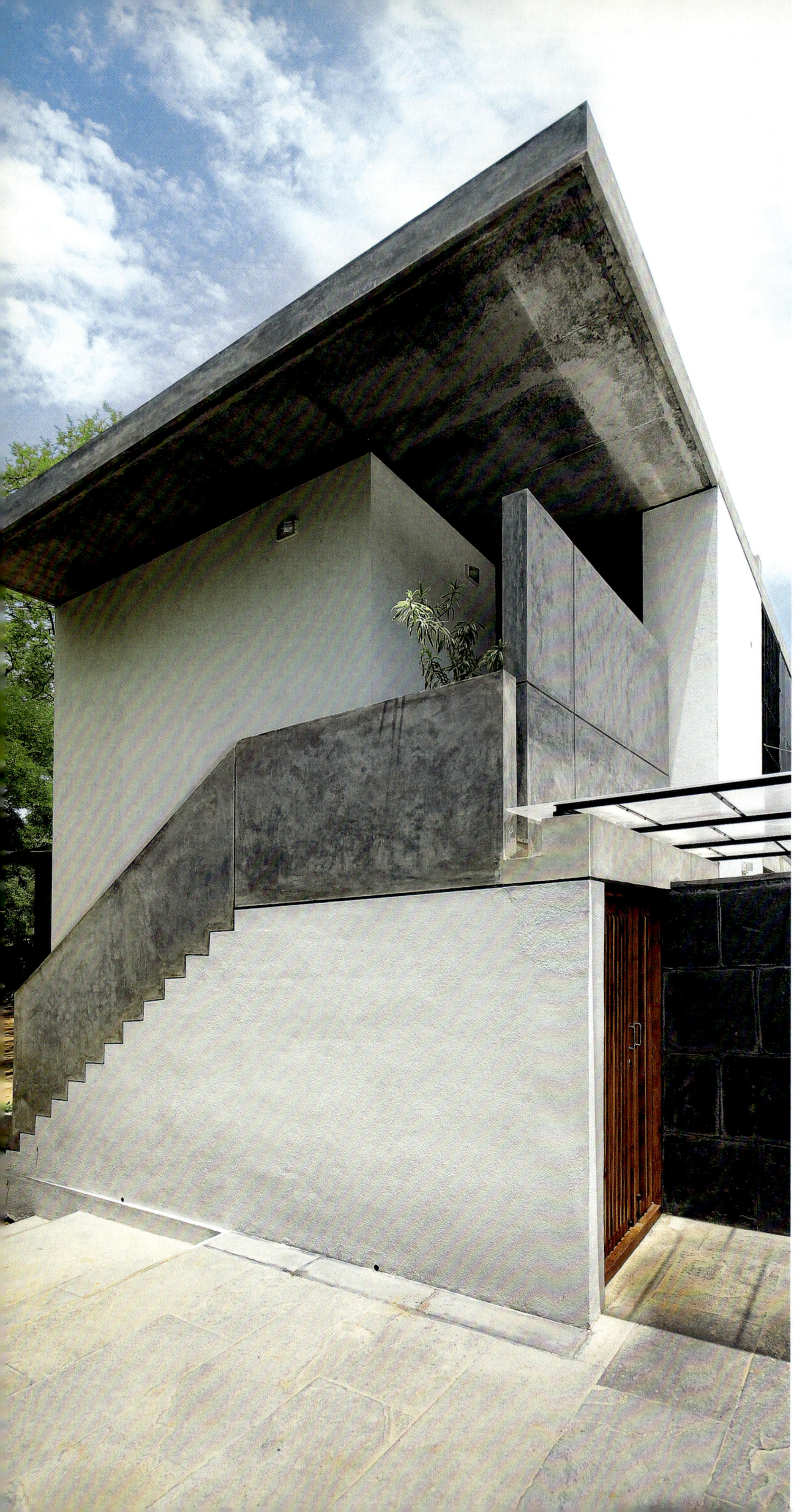

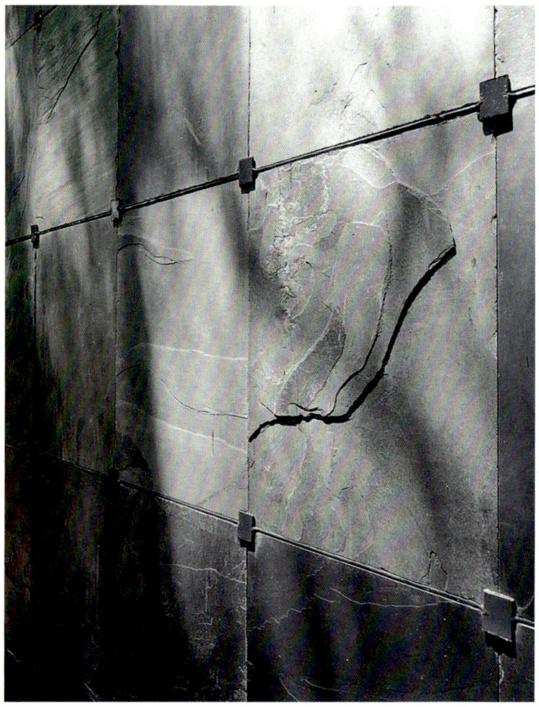

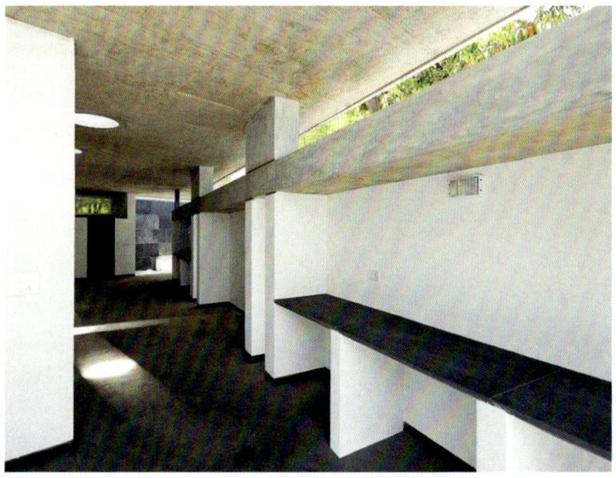

Architecture in India since 1990 | Regional Manifestation

Residential unit on the upper level The school's supervisor has a separate access through this well-articulated entranceway

Detail of exterior wall cladding Granite wall panels are supported by a metal frame to form the external skin

Central wall in the courtyard This modulated wall shields the entrance to the dormitory from the wash areas and allows direct entry into the court. The rear face of the wall integrates storage and usable surfaces

Coloured skylights Circular cut-outs are covered with shades of fibreglass to bring in coloured light over the common wash areas

View of the dining area from the pantry A large uninterrupted area allows the space to be used in a multipurpose way

View of courtyard through a dwelling unit The irregular profiled courtyard integrates a rainwater-harvesting system within its landscaping while serving as an informal meeting area for students

185

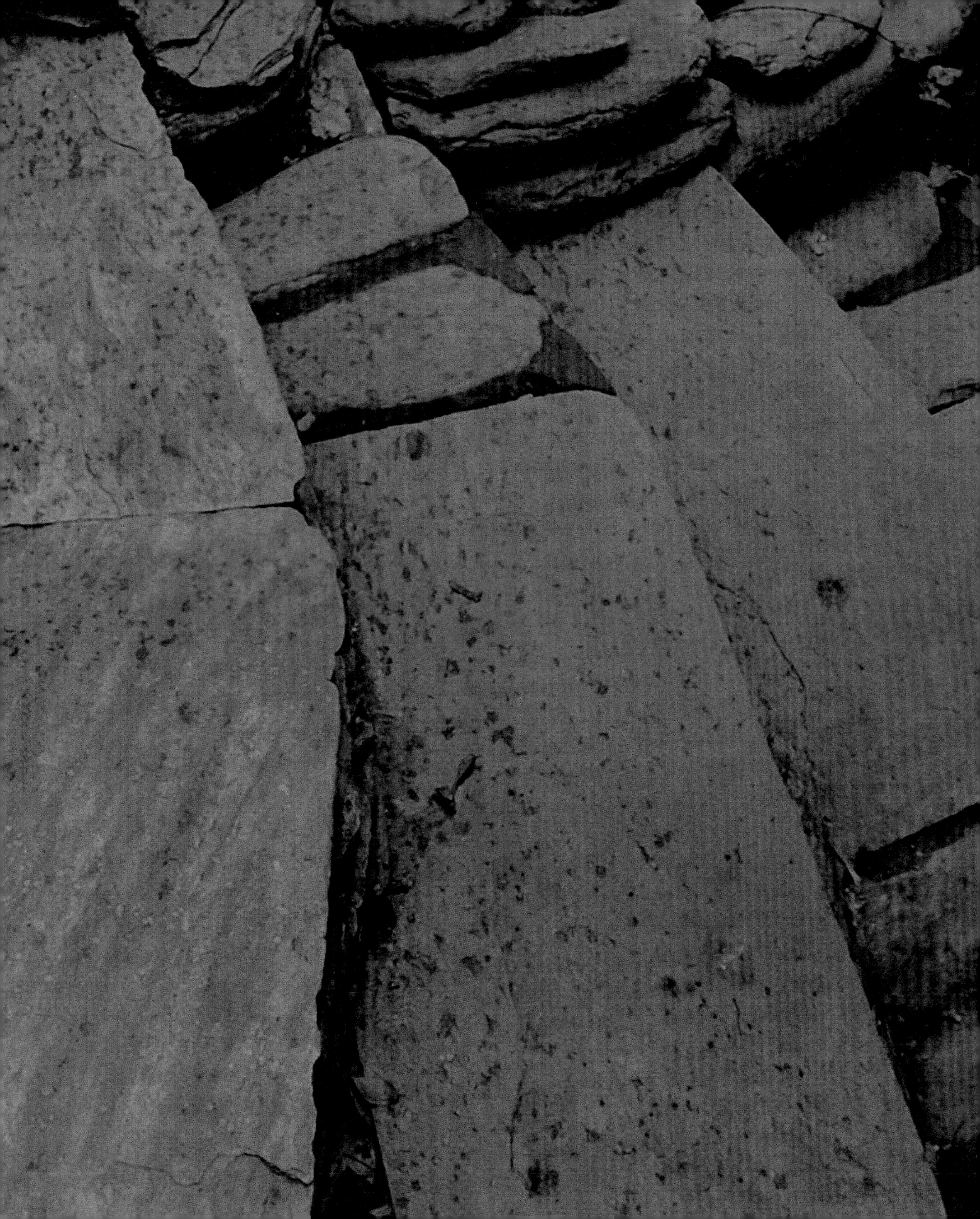

Alternate Practice
Towards Sustainability

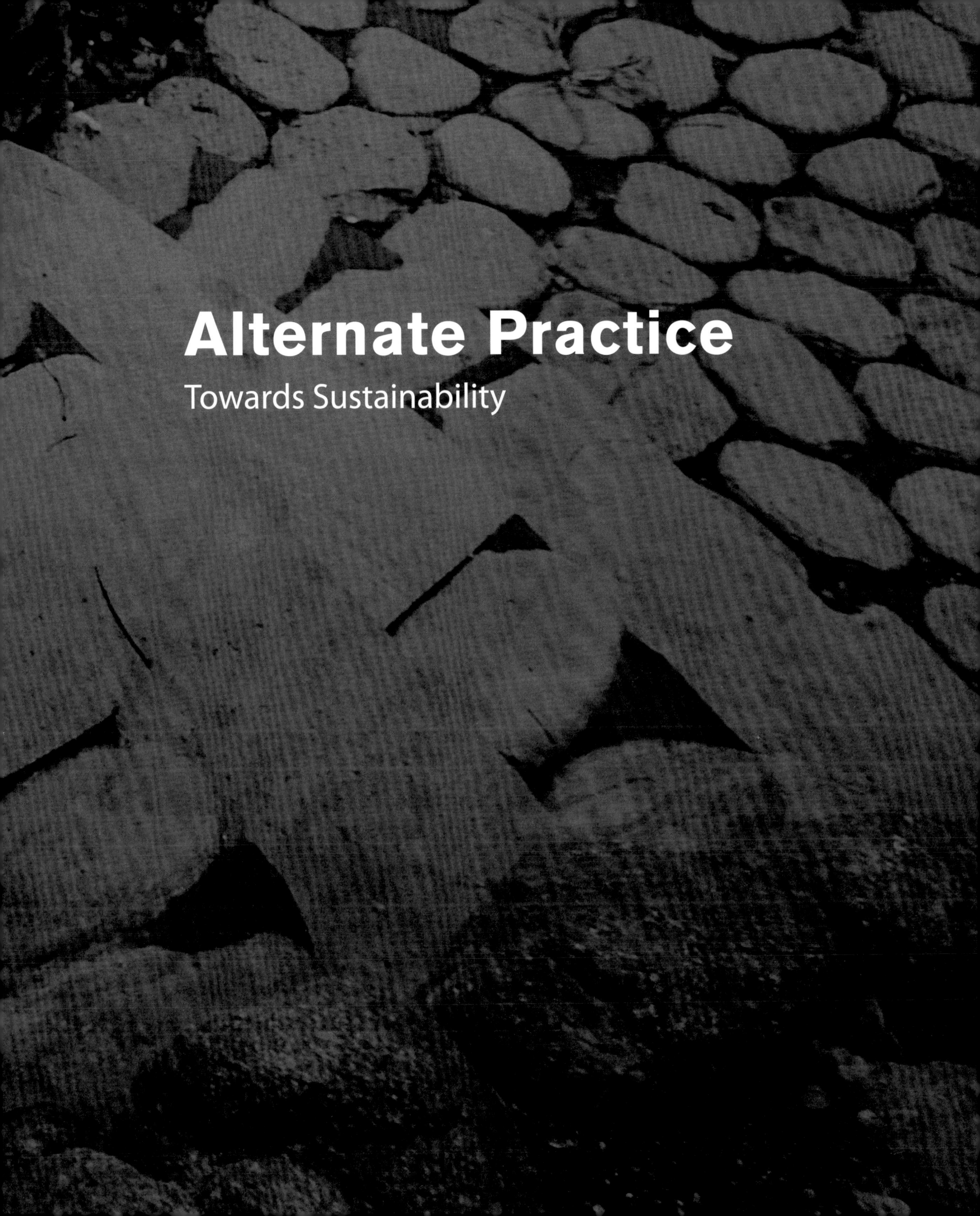

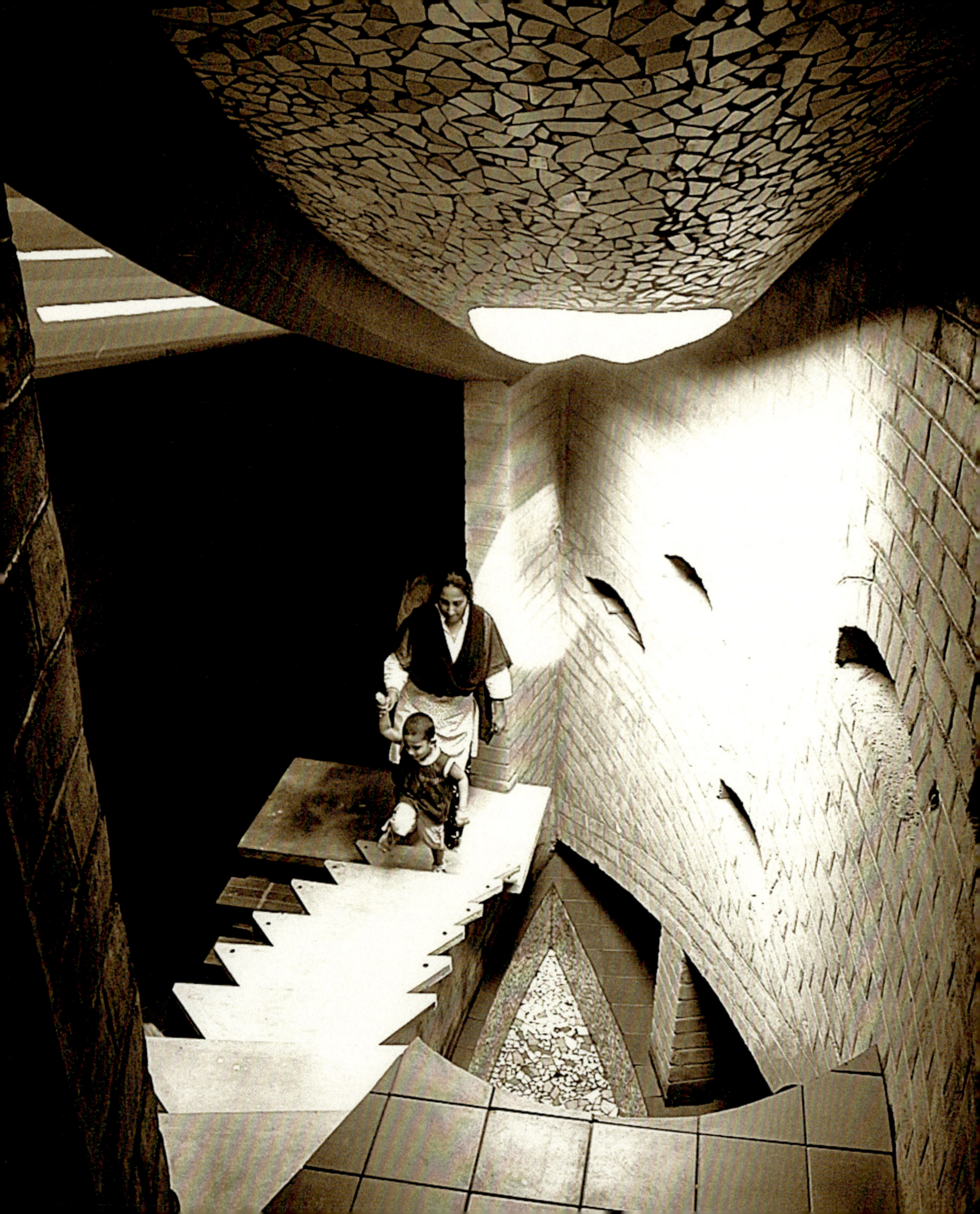

In India, local resistance to the otherwise potentially unifying global flow of capital, building and cultural seduction is unique, takes on many forms. One of the most potent manifestations of this is the work of architectural practitioners committed to the ideals of sustainability in the broadest sense of the built environment and its relationship to nature and people's socio-economic, cultural and aspirational 'pulse'. These practitioners are inspired by the locale, and highly cynical of the universalising trends perpetuated by the ensuing forms of global flows. The single most potent aspect of this alternative practice is that it is essentially a reaction to the displacement of people and their dislocation from the centre of the architectural and development debate.

In some ways, this alternative practice model extends the regionalist architect's approach—moving forward on somewhat moral grounds, in that these practitioners perceive themselves as self-appointed custodians of a region's building ecology and traditions. They believe in the role of architecture as a powerful social and environmental modifier. This trend took root in the late 1960s as the first schools of architecture were being established in post-independence India—institutions where issues of housing and lessons from vernacular architecture were articulated for the first time in the new nation. The early and seminal works and writings of English architect John Turner were extremely influential in moulding this debate. Turner argued that housing should be viewed as a process, not a product, and demonstrated in his writings how the social, economic and cultural are all critical ingredients for robust settlements. Similarly, the works of the Greek planner CA Doxiadis, American architect Christopher Alexander and several others created a potent discourse around these issues in India. Furthermore, the state's direct involvement in questions of housing across a wide spectrum of income groups, as well as the large public sector defining the ideals of a socialist India, created the perfect foundation for intersections between these emerging academic trends and official patronage.

Another growing trend in this period was that of the vernacular as a wellspring for architectural ideas and inspiration. Bernard Rudofsky's seminal exhibition at the Museum of Modern Art in New York from November 1964 to February 1965, entitled *Architecture Without Architects*, was inspirational in bringing attention to the wonderful examples of vernacular architecture encountered worldwide. These buildings had been constructed with the collective knowledge accumulated by anonymous builders over the centuries and challenged architects across the globe to rethink their role in the community. Set as a counterpoint to modernism, and the perceived erasing of tradition that the modern project implied, this model first manifested itself in the form of the architect re-aspiring to assume the role of the craftsperson, working directly with builders and more or less eliminating drawings as a medium for communicating design intentions. This direct communication created a truly participatory process, as craftspeople and builders became integral to the decision-making process. Buildings by practitioners such as Hasan Fathy in Egypt were among the early examples of this mode of engagement with architecture. These structures were characterised by the vigorous use of local materials and vernacular construction techniques.

The earliest celebrated example of this approach was the work of Nari Gandhi, who returned to Mumbai in the early 1960s after working with Frank Lloyd Wright in the United States. Patronised mainly by Mumbai's rich, he built several deftly handcrafted and extremely unusual homes for them in the surrounding countryside. Organic forms and diverse materials produced in

Valsala Cottage (*opposite*) by architect Vinu Daniel. Today's sustainable practitioners clearly attempt to reinterpret regional building traditions and experiment with local materials to create new forms and spaces for contemporary use

Architecture Without Architects **by Bernard Rudofsky** (*right*). The strong impact that this exhibition and book had upon the architectural fraternity worldwide in the 1960s gave rise to an entire generation of practitioners and thinkers, who took lessons from the vernacular to shape their work

conjunction with craftspeople, set in dramatic space configurations all collided in harmonious, though sometimes clumsy, resolution. At a social level, his work ensured sustained income for local craftspeople through long-term commitments of their time over multiple projects rather than with task-based financial reimbursements. It was a decade or so later that Laurie Baker expanded and established this model of practice to Kerala with an ambitious social dimension, focusing on building using local resources and traditional wisdom.

Baker came to India in the mid-1940s; influenced by Mahatma Gandhi he decided to stay and work here. Until the mid-1960s, before settling in Kerala to practise as an architect, he worked as a doctor in the remote and rural Himalayan regions. During his time in the Himalayas, he acquired deep insights into rural India and developed a profound appreciation of the indigenous architecture of these places. Although his initial mandate was to find solutions for housing India's rural poor, he ultimately engaged with a wide spectrum of building types across the state of Kerala ranging from homes, institutional buildings, clinics and hospitals—and even a popular coffee house. In order to make houses affordable, he innovated at the level of the spatial disposition of his buildings and,

Architecture in India since 1990 | Alternate Practice

Jain Bungalow (*these pages*). Nari Gandhi's work in India responds strongly to the landscape and site contours; his houses harmoniously merge with their surroundings. The playful yet refined use of local resources is coupled with experimental forms, which reflect his innate understanding of structure and material. Designed and communicated on site without formal architectural drawings, his work is an early example of alternative ways of building and practice in post-independent India

Indian Coffee House (this page) by Laurie Baker. Economy of materials and cost through innovation in construction techniques allowed Baker a participatory design process and the development of a new visual language. Here, the building is designed as a continuous ramp, which becomes the circulation as well as the seating space of the coffee house. In the interior view, built-in seats and tables can be seen drawing light and ventilation from the external screen wall

most importantly, in the way that they were made. Inventing new techniques for making walls and roofs, he economised in the materials used while also achieving a visual vibrancy. His approach was characterised by flexibility in design intentions and an open-endedness, whereby the final product was defined by the construction process. This facilitated the easy incorporation of various materials, both new and recycled. As very little was predetermined, there was less pressure on the end product, and it also allowed craftspeople to engage in the decision-making process of the building. Non-governmental organisations (NGOs) and cultural institutions were the chief patrons of his services.

Baker's work energised this alternative way of building, and by the late 1970s and early 1980s, his influence was more than evident throughout India, gaining momentum with the support of the popular national press. Despite this growing influence and increasing governmental recognition Baker was unable to alter policy in any significant way for this alternative approach to gain acceptance by the national, or even the regional, bureaucracy at that time. In fact, this form of advocacy planning and activism in architecture was at its nascent stage of growth in India. This is particularly pertinent because policy that affected the built environment for housing and land use, or even for development planning, in the years after independence was borrowed from older democracies (such as the UK and the US) and was cast in a context of technical analysis too abstract for the ordinary Indian citizen to comprehend. An example of this in the late 1960s was the citizen-initiated idea for Navi Mumbai (formerly New Bombay) by two young architects— Pravina Mehta and Charles Correa—and structural engineer Shirish Patel who wrote and lobbied for their own initiative. The appropriation of these efforts by the state and their recasting in the language of the bureaucracy rendered them impotent in the context of their original intent: that of being a people-driven process of city making.

The Navi Mumbai example, was one of an array of efforts to establish new cities or improve existing ones that were devoid of citizens' participation. Most forms of development (whether rural or urban) became bureaucratic operations. Thus, many social groups at a disadvantage in the political framework were rendered even more so when dealing with those who spoke the language of land-use maps, diagrams and statistical tables when planning new settlements. India consequently developed a bureaucracy in the form of municipal corporations and state housing boards, which, unfortunately, often seemed impersonal and alien. Importantly, polemic writings and films against squatter-settlement demolition in the 1970s and 1980s shared the angry suspicion that experts had pulled the wool over the eyes of the ordinary, helpless people. Advocacy planning in India (as in other parts of the world) had its origins in the perception that such groups need architects to make their case and express their aspirations. It was for this new constituency, and the role of the architect, that Baker's work had great implications. However, as his focus was on building in its narrowest and yet most potent sense this question of broader planning policies is one in which he did not have any significant impact.

The first generation of architects born in independent India took the lead in advocacy planning. Jai Sen in Kolkata set one of the earliest examples for this new role of advocacy planning and architecture in the late 1970s, making it prominent among the profession in India. Sen's seminal essay, 'Unintended City', provided an alternate reading of the Indian metropolis. He suggested an understanding of the marginalised or 'invisible' city, and stimulated designers and planners to recognise this as their field of operation and engagement. His organisation, Unnayan tackled questions of housing, employment and the intrinsic link between housing rights, economic development and social well-being. Most importantly, it initiated the campaign for housing rights in India which led to a series of such non-governmental initiatives in Ahmedabad and Mumbai. In these cities, while there existed dynamic educational institutions, the questions of rapid urbanisation were inadequately addressed by the government's delivery system for housing, compelling civil society and academics to become activist. The Ahmedabad Study Action Group (ASAG) founded by Kirtee Shah in the early 1970s, and VIKAS, by Rajesh Shah in 1978, were two of the pioneers that set the foundations for advocacy in the realm of architecture and planning in India. Later, in the 1980s and 1990s, these movements found stronger voices in cities like Mumbai through the Society for the Promotion of Area Resource Centre (SPARC) by Sheela Patel and her colleagues, and the Bombay Environmental Action Group (BEAG) spearheaded by Shyam Chainani. These groups focused on housing, rights for the informal city and its inhabitants, and the environment in general. They became the 'conscience' of civil society in India, and had a large following across the country.

In the 1990s, with the intensification of globalisation and the state's further devolvement in areas of planning and public spaces, several initiatives emerged around the country to address questions of preservation, planning policy and, especially, the creation and maintenance of public space. Two such non-governmental organisations, the Urban Design

Research Institute (UDRI) in Mumbai (first established in 1985, and revived in a new form in 1992) and the Environment Planning Consultants (EPC) in Ahmedabad (1996), served as advocates for questions of planning policy, public space, preservation of historic districts and a general thrust for coordinated planning in cities. This model of engaging academics and professionals in initiatives related to city improvement was quickly adopted by schools of architecture, which set up design cells within their institutions as mechanisms for professors and students to take on such city-related projects (often commissioned by the state) independent of a developer or private client who could bring their own agenda to bear on the process. The state sometimes participated in these partnerships, co-opting these NGOs in contentious projects to create tripartite arrangements between themselves, the advocacy planner or NGO, and those affected by the project. Important examples include the Slum Networking of Indore project (1989-present) initiated by Himanshu Parekh, and the relocation of slum dwellers from the railway lands in Mumbai (1989) in which SPARC played a critical role. The Slum Networking of Indore City project was run in partnership with the Indore Development Authority, and involved the mobilising and coordination of financial and human resources across governmental organisations, NGOs and local communities in a bid to improve the quality of life in Indore's slums. The project involved networking, not only for the physical infrastructure to be workable but also to engage social assets in the community in the form of people's participation as well as the creation of 'feedback loops' for information sharing. Unlike most slum upgrading projects, this one integrated the slum with the larger city fabric by networking at both the physical and social levels. Meanwhile, the SPARC project negotiated with slum dwellers for their relocation to free up the land they occupied for the larger social good of increasing capacity of the Mumbai transportation system. Although this project involved a more complex form of negotiation in Mumbai's contested urban context, its lessons lie in the vital role that advocacy can play in shaping these urban places. It led to a successful alliance between SPARC (an NGO), the National Slum Dwellers Federation (NSDF—a citizen-based concern) and the Mahila Milan (an organisation of poor women). This alliance united the participants on the basis of their mutual concerns, of securing land and access to urban infrastructures. It facilitated a successful exchange between the formal and informal settlements not only in Mumbai city but across national boundaries, with a network of other alliances working with slum dwellers around the world. In addition to enabling the reconstitution of citizenship, these efforts pointed to the dire need for the architectural profession to engage in influencing the city's physical form, especially with the transformation of urban India and the broader built environment at an alarmingly rapid rate.

Mahila Milan housing project under construction. Here, an alliance between a local women's group and the National Slum Dwellers Federation, together with SPARC, empowered women to self-build their houses in a slum-relocation scheme in Mumbai

This approach or model of alternative practice re-energised itself with new vigour in the late 1990s with the onslaught of globalisation and the marginalisation and displacement ensuing from its arrival in an altered economy. Furthermore, with the government divesting itself of the responsibility to deliver housing and social infrastructure, the alternative practitioners aspired to fill the vacuum produced by the state's disengagement. This model of practice engages the architect as activist, wherein a new form of practitioner has consciously chosen to be more reflective, considering the consequences of his or her actions and the

Sketches by Laurie Baker. In the absence of formal architectural drawings, Baker's inventiveness was explored and transmitted through detailed sketches and perspectives, which were improvised upon in dialogue with site workers

ways in which the global flows marginalising both traditions and people can effectively be addressed. They often take up what may be referred to as 'unsolicited commissions', and strive to show how spatial arrangements play a role in the way economic and social processes are realised. Unlike traditional architects these practitioners enter into a potentially more fulfilling relationship with the site, its history, the community of users whose needs they address, and members of the workforce who are their collaborators.

The common thread among these efforts is that they are all based on community participation and on resituating architecture and urban design from formal production processes squarely into the fabric of the lived experiences of their users. This form of practice also acts as an important counterpoint to the protocol-driven corporate pattern. The emphasis is on the intimacy of the scale, a direct involvement with the building and an activist preoccupation with the political and civic issues that impinge on architecture. This model of practice is viewed with great suspicion by mainstream practitioners—perhaps because it challenges the more orthodox patterns and protocols of professional practice? Indeed, these experiments are carried on at the margins of conventional practice. By choosing to operate at the edge of capital's dominant structure, these alternative practitioners have made explicit their moral choices in the face of globalisation. This type of practice is innovative in both patronage and technology; the projects are sometimes supported or commissioned by the state or the corporate sector in a compassionate mood (trusts, foundations, etc.), but more usually by NGOs, charitable trusts and similar patrons. The practitioners themselves reject certain sources of patronage (developers, real-estate speculators) and treat technologies of mass production (reinforced cement concrete and steel) with suspicion.

Over time, two distinct trends within the alternative practice have emerged. While one group focuses on process and the broader question of policy and infrastructure, another stream is concerned with exploring alternative technologies and building methods, attempting to make a critical contribution to India's broader architectural scene. Unhindered by the obsession with speed that characterises global practices and the impatience of capital, they can afford the luxury of experimentation, often to leverage the capital over to more efficient means and applications. Examples of this approach are Baker's early and seminal works in Kerala, where he reinvented methods of construction that proved more economical (rat-trap bond walls; filler-slab roofing; exposed brickwork; the use of natural stabilisers, such as lime, instead of cement) to save on costs, are emblematic of this approach. This not only created a new aesthetic for affordable housing and building construction, but also shaped (on its own terms) a parallel to the exposed brick and concrete aesthetics of the moderns. Baker's architectural skills and his projects demonstrating these techniques are evident in the several houses and institutions he built in Kerala. For example, in Abu Abraham's house (1989) in Thiruvananthapuram (formerly Trivandrum) Baker created a pattern from his new bonding techniques as a new aesthetic in exposed brickwork. In other houses, the filler slabs and roofs were the defining elements. Never repetitive, he rapidly produced dozens of houses in which the aesthetics and formal design moves were subservient to the relevance of technology and its performative aspects. The best catalogue of Baker's entire repertoire

Nrityagram (*this page*) by Gerard da Cunha. The significance of this project lies in its experimental nature in terms of construction techniques and the innovative use of material and fundamental building techniques. At the time the project was undertaken, there were not many examples of such building processes by trained architects, where they worked directly with craftsmen and did not superimpose aesthetic rules for the architecture that emerged. Using traditional building forms, stone, mud and thatch have been used here as the primary construction materials. Modelled on the Indian village cluster, low-rise built forms house the various gurukuls (residential teaching clusters), guest cottages and administrative blocks

is his collection of buildings on the Centre for Development Studies campus in Thiruvananthapuram, starting in 1971 and continuing to 1990. The poetic forms; the variety of the jali, or screen, walls; and the application of multiple building techniques demonstrate not only his dexterity but also the direction for a completely different and unencumbered aesthetic. The modulation of light and passive control of temperatures within these buildings further assert that his was not purely a tectonic exercise, but one that placed the human at the centre of its concerns.

The alternative approach inspired an entire generation of architects in India, and in the late 1970s several practices had already begun to embrace these new values. However, their impact was minimal and it was only in the late 1980s, once Baker's work gained prominence, that people began to acknowledge the significance of these fringe operations. In addition, the natural application of these autonomous processes of building using local crafts seemed to flourish greatly in the "decentralised" locations of Kerala, Auroville, Puducherry and Goa. The lack of an overwhelming large urban centre, coupled with a mainly rural landscape but a sophisticated and educated population that wanted to experiment, soon made these regions the centres for such (sometimes utopian) experimentation. Unfortunately, these experiments began to be consumed as a style and was appropriated by the rich for their weekend villas as they were seen as gentler, eco-friendly interventions than mainstream efforts.

This trend has distorted the ecological and economic concerns from which these approaches originally stemmed and the new challenge for the next generation of alternative practitioners will be to straddle the inherent values and the rapidly changing aspirations of India's middle class.

Anupama Kundoo's Wall House (2000) in Auroville near Puducherry picks up Baker's building tradition, but is more exuberant and less disciplined. It reflects more the autonomous nature of Auroville's context than the stringent constraints that Baker set himself. Similarly, Gerard da Cunha's Nrityagram Dance Village (1994) near Bengaluru is an example of a free, unselfconscious extension of the Baker idiom—in this case, as a school for the dancer Protima Bedi. The forms are alien, the materials sometimes tortured, but the construction is innovative, experimental and free spirited, like the patron for whom it was designed. Thus, as it escapes architectural categorisation it seems to capture the raw energy of the craftspeople who created it and the fresh, and yet naive, attitude of the architect facilitating the process. Similarly, Suhasini Ayer and Ajit Koulagi in Puducherry; Dean D'Cruz in Goa; Natasha and Jeeth Iype, and Gayathri and Namith in Bengaluru; Benny Kuriakose in Chennai; Vinu Daniel, Eugine Pandala, Latha Raman and Jaigopal Rao in Kerala; Ashok B Lall, Pradeep Sachdeva and Sanjay Prakash in New Delhi; and Didi Contractor, in her new avatar at age 80 in the Kangra Valley, are architects who have been concerned with similar questions—albeit with

La Cuisine Solaire (*left, top and centre*) by Suhasini Ayer of Auroville Design Consultants. As a collective solar kitchen demonstrating the use of solar energy for community cooking and use of appropriate technologies, this project uses compressed earth blocks and ferro-cement

Beck House (*left bottom*) and **Nilaya Hermitage Hotel** (*right, top and bottom*) by Dean D'Cruz. The work of Dean D'Cruz in Goa responds to the climate and architecture of the region through the use of local stone and building details that allow rootedness to its tropical setting

an inspiring rigour that transcends the experimental nature of the early works in this mode.

Others have tried to formalise these processes by institutionalising such efforts, training craftspeople in techniques and innovations in building materials, and creating unconventional market mechanisms for the distribution of these alternative technologies. The earliest such attempt occurred within the state itself through the creation of the Central Building Research Institute (CBRI). While it initially promoted innovative techniques and material applications the organisation had atrophied by the early 1980s, being weighed down by its own bureaucracy. In 1983, Baker, together with Dr DR Chandradutt, Dr KN Raj (an economist) and the then Chairman of the Centre for Development Studies, Achutha Menon (former Chief Minister of Kerala), founded COSTFORD, a voluntary concern providing technological assistance for rural development. It was registered as a non-profit voluntary organisation in 1984 and started its construction activities in 1986. Collectively, COSTFORD has been able to realise nearly 20,000 buildings in Kerala based on the principles and techniques that Baker established.

Simultaneously, in the 1970s and early 1980s, privately established foundations began to fill this need to address the development process in a systemic manner, using alternative solutions relevant for India. In 1972, Bunker Roy's practice Barefoot Architects & Neehar Raina established the Barefoot College in Tilonia, a small rural community in the arid north

Good Earth Orchard Homes (*left top*) by Jeeth and Natasha Iype. An attempt to create environmentally and economically sensible societies while returning to the intimacy of community neighbourhoods, this project sensitively weaves together nature, material and local crafts for contemporary living

Dakshinachitra (*left and right bottom*) by Benny Kuriakose. Traditional craftsmen and folk artists worked and performed in the reconstructed period settings of nineteenth-century streets, homes and workshop spaces in South India. Initially guided by Laurie Baker's spatial conceptualisation, the centre echoes his ideas of empowering masons and craftspeople in the building process. Other than serving as a museum of traditional buildings and artefacts, Dakshinachitra also organises craft workshops and cultural events for the local community

Samskrutha Pathshala (*right top*) by Gayathri & Namith Architects. A conscious response to the surrounding landscape resulted in a remarkably open plan, which gradually merged with the outside. Using familiar forms, as well as material used traditionally in the region, the buildings feel organic and rooted to the locale

Dilli Haat, Pitampura (left, top to bottom) by Pradeep Sachdeva. The invention of a new form of marketplace, inspired by traditional spatial organizations but with contemporary facilities, this is a sort of hybrid programme that allows the bazaar to operate with a formal bureaucratic organisation. The use of a sloping roof in stone, supported by metal columns for the walkway, clearly demarcates areas while providing shade for the shoppers and the stalls. Open spaces are multi-levelled, with hard and soft landscaping, seating platforms and lighting that allow multiplicity of use at various times

Inspiration Head Office (right, top and bottom) by Latha Raman and Jaigopal Rao. As a generation inspired by Baker, these young architects are also exploring sustainability and vernacular traditions through experimenting with materials like bamboo and wood

Houses by Didi Contractor (*this page*). Detail of the external paving surrounding the house: where different stones are combined in a collage-like manner to create a rich texture and organic sensibility. The use of mud walls in the interior, with external and more exposed walls in stone—as seen in this view of a stacked stone wall beyond an adobe wall—reflects a deep understanding of the place, local lessons and climatic constraints

Khamir Craft Park (*left, top and bottom*) by Hunnar Shala, designed by Neelkanth Chhaya. Intended to be an interface with the long-term sustainable development needs of the Kutchi communities, this project meant to generate interaction between designers and master artisans in order to create new directions for these traditional crafts. The design and construction processes utilised opportunities to innovate and develop from local building crafts. Through experimentation, using both traditional and new technology with Hunnar Shala and local craftsmen, a new idiom was developed that was responsive to the place

Barefoot College (*right top*) by Barefoot Architects and Neehar Raina. Using local village women and labourers as decision makers, the plans were drawn and redrawn on the spot to accommodate adjustments in dimensions on account of traditional building techniques that were often not considered in the original design

Indian state of Rajasthan, to address the issue of empowering and equipping rural populations by demystifying technology and re-establishing the dignity of manual labour. The college's work ranges from issues of health, water and sanitation to appropriate building technologies. Although the institution's mandate is not restricted to construction, it does form one of its important thrusts in which several explorations to adapt existing technologies for rural application have been undertaken. For example, as there is a depleted supply of wood in rural areas, the architects of the college experimented to make geodesic domes out of scrap metal from discarded tractors and agricultural implements. Several of the campus buildings have been constructed in this way, thus demonstrating these applications. The college's essential mission is self-reliance for the rural poor, the broader implications of which are distress migration of workers to cities, leaving villages deprived of their skilled human resources, and an erosion of their economic bases.

A more contemporary version of this sort of effort is the work of the Hunnar Shala Foundation, established in 2003. Founded by Sandeep Virmani and Kiran Vaghela and based in Bhuj, the foundation is run by engineers and architects committed to sustainable building and settlements. Its most noteworthy projects are the Sardar Nagar Housing projects (2001-present) on the outskirts of Bhuj and the Shaam-e-Sarhad Eco Resort (2006) in nearby Hodka village. The first stemmed from the need to rehabilitate the poorest of the families who lost their homes in the 2001 earthquake in Bhuj. In addition to arranging finance from institutions in Gujarat, Hunnar Shala provided the research and a master plan for construction systems using local mud as the basic resource. Rammed-earth techniques, innovative master planning with hierarchies of public spaces and a well-designed sewage system that also serves as the green space around which schools are clustered, were some of the innovations that infused the project, and engaged the community strategically. In the eco resort, one of the driving ideas was community engagement on a daily basis. The resort was situated among existing houses as one of many village units, with its common space being configured in a way to make it accessible to the villagers as well as doubling as their common village square. Local craftspeople and techniques were

Mati Ghar by Sanjay Prakash & Associates. This project explored a concentric plan form for a gallery space, utilising compressed earth blocks to reduce embodied energy content and an innovative underground ventilation system for passive cooling

used to create the resort's buildings, with the craftspeople leading the design process. Village residents run the kitchen and determine the cuisine. In addition to being completely interwoven in the fabric of the resort in an interdependent relationship, this approach demonstrates a deeper and harmonious participatory process where social development is intrinsic to the creation of a harmonious environment.

Much earlier, in 1983, with similar intentions but with a far more ambitious mandate, Ashok Khosla established the Development Alternatives (DA) World Headquarters in New Delhi with the mission of promoting sustainable national development. DA aimed to innovate and disseminate the means for creating sustainable livelihoods on a large scale, thereby mobilising widespread action to eradicate poverty and regenerate the environment. To this end, it focused on promoting innovation through the design and development of appropriate technologies and institutional systems to make the dissemination of this research possible. The participants first developed this project in their own office building in New Delhi, designed in 1985 by Neeraj Manchanda. Built in mud, the building showed how simple innovations in technology could modulate light and climate to create an ecologically sensitive environment. DA obviously recognised the importance of housing and building as crucial to the broader development processes; consequently, in 1993, it set up the subsidiary Tara Nirman Kendra to focus on alternative technologies for buildings that were resource efficient and accessible to the urban and rural poor. Several such branches were established in the country, as DA building centres, with the mandate to promote alternative building methods and ensure the transfer of low-carbon technologies from 'lab to land'. Although the contributions of these organisations were critical in the formation of alternative practices as a model of engagement, their impact has remained limited in the mainstream of the field. Another associate of DA, Sanjay Prakash designed a seminal project extending this sensibility. This was also a building in mud erected as an exhibition space for the Indira Gandhi National Centre for the Arts in New Delhi, built by his firm Sanjay Prakash & Associates and called Mati Ghar (or House of Mud). It demonstrated the use and potential of this simple and renewable natural material for institutional buildings, challenging the bureaucracy and specifications of the Public Works Department that otherwise held a monopoly on government institution building.

There have been precedents, however, that pre-dated these efforts. Ray Meeker, in the early 1980s in Puducherry, for example, conducted a noteworthy experiment with material and technology, creating houses using fired-mud building techniques. He argued that mud, or rather clay, is easily available as an extremely cheap material resource. He now uses the houses as kilns for his own pottery products in the workshop which he runs with his ceramist wife Deborah Meeker. Although this approach produces a visually sensual and interesting process, the firing of an entire structure is an inefficient use of fuel— a self-professed criticism that he has not yet been adequately able to address. In addition to houses, Meeker has designed other terracotta structures, such as the memorial to Protima Bedi (1997) in Nrityagram near Bengaluru, that constitute surprisingly beautiful artefacts. However, the conflict between the efficiencies of alternative materials and technologies and their visual results have always been, and perhaps continue to be, a point of unresolved tension.

Despite these distortions, the implicit thrust of this body of emerging work within the larger rubric of alternative practices involves constructing new meaning around the question of sustainable design. The dimension it brings to the debate is that of the social as a suitable 'material' for architecture. Such approaches recognise the broader ecology in which the building process is set. Lacking the recognition of these broader ecologies—especially the 'social' in discussions about sustainability in the globalising West—makes the processes triggered by this alternative mode relevant and critical for future architectural imaginations in India. This is particularly appropriate in the light of the international influences within the profession and its patronage. The Western rating approach is an example of how the broader ecology of a building, which includes the social, is ignored in the quest to focus on the materials. Discussions about sustainability in the globalising world have also been pre-empted by high technology; consequently, craft, or the new craft of architecture (especially in the West), builds on the idea of the complete disappearance of traditional skills. In India's context, craft is a continuous and living tradition. These practices pointedly address and celebrate craft in their approach, and the involvement of craftspeople and builders in the design and decision-making process.

In addition to the institutional efforts of Tara Nirman and the Barefoot College, the most potent examples of this approach within mainstream architectural practice are the numerous houses built by Chitra Vishwanath (starting in 1990) across southern India using local materials, a band of trained craftspersons and sustainable design configurations. Her success lies in the manner in which she scaled up her production and replicated this approach in more than 600 houses built between 2005 and 2010. Building on the

Kamath House by Revathi and Vasant Kamath. Their mud house, an embodiment of the architects' building philosophy, sits on what was once a mining site and is now topped by a bamboo roof. The house roof is covered with grass, thereby producing oxygen and absorbing heat while atomisers spray the courtyard and circulate air

aesthetics and sensibilities championed by Baker and the other numerous pioneers of innovative technologies, Vishwanath has managed to make their application work in the face of changing middle-class aspirations in urban centres such as Bengaluru. In many ways her work is closest to the sensibilities, values and challenges that engaged Baker. Vishwanath balances pragmatic requirements with elegance and an ecological sensitivity at a scale that her peers were unable to achieve. Her approach is a systemic one, wherein the ecology of building spans environmental concerns (the appropriate as well as frugal uses of materials and water harvesting) and a social ecology of craftspeople and collaborators that facilitate the scales at which she is able to work. If anyone in the next generation extends the legacy of Laurie Baker it is clearly Chitra Vishwanath.

Meanwhile, Ashok B Lall in Delhi has bridged the gap between various practices emerging from this landscape of resistance. His disciplined approach to reconciling the formalism of modernism (without being weighed down by its aesthetics) with the looseness of the vernacular (and its inevitable hybridism) in combining different material as well as building elements and infusing these with rigorous performance criteria makes his work seminal in the debate about India's sustainable design. In building the DA World Headquarters (2006) in New Delhi he has invented new spatial configurations for shading, integrating airflow mechanisms and natural forms of insulation to create a sustainable and energy-efficient building without the mechanical 'fixes' that characterise global green architecture. Passive cooling, recycled material and touches of visual delight are all seam-lessly orchestrated into this project. Revathi and Vasant Kamath also bring to their work this balance between the integrity of alternative materials and new technologies, and architectural rigour. The several houses, resorts and institutional buildings they have built in and around Delhi demonstrate this skill, and the maturity and coming of age of the alternative practitioner outside the mainstream. Their project for Nalin Tomar's House in Hauz Khas village (1992) demonstrates not only design and construction expertise, but also a sensitivity in intervening in a historical context.

This approach also flourishes in other places facing severe resource and financial constraints, creating new aesthetic sensibilities. Social NGO Manav Sadhna's crèche for slum children (2006), designed by Yatin Pandya, demonstrates another level of engagement with recycled material for both construction and

Lotus Lake View Resort by Parul Zaveri and Nimish Patel of Abhikram. Dry stacked-stone walls such as this one (detail), crafted by local artisans, are a hallmark of these architects' works–a direct and unencumbered engagement of craftspeople as equals on the building site

decoration. Configured like a large traditional village cluster, the building employs filler slabs, walls made from recycled bottles, waste cycle parts for the making of screens and doors, waste flooring from other construction sites and ash from a thermal power station adjoining the site. Similarly, waste items, from broken glass to computer keyboards, are embedded in walls and ceilings to create decoration from familiar discarded objects. The project sharply highlights the visual freedom that is possible when the baggage of predetermined aesthetics is dropped for a looser, more open-ended approach in which the building's image evolves as it is built.

In another vein, Parul Zaveri and Nimish Patel in Gujarat and Rajasthan have demonstrated the potency and continuity of India's craft tradition within the consciousness of the emerging aesthetic without being limited by the sensibilities of modernism. Their work ranges from historic preservation to new buildings, and employs craftspeople and traditional materials with the explicit aim of re-establishing the relevance of traditional decision-making processes in the contemporary context. The traditional craftsperson becomes the central figure in the process, with the architect operating simply as a collaborator and sometimes a mentor who is always mindful of the building's visual integrity. Ancient and contemporary aesthetics are recognised as simultaneously valid in their approach. Parul and Nimish's work ranges from industrial buildings to luxury hotels and boutiques, to small institutional works and historical preservation. Their approach to preservation is unlike that of practitioners trained formally in conservation—who align closer to the regionalist in their approach of formal building processes that include detailed instructions through drawings and tender documents. Instead, Parul and Nimish also work directly with craftspeople, employing oral instructions and collaborative decision making. They have successfully achieved the single-minded application of the same set of values across these scales and diverse commissions. The conservation of resources, the use of appropriate technologies and materials and a deep respect for the craftspeople involved in these buildings make their work special in the context of these alternative practices. Their Torrent Research Centre (1999) in Ahmedabad uses passive cooling and wind towers in the most scientific ways to minimise the use of mechanical systems while creating a unique form and aesthetic sensibility that grows out of the building's functional modulation. At the other end of the spectrum is the Udaivilas Hotel (2003) in Udaipur, which

Torrent Research Centre by Parul Zaveri and Nimish Patel. The use of passive cooling techniques in a facility of this nature and scale demanded an effective and efficient environment that minimised energy consumption in the long run

The Oberoi Udaivilas by Parul Zaveri and Nimish Patel. Within the idea of a contemporary hotel with all modern amenities, this project explores traditional forms and building techniques while remaining true to the ethos of the locale

employs traditional forms and materials while maintaining their integrity at the highest levels.

Such practices emphasise the intimacy of scale, a direct involvement in building and an active preoccupation with the political and civic issues that impinge on architecture. The practitioners make an argument for architectural diversity, and represent the differences critical to the evolution of relevant architecture. Moreover, the recognition of human creativity has acquired special meaning in the face of globalisation, which otherwise can reduce the character of the built form to a thin veneer of glamour. Most importantly, these practitioners perhaps address the issue of sustainability most squarely because they go beyond the physical fabric of the building to encompass, in their imagination, the people who build and inhabit the architecture.

Although the scale at which it operates is often limited, this model of practice is firmly embedded in a region's socio-economic milieu. It facilitates the engagement of social networks in the process of building, and is characterised by cost-effective solutions, often derived from the conversion of social assets into financial ones in terms of how labour is engaged or materials procured. Not overwhelmed by issues of architectural and aesthetic concerns, these buildings are often arranged and conceived with a looseness that allows for flexibility in use of materials and of the building process itself. Nevertheless, although this mode of practice has proliferated, and receives popular support among institutions, NGOs and intellectuals, it lacks the cohesion in its physical articulation as demonstrated by the regionalists and is often reduced to a caricature of regional icons and images. Its output, although robust and vigorous in its moral and ideological stance, suffers from the awkwardness of an architecture in formation or evolution. Disparate elements often clumsily collide to create new hybrid forms. Another discordant note that plagues this mode of practice is that alternative practitioners often forget to acknowledge craftspeople on an equal footing when these projects are celebrated in the media. Thus, while they recognise them as part of the process, the credit in the Western and national press often goes exclusively to the architect!

At any rate, this model of practice holds the potential to negotiate the multiple modernities that have emerged, in order to shape a sustainable direction

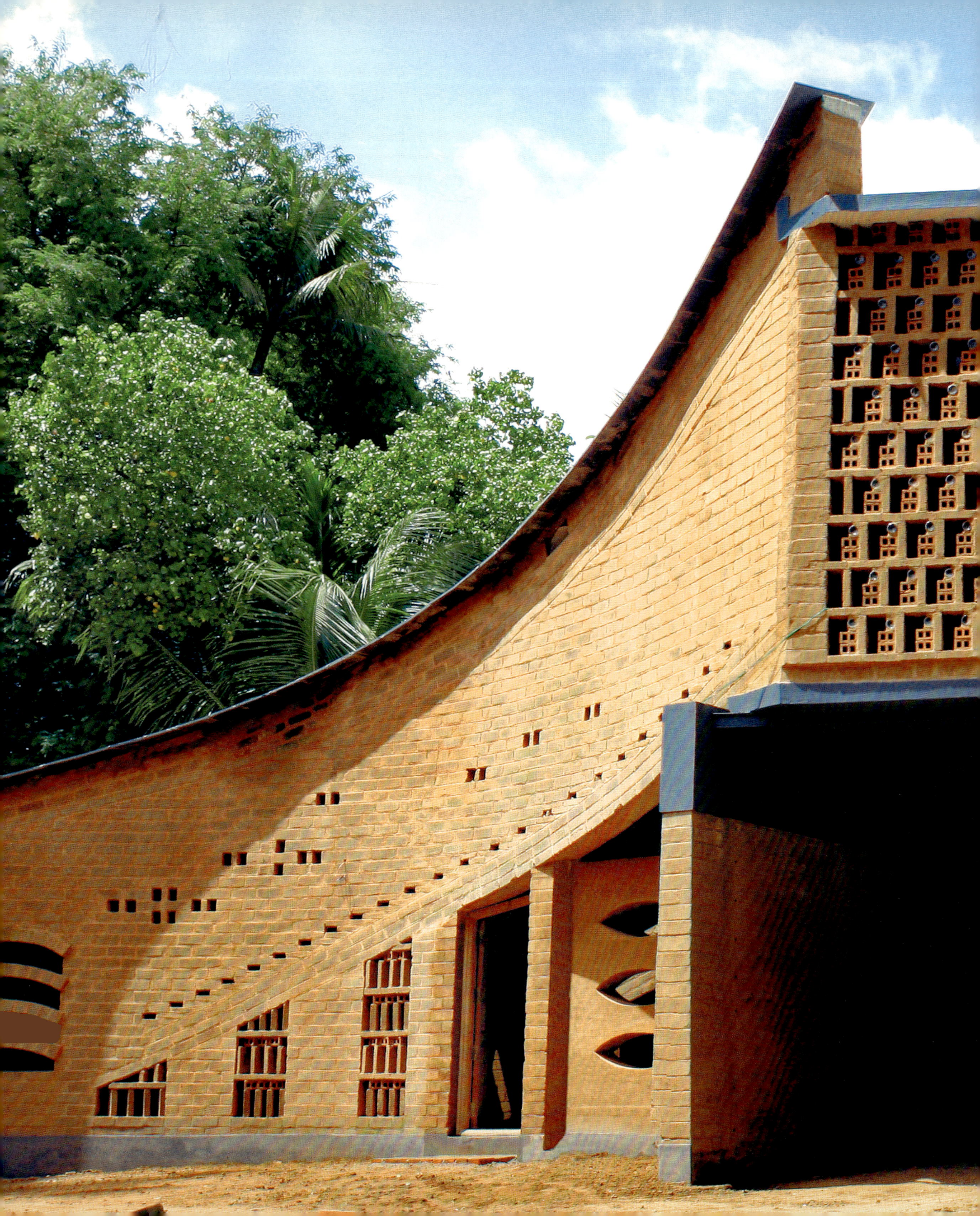

Architecture in India since 1990 | Alternate Practice

for new architecture in India in the coming decades. Its approach is not self-conscious, but rather based on community participation and the resituating of architecture from formal production processes squarely into the fabric of the users' lived experiences. Although this mode of practice seemingly extends traditions and attempts to express an economy of means, its literal visual translation often subverts rather than extends vernacular customs and lacks the aesthetic robustness that makes the traditional idiom timeless. In the coming years, the greatest contribution of this approach to contemporary Indian architecture will be the firm emphasis on the questions and parameters for the debate on sustainability. It is these practitioners who will challenge the hegemony of Western attitudes and set the standards for sustainable design in India.

Valsala Cottage (*these pages*) by Vinu Daniel. Extending the building traditions of Baker and the experiments of Auroville, younger architects like Vinu Daniel are trying to find a new aesthetic for this approach while being conscious of the integrity of the basic materials used and the construction practices of the locale

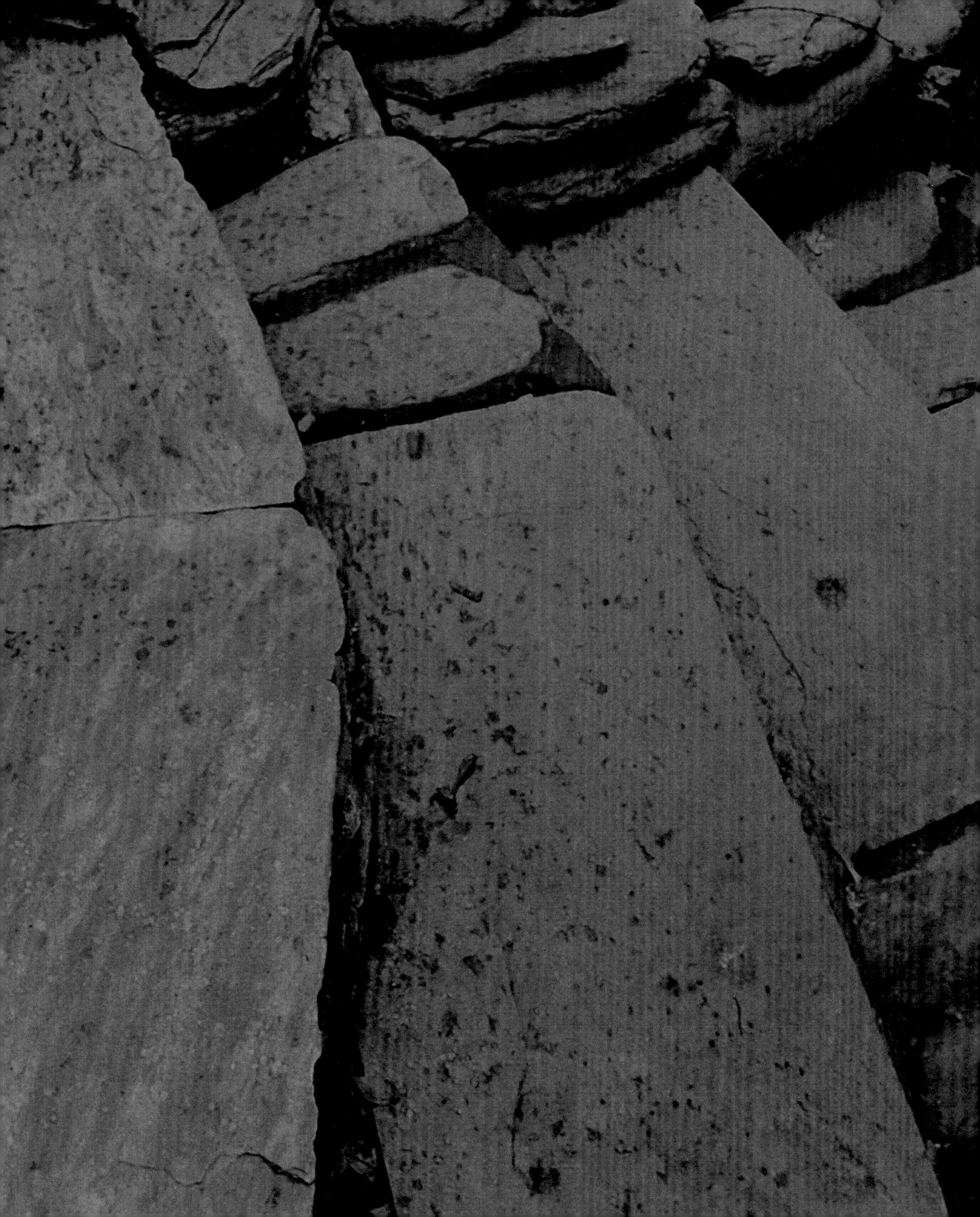

Folios

CENTRE FOR DEVELOPMENT STUDIES	213
LOYOLA CHAPEL	215
ABU ABRAHAM'S HOUSE	217
MALIK HOUSE	219
NALIN TOMAR HOUSE	222
WALL HOUSE	227
MANAV SADHNA	231
DEVELOPMENT ALTERNATIVES WORLD HQ	235
JENNY PINTO'S PAPER MAKING WORKSHOP	239
PETTACHI HOUSE	241
OUR NATIVE VILLAGE ECO RESORT	243
SHAAM-E-SARHAD VILLAGE RESORT	245

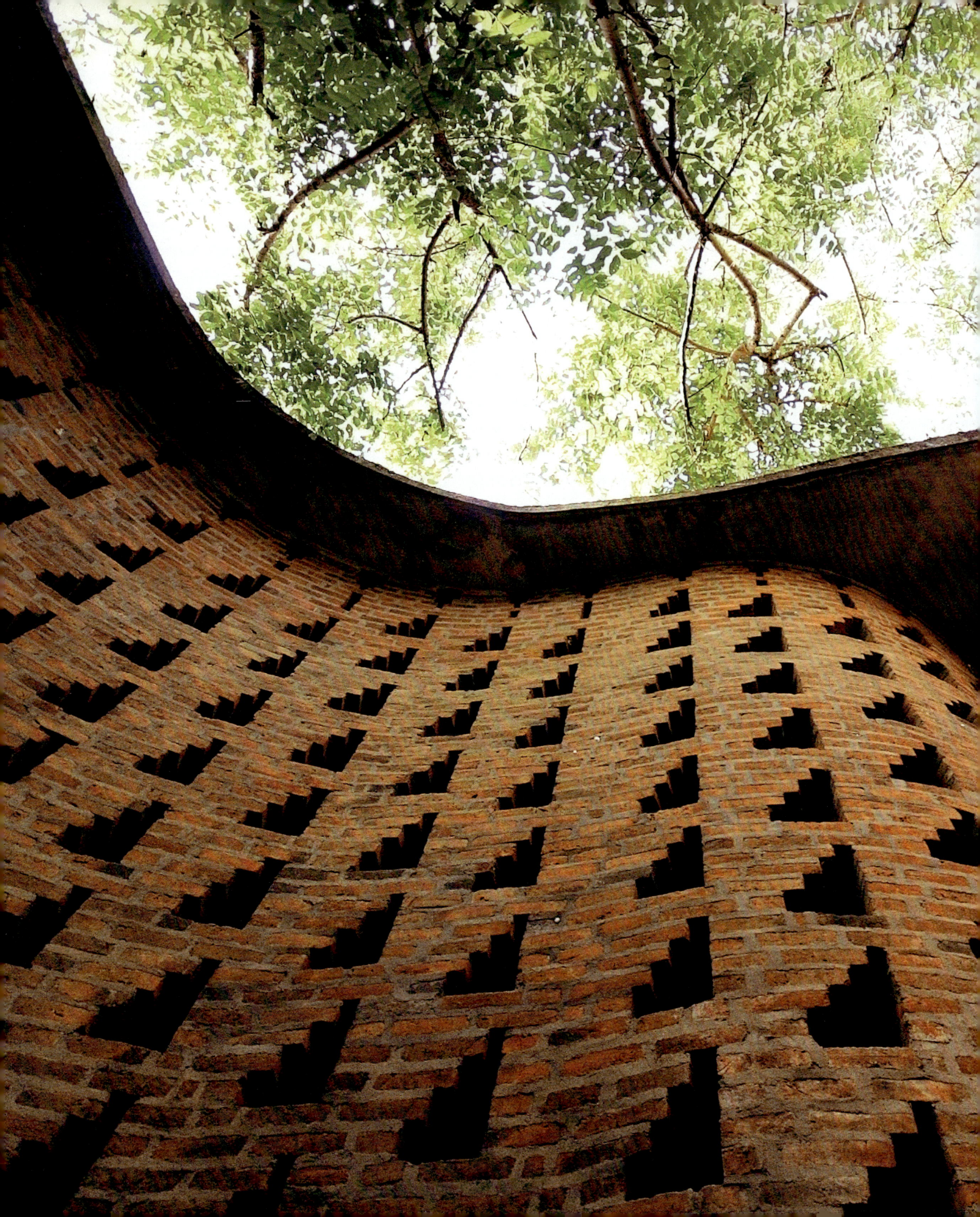

folio 1
CENTRE FOR DEVELOPMENT STUDIES, Thiruvananthapuram

Laurie Baker

The Centre for Development Studies in Ulloor near Thiruvananthapuram is one of Baker's most significant works and a catalogue of the rich architectural vocabulary that he evolved as an architect in India. Situated on a hillside, the site rises steeply to the crest of the rocky hill. Displaying a range of ideas, the campus accommodates administrative offices, classrooms, a library and computer centres, an amphitheatre and housing facilities among other functions.

While cost-effectiveness and economy of means was a concern, the larger aim was to provide a setting that echoed the 'development' thrust of the centre. The seven-storey library forms the centre of the site, with other activities placed organically depending on the land contours and slope. Individual buildings are connected through a series of corridors and landscaped courts, hostel and dining facilities are placed away from this central complex, and the staff quarters lie even further afield. Locally made, fired bricks are used in a variety of ways ranging from curved, corbelled and flat arches, and regular load-bearing walls to sinuously articulated brick screen surfaces that help modulate climate and light, and also form the essential images of the complex.

Façade detail of the women's hostel Curved surfaces increase the structural stiffness of the façade, but also create wonderful diffused and changing light patterns through the jali, or screen wall

View of the campus cluster The overall planning of the campus is based on the natural topography of the land, and the buildings are mainly low-rise brick structures interconnected by corridors. The tower in the background, dominating the campus, is the library building

View of the sanctuary space In spite of the tall volume, acoustic issues were minimised by the use of the textured brick surface, which absorbed reverberations. Light of a mysterious quality washes the space through perforated brickwork on the sanctuary wall. An even, top light adds a glow in the space over the sanctuary

folio 1
LOYOLA CHAPEL, Thiruvananthapuram

Laurie Baker

Situated in the grounds of a college on the outskirts of Thiruvananthapuram, the Loyola Chapel is part of a group of buildings on a campus that was not entirely planned and developed by Baker. He designed individual projects such as dormitories, classrooms, field house and large ceremonial structures for collective gathering. With a programme requirement for the chapel to seat 1,000 persons, Baker's skills in creating low-cost structures was put to a serious test in this building, which required a large interrupted space. Avoiding the use of steel and reinforced concrete, Baker chose to use load-bearing walls and a timber roof frame with asbestos-sheet roofing, which proved to be an economical solution. The use of cross-braced cavity walls addresses the issue of ventilation in a tropical climate, while perforated brickwork near the altar brings in light poetically.

The nave, with sloping wooden ceiling Cross-braced cavity walls in brick and a timber-framed roof create a large uninterrupted prayer space while facilitating natural ventilation

Central landscaped courtyard Forming the core of the house, the arched corridor connects the bedroom and kitchen while the dining area opens directly onto it

Driveway leading to the arrival porch This west-facing portico is characterised by traditional wooden columns flanking the entrance, with platforms for seating and display

Sit-out verandah adjoining the courtyard The informal seating area, with cane furniture, is demarcated by a circular brick column and a bridge on the upper level

folio 1
ABU ABRAHAM'S HOUSE, Thiruvananthapuram

Laurie Baker

This residence for a cartoonist, with its rectilinear plan, sits within an old neighbourhood in Thiruvananthapuram. In spite of the presence of a projecting entrance portico the orientation and focus of the main volume is an internal courtyard, around which most of the spaces of the dwelling are organised. One enters the house through a series of arches that act like screens and layer the sequence of spaces. Openings are positioned to respond to changing daylight conditions, while a hipped roof with ridge ventilation defines the owner's work space. Exposed brickwork and rat-trap bonding create a visual pattern that rests on low random-rubble stone walls which rise above the foundations, creating an impression of a distinct base for the house.

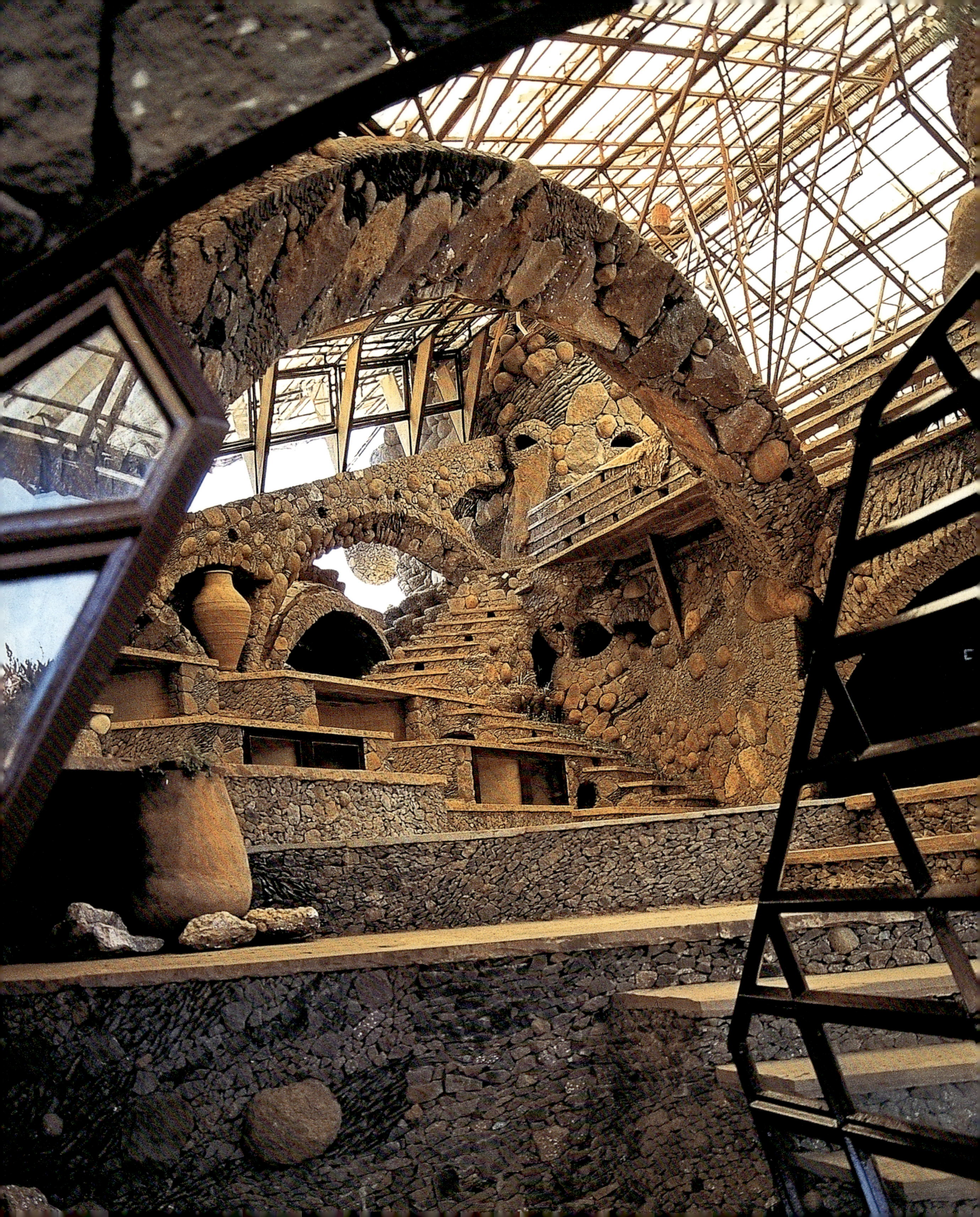

folio 2
MALIK HOUSE, Lonavala

Nari Gandhi

This project in the hilly landscape of Lonavala forms a compelling embodiment of the ideas, principles and approach to architecture that defined Nari Gandhi's life as an architect. Reflective of his earlier training with Frank Lloyd Wright, the Malik House project combines the organic with the precisely crafted. Building without any working drawings or civil engineers to supervise the site progress, the architect maintained an approach comprising oral instructions for all his projects. The house was created by blasting the rocky hill site to generate a series of flat terraces that then accommodated landscaped gardens or dense plantation. Following a more formal, triangular geometry, three arches, spanning nine metres each, create the structure, with a tortoise-shaped wind-catcher and toilets below. The interior elements, fenestration and careful articulation of details resonate an attitude to material that is unique to Gandhi's work.

Approach to the upper terraces The modulation of the ground into a meandering flight of stone stairs connects the various enclosed and open spaces. The diffused light from the roof is bounced off the stone's natural tones to render a warm hue to the space

Enclosed living areas The vertical arrangement of stone slabs creates a porous, louvred enclosure that allows visual connection with adjoining spaces. Terracotta artefacts and landscaped pathways personalise the domestic environment

Architecture in India since 1990 | Alternate Practice

View from main terrace
Large terraces were created to overlook Lake Valvan and the hills that surround the site

Roof over the entire house
Displaying a great clarity of structure and construction, these pure-masonry arches carry the load of the steel roof which forms a large envelope over the several enclosed spaces and terraces that comprise the house

Detail of wall articulation
Decorative panels and an array of stones of different sizes all coalesce within the supporting masonry walls

View of steel sloping roof
The house is spread over three levels, within glass enclosures and a sloping roof. Random-rubble masonry forms the structure and base of each unit

Architecture in India since 1990 | Alternate Practice

folio 3
NALIN TOMAR HOUSE, New Delhi

Kamath Design Studio

This residence is located overlooking the medieval Hauz Khas monument in the Hauz Khas Village in New Delhi. Built on a tight plot of land, the strategy was to build vertically on the basis of a multiple-level plan. Using local Badarpur sandstone, the façade and other interior details express a visual continuum in the language of the neighbouring monument. The 0.75m wide staircase provides the basic module for the house, which at entrance level accommodates the study and bedroom, separated by a level difference. A few steps from the study lead to the kitchen and dining room.

The first flight of stairs, with a fountain on the landing, leads to the living room, which has a view of the monument. The next level leads to the guest bedroom, bathrooms and finally to the terrace. The tree-of-life motif has been utilised extensively in the metal grilles, inlaid terrazzo flooring, lintels and the arches throughout the house. Local crafts and traditional techniques have been widely used in the interiors, which are designed with mirror work decorating the niches. All in all, this is an elegant, contextually successful solution that incorporates the traditional idioms of building effortlessly into this contemporary house.

Site context and surrounds
Responding to the distinctive context of the medieval monuments adjoining the plot was a key concern—and the orientation, architectural vocabulary and texture of the building demonstrates a deep understanding of this historic landscape

View of Hauz Khas monument and gardens
The terrace with its high stone parapet overlooks the monuments outside

View of house and its surroundings A narrow and linear plot resulted in the house being extruded vertically, and towering over the neighbouring properties in the Hauz Khas area

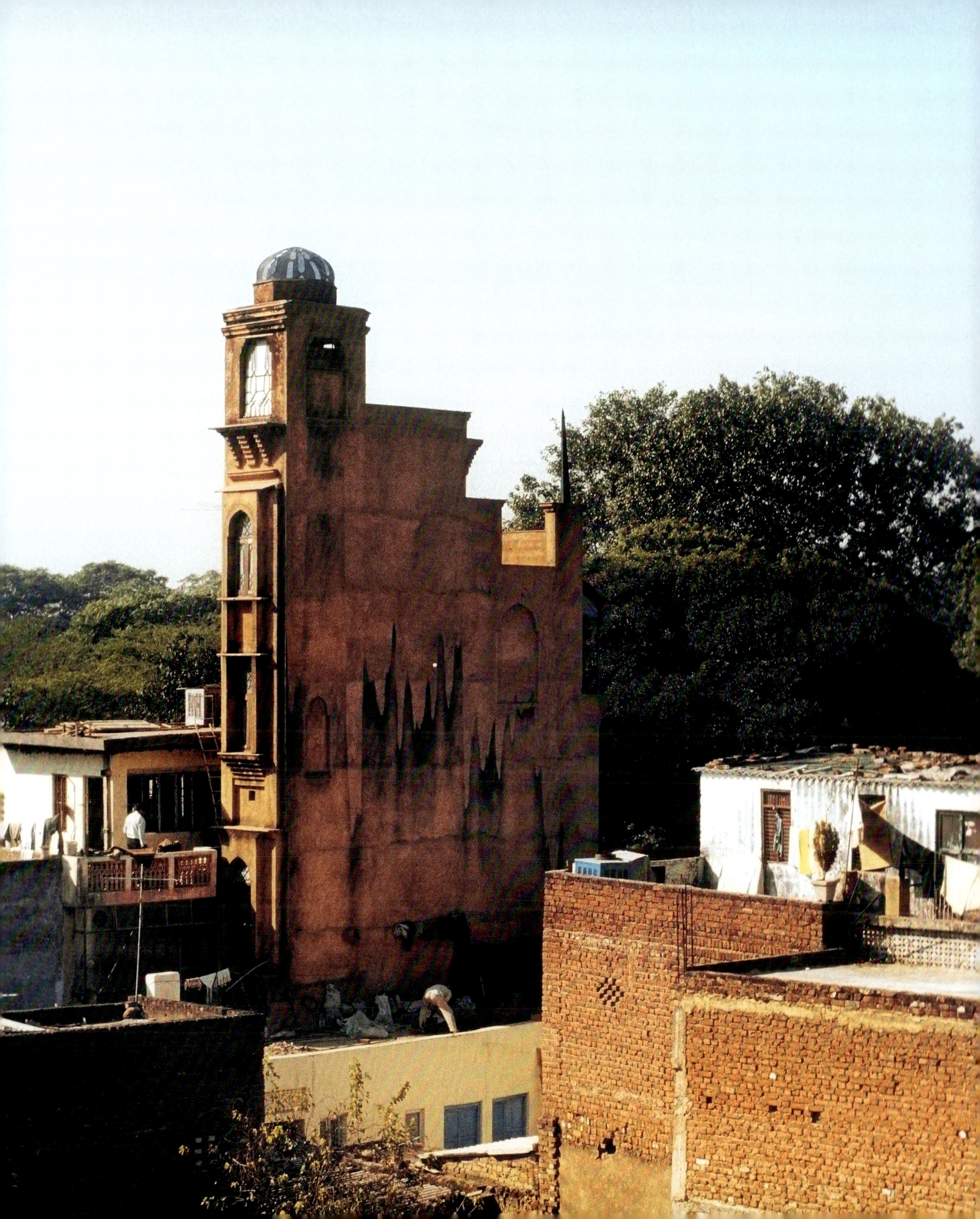

Architecture in India since 1990 | Alternate Practice

Annotated site plan
The location of the house can be seen at different scales across the city of Delhi

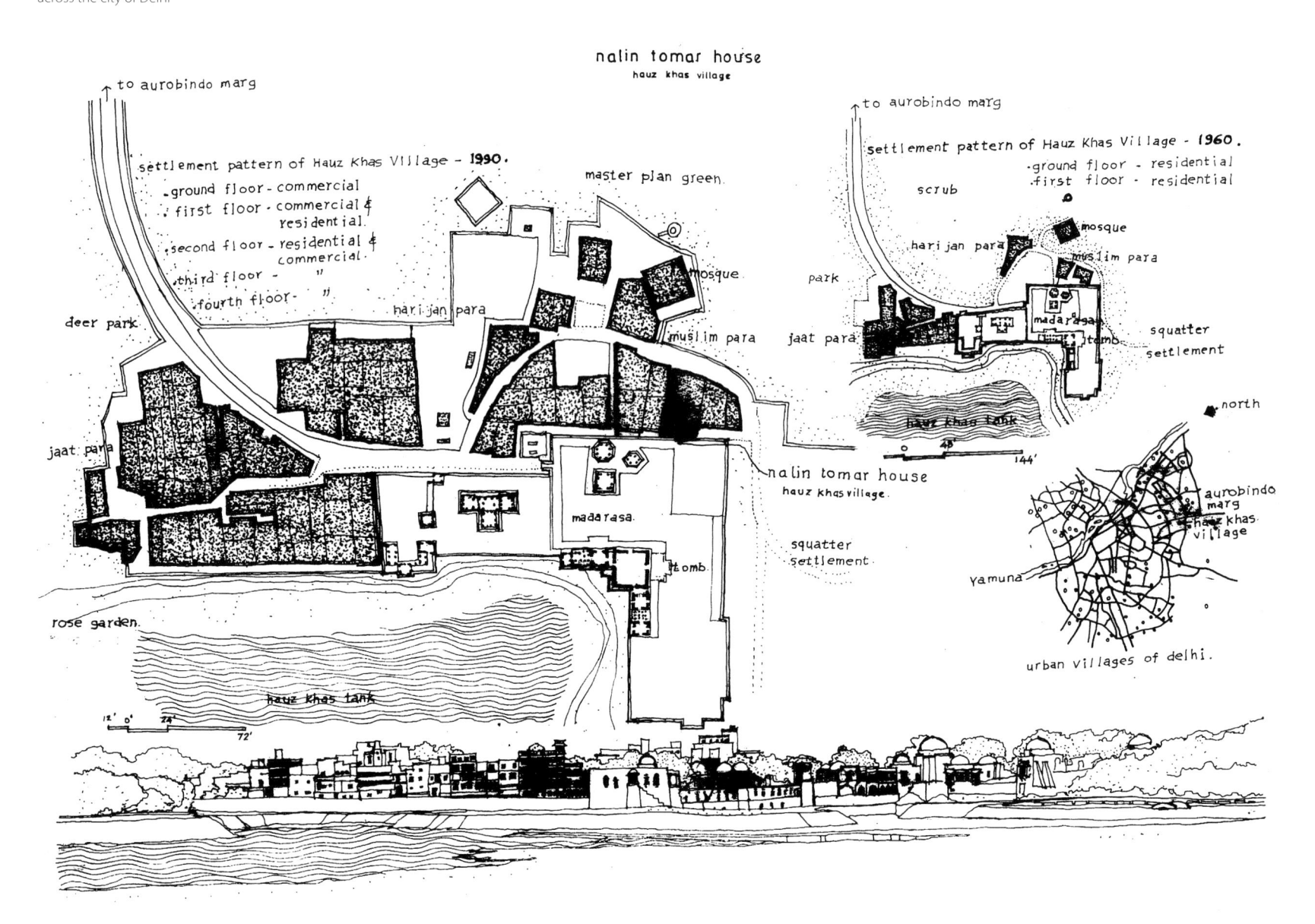

Architecture in India since 1990 | Alternate Practice

The living area The use of archways and wall niches continues the idiom of the neighbouring monument, while the use of traditional crafts and textiles give a distinct character to the space

Building section A series of split levels connected by a central flight of stairs governed the basic spatial planning of the house. These levels alternate between functional areas and leisure pavilions that visually open onto the monument complex

225

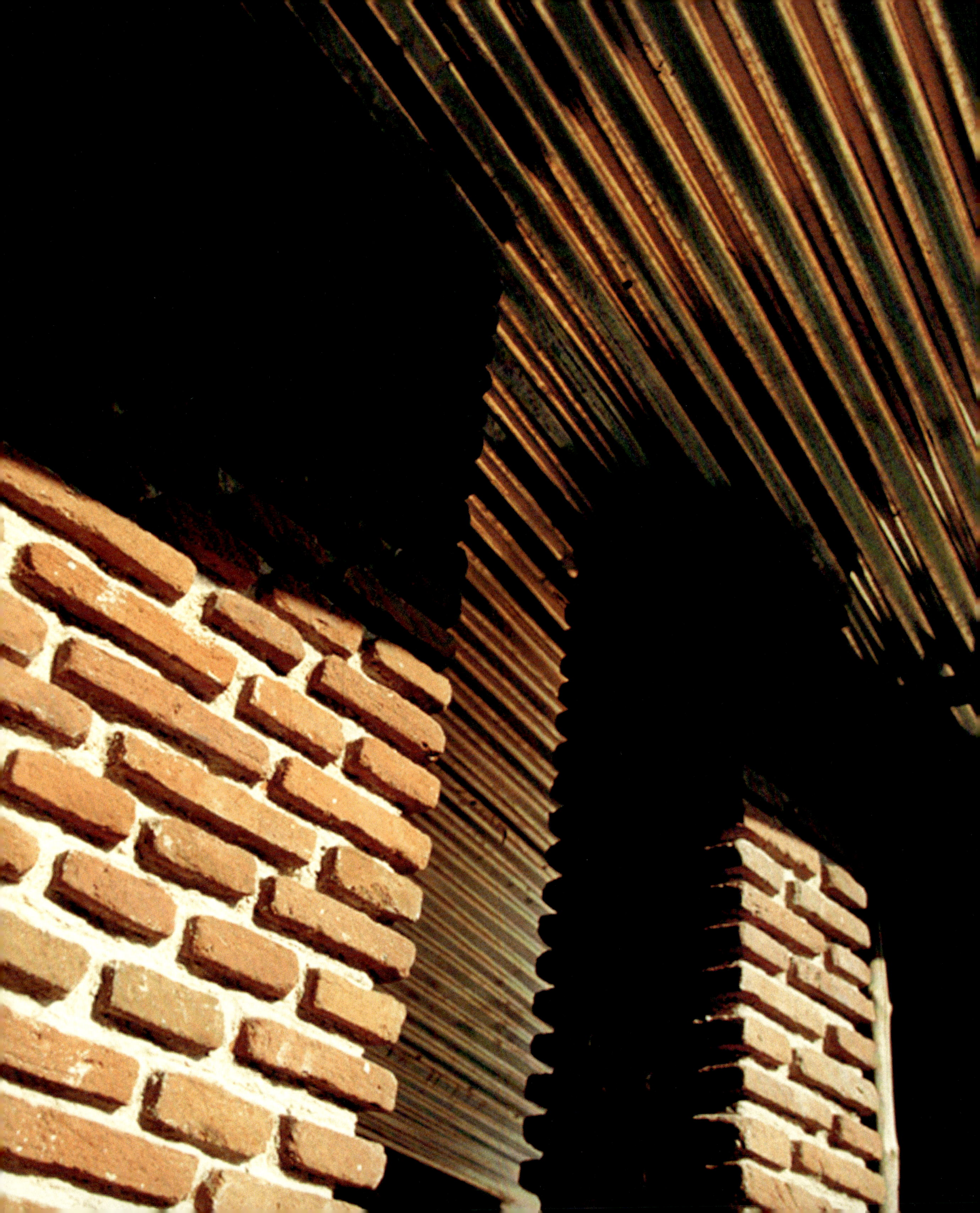

folio 4
WALL HOUSE, Auroville

Anupama Kundoo

Situated within the Auromodele area, outside the planned city limits of Auroville, this house explores experimental ideas regarding innovative construction techniques that the architect has been engaged with for almost two decades. Designed as her own residence, the programme integrated flexibility in planning in order to accommodate variations in use in terms of the number of people the house could accommodate. Minimal furniture, interconnected spaces and semi-enclosed bath areas create fluid spaces and landscape features that make territorial enclosures according to daylight and climatic variations. The project was also seen as a prototype in the quest to arrive at a suitable and relevant building technology for the future development of the region. Constraints of unskilled labour and resources were turned to advantage by using local technologies, such as the ancient practice of brickwork set in lime mortar with raked joints, the use of an insulated catenary roof vault, which was then punctured to allow for light and ventilation.

Detail of wall junction
Exposed-brick piers connect a sheet metal roof that reflects light into the bathing areas

Approach to the house
Set within a wooded enclave and conceived on a linear plan housing the semi-private activities, a double-height vault welcomes the visitor upon arrival

Architecture in India since 1990 | Alternate Practice

The open shower area
This open-to-sky bathroom on the upper level connects to a walk-in wardrobe and study space. An exposed-brick enclosure contains the shower and lounge pool, with a view into the surrounding greenery

View of the dining pavilion
A single flight of green-stained concrete stairs along a louvred periphery opens onto the dining area with its basic wooden furniture. The pavilion ceiling is made of shallow terracotta plates, set in the slab as supporting formwork (for pouring the concrete) as well as for insulation

Construction of the vaulted roof This is a key component of the innovative construction employed in the house. Here, hollow earthen tiles are used in vault form for the central roof of the house, to insulate and economise on costs

Detail at water edge A quality of the handmade emerges in such details, which creatively utilise waste pieces of stone found on site

The sleeping area Surrounded by glass louvres, the sparsely furnished bedroom on the upper level projects out from the linear massing and the principal wall that dictates the form of the house

228

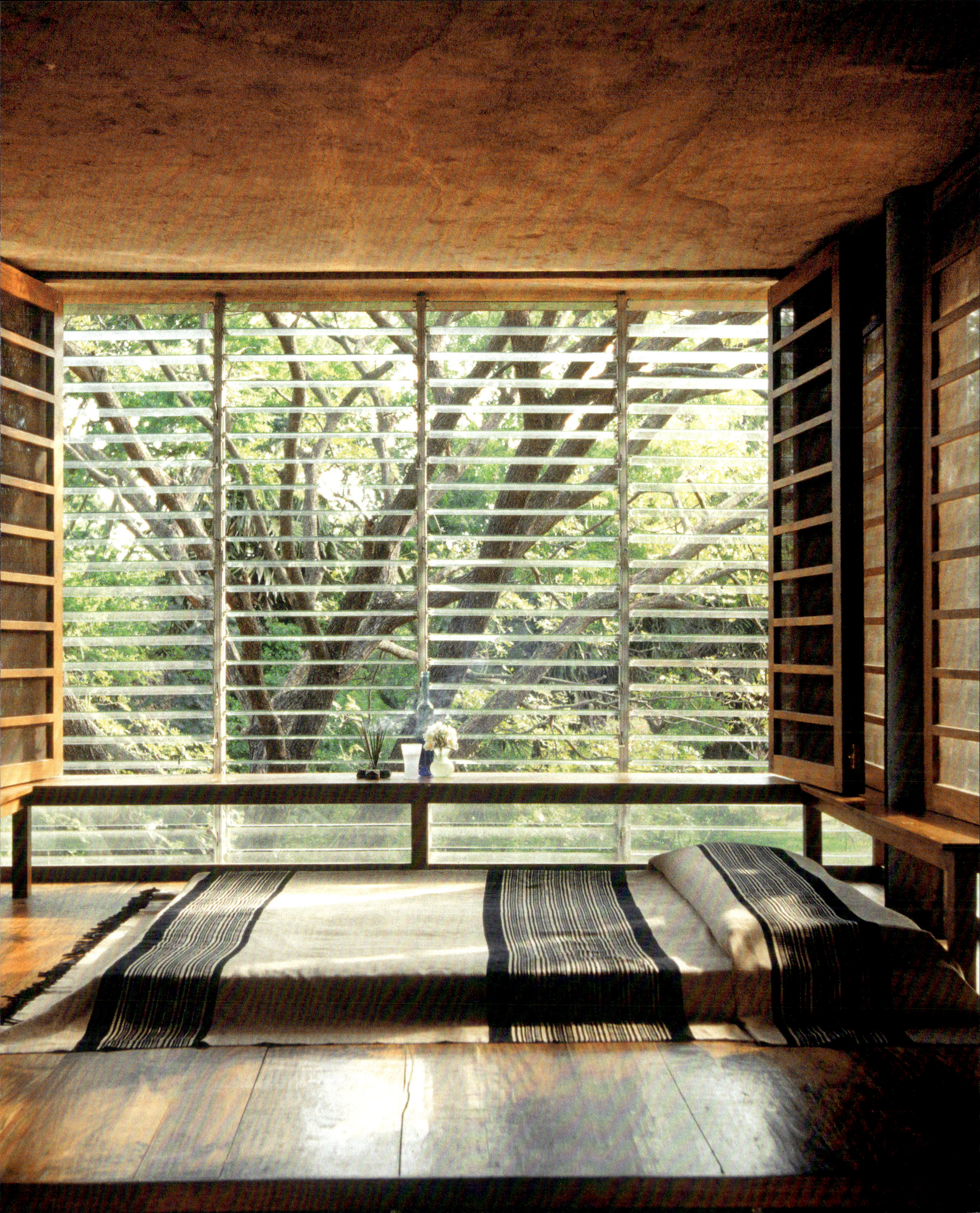

Architecture in India since 1990 | Alternate Practice

Congregation in the central courtyard Aiming to provide vocational training and economic empowerment to residents of the surrounding squatter areas, the central court holds large gatherings during awareness and spiritual programmes

Panoramic view of the site The circular courtyard resonates with the familiarity of a traditional village gathering space under a tree, and is used as the principal venue for meetings at the institute

folio 5
MANAV SADHNA, Ahmedabad

Yatin Pandya and Vastu Shilpa Foundation

This multi-purpose activity centre, located amidst the largest squatter settlement in Ahmedabad, includes a dormitory and an administrative and multi-faith unit. The core activities are an informal school for children, adult education, and training for manufacturing craft-based products by women and elders. The recycling of domestic waste to make building components and generate economic activity for the poor, and created a sense of empowerment for the local craftspeople who erected the buildings.

Recycled components were largely utilised as building materials for walls, floor and roof slabs. Structural walls used cement-bonded fly-ash bricks, mould-compressed bricks from landfill residue and stabilised soil blocks. Internal partitions used recycled glass, plastic bottles filled with ash and waste residue, and wood panelling from material salvaged from vegetable-packing crates. Floor and roof slabs utilised glass and plastic bottles as filler material, as well as bricks, stone slabs and cement-bonded particleboard with a clay tile cover. In addition, surface articulation was achieved using shredded packaging wrappers and coated-paper waste, vegetable-crate wood and oil tins. Developed and produced under monitored laboratory testing for their engineering performance, these materials have been economical, environmentally friendly and participatory, with an aesthetic that expresses alternatives to contemporary material-use practices.

Collage of recycled materials used A diverse range of recycled waste materials was employed within the building to create wall infills, partitions, doors and windows, and surface articulation

Ceiling in waste fabric A framework for a false ceiling supporting panels of waste fabric, which are collaged to create a tent-like enclosure

Wall surfaces using disposed glass bottles Disposed glass bottles were set within a fly-ash wall, bringing a diffused glow of light into the space

Recycled wooden crates for doorway panelling Wood salvaged from vegetable-packing crates has been recycled into panelled door shutters, fixed along a hinge

Filler slab using plastic bottles Discarded plastic bottles were embedded within the slab shuttering before the casting process, to economise on the amount of cement used and to add a wonderful texture

Architecture in India since 1990 | Alternate Practice

Fly-ash brick wall as place of worship Located at one end of the site, this wall also becomes a place of reverence for the local community

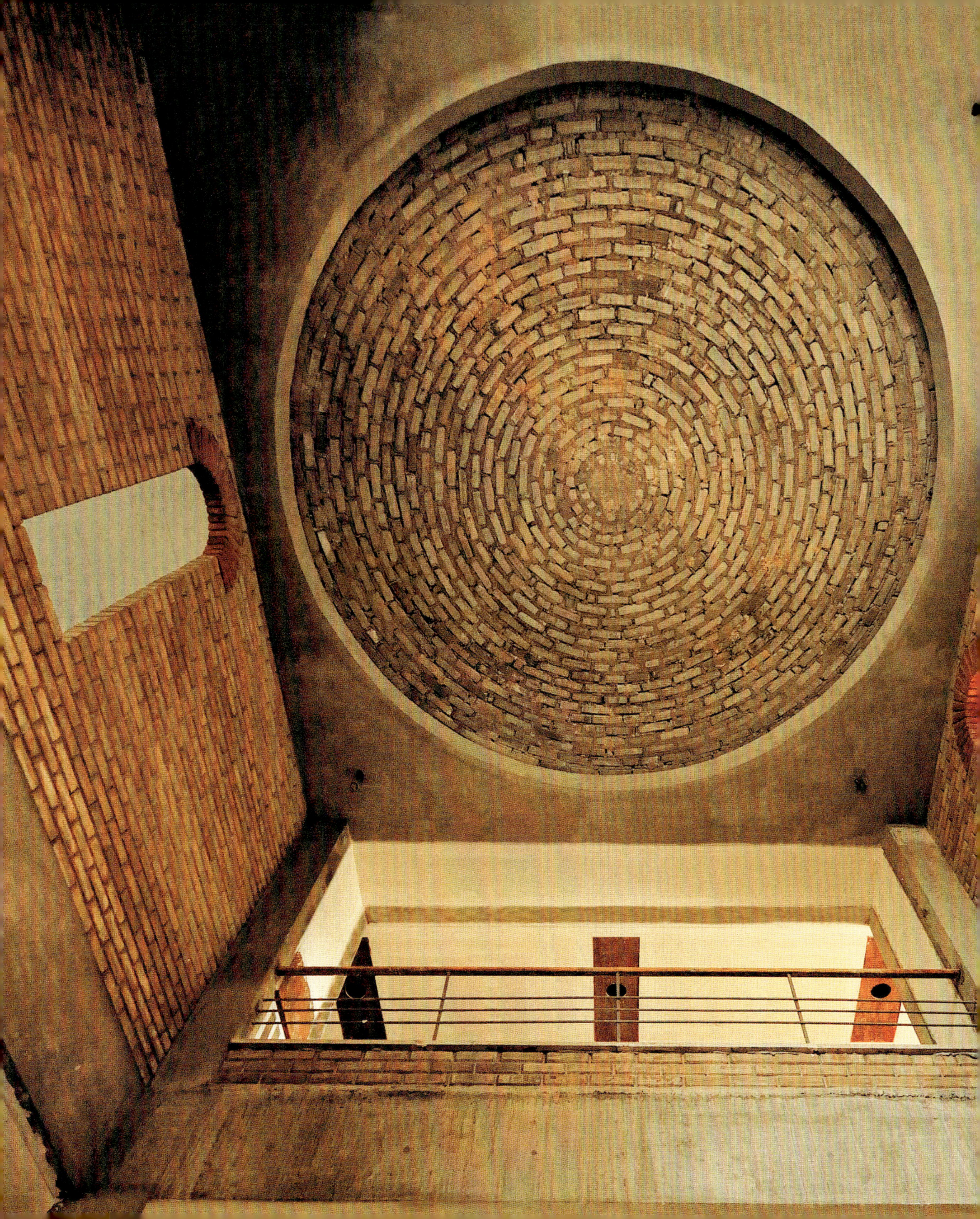

Architecture in India since 1990 | Alternate Practice

folio 6
DEVELOPMENT ALTERNATIVES WORLD HQ, New Delhi

Ashok B Lall Architects

This project seeks to exemplify an imaginative and innovative design solution within generally perceived parameters of sustainable design in the context of contemporary urban development. The building is designed as the world headquarters of Development Alternatives, an organisation advocating an equitable and sustainable model for social and economic development in India. Replacing an earlier facility which had outgrown functional requirements, this new complex in the Qutub Institutional Area near the Qutub Minar was designed to house about 200 occupants.

The forms of the new building resonate with traditional construction elements such as domed lobbies, vaulted ceilings and courtyards. The building is made of cement-stabilised compressed-earth blocks and cement-stabilised fly-ash lime gypsum blocks. Vaulted precast-concrete deck elements are used to span most spaces. Five-metre spacing between columns makes for flexible office spaces while reducing steel consumption. Insulated walls, shaded courts and other passive cooling techniques minimise air-conditioning requirements.

Dome over the entrance atrium Masonry domes, constructed using traditional techniques and earthen forms, punctuate the ceiling of the building periodically

Façade detail In stark contrast to mainstream industrial architecture of metal and glass, the DA office demonstrates that low-energy materials and construction methods can produce effective urban buildings

Architecture in India since 1990 | Alternate Practice

Basement level leading to the *baoli* (well) The gathering space for the office staff descends to a pool of water. The dome over this *baoli* is a nostalgic gesture that draws on the office building located earlier on this site

Rear façade with back entrance The primary building material is cement-stabilised compressed earth blocks: an alternative construction material that is more energy-efficient than conventional masonry

Parapet detail Playful, decorative moments such as this punctuate the building, adding a richness of texture and localised references

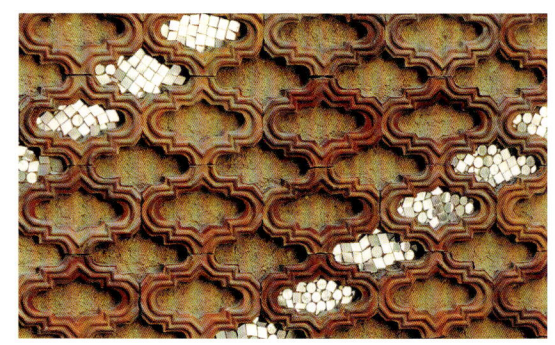

Architecture in India since 1990 | Alternate Practice

External wall detail Multiple building elements coalesce here, unified by the texture of the materials used

Ceiling detail In some areas of the building, the combination of plastered surfaces and exposed fly-ash brick ceilings, such as this one, are used as opportunities to decorate through pattern making

Interior view of office areas Environmentally controlled, flexible spaces allow variations in use while enabling independent climatic control for each wing

Architecture in India since 1990 | Alternate Practice

Detail of leaf motif set within flooring Taking reference from the paper making process, large leaves were cast within the wet flooring to create a lasting imprint of their veins

Primary workshop space Furniture and work surfaces have been pushed towards the periphery to achieve a large, clear work space in order to accommodate this largely floor-based activity

Verandahs around the court This L-shaped verandah exudes a warm hue, owing to the pigmented cement floor and mud-block walls

folio 7
JENNY PINTO'S PAPER MAKING WORKSHOP, Bengaluru

Chitra Vishwanath with Sajitha Sunil

Conceived as a workshop, along with administrative and storage requirements, the design of this paper making studio responded to the rich biodiversity that exists on this lakefront property. However, by the time the workshop was completed the verdant character of the original site had changed substantially due to rampant construction. To compensate for this, the architect used the resultant debris to isolate the studio by moulding the landscape into a series of mounds that were covered with intensive planting.

The studio is designed as a large floor space where paper making can take place, with long windows that stretch to the floor and allow maximum light. Furthermore the windows are covered with paper that is sandwiched between the glass to create translucency and thus a softer and more even light quality. Made entirely of mud blocks combined with granite slabs for stairways and planters, the design, through such choice of materials, utilises passive cooling and does away with fans and air conditioners. Paper making being a highly water-intensive process, recycling of water was required to be integrated within the site. Hence, a rainwater-harvesting system was employed to either irrigate the organic garden or for use in the paper making process.

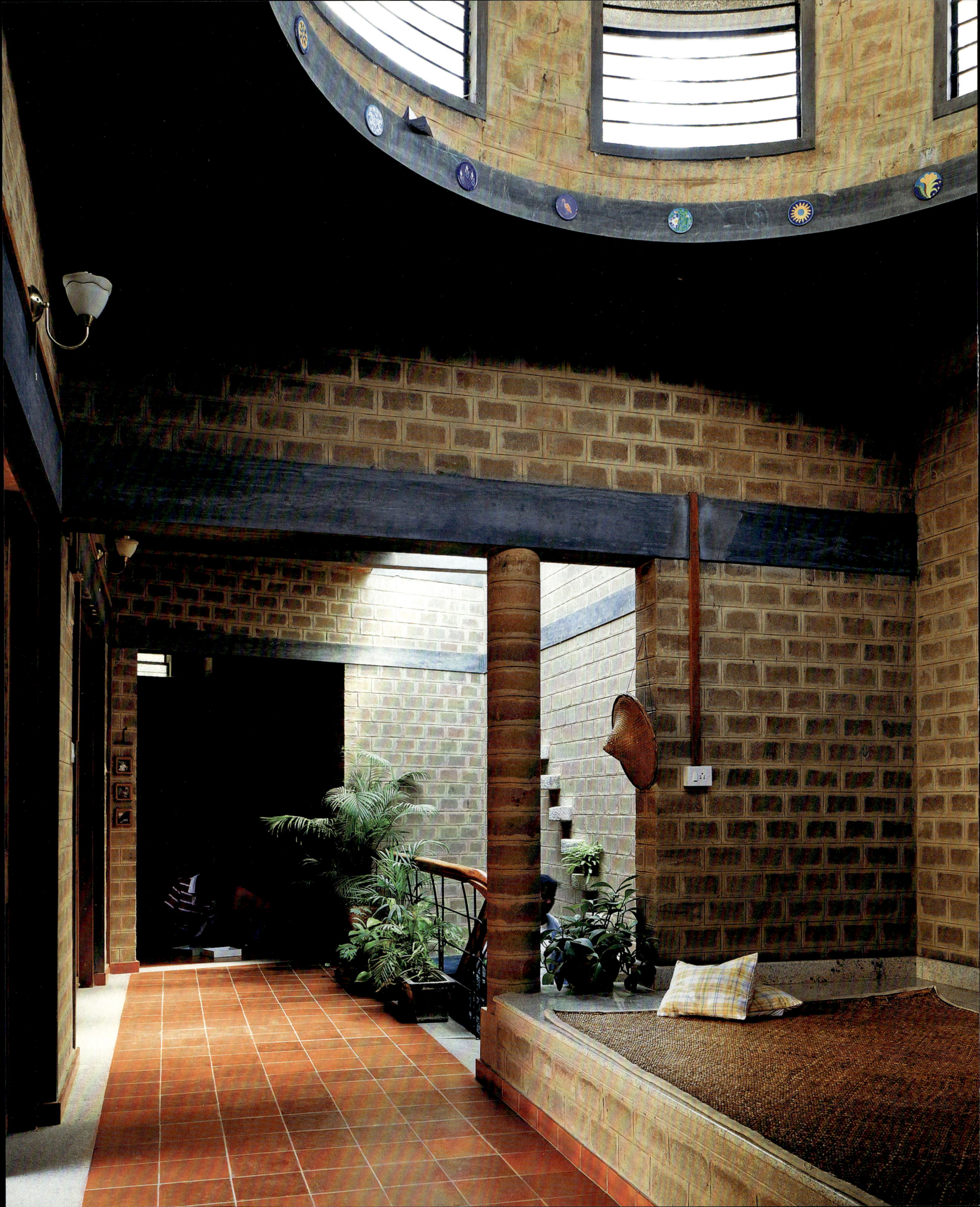

folio 7
PETTACHI HOUSE, Bengaluru

Chitra Vishwanath with Chandrakumari

Designed for a single family that was relocating from their ancestral town of Chettinad to Bengaluru, this house was inspired by the idea of evoking the memory and ambience of their earlier residential environment. Like in the traditional Chettinad house, this was organised around a courtyard and employed as a key element at the entrance a *mittam* (deep platform), which then leads to the living and dining areas. All other spaces overlook the central court while also responding to the street-side location. An overriding decision to build with sun-dried mud blocks governed the construction logic of the project. Sourcing recycled woodwork from traditional, now dismantled, houses for fenestration and entranceways helped collage remnants of the past into the new. The courtyard provides light and ventilation to all adjoining spaces which rarely require any form of artificial cooling. Skylights over the stairway and *mittam* accentuate the volume of these spaces with a warm glow throughout the day.

The *mittam* seating area The entry court leads to this zone where traditional seating under a high, skylit volume creates an informal gathering space while connecting to the various parts of the house

Living area on one side of the courtyard Sun-dried mud blocks and terracotta flooring root the house to the locale. An eclectic mix of furniture fills this area

Architecture in India since 1990 | Alternate Practice

folio 7
OUR NATIVE VILLAGE ECO RESORT, Bengaluru

Martin Lafferiere at Chitra Vishwanath Architects

Located in Hessargatta, on the outskirts of Bengaluru, this resort demonstrates several sustainable solutions while promoting eco tourism in the hospitality sector. Solar energy, rainwater harvesting and biogas utilisation are the major components which drive key functions in the resort. These, coupled with traditional building materials and techniques utilising local skills, further propel the idea of a sustainable method of building. The clay dug out for the foundations was utilised to make bricks in a carefully calibrated process. While all guest rooms are naturally cooled, renewable power from the windmill and the solar panels accounts for seventy-five to eighty per cent of the energy for the rooms. All requirements for water are met by harvesting rainwater while recycled grey water from service areas is fed into the gardens, ensuring that they are lush through the year. Organic farming and a biogas plant on site ensure that kitchen operations also contribute to this model of energy sustainability.

View of the resort campus
Set in a suburban location, the resort is organised around a large pond with a reed bed that is linked to the water-purification system.
A colonnaded verandah skirts all enclosed functional areas, while sloping thatched roofs add to the bucolic charm of the buildings

Architecture in India since 1990 | Alternate Practice

Compound of each traditional *bhunga* suite Wattle-and-daub walls with thatched conical roofs characterise this accommodation group, where a curved adobe platform forms the base of the circular, mud-hut *bhunga* dwelling unit

Site plan of the tourism centre The centre weaves itself within an existing traditional Banni community in Hodka village by responding to the settlement-planning principles of the region. Clusters of circular *bhungas* and tents dominate the landscape, and are connected by open courts and plazas

Sunken library space The sunken ground is surrounded by continuous, amoeboid seating platforms in lime plaster for an informal reading space that adjoins the reception and dining area

folio 8
SHAAM-E-SARHAD VILLAGE RESORT, Hodka

Hunnar Shala

Located near the Rann of Kutch, this project was sponsored by the Government of Gujarat in collaboration with the NGO, Kutch Mahila Vikas Sangathan. Seen as an experiment with endogenous tourism, it was built and operated by the village community of Hodka in Banni. Envisaged with a view to the local community not only becoming a partner and deriving benefits, but also being empowered to interpret their own culture, Shaam-e-Sarhad is an organic cluster of *bhungas*, traditional huts of the region, and tents to be used as individual tourist accommodation. These are connected by a central open space used for activities like music performances and gatherings. The process of design and construction was undertaken in partnership with artisans from the village, in coordination with the Hunnar Shala Foundation. For the tourist facilities local building technologies like adobe, wattle-and-daub walls, thatched roofs with wooden substructures, and mud plaster have been utilised. Artisanal skills such as wood carving and the use of lacquer finishes, lime plaster, locally woven textiles and mural paintings are used for furniture and other interior elements.

Architecture in India since 1990 | Alternate Practice

Plaza fronting the tent accomodation Low seating platforms lead to the tent accommodations that are grouped near the *bhunga* suites

***Bhunga* clusters** Echoing the spirit of the Banni village, an honest approach to materials and construction methods allows this effort at endogenous tourism to move beyond a mere visitor facility

Walkway leading to the reception area High embankments on either side create an arrival path into the reception area, and, further on, to the dining pavilions

Architecture in India since 1990 | Alternate Practice

Wall art reflecting the local culture Lime-plastered walls are embellished by the local residents in mud and mirror to represent traditional Kutchhi clothing, which is renowned for its mirror work and embroidery

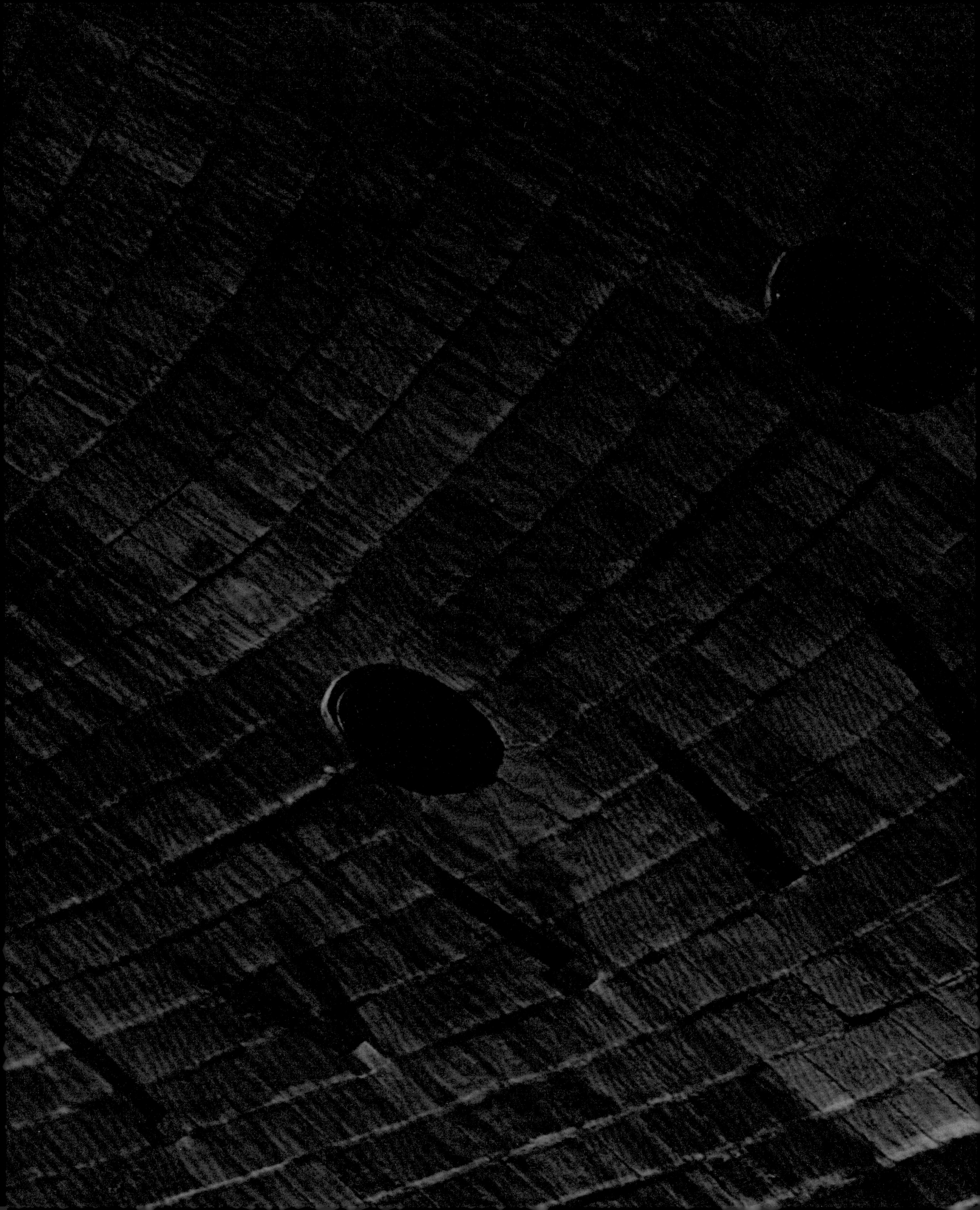

Counter Modernism
Resurfacing of the Ancient

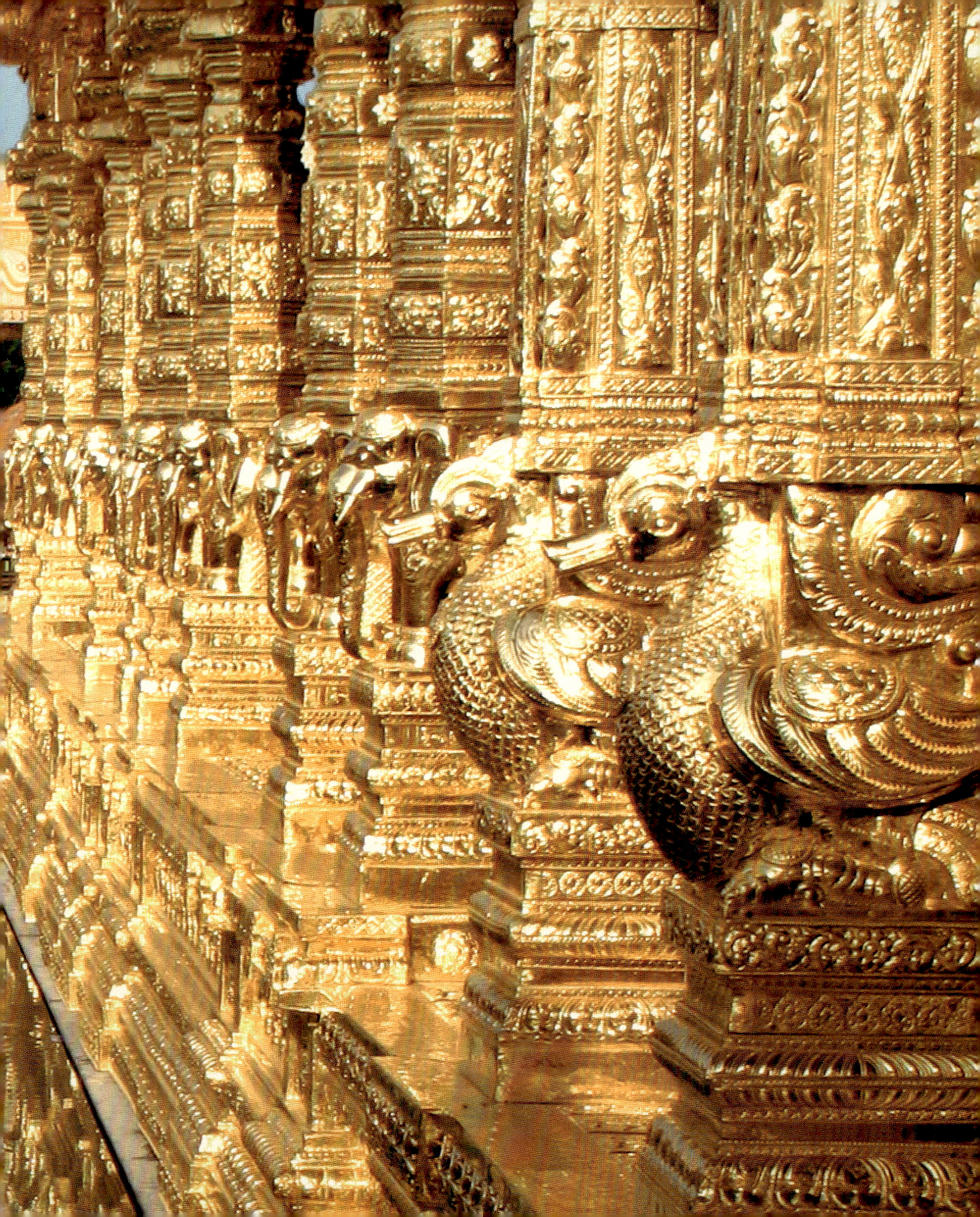

The demolition of the Babri Masjid, the Mosque of Babur, on Ramkot Hill (Rama's fort) in Ayodhya in 1992, marked a significant moment for contemporary India in relation to the powerful ancient symbolism that was embedded in the architecture of the country. The mosque was destroyed when a political rally developed into a riot involving 150,000 people. More than 2,000 people were killed in ensuing riots in major cities, including Mumbai and Delhi. India had only just signalled significant policy shifts towards economic liberalisation (accelerated by the information technology boom) when, with the destruction of the mosque, an old religious battle re-emerged. The demolition of the Babri Masjid was in fact emblematic of a broader condition in contemporary India: the resurfacing of the ancient.

The India of today faces a growing phenomenon perpetuating the reappearance of ancient practices in numerous temples and an entire range of institutional buildings being constructed across the country. In addition to constituting clear strains of resistance to modernity, these trends are symbolic of the collision course that religious chauvinism is on with the integrative mechanisms of globalisation. Many religious buildings are powered by capital from the Indian diaspora, which frequently places nationalism at the centre of its agenda, blurring the lines between religion, politics and ungrounded or misplaced nostalgia. Furthermore, with globalisation, communities, especially marginalised ones, have become increasingly concerned about threats to their identities as well as to their autonomy. This phenomenon questions the very foundation of the nation state and its time-tested capacity to absorb influences from the wider world in constructing, enriching and perpetuating its own identity. In addition to religion-driven fundamentalism and the resurrection of religious architecture, the quest for greater economic mobility has also triggered a resurgent interest in ancient treatises, with India's industrialist and business community seeking refuge in the security of ancient 'props'; in such a context, pre-industrial—even primitive—images and practices are confidently labelled as being integral to regional identity. The resurrection of the Vedic principles of the Vastu Shastra, or the art of building, has swept India via a new set of building practitioners who interpret designs from these rules, and audit and sanctify a large proportion of the new buildings in India.

Details of the gold plated columns at the **Sripuram Golden Temple** (*opposite*) by Sri Sakthi Amma

Babri Masjid (*right*) Demolition of this mosque in 1992, and the ensuing political turmoil in the country, was a turning point in the resurgence of religious architecture with a vigour that was seen across the country in the ensuing years

Architecture in India since 1990 | Counter Modernism

Anandi Ma Temple (*left, top and centre*) by Ashok D Desai Architects. Strongly adhering to rich religious symbolism and forms, several new temples dot the Indian countryside. These employ ancient tenets of temple building and adapt them for contemporary building practices

Vipassana International Academy (*right top*) headed by SN Goenka. Alternative forms of awakening have brought in newer ideas of spiritual practice through meditative and contemplative spaces

Sripuram Golden Temple (*left and right bottom*) by Sri Sakthi Amma. In keeping with South India's penchant for monumental temple building, a semi-covered star-shaped path, representing divine energy on the Earth with twelve 'auspicious' vertices akin to the sacred *Srichakra*, forms the primary circulation of this gold-covered temple

This approach to architectural production, founded on re-manifesting ancient practices, is visible in many forms. The first and most evident examples are the religious buildings built by master craftsmen (often a hereditary occupation) employing ancient imagery as a natural expression of the growing interest in the spiritual as well as the fundamentalism coinciding with the globalisation process. Some celebrated examples of this phenomenon are the Oneness Temple in Andhra Pradesh (2008) conceptualised by Amma Bhagwana; the Anandi Ma Temple in Nikora in Gujarat (2006); the Radhasoami Samadh Dayalbagh in Agra (ongoing), built to rival the Taj Mahal in scale; the Vipassana International Academy in Igatpuri (1979-94); the Sripuram Golden Temple (2007) by Sri Sakthi Amma; the ISKCON Sri Radha Krishna-Chandra Temple in Bengaluru (2007) by Sri Madhu Pandit Dasa, Sri Jagat Chandra Dasa and Smt Bhakti Lata Devi Dasi; the Akshardham temples in Delhi (2005) and Gandhinagar (1992) by Bochasanwasi Shri Akshar Purushottam Swaminarayan Sanstha; Shri Swaminarayan temple in Bhuj (2010) by BAPS

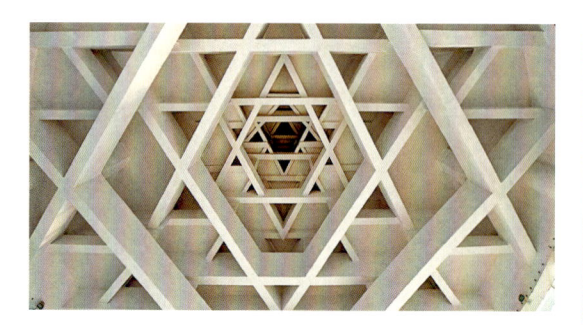

Sri Mayapur Vedic Temple and Planetarium (*left, top and bottom*) by Adam Hardy and Madhu Pandit Dasa. Projected to be the tallest Hindu temple on earth, this campus at the ISKCON headquarters at Mayapur is an eclectic interpretation of ancient Nagara (northern) and Kalinga (of Orissa) Hindu temple design, while also housing extensive gallery facilities

Akshardham Temple (*right top*) by BAPS Swaminarayan Sanstha. The internationally prolific Swaminarayan sect is famous for its organised and expansive temple-building infrastructure, based in Gujarat and Rajasthan, which caters to planning, crafting, shipping and assembly of various parts on and off site and across continents

Shri Swaminarayan Mandir (*right, centre and bottom*) by BAPS Swaminarayan Sanstha. This recently inaugurated temple in arid Kutch is another ambitious expression of the Swaminarayan sect, dominating the landscape through its high plinth and generous use of white marble, intricately carved and assembled on site

Swaminarayan Sanstha; and the Sri Mayapur Vedic Temple and Planetarium in West Bengal (ongoing), by Adam Hardy and Madhu Pandit Dasa, where plans are underway to build the largest temple in the world. In addition, there exist, or are being built, hundreds of smaller temples across urban and rural India which exemplify the fervour with which this counter-modernity is asserting itself on the landscape. Mosques and gurdwaras are also being built, albeit in smaller numbers. The Dadamiyan Mosque in Ahmedabad (2002), built by a trained architect Hiren Patel, is a case in point, and has become emblematic of the political agencies at play in facilitating such construction in zones fraught with religious tensions.

In other cases, like the Akshardham complex in Delhi, antiquity is mined in more literal ways. Perhaps the largest contemporary Hindu temple complex in the world, Akshardham has a footprint of 8,634 sq m. The temple is 96m wide, 108m long and 43m tall and is hand carved in marble and pink sandstone, constructed using ancient techniques of stacking stone. Steel is not used in the building to reinforce or span structural members; rather, more traditional ways of supporting roofs through interlocking and stone corbelling are employed. In order to build the Akshardham complex, workshops were set up in Pindvara and Sikandra in Rajasthan and the numerous surrounding villages where traditional craftspeople could be sourced. Preliminary shaping of the stone for the building was done by machine, with final polishing and sculpting carried out by hand. Complex computer programs tracked the trucks carrying the stone to the building site, where 4,000 volunteers carried out the work, thereby creating an unusual mix of ancient and modern management and execution techniques. The design incorporates 234 intricately carved pillars and nine ornate domes, all resting on a plinth which is used as an instrument for narration. It contains 20,000 hand-carved sculptures depicting elephants and the spectrum of India's great sadhus, devotees and teachers. In addition to this integrated sculpture, the monument contains a series of dioramic exhibitions that capture Vedic life and culture.

The politics of representation in the case of the Akshardham complex are multifaceted. Interestingly, in the official literature on Akshardham the word 'temple' is not used to describe the complex. Instead, it is referred to as a 'monument'. This neutralising of religious affiliation has occurred in reform and nationalistic movements in the nineteenth and twentieth centuries. The Arya Samaj, for example, unequivocally condemned practices such as polytheism, iconolatry, animal sacrifice, ancestor worship, pilgrimage, priest-craft, the belief in avatars or incarnations of God, the hereditary caste system, untouchability and child marriage on the grounds that all these lacked Vedic sanction. Such movements were more interested in the idea of the culture of Hinduism than the religion per se; as such, the preoccupation with representing Vedic culture and the rich depiction of the personalities and events that make up this meta-narrative is not surprising as it de-emphasises ritual. Consequently, Akshardham emphasises decorative representation and imagery that alludes to the richness and deep traditions in Vedic culture.

As more segments of civil society—politicians and even some state governments—become active as guardians, and, by extension, interpreters, of Hinduism, Buddhism or Islam, the emergence of the representation of multiple narratives and their aesthetic reinterpretation becomes more visible. The renowned Indologist Dr Jyotindra Jain explains this by situating it in a historical context: "Processes of religious transformation, reconstruction, reinterpretation, revival and resurgence have been common in Hinduism in the past and are active even today. Nevertheless, when these processes are prompted by political objectives, they follow different trajectories."

Numerous such examples of technological and representational trajectories are visible given the surge of temple building in the country facilitated by diverse groups of civil societies, political agendas and sometimes the state. The Vallabh Smarak Temple in New Delhi (1995), by Chandulal P. Trivedi, is a Jain temple that demonstrates complex structural engineering techniques executed by the *sompuras* (traditional master craftsmen) in compliance with the formal norms of representation. Others, such as the Maidevi Temple in Nadiad in Gujarat (2000), inspired by the Meenakshi Temple in Madurai project a new visual palette

Nrityagram Fired Temple (*this page*) by Ray Meeker. The use of 'fired building' technology by the architect, as an experiment in pursuit of eco-friendly construction approaches, was adopted in this temple at Nrityagram Dance Village

which when rendered in materials such as reinforced cement concrete, result in images amounting to kitsch. Another such example of pastiche is the Chattarpur Temple complex in New Delhi by Swami Nagpal Maharaj (1998), which is undisciplined in its disposition and distorts and combines the ancient images through superficial treatment in a manner that renders the sources unrecognisable.

Perhaps a more significant example of the demonstration of ancient imagery using modern techniques is the Maitreya project in Kushinagar in Uttar Pradesh, by Aros Ltd of London (2004-present). This 152m tall bronze statue of the Buddha (more than three times the height of the Statue of Liberty!), together with a meditation centre, hospital, museum and international university, stands adjacent to a hotel complex and an amusement park. The project straddles a thin line between a serious dedication to Lord Buddha and his teachings and a slipping into the realm of entertainment, amusement and tourism. In any case, it evokes ancient images to establish its presence as well as legitimise the spectacle through religion. The Maitreya Buddha project, while founded on the religious resurrection of Buddhism, is in this case driven by a global demand to celebrate Buddhism in India. Supported by the Maitreya Foundation of Japan, the edifice was originally intended to be constructed in Bodhgaya in Bihar, where the Buddha attained enlightenment, but was moved to its present site after the local farmers protested over land-acquisition issues. Clearly the farmers saw this not as a religious gesture, but one of commercial enterprise.

On a completely different scale is the tiny shrine designed and built in Nrityagram near Bengaluru by the American ceramicist Ray Meeker in homage to the dancer Protima Bedi. Here, the references to iconography, form and disposition are purely aesthetic, yet the temple is innovative in that it employs completely new material and techniques for its fabrication. Designed and built at Meeker's studio in Puducherry, the building was conceived as a hollow lingam with a series of lingam forms stacked up to create its final form. The temple was constructed using a technique that Meeker had honed over the previous decades: casting the structure in mud, and then firing it by treating the final building itself as a kiln. Originally designed to be a Shiva temple, and dedicated to 'space', the form was adjusted to incorporate sculpted images of Bedi after her sudden death in 1998, becoming a memorial to her contributions to dance and her establishment of the dance academy in Nrityagram. Set in a verdant environment, this small building does not visually overpower, but yet exerts its presence. More importantly, it is also emblematic of another application of the resurrection of ancient imagery: memorialisation.

Another important and more recent example of this attempt at a contemporary interpretation of ancient imagery is the Shiva Temple by Sameep Padora in Wadeshwar in Maharashtra (2009). Here, a traditional

Isha Yoga Ashram by Sadhguru Jaggi Vasudev. As institutionalised campuses under a spiritual teacher, such centres of well-being are gaining popularity through the country, as places where ancient philosophy, yoga and architecture converge

form is reinterpreted in contemporary materials with modern sensibilities. Designed and built by devotees donating their time to the temple trust, the processes of construction, the rituals for sanctifying the site, its essential components and basic form all comply with the traditional norms. However, its construction in a minimalist aesthetic makes it a significant piece of contemporary architecture.

Aside from these religious resurrections, another emergent force resurfacing with renewed vigour is that of spiritualism and a sort of faith-based paradigm which is also fast becoming a political force. Baba Ramdev and a host of such spiritual practitioners have in the new India mobilised media and communications to spread their faith and following—in the process emerging as a significant 'third force' in the political landscape of contemporary India. These movements have thus far not found significant architectural expression, but are evidenced in more moderate forms of faith-driven structures in different parts of the country. Examples are the Isha Yoga Ashram by Sahdguru Jaggi Vasudev in Coimbatore (2003) and Sri Sri Ravi Shankar's Art of Living Ashram in Bengaluru (2003), which emphasises well-being as its core focus and has developed a powerful following around the world. Other, and perhaps more significant and elegant examples of this are the Baha'i House of Worship (1976-86) in New Delhi designed by Fariborz Sahba, the Matri Mandir in Auroville (2008) designed by Roger Anger. While the first two projects took over a decade to build and were initiated before India's liberalisation policies were implemented, they were emblematic of the power of faith and its affirmation in the physical form. The Matri Mandir was built at the behest of the Mother, the spiritual leader of the faith inspired by the teachings of Sri Aurobindo. It was the result of a vision that she had which moved her to create an inner chamber for meditation at the centre of Auroville, the new community that she instituted near Puducherry. The Matri Mandir took thirty-seven years to build, from the laying of its foundation stone at sunrise on 21 February 1971 (the Mother's ninety-third birthday) to its completion in May 2008. It is surrounded by twelve pedestals in the form of a huge sphere. The central dome

Visalakshi Mantapa Art of Living Ashram (*left*) by Sri Sri Ravi Shankar. An immensely popular movement in India based on well-being, the lotus-inspired Visalakshi Mantapa forms the centre point of their Bengaluru headquarters

Bahai' House of Worship in Delhi (*right*) by Fariborz Sahba. Dating from India's pre-liberalised economic era, this early project heralded a new era and architecture for faith-based practices, with its rigorous approach to the form, geometry and symbolism embedded within. The construction techniques were sophisticated, employing computer-generated cutting techniques to shape the marble cladding and the complex geometries of the structural system

is covered by golden discs that reflect sunlight, giving the structure its characteristic radiance. Inside this central dome is the inner chamber, a meditation hall that contains the largest optically perfect glass globe in the world. The Matri Mandir and its surrounding gardens are referred to as the Peace Area, and are an evolving landscape for meditation. An absolutely stunning piece of architectural conception, the Matri Mandir is devoid of any explicit symbolism but contains deep symbolic and traditional values embedded in its articulation. These values relate to the broader goals of universal peace and harmony, and are free from any myopic political agendas. The Matri Mandir embodies the broader aspirations of the Auroville community; although utopian in its motivation, it has demonstrated the moderation and autonomy with which faith-based practice can also find rich architectural expression.

A significant example of this faith-based architectural expression is the Global Vipassana Pagoda that was built to operate as an icon in Mumbai's landscape. Built by Shah and Dumasia Architectural Consultancy in 2008, and costing approximately US$ 70 million, it rises 100m into the air and covers an area of 6,300 sq m. The building was designed and supervised by Chandubhai Sompura, a traditional temple architect from the familial tradition of master craftsmen, and was constructed using traditional techniques of self-supporting interlocking stones, thereby avoiding any form of shuttering. Rather than being called a religion, Vipassana could more aptly be described as a practice. Founded on a technique of meditation (through controlled breathing) that was invented and evolved by the Buddha, it had long disappeared (but

Architecture in India since 1990 | Counter Modernism

Amarnath Cave Shrine (original) (*left top*). Drawing innumerable pilgrims and devotees each year through difficult terrain, trying weather conditions and security lapses, the Amarnath caves retain their sanctity while also allowing the decentralising of their presence via replicas in different locations in the country

Amarnath Cave Shrine (replica) (*right top*) by Bakul Sompura. Initiated by the survivors of a terrorist attack on the original site, Ahmedabad was the first place to where an Amarnath cave replica was created within city limits, to counter the increasing number of pilgrims yearly

Palitana Temples (*left, centre and bottom*) by generations of the Sompura family. Repair and renovation of the group of temples within this major Jain pilgrimage centre was conducted by the Sompuras, a family of master craftsmen with a long history of traditional temple building in Gujarat and Rajasthan

survived in Burma), and has now found its way back to India and some other parts of the world. Although this particular building has little to do with religious fundamentalism, the resurgent popularity of the ancient Vipassana meditation techniques can be attributed to its ability to provide respite from the onslaught of globalisation, economic frenzy and stress and their inherent disruptions. In the Vipassana Pagoda, patrons of this faith have dug deep into the past, situating the building intelligently and with a sensibility that embraces the present, thereby creating a poetic expression for contemporary India.

With a liberalising economy in contemporary India, faith is on the rise. Religion and faith are perceived as stabilising forces in a landscape saturated with the competitive spirit; as the will to survive and succeed becomes increasingly intense, so does faith. *The Times of India* in its issue of 23 January 2009 reported statistics that donations to temple trusts have increased by twenty-five per cent since the 1990s. In addition to the construction of new temples, the restoration, expansion and replication of temples have also experienced an increased fervour. The 2009 announcement by the Tirupathi Temple Trust that it intended to commission Tirumala Tirupati Devasthanam for the construction of an exact replica of the original Tirupathi Temple (Andhra Pradesh) in Chennai (on the East Coast Road, or the 'IT corridor') on a 4-hectare property is an interesting idea. The notion that 'darshan' (or seeing the divine) could be detached from its sacred location in an effort to decentralise the crowds that throng this sacred site points to the commercialisation of faith. The present waiting list for darshan at the original site of the Tirupathi Temple is three years, and for some special events it runs into decades. Similarly, Bakul Sompura's replicas in Gujarat of the Amarnath Cave shrine (2001) and Vaishno Devi Temple (2002), the originals of which are both in Jammu and Kashmir, are examples of the commodification of worship. This decentralisation of worship and the resulting construction of replicas are also a consequence of the concern for the safety of visitors that surrounds these sites due to the massive increase in their numbers. From 1998 to 2008 more people died in stampedes at sacred sites than perished in terrorist attacks in India (875 killed in stampedes at sacred sites as against 767 killed in terrorist attacks). It is with this very safety in mind that the replica of the Amarnath shrine in Gujarat

Architecture in India since 1990 | Counter Modernism

Temple Yard (*this page*). Scaled drawings are translated into full-size stencils for all repetitive elements and ornamentation. Using rather rudimentary tools to shape and carve the stone blocks, large mock-ups are erected at workshops in southern India. These mock-ups are often transferred onto the workshop walls to map the basic grid before the stone blocks are cut and shaped to size. This precision and quasi-factory-line production process leads to each section of a designated temple form, being numbered and packed in cartons, sometimes for long-distance transportation

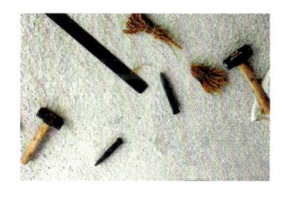

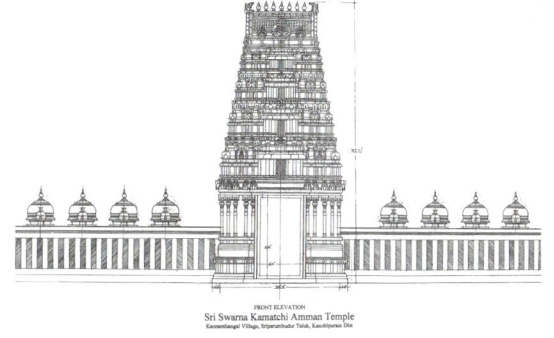

was initiated by survivors of the terrorist attacks on the original shrine in Amarnath, in 2001.

This entire range of religious and faith-inspired buildings is being driven by practitioners who are not on the radar of architects in the mainstream of practice. The Sompuras are one such family or guild of master craftsmen engaged in building numerous new temples in contemporary India. Brahmins by birth, the Sompuras originated in Gujarat and were earlier known as acharyas (or teachers). They derived the present-day nomenclature from the Somnath Temple, which they helped rebuild following periodic onslaughts from the marauding armies of Mahmud Ghaznavi and others. Approximately 200 families of these temple architects still exist in Gujarat. After undertaking the construction of the temple in Somnath, the succeeding generations moved on from there when Gujarat's rulers set up new capital cities—namely Champaner, Patan and Palitana—and built more temples like the original one.

The Sompuras traditionally follow strict rituals before commencing work on a temple. The plot is first divided into eighty-one equal squares, followed by excavation for *bhoomishuddhi* (purifying the land), during which strands of hair, bone and iron pieces in the excavated earth are removed. As a symbolic gesture a time capsule containing precious metals and stones is immediately embedded in the ground, for, in future should the temple become derelict and the devotees unable to undertake reconstruction or renovation,

259

Sree Venkateshwara Temple in Oldbury, England (*top and centre*) by Adam Hardy. The resurrection of this ancient Indian temple imagery has proliferated across continents, especially in the UK and the US where multiple religious sects build for the Indian diaspora

Shree Krishna Temple in West Bromwich, England (*bottom*) also by Adam Hardy. Reconnecting with the past, these temples use an eclectic architecture that staunchly adheres to ancient treatises of temple building but sometimes combines the components in new ways

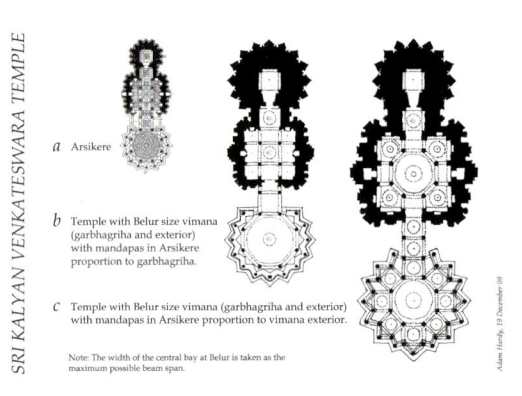

this treasure would be available to them. Similarly, they still employ traditional methods for assembling the structure using an interlocking system of stones in which each piece of a pillar is carved separately, the 'male' stone is locked within the 'female' stone, to create a garland-like structure. Similar guilds exist in Rajasthan, Andhra Pradesh and Tamil Nadu, where numerous yards are being set up for the production of components for temple buildings. Drawings are all produced at a 1:1 scale, and often-repetitive elements are mocked up to create stencils.

A more formalised version of this institutional framework exists in Mahabalipuram in Tamil Naidu, where the College of Architecture and Sculpture headed by Ganapati Sthapati (from 1961 to the early 1990s) offers formalised education for the traditional craft of building. The three-year program includes courses in music, dance, philosophy, Sanskrit literature, art aesthetics and the history of Hindu art and architecture as well as temple conservation. Fifteen students a year graduate from the institution, and they usually going on to join the studios of other *sthapatis* or master craftsmen. The college is founded on the belief that the traditional texts of Vastu Shastra addressed the question of creating a harmonious relationship and spatial expression to unify man and God. This is a tradition in which the spiritual aspect of the art must take precedence, free of all political preoccupations and constraints. Sthapati and his followers believe that India is going through a second colonisation that is more complete than the first one under British rule, as this time, with globalisation, both the Indian body and mind are colonised. These followers react to modernity and make the case for a search of ancient truths. The proponents of this approach clearly see themselves as the custodians of the classical traditions of Indian temple architecture; this ownership implies that they safeguard tradition and that their work adheres literally to classical traditional forms and models of practice.

The growing Indian diaspora has also fuelled interest in, and a demand for, the ancient imagery of temples. The temple-building yards in India have a booming business exporting temple components for consumption in the UK, the US and some parts of Europe as well Singapore, Malaysia, Japan, Fiji, Mauritius and Canada, where more historically the Indian diaspora has historically been practising its faith. The Ganesh temples in New York; the Bochasanwasi Shri Akshar Purushottam Swaminarayan Temple in Houston, Texas; and others in Pittsburgh, Nashville, Poughkeepsie, Detroit and Chicago are some examples of the resurrection of these ancient images at a rather rapid rate—even outside India. Similarly, the Swaminarayan Temple in Neasden, England (1995) and the Shree Venkateswara Temple near Oldbury (2001) as well as the Shree Krishna Temple in West Bromwich (2010) all emulate these principles. In fact, the temples in England were designed by Dr Adam Hardy at De Montfort University, where he established the Practice, Research and Advancement in South Asian Design and Architecture

(PRASADA) Institute. In the words of the eminent architectural scholar and critic AG Krishna Menon, "Hardy's designs are purposefully eclectic because they derive from formal academic analysis of the principles of temple design, and he uses modern construction materials and technology in his projects. His works are perhaps the most innovative in the formal context of contemporary temple building, though it is another matter that the final outcome cannot be distinguished from the pastiche he so assiduously tries to avoid. His work along with the works of the sompuras and Ganapati Sthapati are serious attempts to establish links with the past and constitute a major trend in religious architecture."

In another vein is the emergence of the ancient with a new fervour through events or enacted moments that produce a temporary manifestation of architectural form. Although these do not leave a permanent memory on the landscape as does conventional architecture, it informs, moulds and creates the representation of a new popular culture. In fact, the increased popularity of festivals has emerged as pageants of contemporary India and their presence on the everyday landscape pervade and dominate the popular visual culture of Indian cities. They all produce a temporary architecture and a re-articulation of space that have a profound meaning. The cities and villages involved are reconfigured temporarily to support the event. Tents and barricades redefine public and private spaces, as they are reconfigured for the festival—albeit only temporarily. The burning of large effigies of Ravan on Dussera or the Jagannath Rath Yatra in Puri, in which life-size replicas of the temples are taken out in processions that weave through the city, are both examples of these architectural extravaganzas. Similarly, the Tazia processions during Muharram in Surat and Ahmedabad, the Ganesh festival in Mumbai and the Durga Puja in Kolkata have in recent years configured urban spaces in substantial ways in the cities in which they are performed, temporarily creating evocative visual juxtapositions with the permanent city and its architecture.

Large gatherings such as the Kumbh Mela as well as those in Tarnetar, Pushkar and other locations in Hindu geography have all had an influence on the resurrection of ancient imagery and rituals as spectacles in the contemporary Indian imagination. The recent surge in the populace engaging with the Kumbh Mela is a key example. Today, more than a hundred million people participate in the ritual at multiple locations across the country. The Festival is celebrated every four years along the Ganges: the Ardh (half) Kumbh Mela occurs every six years in Haridwar and Allahabad (formerly Prayag), and the Purna (complete) Kumbh takes place every twelve years in Allahabad, Haridwar, Ujjain and Nasik. The Maha (great) Kumbh Mela that comes after twelve Purna Kumbh Melas (every 144 years) is held in Allahabad.

Resurfacing of the Ancient
Concurrent building developments often create strong juxtapositions within the urban landscape

Architecture in India since 1990 | Counter Modernism

Rath Yatra (left). Indian festivals and other regional celebrations create an urban spectacle that powerfully contests the built landscape, and witnesses a participation and fervour that built environments seldom command

Tazia (right, top and bottom). Envisaged as disposable sacred art, these mobile replicas of tombs are carried around the city in a grand procession, through narrow alleys and main thoroughfares. Often competing with the surrounding built form, these heavily embellished structures dominate the city's visual character during Muharram

Ganesh Festival (opposite, top and centre rows). The temporary architecture created through pandals and processional structures for the Ganesh festival reflects the coexistence of a popular culture and ethos overlaid upon the splendor of the static city. Large Ganesh idols and decorated tableaus with rich narratives move through the city's streets before their final immersion, while neighbourhoods are temporarily transformed through lights, installations and colourful enclosures

Kumbh Mela (opposite, bottom row). As the most significant pilgrimage for Hindus, the periodic occurrence of the Kumbh Mela across designated locations witnesses crowds and functions that completely reconfigure each venue. The formation of a temporary 'citadel', with multi-tiered planning and management at work, makes the complexity of this networked system difficult to understand and experience

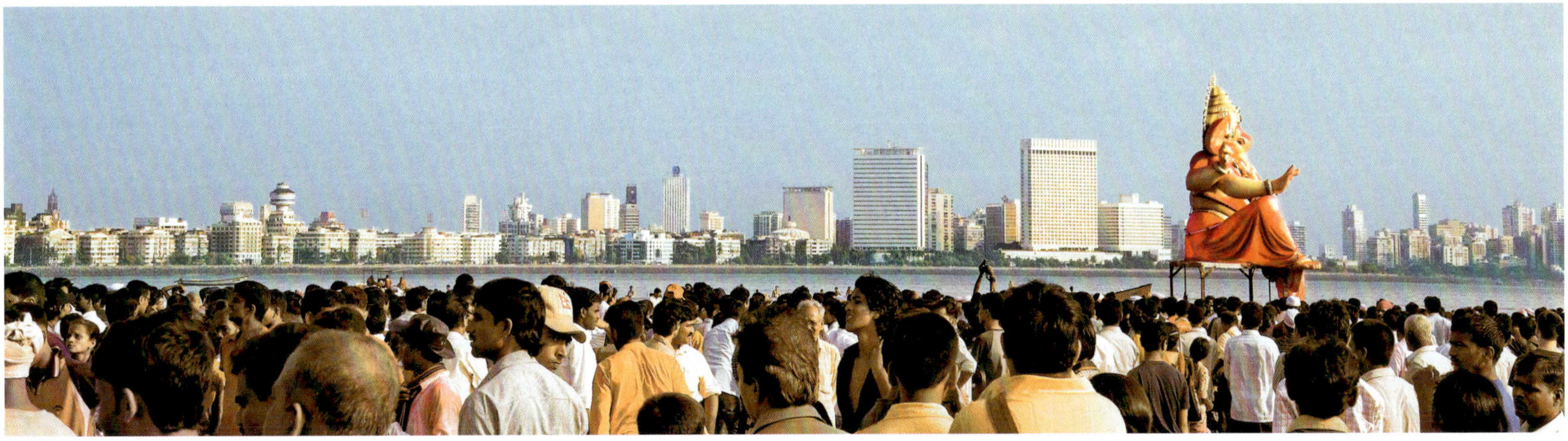

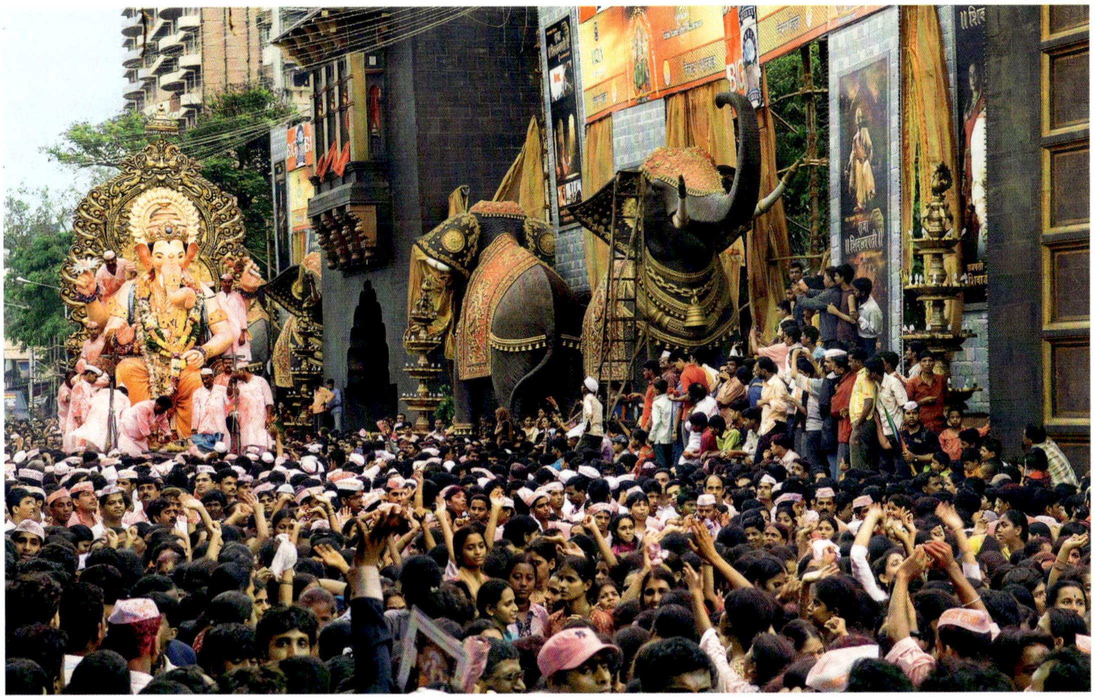

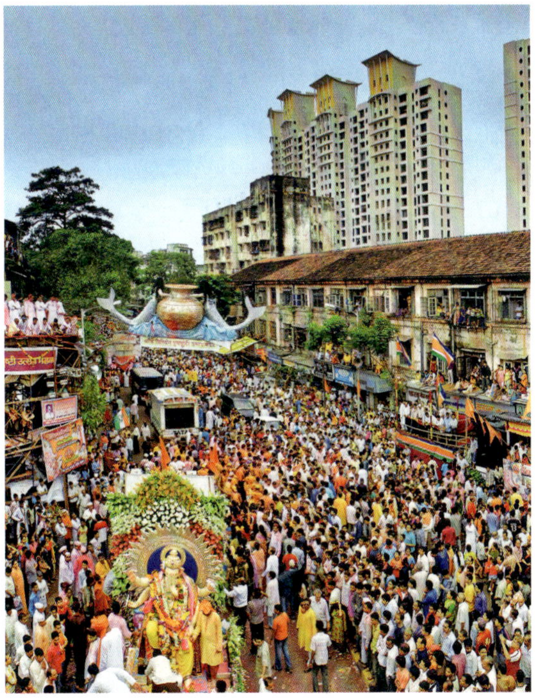

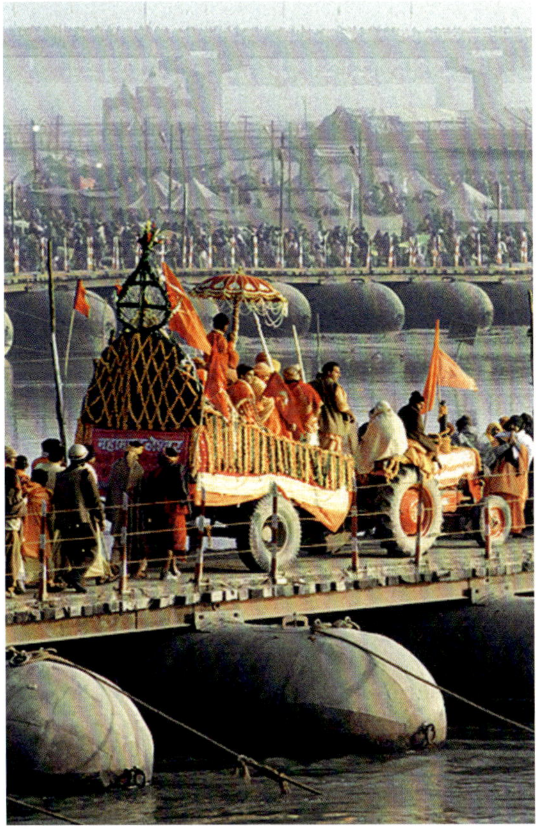

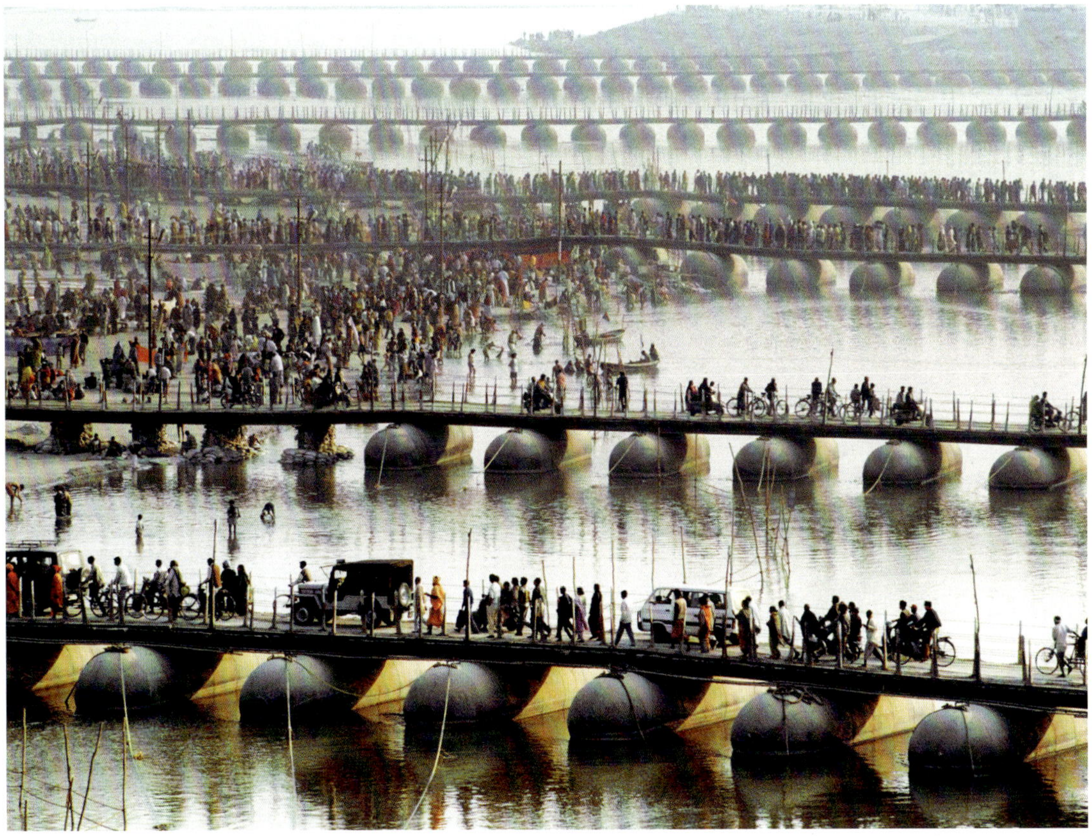

The last Maha Kumbh Mela, held in 2001, was attended by nearly sixty million people, making it the largest gathering anywhere in the world in recorded history. The highlight of the festival is the ritual of bathing along the banks of the river in whichever town it is being held. Other activities include religious discussions; devotional singing; mass feedings of holy men, women and the poor; and religious assemblies, at which doctrines are debated and standardised. Considered the most sacred of all pilgrimages, the Kumbh Mela, is attended by thousands of holy men and women. Sadhus are seen clad in saffron sheets with ash and powder dabbed on their skin according to the tenets of ancient traditions. Some, called *naga sanyasis*, may not wear any clothes—even in the most severe winter. An entire city is erected on a grid, with pontoon bridges to cross over rivers and access water. The settlement, which houses millions, is broken up into sectors for ease of administration and has a commissioner and police unit that monitors its smooth functioning. Both large and small tents, as well as enclosed courtyards defined by bamboo and cloth, and a host of temporary articulations of space create a wonderfully rich sense of impermanent occupation. This incredible faith-based gathering and ritual of cleansing in the holy waters is a "production" that is set up as an enacted event, leaving no trace of its built manifestation.

In the same way that temples are an expression of faith-based fundamentalism and often a political response to modernity and its variants in the global condition, festivals create a forum through which the fantasies of the subalterns are articulated and even organised into political action. In Mumbai, for example, the popularity and growth of the Ganesh festival have been phenomenal. During the festival, which occurs in August or September, numerous neighbourhoods transform temporarily through lights and decorations. New spaces are created to house the idol of Ganesh for ten days. A temporary architecture emerges that seems to expand the margins of the city for a short period of time for a new use. During the festival period, family, neighbourhood and city events mark the celebrations.

On the last day, large groups of people carry the idols in long processions to the sea, where they are ultimately immersed. Each procession carries a tableau, depicting the images of Lord Ganesh set in dioramas depicting current events of national as well as international interests thus mediating both local as well global concerns. This representation is not based on formal scriptures or predetermined rules; instead, human ingenuity breaches the boundaries between the local and the global, the historical and contemporary. These images convey the hybrid urgencies of metropolitan India. Neighbourhood processions weave through predetermined routes in the city, each vying with the other to showcase the intensity of its faith. Set against the backdrop of the static city where architecture is the primary spectacle the procession culminates in the immersion of the idol, bidding farewell amidst chants inviting Ganesh to resurrect his presence the following year. Immersion becomes a metaphor for the spectacle of the city. As the clay idol dissolves in the water of the bay, the festival comes to a close. There are no static or permanent mechanisms to encode the event. Here, the memory of the city is an 'enacted' process, a temporal moment as opposed to buildings that contain the public memory as a static or permanent entity, underscoring the fact that contemporary India's architecture is not homogeneous and cannot contain a single meaning. In the emergent landscape, meanings are not stable and spaces get consumed, reinterpreted and recycled. The ancient and contemporary consume each other to create new orchestrations of urban space.

This manifestation of the aspiration of the subalterns also takes on an interesting form in the way in which the architecture of statues is emerging in India, facilitated by identity politics. First it was the lame attempt by the Shiv Sena (a right-wing Hindu party) in Mumbai to consistently resurrect ideas about bigger and better statues of the warrior king Shivaji across the urban and rural landscape of Maharashtra. Recently, Mayawati the Chief Minister of Uttar Pradesh put forth a project to populate the state with statues of the great Indian leader BR Ambedkar (the chief architect of the Indian Constitution) as a permanent expression of political assertion. The movement for the emancipation of the Dalits (the lowest class in the Hindu caste system)

Mayawati statues by sculptors from Sukhuapada Village, Orissa. The institutionalising of memory and the appropriation of symbols through architectural representation is being practised with new fervour by political parties in the new, economically liberalised India

was inspired by Ambedkar and carried forward by Mayawati's political mentor Kanshi Ram. The difference between them was the path to this emancipation. While Ambedkar favoured empowerment of the Dalits by building their intellectual capacity, the others imagined them gaining a place in history by confronting the rich in a sort of class war. In fact, it was to avoid such a confrontation that Ambedkar urged the Dalits to embrace Buddhism, itself a reform movement of Hinduism that implicitly challenged the caste system. He saw this as an important step in achieving equity and moving India toward an economic democracy beyond the political one that the country had inherited. Ambedkar thus favoured education over memories and memorials. In contrast, Mayawati promoted and built hundreds of statues of Buddha, Ambedkar, her mentor Kanshi Ram and herself! The high point of this exercise was the creation of Ambedkar Park in Lucknow, an assemblage of more than 20,000 statues which betrays the ideals of Ambedkar, who was known to have rebuked his supporters for erecting statues.

The irrational scale and spectacle of these movements are potent symbols of a megalomaniacal attempt at reversing history, of striking back in an ancient battle and of signalling a shift in Dalit perceptions, as well as an attempt at reversing the ills of history and hundreds of years of prejudice. They are a symbolic retribution for past traumas—traumas so intense that they necessitate the expression of their retribution to be expressed in public spaces, parks, squares and streets as a gesture of their victims regaining their place and claiming the city both symbolically and physically. Mayawati turns this, just like the numerous festivals in India, into a spectacle—albeit a more enduring one. In this case the spectacle is aimed at leaving a permanent mark: institutionalising memory. It is a powerful statement of the resurfacing of ancient religious, political and social tensions and their manifestation on the contemporary built environment of India.

Another powerful manifestation of this counter-modernity takes a subtler, but perhaps more potent form: the invisible setting of rules that allude to a sacred or hidden order. The amazing resurrection of the belief in Vastu (the sacred rules of building) is a case in point. Much like feng shui (which is founded on the idea that the arrangements of landscapes and objects have a bearing on well-being), Vastu probably also had its roots in geomancy. Being subsequently codified in religion, the interpretation of its code lay with the upper classes, or Brahmins. Today, specialised practitioners hold this power of interpretation and have turned it into a full-blown practice. These practitioners engage in the design of hospitals, factories, hotels and offices as well as large homes. It is a practice in which locational attributes predetermine the layout of the building. Direction of entry and the location of sleeping areas, cooking areas, water bodies and of services such as generators or machinery like pumps—as well as the topography of the site and the building that sits on it—are imagined by these practitioners in abstract terms but in great detail. Often these codifications are verbally described with a supporting line diagram, stipulating quadrants rather than spatial proportions. It is a form of depiction that challenges the principles of Western spatial representation, upon which all architectural training in the country is founded. Its portrayal is invisibly embedded within

Architecture in India since 1990 | Counter Modernism

Ambedkar Park by Design Associates (detail). The blatant use of election symbols belonging to the political party that created the park indicate the emergence of architecture in the representation of power—wherein the resurfacing of ancient symbolism and politics are folded into each other

Vastu. Renewed faith in the tenets of Vastu, the sacred rules of building, often supersedes and predetermines decision making, often limiting the role of architects. Intensive practices and rules also determine the site selection and purification rituals in order to ensure the well-being of the land owner

the built form, making its presence subtle yet strong in the way it sometimes challenges more conventional spatial designations. Although Vastu's use and application are folded into, or camouflaged by, seemingly global forms and imagery, the rules and icons of the ancients are visible resistances to the universalising landscapes of global flows.

The increased interest in Vastu coincides rather accurately with the opening up of the Indian economy in the late 1980s and early 1990s—just when global flows were sweeping across the Indian landscape. Today, most middle- and higher-income families would follow the Vastu principles in the design of their habitat. Although this has no particular physical expression, Vastu is often limiting in what it does and does not permit. The practice of Vastu and its popularity is clearly bringing a new conservatism to the practice of architecture and the innovations of form—not necessarily challenging the emerging vocabulary and imagery of global identities, but setting some rules for its operation and thereby attempting to localise its spirit.

This space of the sacred and, more importantly, faith-based practice of architectural production is continuing to assert itself convincingly on the Indian landscape. The resurfacing of the ancient that has been co-opted by most faith-based practices challenges architects in India. The literal application of ancient imagery by practitioners not formally trained in the tenets of architectural education implicitly mocks the quest of the regionalist practice to consistently refer to the un-modern in order to localise their designs. References to ancient cities and buildings as points of departure or to the *vastu purush mandala* (sacred cosmic diagram) as a visual and sometimes legitimising device are inverted by these new and literal caricatures. Indian architect Romi Khosla refers to the props of these images as the paraphernalia of the ancient futurologists. Interestingly, this phenomenon is more evident in the resurrection of faith-based architecture among the Hindu and Islamic communities of India. Other faiths moderate their architecture with more critical explorations, such as the Vipassana Pagoda or the several examples of contemporary churches built by the Christian community. In the words of AG Krishna Menon, "in sum, these neo-traditional temples are pale imitations of ancient monuments, sitting anachronistically in a new cultural landscape, unable to emulate the spirit that spurred the past, and unwilling to come to terms with the forces fuelling the future. That they are still built in this day and age, in complete sincerity and reasonable verisimilitude, is perhaps the main element of cultural significance. It is indicative of a cultural continuity of a kind, which was wiped out in other societies with the onset of modernity. But the tragedy in architectural terms is that we have been unable to translate this valuable cultural resource into critical architecture. The blind worship of a known reality only represents resistance to change."

This conservatism is also, perhaps, what makes this approach and attitude so susceptible to being co-opted into the political manoeuvres of fundamentalism. All these practitioners of faith-based architecture are mindful of their own quest for authenticity, of a belief in an invisible and underlying order that is not part of the mainstream architectural discourse in India and of the sacred space in which many Indians spend a greater part of their lives. This is, after all, a nation where meetings and marriages are often set up according to astrological predictions and projections. The landscape of faith that facilitates this resurfacing of the ancient, with its many layers of mystic codification, is a fascinating architectural attitude particular, perhaps, to India. It is a phenomenon that cannot be ignored: a hybrid condition exerting a powerful presence in the emergent and highly pluralistic architectural landscape of contemporary India.

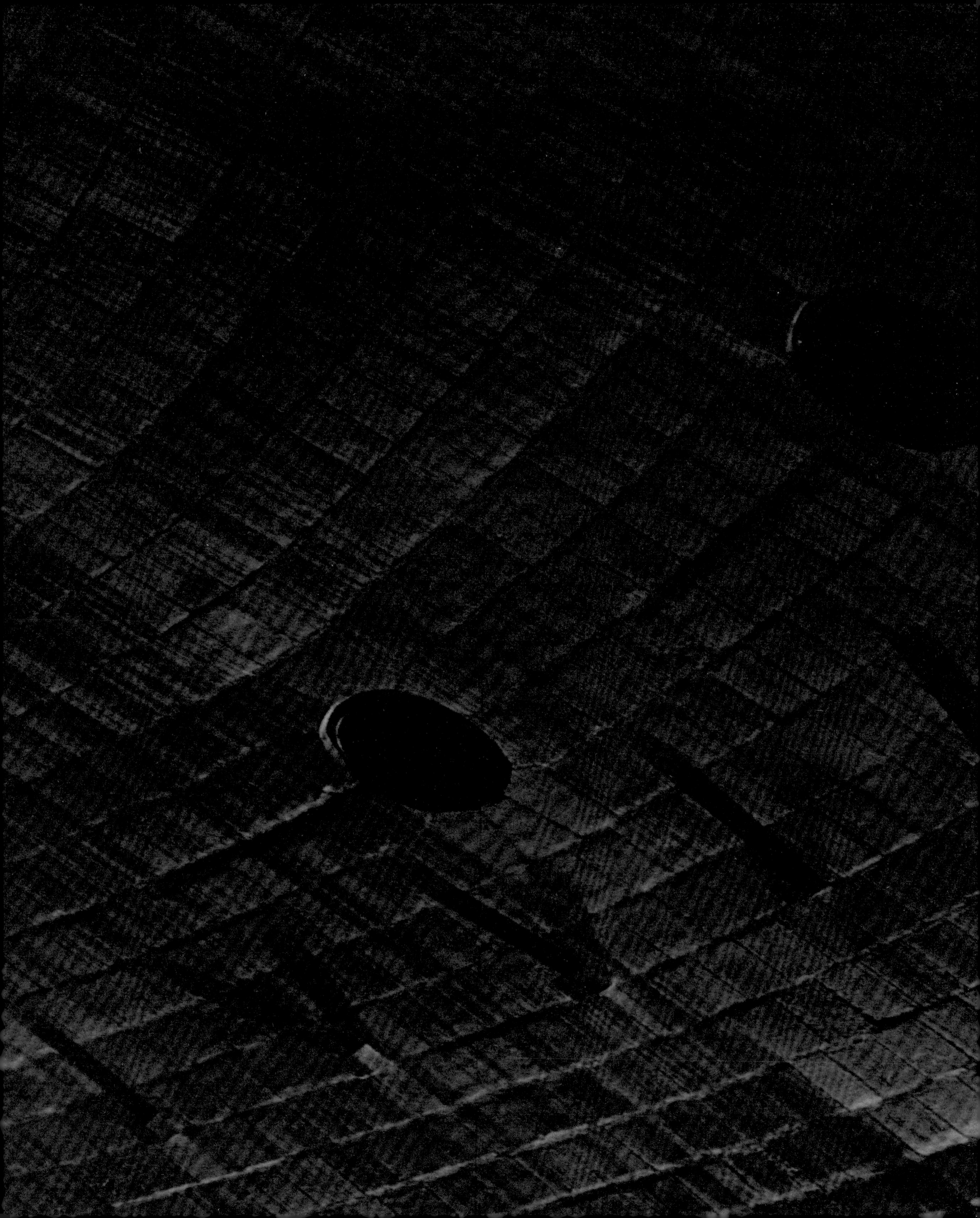

Folios

SWAMINARAYAN AKSHARDHAM TEMPLE	271
GLOBAL VIPASSANA PAGODA	275
ISKCON SRI RADHA KRISHNA-CHANDRA TEMPLE	278
ONENESS – HALL OF AWAKENING	283
MATRI MANDIR	287
DADAMIYAN MOSQUE	291
RADHASOAMI SAMADH	295
SHIVA TEMPLE	299

Architecture in India since 1990 | Counter Modernism

Detail of carved inner dome This marble ceiling with its supporting pillars in the main hall is an example of the intricate carvings that adorn the temple interior

Colonnade and steps leading down to the Narayana Sarovar Believed to contain holy waters from 151 rivers and lakes sanctified by Lord Swaminarayan, these sandstone pavilions and colonnade connect to the adjoining lake while providing a view of the main shrine

folio 1
SWAMINARAYAN AKSHARDHAM TEMPLE, New Delhi

Bochasanwasi Shri Akshar Purushottam Swaminarayan Sanstha

This temple is the prime focus of the Swaminarayan Akshardham Cultural Complex, occupying 42 hectares on the banks of the Yamuna in east Delhi. Tracing its origins to the life and teachings of Lord Swaminarayan (1781-1830), a Vaishnava saint from Gujarat and founder of the sect that bears his name, this temple surpasses the first Akshardham built in Gandhinagar. The 43m tall, nine-domed monument aims to instil a sense of pride and identity in devotees while deepening their connection with the ideals of the sect.

A team of eight sadhus formed the core group that designed, coordinated, managed and executed the project—even travelling overseas, including to Cambodia, to seek inspiration from ancient monuments for the domes, walls, plinths and sculptures. They supervised over 3,000 volunteers and 7,000 craftspeople, including drought-stricken farmers and tribal women, on site and in large workshops that were established in Pindwara and Sikandra in Rajasthan. The preliminary shaping was carried out on machines, and the detailed carving done by hand.

Architecture in India since 1990 | Counter Modernism

Exhibit at the Hall of Values
Featuring 15 dioramas through robotics, fibre optics, light-and-sound effects, dialogues and music, this exhibition, also called 'Sahajanand Pradarshan', narrates incidents from Swaminarayan's life and teachings

Carving details Manually sculpted by an expansive workforce, the iconography draws inspiration from traditional Hindu temples

Architecture in India since 1990 | Counter Modernism

Circumambulatory path following the Elephant Plinth
A high plinth surrounds the main temple, whose carved sandstone base depicts an elaborate procession of elephants, palanquins and soldiers

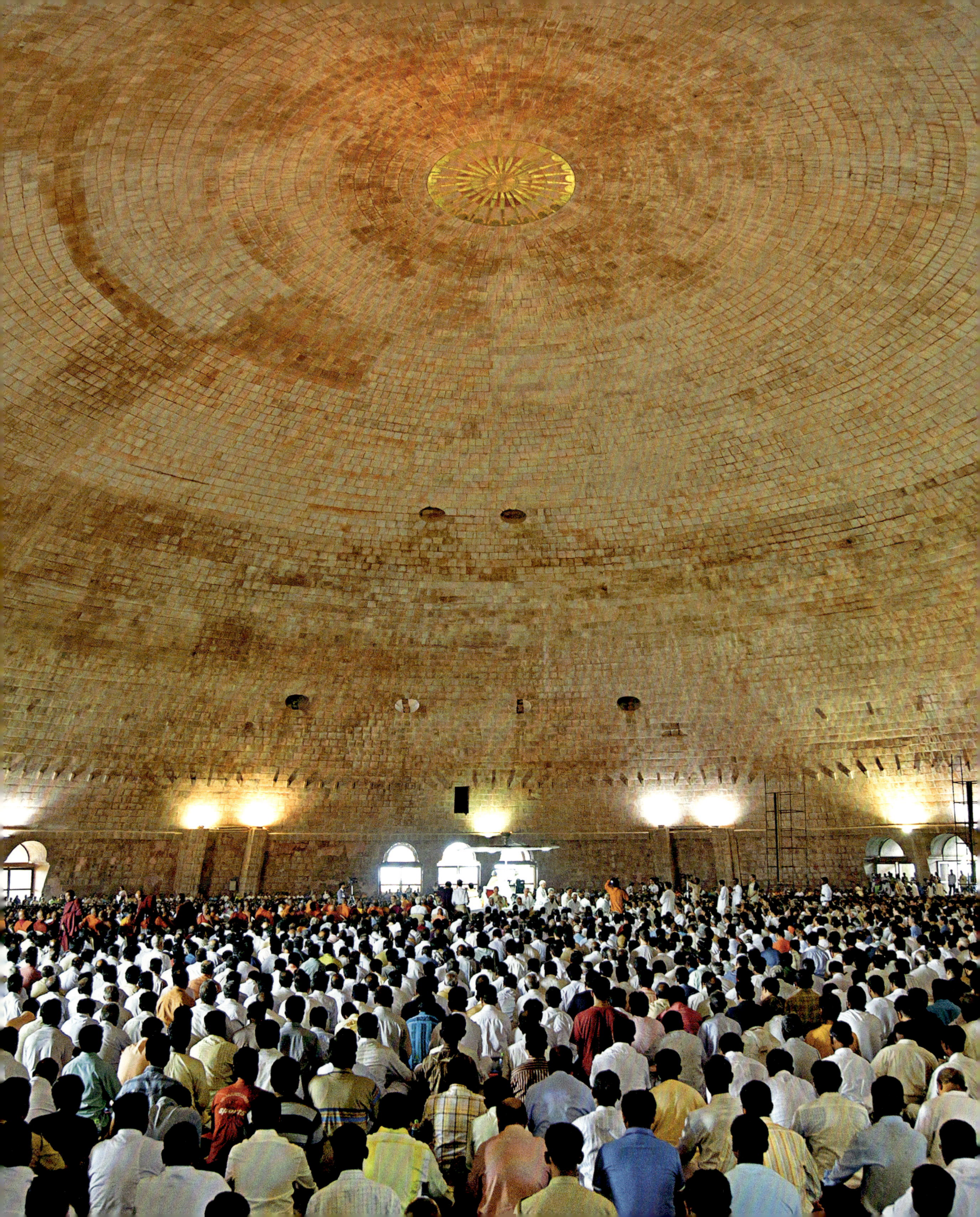

folio 2
GLOBAL VIPASSANA PAGODA, Mumbai

Shah & Dumasia Architectural Consultancy

Designed to replicate the Shwedagon Pagoda of Yangon, as a gesture of gratitude to Myanmar for preserving the non-sectarian Vipassana meditation technique in its pristine purity, the Global Pagoda is located in Goregaon in suburban Mumbai. This place for meditation and the practice of Dhamma, with a capacity of holding 8,000 people, houses exhibition galleries, restrooms, guest accommodation and basement parking. The 100m tall pagoda tower covers 20,000m² of built and landscaped area.

Abandoning an earlier idea for construction in steel and concrete, the pagoda uses the technique of interlocking stones to achieve a clear, column-free interior space for meditation. Technical assistance from the master craftsman Chandubhai Sompura helped establish the horizontal and vertical grooves on each stone block, allowing it to interlock without the need for shuttering. This 85m diameter space supports the dome of the pagoda, which reaches a height of 100m. Approximately 2.5 million tonnes of Jodhpur sandstone, for the inner dome and outer serrations, was transported, sized, shaped and erected on site. The result is a building that uses traditional methods but integrates them seamlessly into a contemporary condition.

Central meditation area With a seating capacity of 8,000 people, the dome is artificially lit through peripheral ceiling lights

Process models highlighting structural logic Following an interlocking principle, wherein grooves were cut into each stone in both the horizontal and vertical directions, a large column-free meditation space was achieved

Architecture in India since 1990 | Counter Modernism

View of the pagoda looking towards the Gorai creek Surrounded by dense vegetation, the built form is modelled on the Shwe Dagon Pagoda of Myanmar, which preserves the non-sectarian Vipassana meditation practice. The building is situated at the edge of the city but is visible for miles, thus exerting a presence in the landscape of Mumbai

Architecture in India since 1990 | Counter Modernism

folio 3
ISKCON SRI RADHA KRISHNA-CHANDRA TEMPLE, Bengaluru

Sri Madhu Pandit Dasa, Sri Jagat Chandra Dasa and Smt Bhakti Lata Devi Dasi

This three-hectare rocky site, earlier considered as wasteland due to its rough terrain, was acquired by ISKCON to build their temple complex. Renamed as Hare Krishna Hill, it also houses their Bengaluru headquarters together with this key place of worship. Designed and executed by the in-house team at the ISKCON Construction Department, the project employed 600 skilled craftspeople and introduced a vocabulary previously unexplored in temple building, of traditional techniques alongside modern materials such as glass. For example, glass façades connecting the four traditional *gopuram* towers were devised as a way of synthesising, as well as separating, the old techniques and forms from the new.

Elements of the traditional temple architecture of Karnataka were coupled with a fresh aesthetic that incorporated the use of newer construction technology. Ferro cement for the *gopurams* and a steel frame for the temple structure were some of the major deviations from traditional temple building. A 150mm concrete skin then covered the structure, being finished and profiled in stone and mortar.

Gopuram towers marking the central shrine adjoined by the temple tank The traditional *gopurams*, facing the cardinal directions, have been restructured with the use of curtain glazing on all sides to obtain the enclosed main hall. The path to the temple is through an undulating landscape

Courtyard with *mandapas* leading to the subsidiary shrines Remaining true to the tenets of Dravidian temple architecture, a linear movement through the colonnaded *mandapas* lead to the two smaller shrines of Sri Prahlada Narasimha and Sri Srinivasa Govinda

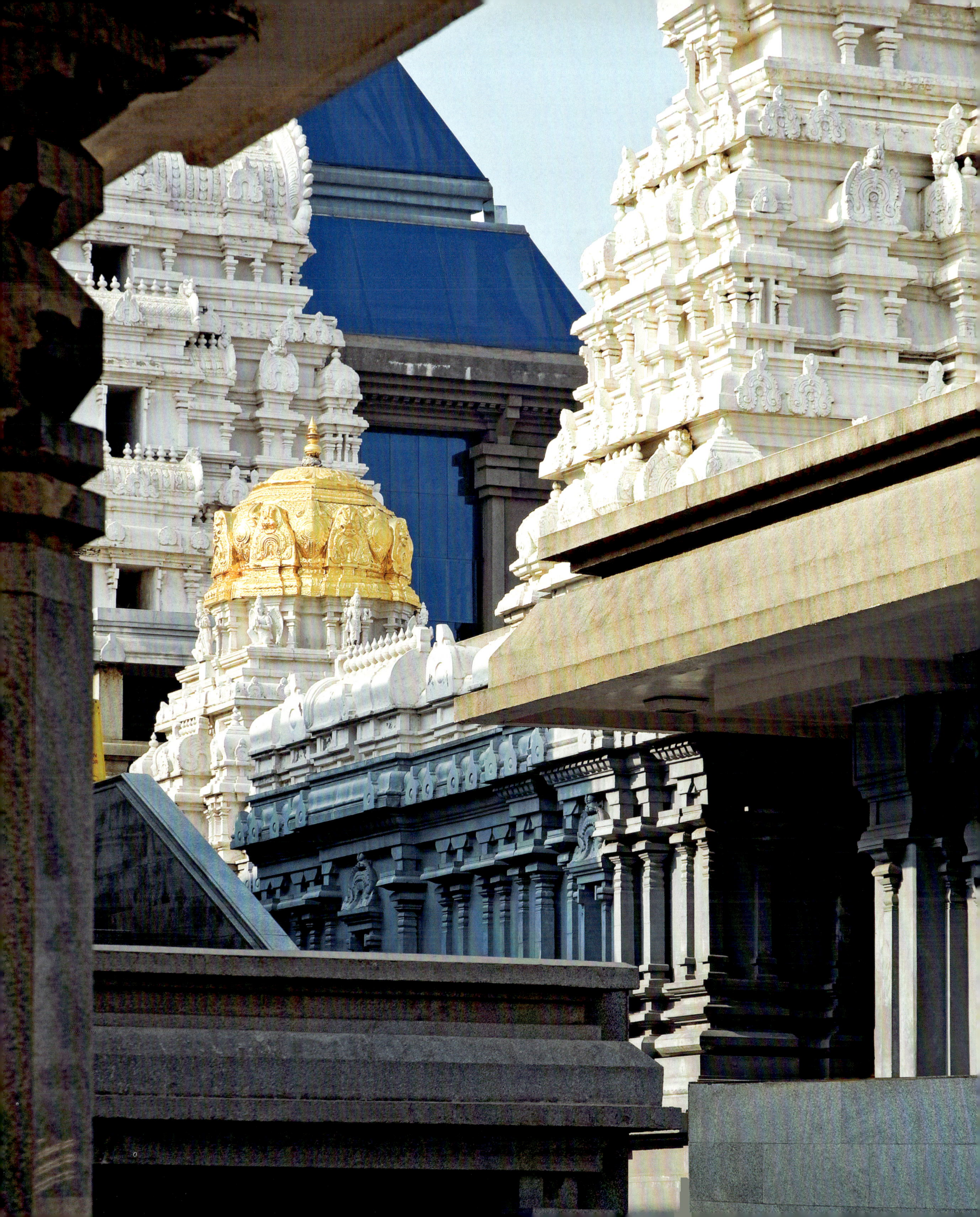

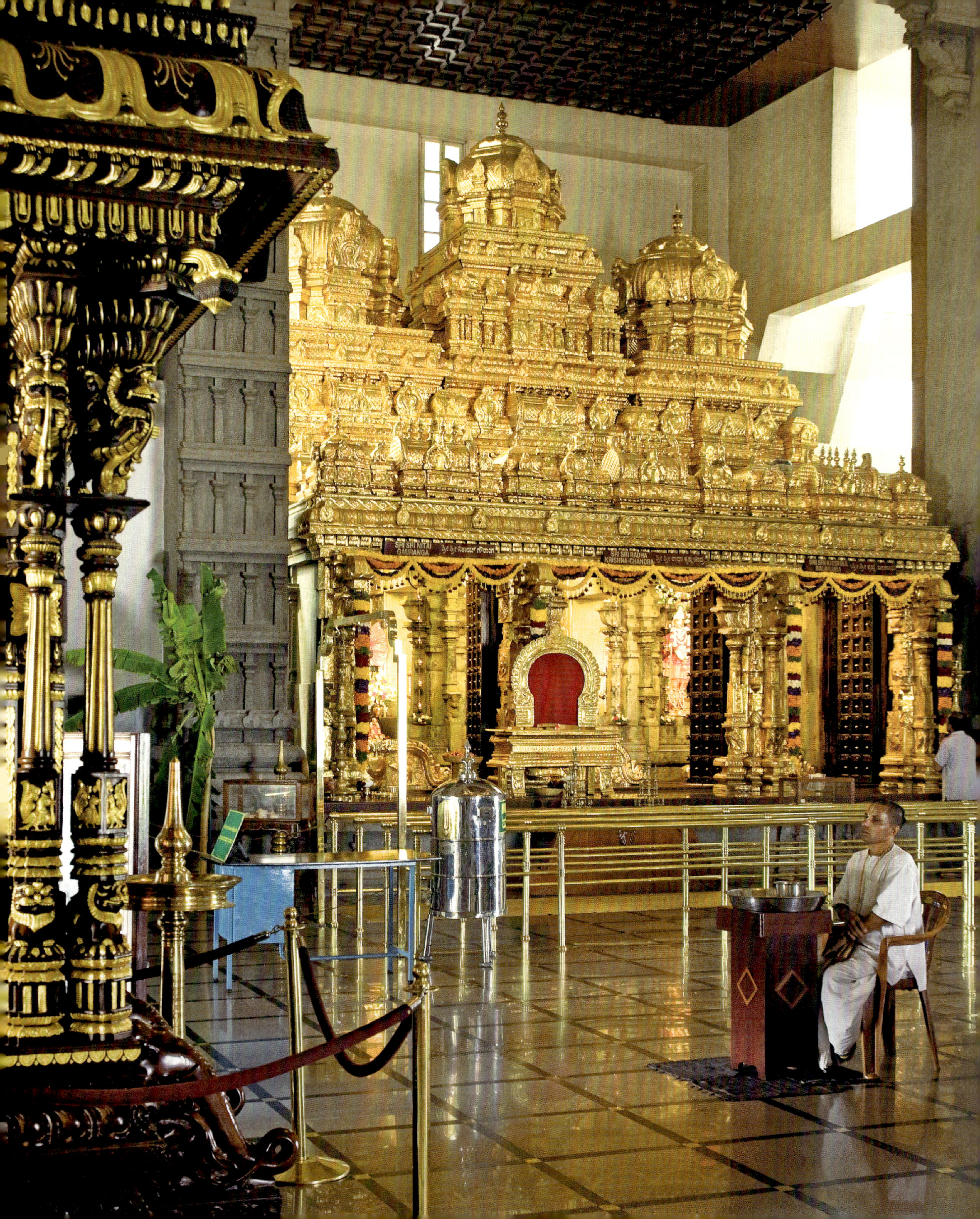
SRI SRI NITAI
GAURANGA
SRI SRI RADHA
KRISHNA-CHANDRA

Architecture in India since 1990 | Counter Modernism

***Garbhagriha* with the deities**
Signifying the spiritual universe, or 'Goloka Vrindavana', in these gold-plated shrines reside Sri Nitai Gauranga, Sri Radha Krishnachandra and Sri Krishna Balarama

Spire detail over central dome This gold-plated finial caps a petalled dome over the central hall

Detail of *gopuram shikhara*
The towering *gopurams* which taper upwards are capped with ornate plaster work on a barrel vaulted roof with bulbous stone finials (*amalaka*)

281

Architecture in India since 1990 | Counter Modernism

Corner view of the Hall of Awakening Surrounded by a narrow moat, this outer marble enclosure capped with domed pavilions has three entranceways leading up to the main level

Flooring depicting the Sri Yantra within the interior space The entrance hall uses the Sri Yantra to address the idea of Man's spiritual journey from the stage of material existence to ultimate enlightenment

folio 4
ONENESS – HALL OF AWAKENING, Varadaiahpalem

Dr Prabhat Poddar

The Oneness temples, conceptualised by Sri Amma Bhagwana as elements of a spiritual movement through meditation and self-awakening, form part of a number of satellite towns and universities developed for this purpose across South India. The centrepiece of this 17-hectare site in Varadaiahpalem in the southern state of Andhra Pradesh, embodying and upholding the philosophy of the movement, is the Hall of Awakening. Transcending diverse faiths from across the globe, this temple follows ancient Vedic geometric patterns in order to potentially generate extraordinary sacred energy.

A moat and other water bodies separate this three-tiered structure, with its waiting halls at the ground and middle level and a meditation hall at the top, from the rest of the landscaped campus. Following the tenets of Vastu Shastra in its planning, entrances occur at cardinal directions with octagonal staircases at each corner, attempting to balance static and dynamic energies within the space. Large spans and the monumental heights of the meditation halls, capable of accommodating 28,000 people at a time, were achieved using pre-stressed reinforced-concrete beams.

A diverse array of materials, ranging from white marble and semi-precious stones to enduring metals and local timber, was employed for surface finishes. Rich symbolism derived from the human body defines the meditation hall entrances, while the nine domes, or *kalashams*, carry pinholes to signify the *bindu*, which allows the flow of cosmic energies.

Architecture in India since 1990 | Counter Modernism

View of the Oneness Temple
Displaying an eclectic mix of architectural styles, the roof profile of this symmetrical structure draws from multiple faiths and building traditions

Detail of dome profiles An array of roofs in marble, varying from *chatris* and *shikharas* to vaults and arcades

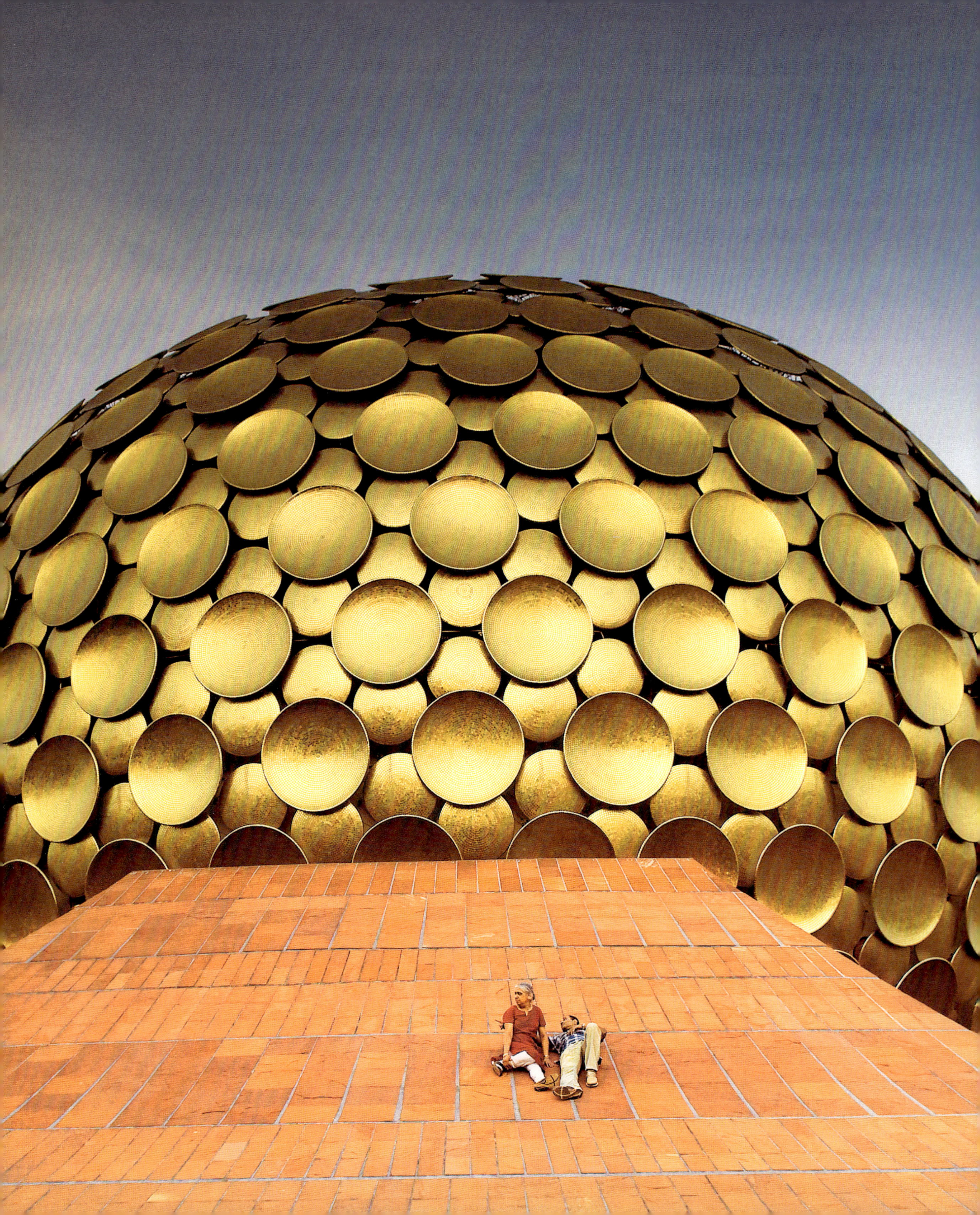

Architecture in India since 1990 | Counter Modernism

folio 5
MATRI MANDIR, Auroville

Roger Anger

Auroville, an experimental universal city, was envisioned by the Mother, the spiritual head of the Aurobindo Ashram near Puducherry. At the spiritual and physical heart of Auroville is the Matri Mandir, a spherical structure dedicated to the Universal Mother. This edifice, which was under construction for over three decades, is a flattened dome spanning 36m in diameter and containing meditation rooms, surrounded by gardens and an amphitheatre. Radiating from the Matri Mandir are its gardens, landscaped in three ways: those around an existing banyan tree, an urn containing soil from different countries to symbolise the internationalism of Auroville, and finally the red sandstone paving around the structure.

Four massive concrete columns support an inner circular chamber—with a floor at 14m above ground level and the roof at 29m. The outer edges of the columns create a circle, whereby the triangular space frame forming the outer skin of the structure resembles a flattened globe. This skin is covered by a mesh of gold-encased discs, while the inner chamber is lined with a layer of tinted glass. From the entrance, two helical ramps lead to the inner chamber, in the centre of which is a crystal globe illuminated by a single ray of light from the heliostat mounted on the roof.

Detail of stone clad 'petals' around the Matri Mandir Twelve sandstone-clad petals encircle the Matri Mandir, while containing meditation rooms within them. Between each petal is a pathway, either leading up to the central meditation chamber of the mandir via a flight of stairs or moving down to the lotus pond below

View of the circular façade with gold discs No less than 852 concave and convex discs are mounted onto the inner space-frame structure using metal rods. While addressing shading and durability as key criterion, these gold discs are encased between two thin layers of glass and were manufactured in Germany

Architecture in India since 1990 | Counter Modernism

View of the marble pond below Matri Mandir Eight entrances from the stone petals lead to this contemplative space with a floral marble pond

Architecture in India since 1990 | Counter Modernism

Detail of the Matri Mandir
Viewed through the adjacent grove of trees, the building glistens when perceived through the shade of the foliage

Plan of Auroville with Matri Mandir as the nucleus Seen as the 'city of the future', which was to be truly universal in its approach, a galaxy-shaped integrated master plan was conceptualised by architect Roger Anger

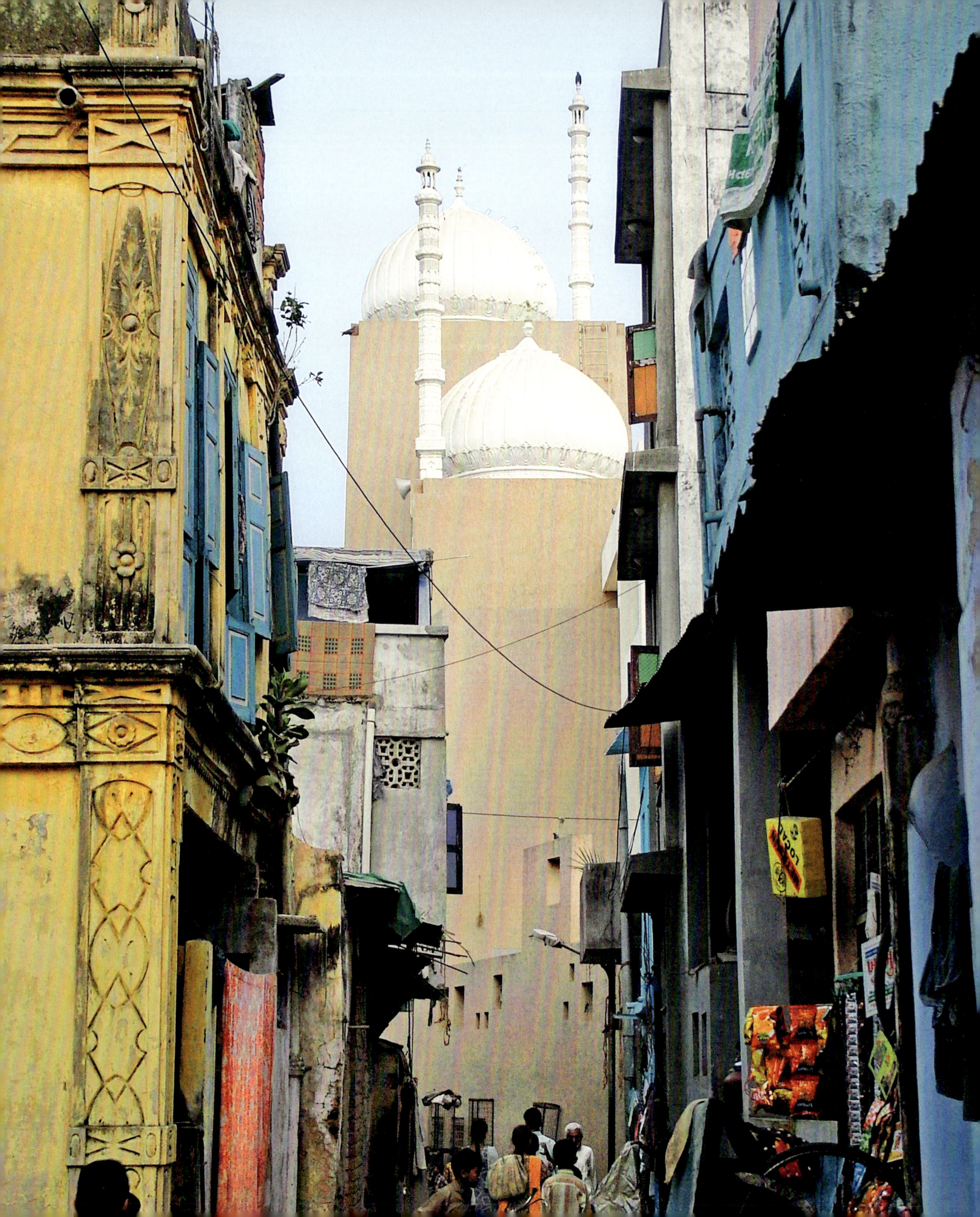

folio 6
DADAMIYAN MOSQUE, Ahmedabad

Hiren Patel Architects

An 800m² plot in Dariapur, within the walled city of Ahmedabad, forms the urban context for this new mosque. The generating force behind the project was to create an institutional presence in the context of the inner city of Ahmedabad. Designed to accommodate 2,700 people, it uses reinforced concrete and brick, covered with a rough-textured plaster as finishing material.

This contemporary mosque is designed around two central themes—those of the central prayer hall and the peripheral wall. The plan establishes a strong physical and visual link with the surrounding streets, while the prayer hall emphasises the shape and nature of the open terraces. A double-height volume, towards the rear, accommodates the *hauz*, or ablution tank, and links to the main entrance with a bridge. The west wall with the mihrab, the basic architectural element in Islam, is used as a bold gesture in the urban context. The prominence of this religious structure and its functions within the dense city fabric is heightened through tapering masonry masses along the external façades of the mosque. A central open courtyard with full-height openings on three sides allows the penetration of natural light deep into the prayer areas.

Approach lane leading to the mosque Devoid of exterior fenestration, this narrow by-lane provides a glimpse of the monolithic mass, thereby highlighting the domes and minarets as key elements in the urban landscape

Surrounding built context in Dariapur The mosque towers over the low-rise neighbourhood as a harmonious blend, in spite of being a contemporary insert

Architecture in India since 1990 | Counter Modernism

Double-height arrival spaces This volume leads to the western *mihrab* wall and main prayer area via flights of stairs on either side

Interior view of central prayer hall This matted prayer hall opens onto terraces that overlook the street on all three sides, while allowing diffused light into the space

Building drawings by the architect A central open court has been critical in allowing light into the mosque, while the three-domed towers add a monumental dimension to the built form

Front façade with entrance archway This triple-volume central archway with overlooking balconies is connected to the ablution space through a bridge, and, further on, to the prayer hall

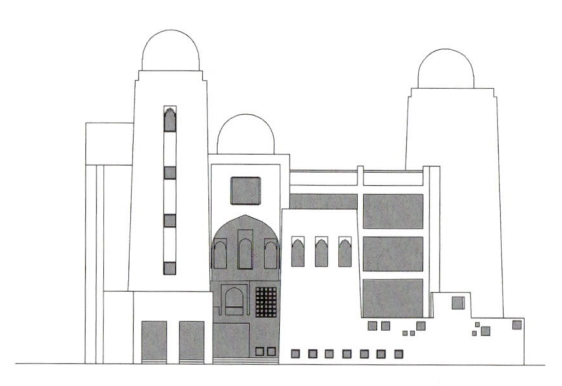

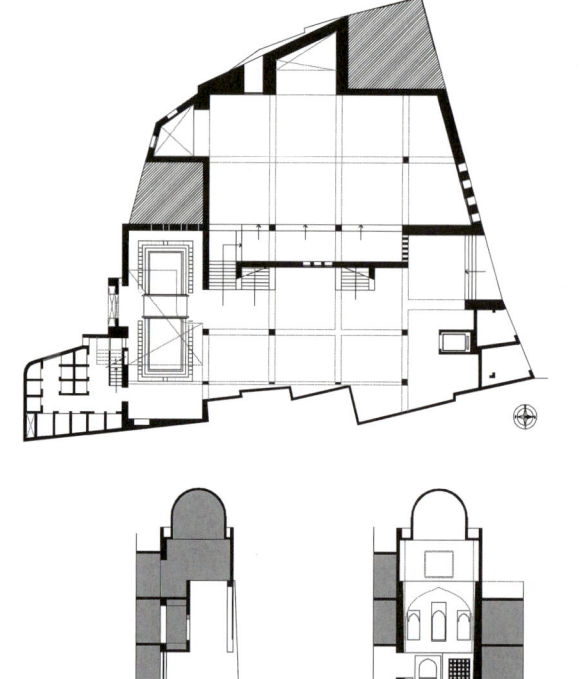

292

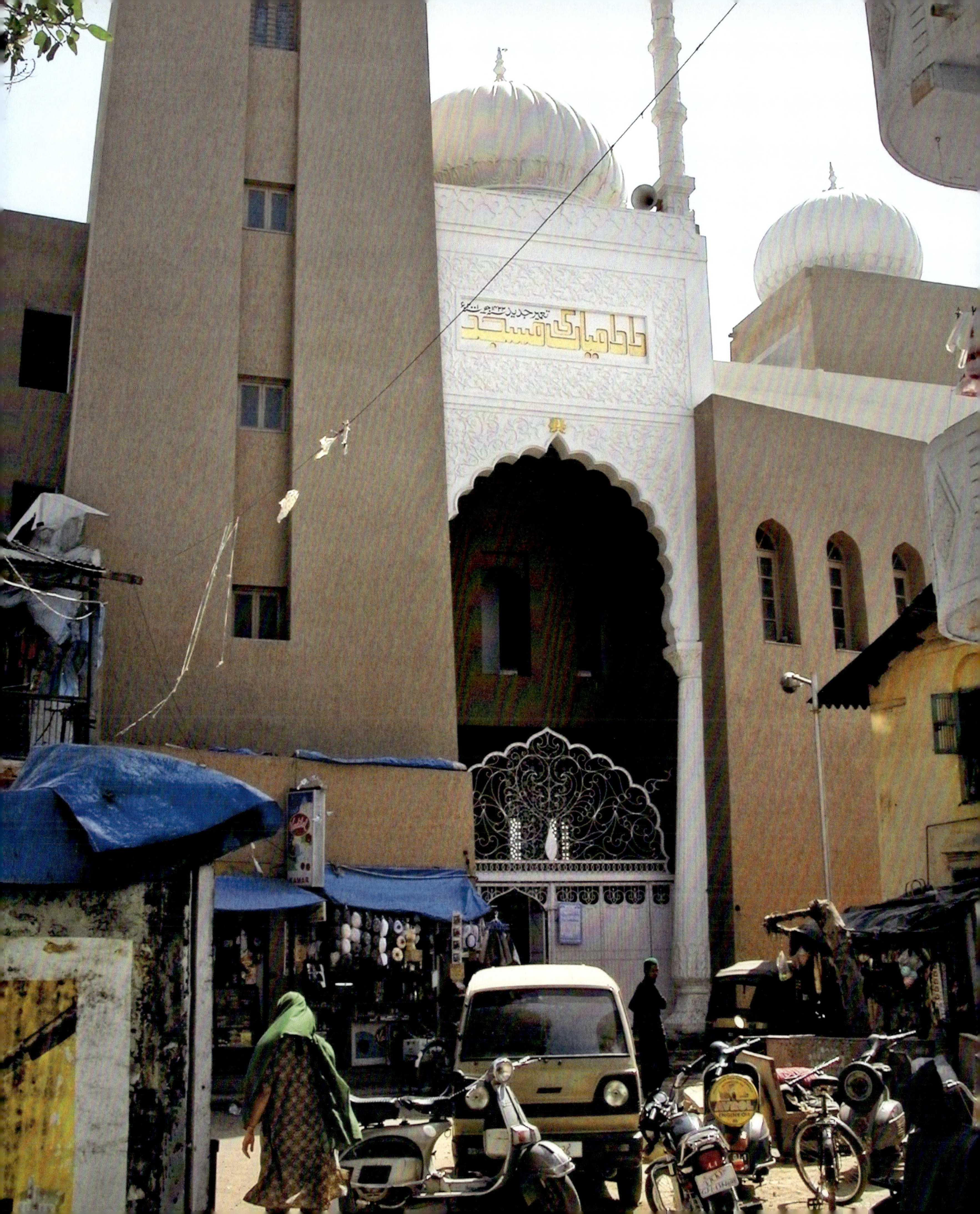

यहाँ बैठना मना है ।

Architecture in India since 1990 | Counter Modernism

folio 7
RADHASOAMI SAMADH, Agra

Anonymous British Architect and Collaboration of Devotees

The Radhasoami Central Satsang and the memorial of the movement's founder, Soamiji Maharaj, has been under construction outside Agra for over a century now. It aims to surpass its significance as a 'mere' place of worship into a space for spiritual renaissance, meditation and contemplation. This project was commissioned by the founder of the sect, aided by a British architect, and carried forward by three successive generations of the founder's family.

The main memorial occupies an area of 1,100m² and sits on a 6m high plinth with an ambulatory path 17m long around it, while proposed to be rising to a total height of 58m. Although the ground floor was constructed in 1935, until 2006 the work had only reached the fourth floor, adhering to a belief that this memorial should always remain in progress.

Marble has been extensively used, both as surface cladding and as ornamentation. Stone workshops set up in Makrana, Pindwara (in Rajasthan) and Agra employed skilled craftspeople to execute the designs, which utilise inlay, relief and latticework as their key techniques. Individual pieces relating to each architectural element—arches, columns, screens, domes, minarets and their components—are carved at the workshop, transported and then erected on site in a highly labour-intensive process.

Latticed screens along the upper corridors Intertwined foliage motifs in marble, which filter light into the corridor spaces, are intricately carved by craftsman on site

Arched entranceway leading to the central *samadh* The incomplete lower archway in marble is meant to form an outer wall that shields the inner *samadh* building

Architecture in India since 1990 | Counter Modernism

Details within the inner courtyard Arched colonnades dominate most vertical surfaces, which contain either doorways or screened *jalis*, along the inner edges of the court

Architecture in India since 1990 | Counter Modernism

Detail of column capital
Marble reliefs on the capitals depict vignettes and other flowered creepers

Detail of carved archway over the main entrance This series of Gothic arches is overlaid with stone inlay and plaster relief, demonstrating the synthesis of architectural styles within the *samadh*

Carving work in progress
While this building has been in progress for several generations, all the work is undertaken in and around the site itself by devotees and volunteers

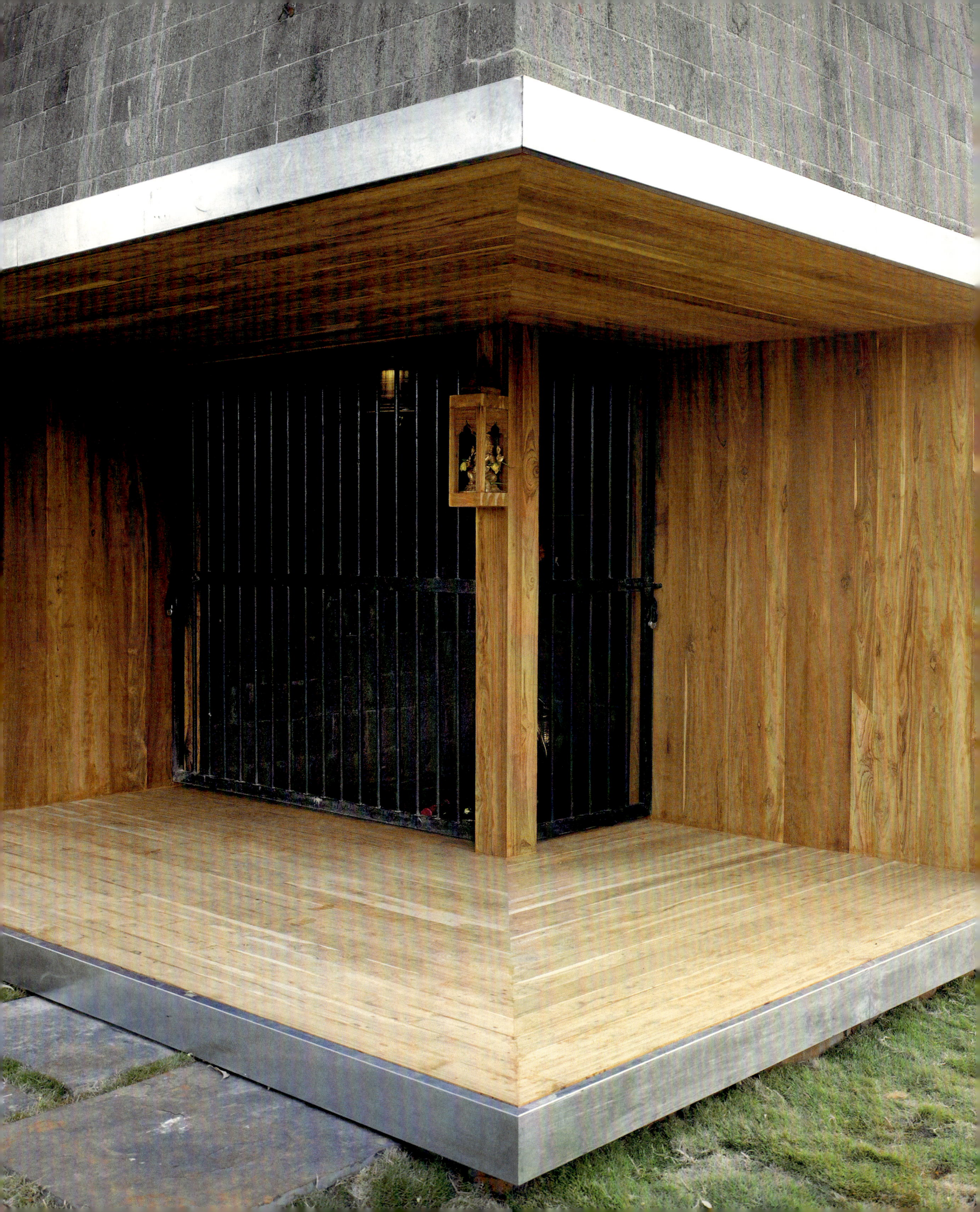

Architecture in India since 1990 | Counter Modernism

folio 8
SHIVA TEMPLE, Wadeshwar

Sameep Padora & Associates

This temple in Wadeshwar village, on the outskirts of Pune, is an architectural work that consults and collaborates with the temple priest and people from surrounding villages. Based on the idea of *shramdaan* (donating labour), the team utilised laterite stone donated by a nearby quarry as the key resource.

Adhering to planning principles of traditional temple architecture, the project discarded all embellishment other than those integral to its key symbolism.

Entry to the sanctum is through an exaggerated threshold space, reflecting a contemporary aesthetic, lined in timber and framed in stainless steel. Religious iconography in the form of statues of the holy cow, Nandi, and Lord Vishnu's avatar as a turtle become installations in the landscape while the *kalash* (jar) on the *shikhara* tower, a finial cast from *ashtadhatu* (an amalgam of eight different metals), reinforces its relationship with the cosmos. Stepped seating on the southern edge of the site negotiates steep contours while transforming the purely religious space into a socio-cultural one used for festival and gatherings.

Detail of the doorway As a minimal yet contemporary insert, this timber-and-steel threshold alters the formal dimensions of an otherwise traditional temple form

Section through the forecourt The basic orientation and spatial planning of the site and temple were governed by its strategic location in an existing, dense grove of trees

Section through temple and landscape By retaining only the *garbhagriha* and *shikhara*, the temple design respects key traditional spatial features while adding contemporary treatment in the details of the threshold, which mediates between the structure and the landscape

Approach to the temple ground The site is steeply sloped on its southern side, and this is modulated into stepped platforms for community use

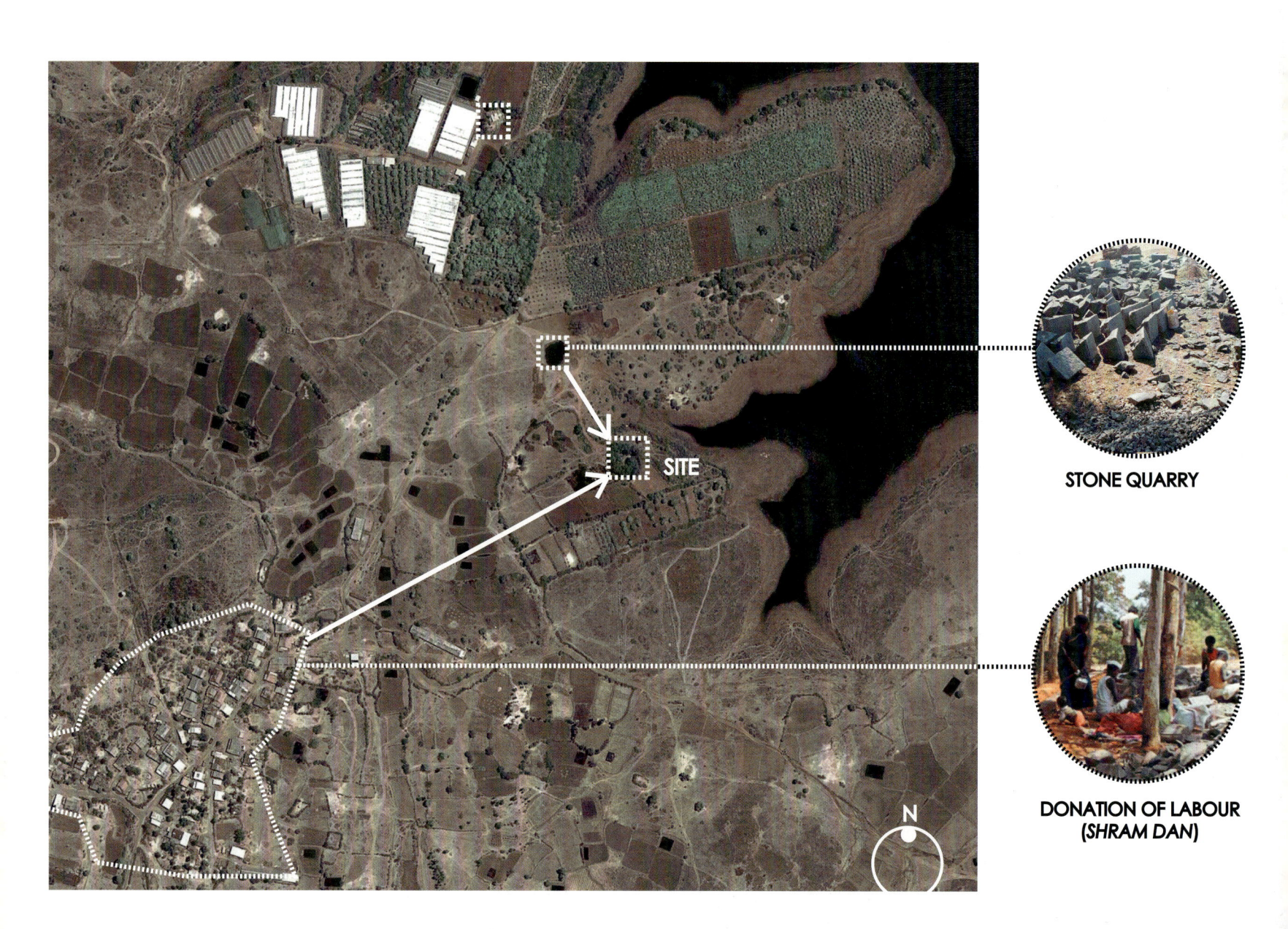

Architecture in India since 1990 | Counter Modernism

STONE QUARRY

DONATION OF LABOUR (SHRAM DAN)

Diagram illustrating the idea of *shramdaan* Working on the idea of donated labour, the temple sourced laterite from the nearby quarry and labour from the neighbouring village—thus reinforcing a traditional social pattern and form of community engagement in the construction of temples in India

The threshold space Timber and stainless steel lines the threshold as a contemporary addition to the basic form of the traditional temple *shikhara*

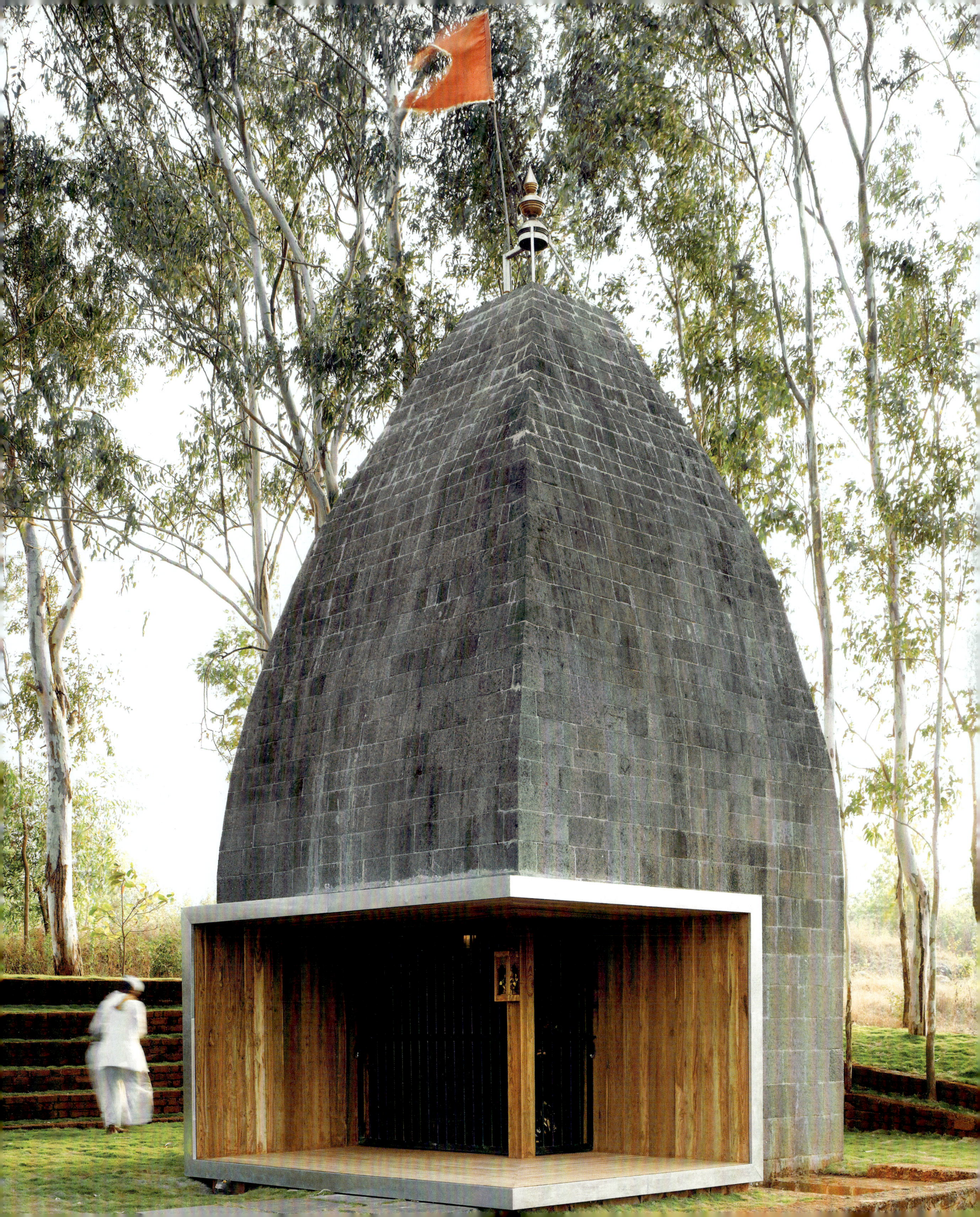

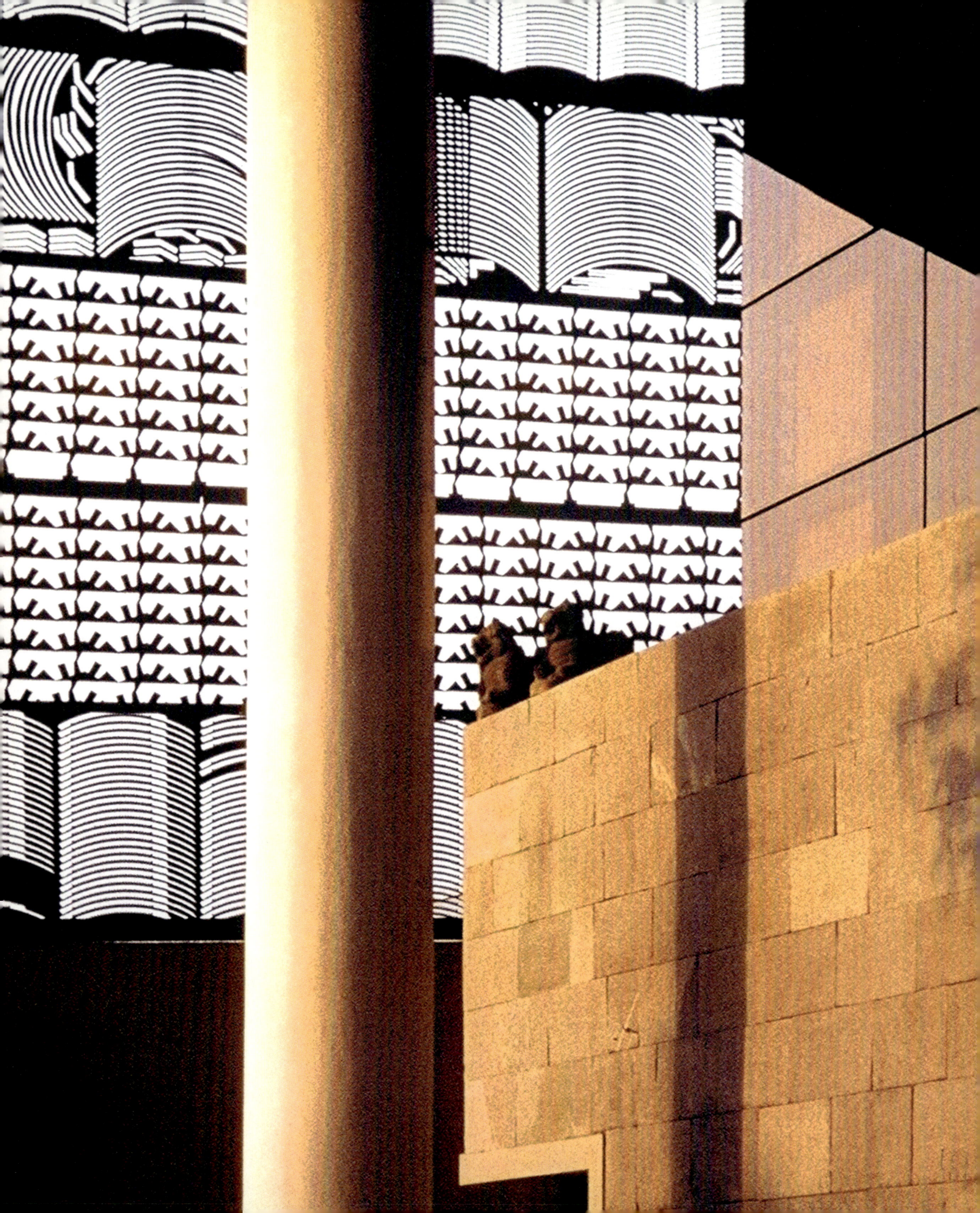

ENVOI

As the world—and India, in particular—becomes increasingly globalised, we must be cautious about not accepting and working with difference when things progressively begin to look more alike, as a superficial overview of India's emerging architectural landscape might suggest. With the influx of foreign capital and the many architectural firms that have followed, most readings of the contemporary Indian architectural scene have unfortunately locked their gaze on the narrow spectrum of an evolved and mutated modernist aesthetic. This reading has been perpetuated by the architectural media, both nationally and internationally, which has been obsessed with representing a new Indian identity premised on India's position in a globalizing world. In fact, on the contrary the architectural landscape in India has been freed from the burden of this singular pan-national identity, and instead is forging one that is grounded in multiple realities, beliefs and aspirations across the diverse regions of the country. A deeper exploration of the Indian condition, by mapping disparate forms and modes of practice, results in a richer view. In this perspective, the pluralism in the emerging landscape becomes more striking than before—even though we would assume that the differences would have become indistinguishable by the globalisation process.

India's architecture has clearly developed its own strategies of resistance to the phenomenon of globalisation, creating a kaleidoscopic representation of its coexisting multiple modernities. Thus, any reading of this highly pluralistic condition in India (and perhaps all of South Asia) requires a continual negotiation and mapping of differences in order to present a clear picture of the emerging landscape. Within India's democratic political framework, diverse aspirations express themselves in completely different ways architecturally rather than allowing one entity to prevail and remake the landscape in its image. This intrinsic resistance to any singular force—global capital or political ambition—reforming the other is what could, and perhaps already does, distinguish India's architecture from that of, say, China or the Middle East, where upto now, it grows from more autocratic regimes and often limited types of patronage. In fact, this expression of human societies that can live with difference rather than becoming a homogeneous national construct is what makes the Indian experiment extraordinary. And it is from this condition that an architecture of resistance is born: an architecture of inherent pluralism, which is a true expression of Indian democracy and unique in the emerging global landscape.

Rahul Mehrotra
April 2011

CHRONOLOGY

YEAR OF COMPLETION	GLOBAL PRACTICE	REGIONAL MANIFESTATION
1990		
1991		
1992		IUCAA, Pune
1993		
1994		
1995		Husain Doshi Gufa, Ahmedabad,
1996		
1997		
1998		
1999		Devi Garh Fort Palace, Udaipur
		Karunashraya Terminal Care Centre, Bengaluru
2000		Ashwini Kumar Crematorium, Surat
2001		
2002		Sua House, Bengaluru
2003		ITC Sonar Bangla, Kolkata
		Parliament Library, New Delhi
2004	Sri Siddhartha Institute of Technology, Tumkur	
2005		Residence for Jacob George, Kochi
2006	Infosys Software Development Block 4, Mysore	
2007	Indian Institute of Management, Ahmedabad	
2008	Pearl Academy of Fashion, Jaipur	Tara House, Kashid
	Chhatrapati Shivaji International Airport, Mumbai	
	Castro Cafeteria, New Delhi	
2009	Tote, Mumbai	Rishi Valley School, Madanapalle
2010	Park Hotel, Hyderabad	
	Tamil Nadu Legislative Assembly Complex, Chennai	
	Khalsa Heritage Centre, Anandpur Sahib, Punjab	

The chronology illustrates the simultaneous development of India's extremely disparate forms of architectural expression during the period covered in this book. It is interesting to note that the regional manifestations and alternative practices described in this text followed through from the preceding decades with vigour and continuity. These models of practice and operation have their roots in the 1970s. The two extreme expressions resulting from the process of globalisation—global practices and the expressions of a counter modernism—took a few years after the liberalisation of the economy to exert their presence in India. They began to emerge in the mid- and late 1990s, once the effects of economic liberalisation were in place, and the reactions to it were also in play. The relationships between these two groups of practice is best manifest in the format of a chronology. Here, a simultaneous viewing makes evident the pluralism in the architectural landscape of India in the decades from 1990 to 2010.

YEAR OF COMPLETION	ALTERNATE PRACTICE	COUNTER MODERNISM
1990	Abu Abraham's House, Thiruvananthapuram	
	Loyola Chapel, Thiruvananthapuram	
1991		
1992	Nalin Tomar House, New Delhi	
	Centre for Development Studies, Ulloor	
1993	Malik House, Lonavala	
1994		
1995		
1996		
1997		ISKCON Sri Radha Krishna-Chandra Temple, Bengaluru
1998		
1999	Wall House, Auroville	
2000		
2001		
2002		Dadamiyan Mosque, Ahmedabad
2003		
2004		
2005		Swaminarayan Akshardham Temple, New Delhi
2006	Jenny Pinto's Paper Making Workshop, Bengaluru	
	Pettachi House, Bengaluru	
	Manav Sadhna, Ahmedabad	
	Shaam-e-Sarhad Village Resort, Hodka	
2007		
2008	Our Native Village Eco Resort, Bengaluru	Global Vipassana Pagoda, Mumbai
	Development Alternatives World HQ, New Delhi	Oneness – Hall of Awakening, Varadaiahpalem
		Shiva Temple, Wadeshwar
		Matri Mandir, Auroville
2009		
2010		Radhasoami Samadh, Agra (ongoing)

PROJECT DATA

GLOBAL PRACTICE

Infosys Software Development Block 4
Location Mysore
Name of Firm Architect Hafeez Contractor, Mumbai
Principal Hafeez Contractor
Project Team Anupam De, Rupa B D'Souza
Project Period 2005-06
Built Area 42,000m²

Park Hotel
Location Hyderabad
Name of Firm Skidmore, Owings and Merrill, New York
Project Team Roger Duffy
Project Period 2010 (completed)
Built Area 54,000m²

Sri Siddhartha Institute of Technology
Location Tumkur
Name of Firm Geodesic Techniques (P) Ltd, Bengaluru
Principal Srinidhi Anantharaman
Project Period 2004 (completed)
Built Area 400m² (approx)

Chhatrapati Shivaji International Airport, Terminal 1B
Location Mumbai
Name of Firm Architect Hafeez Contractor & DV Joshi and Co, Mumbai
Architect Hafeez Contractor & DV Joshi
Project Period 2005-07
Built Area 45000m²

Tamil Nadu Legislative Assembly Complex
Location Chennai
Name of Firm gmp · von Gerkan, Marg and Partners · Architects. gmp International GmbH architects and engineers in cooperation with the local consultant Archivista Engineering Projects Pvt Ltd as well as Schlaich, Bergermann & Partner, Stuttgart for the structural engineering of the dome
Design Volkwin Marg and Hubert Nienhoff with Kristian Spencker
Principal Gerkan, Marg and Partners Architects
Project Period 2008-10
Built Area 170,000m²

Indian Institute of Management
Location Ahmedabad
Name of Firm HCP Design and Project Management Pvt Ltd, Ahmedabad
Principal Bimal Patel (Director)
Project Team Bimal Patel, Gajanan Upadhyay, Jayant Gunjaria, Brijesh Bhatha, Niki Shah, Samarth Maradia
Project Period Phase 1 – 2007, Phase 2 – ongoing
Built Area 55,000m²

Pearl Academy of Fashion
Location Jaipur
Name of Firm Morphogenesis, New Delhi
Principal Manit Rastogi and Sonali Rastogi
Project Team Sonali Rastogi, Rudrajit Sabhaney, Anna Kristiana Bergbom, Shruti Dimri, John Alok Decruz
Project Period 2008 (completed)
Built Area 11,745m²

Khalsa Heritage Centre
Location Anandpur Sahib, Punjab
Name of Firm Safdie Architects, Boston and Ashok Dhawan, New Delhi
Principals Moshe Safdie and Ashok Dhawan
Project Period 1998-2010
Built Area 23,225m²

Castro Cafeteria
Location New Delhi
Name of Firm Romi Khosla Design Studio, New Delhi
Principals Romi Khosla and Martand Khosla
Project Team Praveen Rajput, Maulik Bansal
Project Period 2006-08
Built Area 1,150m²

Tote
Location Mumbai
Name of Firm Serie Architects, Mumbai
Principal Chris Lee and Kapil Gupta
Project Team Yael Gilad, Dharmesh Thakker, Suril Patel, Purva Jamdade, Advait Potnis, Vrinda Seksaria, Udayan Mazumdar, Mayank Ojha and Atish Rathod
Project Period 2006-2009
Built Area 2,500m²

REGIONAL MANIFESTATION

ITC Sonar Bangla
Location Kolkata
Name of Firm Kerry Hill Architects, Singapore
Principal Kerry Hill
Project Team Kalyan Biswas Architects, Kolkata
Project Period 1998-2003
Built Area 35,409m²

IUCAA (Inter-University Centre for Astronomy and Astrophysics)
Location Pune
Name of Firm Charles Correa Associates, Mumbai
Principal Charles Correa
Project Period 1988-92
Built Area 15,000m²

Husain Doshi Gufa
Location Ahmedabad
Name of Firm Vastu Shilpa Consultants, Ahmedabad
Principal Balkrishna V Doshi
Project Period 1990-95
Built Area 420m²

Karunashraya Terminal Care Centre
Location Bengaluru
Principal Sanjay Mohe
Project Period 1999 (completed)
Built Area 3,500m²

Ashwini Kumar Crematorium
Location Surat
Name of Firm Matharoo Associates, Ahmedabad
Principal Gurjit Singh Matharoo
Project Team Komal Mehta, Hetal Pandya
Project Period 2000
Built Area 2300m²

Devi Garh Fort Palace
Location Udaipur
Architectural Renovation Gautam Bhatia and Navin Gupta
Interior Design Rajiv Saini
Landscape Design Bhagwat Associates
Project Period 1993-99
Built Area 10,220m²

Parliament Library
Location New Delhi
Name of Firm Raj Rewal Associates, Delhi
Principal Raj Rewal
Project Period 1993-2003
Built Area 60,460m²

Tara House
Location Kashid
Name of Firm Studio Mumbai Architects
Principals Bijoy Jain and Priya Jain
Project Period 2006-08
Built Area 930m²

Residence for Jacob George
Location Kochi
Name of Firm Design Combine, Kochi
Principal Jacob George
Project Period 2004-05
Built Area 220m²

Sua House
Location Bengaluru
Name of Firm Mathew & Ghosh Architects
Principals Soumitro Ghosh and Nisha Mathew Ghosh
Project Period 2002
Built Area 700m²

Rishi Valley School
Location Madanapalle
Name of Firm Flying Elephant Studio
Principals Rajesh Renganathan and Iype Chacko
Project Period 2006-09
Built Area 1,300m²

ALTERNATE PRACTICE

Laurie Baker Projects

  a. Centre for Development Studies
Location Ulloor
Project Period 1967-1992
Total Area 9 acres

  b. Loyola Chapel
Location Thiruvananthapuram
Project Period: 1970-1990
Built Area 930m^2

  c. Abu Abraham's House
Location Thiruvananthapuram
Project Period 1990 (completed)
Built Area NA

Malik House
Location Lonavala
Name of Firm Nari Gandhi
Project Period 1993 (completed)
Built Area NA

Nalin Tomar House
Location New Delhi
Name of Firm Kamath Design Studio, New Delhi
Principal Revathi & Vasanth Kamath
Project Period 1992 (completed)
Built Area 33m^2

Wall House
Location Auroville
Architect Anupama Kundoo
Project Period 1999 (completed)
Built Area 240m^2

Manav Sadhna
Location Ahmedabad
Name of Firm Yatin Pandya and Vastu Shilpa Foundation, Ahmedabad
Project Team Yatin Pandya
Project Period 2005-06
Built Area 515m^2

Development Alternatives World HQ
Location New Delhi
Name of Firm Ashok B Lall Architects, New Delhi
Principal Ashok Lall
Project Team Rakesh Dayal, Anjali Jyoti
Project Period 2005-08
Built Area 4,775m^2

Chitra Vishwanath Projects

  a. Jenny Pinto's Paper Making Workshop
Location Bengaluru
Principal Chitra Vishwanath
Project Team Sajitha Sunil
Project Period 2006 (completed)
Built Area 300m^2

  b. Pettachi House
Location Bengaluru
Principal Chitra Vishwanath
Project Team Chandrakumari
Project Period 2006 (completed)
Built Area 200m^2

  c. Our Native Village Eco Resort
Location Bengaluru
Name of Firm Chitra Vishwanath Architects, Bengaluru
Principal Chitra Vishwanath
Project Team Martin Lafferiere
Project period 2006-2008
Built Area 2.4 acres

Shaam-e-Sarhad Village Resort
Location Hodka
Name of Firm Hunnar Shala Foundation, Bhuj (NGO)
Principal Sandeep Virmani
Project Team Vaghabhai, Ramaben, Hirabhai, Mangubhai and other local artisans from Kutch
Project Period 2004-06
Built Area 200m^2

COUNTER MODERNISM

Swaminarayan Akshardham Temple
Location New Delhi
Name of Firm Bochasanwasi Shri Akshar Purushottam Swaminarayan Sanstha (BAPS)
Project Team Sadhu Anandswarup Das, Brahmavihariswami
Project Period 2000-05
Built Area 11,000m^2

Global Vipassana Pagoda
Location Mumbai
Name of Firm Shah & Dumasia Architectural Consultancy, Mumbai
Principal Parvez Dumasia
Project Period 1997-2008
Built Area 6300m^2

ISKCON Sri Radha Krishna-Chandra Temple
Location Bengaluru
Name of Firm Construction Department of International Society for Krishna Consciousness (ISKCON)
Project Team Sri Madhu Pandit Dasa & Sri Jagat Chandra Dasa and Smt Bhakti Lata Devi Dasi
Project Period 1990-97
Built Area 15000m^2

Oneness – Hall of Awakening
Location Varadaiahpalem
Conceptualised by Amma Bhagwana and
Designed by Dr Prabhat Poddar
Project Period 2002-08
Built Area 14,000m^2

Matri Mandir
Location Auroville
Principal Roger Anger, Auroville
Project Period 1970-2008
Built Area 2,513m^2

Dadamiyan Mosque
Location Ahmedabad
Name of Firm Hiren Patel Architects, Ahmedabad
Principal Hiren Patel
Project Team Nidhish Nair, Nitin Jain and Niki Shah
Project Period 2000-02
Built Area 2,513m^2

Radhasoami Samadh
Location Agra
Architect Anonymous British architect and collaboration of devotees
Project Period 1904-present
Built Area NA

Shiva Temple
Location Wadeshwar
Name of Firm Sameep Padora & Associates
Principal Sameep Padora
Project Team Minal Modak, Vinay Mathias
Project Period 2008 (completed)
Built Area 15m^2

ACKNOWLEGEMENTS

My deepest acknowledgements are to my teachers—they inspired this book in ways that are hard to describe, but I hope they recognise their influence and contributions and accept my gratitude.

I would like, at the outset, to acknowledge those who have led the discussion about architecture in post-independence India—their seminal writings have formed the foundation for this book: Balkrishna Doshi, Charles Correa and Raj Rewal have been the pioneers in presenting, through their monographs, exhibitions and writings; a schema of patterns, issues and questions for the architect working in post colonial India. Acknowledgements are also due to Vikram Bhatt and Peter Scriver, , Gautam Bhatia, Madhavi and Miki Desai, Jon Lang, Kulbhushan and Meenakshi Jain, William Curtis, Brian Taylor, Giles Tillotson, Romi Khosla, Jagan Shah, Satish Grover the Bahga brothers (Sarbjit, Surinder and Yashinder), Himanshu Burte, Vikram Prakash and Peter Gast for their writings and documentation on contemporary architecture in post-independence India. Romi Khosla, Ashish Ganju, Malay Chatterjee, AGK Menon, KT Ravindran and Prem Chandavarkar have additionally prompted the debate with underpinnings of theoretical questions. The care as well as passion with which these practitioners and scholars have researched, articulated and framed the discourse for contemporary Indian architecture will be appreciated even more deeply with the passage of time and by generations to come.

For the essential ideas in this book, I am most grateful to the late Raghubir Singh who first challenged me in the mid-1990s with the idea of the validity of plural practices and modes of engagement in the making of the built landscape. Raghubir perceived the 'barefoot architect' model (then popularised by Laurie Baker) as the one challenging the accepted paradigms of architectural production. He first planted the idea in my mind of looking at models of practices as they set up their own self-perpetuating cultures, which he believed would be the way to discern the future of architecture in India. However, since then this idea has taken on more dimensions, partly inspired by my conversations with Romi Khosla and his critical writings on 'Ancient Futures'. Romi's insights prompted me to detach notions of modernity and the aesthetics of modernism. With this approach, in which one delinks procedures and process from expected formal and aesthetic outcomes, an entire new landscape of architecture becomes visible for consideration and simultaneous validation. In my struggle with these questions, and especially the essay on Counter Modernism, Aromar Revi encouraged me to use faith, not religion, as a more encompassing category just when I was stuck and could not close the loop with the last section—this unlocked renewed energy in finishing the book. I am particularly appreciative of the invitation Peter Scriver extended to me to visit Adelaide in 1999, and of the time he spent there with me in several discussions about conservation and architecture in India. The one seminal idea I came away with was the notion of 'constructing significance', when he described my conservation work in those terms at his introduction to my lecture at the university. I had not viewed this as clearly as he presented it, and it was a critical turning point for me in viewing my own work but also in seeing this as the point where conservation and new imaginations intersect. To the intellectual generosity of Raghubir, Romi, Aromar and Peter, I will be always indebted.

I would similarly like to acknowledge the contribution of Ram Guha, Sunil Khilnani, Suketu Mehta, Arjun Appudarai, Ravi Sam and Ranvir Shah. My understanding of India has been deeply influenced by their writings and my several conversations with them over the years—these exchanges, without ever placing this book project at the centre of the discussion, have been influential in recognising the importance of the breath of architectural production that I have attempted to represent in this work.

The formulation of the specific contents for this book first started when I was invited by Prof Kenneth Frampton to edit one of the books in the ten-volume series that he guest-edited on the architecture of the twentieth century. Subsequently, it was at the prompting of Luis Fernandez-Galiano (at the behest of Prof Peter Rowe) that I focused my thoughts on the more recent production of architecture in India. I expanded these ideas in the two volumes that Luis compiled for the Fundacion BBVA in Spain (the Atlas on Global Architecture 2000 and Architectures of the twenty-first century: Asia and Pacific), which helped me expand my research and thinking about the emergent architectural landscape of India. I am grateful to them all for the invitations to participate in these projects.

I would like to extend my gratitude to all the architects and building owners who shared their projects, images and time in order to make this publication possible. Nonethelesss, different sections of this book benefited specifically from the contributions of some people whom I would like to single out for thanks. For the first section I am grateful to Satyendra Pakhale for making available to me a copy of the India Report by Ray and Charles Eames and reminding me that Indian designers and architects needs to be more ambitious in their thinking. The section on Global Practice gained a great deal from my conversations with Sudhir Jambekar and James Beaullardo, and their enthusiasm to capture what was being created by foreign firms working in India today. I am thankful to Harsh Neotia for his introduction to Rakhi Sarkar, who so generously shared with us the ambitious project for KMOMA (Kolkata Museum of Modern Art) that she is spearheading in Kolkata. I am also grateful to Hafeez Contractor, who shared his time and material with great openness once he got over the initial fear of criticism! For the section on Alternative Practice, I am particularly grateful to two individuals: Ranjit Hoskote and Sanjay Prakash. Ranjit Hoskote was a fellow traveller on a journey I embarked on 15 years ago: in the course of it, we aspired to put together a book on 'Alternative Practices in India' based on a conference with the same title I had organised with the Urban Design Research Institute (UDRI). Funds were never available for this endeavour, and so after a year of struggling to put it together we abandoned the project. The beginnings of that section of this book were clearly based on and inspired by that experience. To Sanjay Prakash, I am grateful for his having made me see the debate around 'sustainability' more critically and perhaps more cynically! His insights about the various 'shades of green' and his directing me to the different architects working with the sensibilities that make for sustainable approaches are his contribution to the book. I am most thankful to him for this, and—by extension—also making me ask such questions more clearly in my own work. For the section on Alternative Practice, I am also grateful to Rahul Gore for having shared his research on the work of Nari Gandhi. The last, and perhaps the most difficult, section on Counter Modernism benefited from the ideas and discussions generated by several people, but most particularly: Romi Khosla, Dr Jyotindra Jain and Prof RJ Vasavada. Their writings and insights on the encoding of the ancient in our popular visual imagination are a crucial contribution to the understanding of architecture in India today. I am grateful to them for making their thinking so open and accessible through their writings.

Many thanks, too, for the support of friends: Sharada Dwivedi, Sarita Vijayan and Dinesh Mehta—all of whom would have loved to be more a part of this project than they could. A special acknowledgment to all my colleagues at RMA Architects, who have been extremely patient and supportive of the research and been accommodating of my sometimes ridiculous work schedules across time zones.

My thanks also to Bharath Rammrutham for his early involvement as well as Ram Sinan and his colleagues at Trapeze, who painstakingly processed and helped curate the hundreds of images that were sent their ways. To Anne Marie, who stepped in with little time at hand to make visual sense of the pluralism of architecture in India, which is not an easy task—many thanks, Anne Marie! And finally, within the design team, the book would never have been woven together so skilfully had it not been for the calm, steady and wonderful disposition that Fravashi Aga brought to the process—fusing disparate opinions seamlessly into visual consensus!

Similarly, a very heartfelt appreciation and thanks to Kamalika Bose, who assisted with the research and patiently fact-checked as we gathered material from disparate sources. Her persistence with research was greatly appreciated by all involved. Lastly, to our editors: Nayana Kathpalia, who deftly filtered the jargon and tweaked the text to be more assertive, while being super-sensitive to the tone and style that makes this a personal account. And a sincere thanks to Ian McDonald, whose immense patience and final onslaught of sophisticated questions on the content as well as the text clarified and sharpened many arguments.

Of course, none of this would be possible without the support of two individuals. Jemma, Project Manager, PICTOR, who managed the project over the last two years, contacted hundreds of individuals in search of material and solicited permissions and rights. She acted as the photo researcher and fact checker rolled in one. Her severe organisational abilities and mild manner are an awesome combination! This book truly owes a great deal to her contribution. And lastly, many thanks to my publisher, Padmini Mirchandani, who, in spite of the several transitions her enterprise was undergoing, ensured this book was possible. Her enthusiasm, support, patience and engagement in all aspects of the work—and her banking on the project despite the inherent risks of presenting such a non-standard view of architecture in India—is something I sincerely appreciate and for which I will always be grateful. Padmini thanks for keeping the faith!

And finally my deepest thanks to—Ayesha, Neel and Nondita—their love, patience and support, as always, has been invaluable and impossible to describe in words.

PHOTO CREDITS

1960 Eames Office, LLC (www.eamesoffice.com) 44tl
Abhijit Barua 45 bl
Abhikram 205; 207
Adam Hardy 253lt&b, 260t&c
Adnan Goga 262rb
AFP/Getty Images 251, 267
Age/Dinodia 16l, 263 far bl&br
AKAA/John Paniker 153
AKAA/Justin FitzHugh 39rt, 121lb
AKAA/Rajesh Vora 201rt
AKAA/Timothy James Bradley 47
AKAA/Wayne Caravella 206
Alan Abraham 71ct&b
Albert Lim KS 124, 140, 142, 143 lt&b
Ambuja Realty Development 126
Amit Mehra 162, 165b
Amit Pasricha 164, 165lt&r, 256, 263cl&r, 286, 288, 289t
Andre J Fanthome 101, 103tl&r
Andreas Deffner 226, 228l, 228 rt, 228 rc, 229
Anil Dave/Dinodia 20rt, 21r, 27l, 27rb, 34l, 121rb, 34l, 121rb
Anupam Poddar 163
Anupama Kundoo 227, 228 rb
Apeejay Surrendra Park Hotels Ltd 80, 81, 82lc&b, 82r, 83
Architect Hafeez Contractor 61t, 77t
Architectural Research Cell 123rt,125rt&b, 167b, 169r
Ariel Huber 128lt&b
Arun Mishra/Dinodia 10
Asim Waqif 132
Ayers Saint Gross and Dhiru A Thadani 67rt&b

BAPS Swaminarayan Sanstha 253rt, 270, 271, 272, 273
Bharath Ramamrutham 2, 20rb, 21lb, 23rt, 23rbl&r, 26lt, 26lb, 42, 86, 87, 157, 197 rb, 198bl&r, 259, 275, 279, 280, 281l, 282, 283, 284, 285, 302

Chandavarkar & Thacker Architects 134t
Charles Correa 44br, 45t, 45bc&r, 144r
Clare Arni 130lc, 134lc&b
Collages ©David Wild from Fragments of Utopia, Hyphen Press, 1998 41, 43l

David D'souza 133ct, 133rt
Debasish Banerjee/Dinodia 262l
Design Combine 130lb, 174, 175,176, 177
Dinesh Mehta 26r, 46, 64lb, 64ct, 68bl&r, 82lt, 84, 85, 87rt, 87bl&r, 96-97, 97, 98lt&b, 98rb, 99, 116-117, 121rt, 125lt&c, 130r, 138-139, 158,160lb, 161,197 lb, 197rt, 248-249, 252lt&b, 252rt, 253rc&b, 265, 268-269, 274, 276-277, 294, 295, 296, 297
Director Sripuram Golden Temple 250, 254bl&r
Dmitry Kalashnikov 129rt&b
Dominic Dube 118, 133l, 133cb
Dr Vivek M 240, 241
Dudaney 189

Edmund Sumner 100, 102-103
Edmund Sumner/VIEW 38, 69lt, 112, 114-115, 121lt, 131l, 131ct, 150, 152, 298, 301

FLC/ADAGP, Paris 2011 36, 37, 39rb, 40, 43r
Frank Lloyd Wright Foundation, Scottsdale, AZ/Artists Rights Society (ARS), NY 39l
Fram Petit 56-57, 58, 71rt&b, 74-75, 113, 115tl&r
FXFOWLE 60 lc, 64r, 66 rt&b

G K Waghela/Dinodia 258lt
gmp 95tr
gmp/photo: Christian Gahl 95tl
gmp/photo: Florian Illenberger 92
gmp/visualization: MACINA 93, 94-95, 95b
Golconde: The Introduction of Modernism in India (Urban Crayon Press, 2010) Courtesy of Vir Mueller Architects 28r, 29

H Satish/Dinodia 22l
HCP Design & Project Management 96, 98rt
Helene Binet 170, 171, 172
Henrik Storm 192
Herzog & de Meuron and Mrs Rakhi Sarkar of The Kolkata Museum of Modern Art 68lt
Hiren Patel Architects 290, 291, 292, 293
HOK 63lt, 66 lt-b, 66c

IndiaTodayImages.com 258rt
Inspiration 199rt&b
ISKCON-BANGALORE 278, 281r

Jatinder Marwaha 72-73
JAYBEE 266
Jeeth Iype 198 lt
Jenny Pinto and Navroze Contractor 238, 239
Jino Sam Panayil 188, 208, 209
Joginder Singh 186-187, 199 lt-b, 200, 210-211, 236, 237
Joseph St Anne 127b

Kamath Design Studio 224, 225r
Karthikeyan Narayanan 60lt
Kiran Aditya 60rt-b, 76-77, 78, 79

Lavannya Goradia 242-243

M Hamid 44ct
Madan Mahatta 125lb
Madheswaran Periyasamy 196
Mahendra Sinh 44cb,145, 147t, 149t
Mallikarjun Katakol 136, 137, 178l, 179
Manav Parhawk 204
Manoj Navalkar/Dinodia 22r, 263bl
Manoj Sudhakaran 134rc&b, 182, 183, 184, 185
Manu Rewal 166, 167t, 168, 169l
Marathe & Kulkarni 27rt
Matharoo Associates 8-9, 131rt, 159, 160lt, 160r
Mathew & Ghosh Architects 178r
Maulik Bansal and Praveen Rajput 108b
Michael Portman 2004 67lt&b
Mindspace 130lt, 154,155,156
Morphogenesis 103b

Moshe Safdie 105r

Nitin Kelvalkar/Dinodia 35l
Noshir Gobhai 60lb, 64lt, 88,89, 90, 91
Nutan Varma 198rt

Oneness 283r

Pallon Daruwalla 180t
Pankaj Anand 133rc&b
Patrick Bingham-Hall 141, 143r
Pei Cobb Freed & Partners LLP, New York 64lc
Phillips Antiques 16r, 17, 19lt, 19ct, 19cbl, 19cbr, 19rb
Pradip Gupta/Dinodia 257r
Pranlal Patel 120tl

Rahul Gore 190, 191, 218, 219, 220, 221
Rahul Mehrotra 13, 18, 19lbl, 19lbr, 19cbc, 19rt, 20l, 28lt, 28 lbl&r, 35r, 44bl, 44ct, 44tr, 53, 120 bl, 122lt&b, 123l, 144l, 146, 147bl&r, 148, 149 r, 151, 195, 261, 287, 289rb
Rajesh Vora/Dinodia 262rt
Rajeev Kathpalia 129lt&b
Rajeshwari Prakash 202-203
Raju Shukla/Dinodia 23rbc
Ram Rahman 23l, 104-105, 106, 107
Ramprasad Akkisetti 123rc&b
Ray Meeker 255
RMJM 68lc
Rohinton Irani 120r

Saibal Das courtesy Tasveer 180bl&r, 180-181
Sameep Padora 299, 300
Samir Pathak 258lc&b
Sanjay Puri Architects 68rt
Sanjeet Wahi 13cb, 131rc&b
Saurabh Pandey 71lt&b, 108t, 109, 110, 111
Schwartz Architects/Gensler/Creative 63lb, 63rt&b
Seema Krishnakumar 212, 213, 214, 215, 216, 217
Senthil M 257l
Serie Architects 115b
Simon Shepheard/Dinodia 260b
Skidmore, Owings & Merrill, rendering by CrystalCG 62
Soumitro Ghosh 135
SPA Design 128r
SPARC 194
Studio Mumbai Architects 173
Sunhil Sippy 263
Sunil Jain 197lt&c

Taj Mohammad 61b
Tod Williams Billie Tsien Architects 69lb, 69rt-b

Vasanth Kamath 222, 223, 225l
Vastu Shilpa Foundation 122r, 127t
Vithalbhai Collection/Dinodia 26lb, 34r

Yatin Pandya 230, 231, 232, 233

309

BIBLIOGRAPHY

Landscape of Pluralism

Appadurai, Arjun. *Modernity at Large: Cultural Dimensions of Globalization*. Minneapolis, University of Minnesota Press, 1996

Bahga, Sarabjit and Surinder Bahga. *Le Corbusier and Pierre Jeanneret: Footprints on the Sands of Indian Architecture*. New Delhi, Galgotia Publishing Company, 2000

Bahga, Sarabjit, Surinder Bahga and Yashinder Bahga. *Modern Architecture in India, Post-Independence Perspective*. New Delhi, Galgotia Publishing Company, 1993

Batley, Claude. "Indian Architecture Today", *Journal of the Indian Institute of Architects*, 20(3),1954

Begg, John. "Architecture in India", *Journal of the Royal Institute of British Architects*, (3-14), 1913

Bhabha, Homi. *The Location of Culture*. London, Routledge, 1994

Bhatia, Gautam. *Punjabi Baroque and Other Memories of Architecture*. New Delhi, Penguin Books Pvt Ltd, 1994

Bozdogan, Sibel. *Modernism and Nation Building*. Seattle, University of Washington Press, 2001

Brown, Rebecca M. *Art for a Modern India: 1947 – 1980*. Durham, NC and London, Duke University Press, 2009

Chandavarkar, Prem. "Architecture and the Expression of Meaning", *Architecture + Design*, Vol IV, No 5, July 1988, pp 94-99

Chatterjee, Malay. "Options after Independence", *Inside Outside*, February-March 1986, p 47

– "Physical Design for the Next Century", *Architecture + Design*, Vol XIV, No 1, Jan-Feb 1997, pp 120-22

– "The Evolution of Contemporary Indian Architecture" in *Architecture in India*, eds. R Rewal, JL Veret and R Sharma, Paris, Electa Moniteur, 1985

Correa, Charles. "Chandigarh: The View from Benares", *Architecture + Design*, 3(6), Sept-Oct 1987, pp 73-75

– "Quest for Identity" in Proceedings of the Seminar: *Exploring Architecture in Islamic Cultures 1: Architecture and Identity*, The Aga Khan Award for Architecture, 1983

Curtis, William. "The Ancient in the Modern" in *Architecture in India*, eds. R Rewal, JL Veret and R Sharma, Paris, Electa Moniteur, 1985

– *Le Corbusier in India, The Symbolism of Chandigarh: Ideas and Forms*. New York, Rizzoli, 1986

– "Towards an Authentic Regionalism", *Mimar*, No. 19, 1986

Dalvi, Smita. "Shapes of Salvation", *Time Space and People*, June 2005, pp 20-24

Gast, Klaus-Peter. *Modern Traditions: Contemporary Architecture in India*. Basel and Boston MA, Birkhauser, 2007

Grover, Satish. *Building Beyond Borders: Story of Contemporary Indian Architecture*. New Delhi, National Book Trust of India, 1995

Gupta, Pankaj V, Christine Mueller and Cyrus Samii. *Golconde: The Introduction of Modernism in India*. New Delhi, Urban Crayon Press, 2010

Jahanbegloo, Ramin and Raj Rewal. *Talking Architecture*. New Delhi, Oxford University Press, 2010

Kagal, Carmen, ed. *Vistara – The Architecture of India*. Catalogue of the exhibition, Mumbai, The Festival of India, 1986

Khilnani, Sunil. *The Idea of India*. New Delhi, Penguin, 1997

– "The India Project", *Made in India* edition of *AD*, Vol 77 no 6, 2007

Lang, Jon. *A Concise History of Modern Architecture in India*. New Delhi, Permanent Black, 2002

Lang Jon, Madhavi Desai and Miki Desai. *Architecture and Independence: The Search for Identity – India 1880 to 1980*. New Delhi, Oxford University Press, 1997

Mehrotra, Rahul. "Bangalore: Dysfunctional Boom Town", *Harvard Design Magazine*, Spring/Summer 2007

– "Between Computers and Geomancy – India Global Flows and Local Assertions", *Atlas: Architecture of the 21st Century – Asia and Pacific*. Madrid, Fundacion BBVA, 2010

– "Emergent Landscapes: Contemporary Architecture in India 1990-2006", *Atlas: Global Architecture circa 2000*. Madrid, Fundacion BBVA, 2007

– "Negotiating the Static and Kinetic Cities" in *Urban Imaginaries*, ed. Andreas Huyssen, Durham, NC, Duke University Press, December 2007

– "Response to a Tradition: A Study of Architectural Attitudes during the British Intervention in India". unpublished thesis, Ahmedabad, CEPT, 1985

– "Simultaneous Modernities" in *The Ruins of Modernity*, eds. Julia Hell and Andrea Schonel, Durham, NC, Duke University Press, 2007

– ed. *World Architecture A Critical Mosaic 1900-2000 – Volume VIII, South Asia*. General editor: Kenneth Frampton, Beijing, Architectural Society of China and Union of International Architects, 2000

Mehrotra, Rahul, Prasad Shetty and Rupali Gupte. "Architecture and Contemporary Indian Identity" in *Constructing Identity in Contemporary Architecture – Case Studies from the South*, eds. Peter Herrle and Stephanus Schimitz, London, Transactions Publishers, 2009

Menon, A G Krishna. "Interrogating Modern Indian Architecture", *Architecture + Design*, Vol XVII, No 6, Nov-Dec, 2000, pp 24-28

– "The Invention of the Modern Indian Architect", *Architecture + Design*, 2008, pp 46-54

Nehru, Jawaharlal. *The Discovery of India*. Kolkata, The Signet Press, 1946

Parhawk, Manav and Rahul Khanna. *The Modern Architecture of New Delhi, 1928-2007*. Noida, Random House Publishers India, 2008

Pieris, Anoma. "The Search for Tropical Identities: A Critical History" in *New Directions in Tropical Asian Architecture*, ed Patrick Bingham Hall, Singapore, Periplus, 2005

Ravindran, KT. "Contemporary Architecture: An Uncomfortable Glance in the Mirror", *Architecture + Design*, Vol XIV, No 1, Jan-Feb 1997, pp 26-28

Rewal, Raj, ed. *Architecture in India*. Paris, Electa Moniteur, 1985

Sassen, Saskia. "Whose City Is It? Globalization and the Formulation of New Claim", *Public Culture* 8.2, 1996, pp 205-23

Scriver, Peter and Vikram Bhatt. *After the Masters: Contemporary Indian Architecture*. Ahmedabad, Mapin, 1990

Sen, Amartya. "Culture Matters and How", in special issue on Culture and Development, *Humanscape*, April 2002

– *Identity and Violence: the Illusion of Destiny*. London, Penguin Books, 2006

Smith, Roger T. "On Building for European Occupation in Traditional Climates Especially India", *Royal Institute of Architects Transactions*, 1st series, Vol 8, 1867/68

Sundaram, Ravi. "Recycling Modernity: Pirate Electronic Cultures in India" in *Sarai Reader: The Cities of Everyday Life, The Public Domain*, New Delhi, 2001

Tagore, Sundaram. "The Legacy of Anti-Tradition", *The Art News Magazine of India*, Vol II, Issue I, July 2006

Tillotson, Giles. "Paradigms of Indian Architecture: Space and Time in Representation and Design", *SOAS Collected Papers on South Asia: 13*, 1997

– *The Tradition of Indian Architecture: Continuity, Controversy and Change since 1850*. New Delhi, Oxford University Press, 1987

Tzonis, Alexander and Liane Lefaivre. "Why Critical Regionalism Today?", *Architecture and Urbanism*, May 1990, p 236

Wild, David. *Fragments of Utopia: Collage Reflections of Heroic Modernism*. London, Hyphen Press, 1998

Global Practice: Expression of Impatient Capital

Editorial. "A Landmark Arising", *Madras Musings*, 16-31 March 2010, p 1

Editorial. "Calcutta City", *DesignToday*, December 2006, pp 142-45

Editorial. "The Indian School of Business", *Inside Outside*, October 2000, pp 182-83

Gupta, Kapil and Christopher Lee. *Working in Series*. London, AA Publications, 2010

Hattangadi, Maanasi. "New Integrated Terminal, Vadodara, India", *Indian Architect & Builder*, August 2010, p 46

Indrasimhan, Lakshmi. "Future Systems", *Society & Lifestyle*, 31 May 2008, p 56

Mitra, Dola. "Room for Art", *Outlook*, 13 October 2008, p 92

Moses, Nalina. "Sun, Stone, Glass, and New Wealth", *Harvard Design Magazine*, Spring/Summer 2009, pp 1-6

Raaj, Neelam. "Foreign Hands Building India", *Times of India*, 15 June 2008, p 16

Rathod, Aruna. "Sky's the Limit", *Architect and Interiors India*, September 2010, pp 24-26

Ravimohan, Amrita. "Not Getting 'Type' Cast", *Indian Architect & Builder*, December 2009, pp 2-14

Ravindran, Shruti. "Kings of Xeroxia", *Outlook*, 9 November 2009, pp 56-59

Regional Modernism: Local Assertions

Ashraf, Kazi Khaleed, ed. *Made in India* edition of *AD*, Vol 77 no 6, 2007

Curtis, William. *Balkrishna Doshi: An Architecture for India*. New York, Rizzoli, 1988

Editorial. "India: Global Architecture", *Architecture and Urbanism*, 07:10 #445

Frampton, Kenneth. *Charles Correa*. Mumbai, The Perennial Press, 1996

Khan, Hasan-Uddin, ed. *Charles Correa: Architect in India*. Singapore, Concept Media, 1984

Khosla, Romi. "Current Architecture in India", *Mimar* 41, December 1991

Menon, AG Krishna. "A Modern Building with Distinctly Indian Roots for the New Parliament Library in New Delhi", *Frontline*, 19(11), 25 May – 7 June 2002

– "Interrogating Modern Indian Architecture: Critical Regionalism" *Architecture + Design*, Vol XVII, no 6, Nov 2000, pp 24-28

Prakash, Vikramaditya. "Identity Production in Post-colonial Indian Architecture: Re-Covering What We Never Had" in *Post-colonial Space(s)*, eds. GB Nalbantoglu and C T Wong, New York, Princeton Architectural Press, 1997

Ravindran, KT. "Architecture and Identity" in *Architecture in India*, ed. R Rewal, Paris, Electa Moniteur, 1985

Rossl, Stefania. *Architettura Contremporanea: India*. Milan, Motta Architectura, 2009

Shah, Jagan. *Contemporary Indian Architecture*. New Delhi, Lustre Press/Roli Books, 2008

Taylor, Brian. *Raj Rewal*. Mimar Publications, London, 2002

Alternative Practice: Towards Sustainability

Baker, Laurie. "The People and Architecture", *Journal of the Indian Institute of Architects*, 55(1), January 1985

Bhatia, Gautam. "He lived and worked alone, without rewards", *Times of India*, 3 April 2007

– *Laurie Baker: Life, Work, Writings*. New Delhi, Penguin Books, 1991

Burte, Himanshu. "Building Sustainability through the Mud Path", *Buildotech*, June 2010, pp 36-41

– "Sustainability through Participation", *Buildotech*, March 2010, pp 36-40

Editorial. "A House For Every Man", *Sunday Mail*, 27 October 1990

Editorial. "Architecture with a Global Conscience", *Indian Architect & Builder*, March 2009

Editorial. "The Art of Living", *Architect & Interiors India*, April 2010

Editorial. "House of Arches: The Works of Vinu Daniel", *Buildotech*, June 2010, pp 54-57

Editorial. "Simple homes are back", *The Economic Times*, 24 August 1990

Gore, Rahul. "A Brush with Life: The Works of Nari Gandhi", *Indian Architect & Builder*, May 1998, pp 29-50

Lall, Ashok. "The Potential of Sustainability for Architectural Practice in India", *Architecture + Design*, September 2008

Pandya, Yatin. "Structured from Waste", *Architecture + Design*, Vol XXVI, June 2009, pp 60-64

Patil, Ramu. "To Greener Tomorrows", *The Week*, 29 June 2008, pp 158-60

Putiyan, Ashok. "Social Perspective: Remembering Laurie Baker", *Architecture + Design*, August 2007, pp 50-52

Srivathsan, Dr A. "Remembering Laurie Baker", *Journal of Landscape Architecture*, 2007, Vol 5, Issue 2, pp 57-59

Counter Modernism: Resurfacing of the Ancient

Ahmed, Farzan. "Back to the Stone Age", *India Today*, 13 July 2009, pp 37-40

Babu, Niranjan B. *Vastu: Relevance to Modern Times*. New Delhi, UBS Publishers Pvt Ltd, 2001

Bhatia, Gautam. "Go Into The Art of the Matter", *Times of India*, 10 October 2009

Dalrymple, William. *Nine Lives*. London, Bloomsbury Publishing, 2009

Desai, Santosh. "Understanding Mayawati's symbols", *Times of India*, 5 April 2010

Eck, Diana. "American Hindus", *SPAN*, November-December 2002, pp 3-8

Editorial. "Interview with Subhash Chandra", Bombay Times, *Times of India*, 30 October 1997

Gandhi, Bharat. *Vastushastra and the 21st Century*, Second Edition. Mumbai, Unnaty Vastu Consultants, 1996

Ghosh, Ashim. *Kumbh Mela*. New Delhi, Rupa & Co, 2001

Hindustan Times. "Gorai Pagoda Reaches for the Heavens", *Sunday Hindustan Times*, 8 February 2009

Jain, Jyotindra. "Curating Culture, Curating Territory: Religio-Political Mobility in India" in *Art and Visual Culture in India (1857-2007)*, ed. Gayatri Sinha, Mumbai, Marg Publications, 2009

Khosla, Romi. *The Loneliness of a Long Distant Future: Dilemmas of Contemporary Architecture*. New Delhi, Tulika Books, 2002

– "The Persistence of Pre-Modernism" in *Contemporary Architecture and City Form: The South Asian Paradigm*, ed. Farooq Ameen, Mumbai, Marg Publications, 1997

Krishna, KVS. "A Modern Temple Builder", *Madras Musings*, 31 January 2007, p 5

Kundoo, Anupama. "Devoted to Dance", *Inside Outside*, October 2000, pp 144-51

Menon, A G Krishna. "Contemporary Patterns in Religious Architecture", *Architecture + Design*, Vol XIV, No 6, November 1997, pp 23-29

Narayan, Badri. "Message For Mayawati", *Times of India*, 1 July 2009, p 10

– "What the Statues Say", *Times of India*, 21 December 2009

Pais, Arthur J. "The Temple Faith built", *India Abroad*, 24 July 2009: pp A30

– "Welcome to New York's New-look Landmark", *India Abroad*, 24 July 2009: pp A32

Patra, Reena. *Vaastu Shaastra*. New Delhi, Prakash Books, 2007

Pennick, Nigel. *The Ancient Science of Geomancy*. London, Thames and Hudson, 1979

Radhakrishnan, MG. "Flower Power", *India Today*, 16 August 2010, p 11

Sebastian, Sunny. "Working to a Plan", *Frontline*, Vol. 15, No. 13, 20 June-03 July 1998